Latinos in New York

Sloy
756-2449

853-4262

Latinos in New York

Communities in Transition

Edited by
GABRIEL HASLIP-VIERA
SHERRIE L. BAVER

University Of Notre Dame Press
Notre Dame

Manufactured in the United States of America

Paperback in 1997; reprinted in 1999, 2002

Library of Congress Cataloging-in-Publication Data

Latinos in New York: communities in transition / edited by Gabriel
    Haslip-Viera and Sherrie L. Baver.
        p.   cm.
    ISBN 0-268-01305-5 (cloth)
    ISBN 0-268-01315-2 (paper)
    1. Hispanic Americans—New York (N.Y.)   2. Hispanic Americans—
New York Region.   3. New York (N.Y.)—Social conditions.   4. New
York Region—Social conditions.   I. Haslip-Viera, Gabriel.   II. Baver,
Sherrie L.
    F128.9.S75L37   1994   94-15936
    974.7'100468—dc20   CIP

∞*This book is printed on acid-free paper.*

To My Parents
—GHV

To Chris and Nicholas
—SB

Contents

Part Two: Policy Issues

Part Three: Conclusion

Contributors

SHERRIE L. BAVER is an Associate Professor in the Department of Latin American and Hispanic Caribbean Studies at the City College of the City University of New York. She is a specialist in the political economy of Puerto Rico and has also written extensively on Latino and Puerto Rican migration and politics. Professor Baver is the author of *The Political Economy of Colonialism: The State and Industrialization in Puerto Rico.*

ANA MARÍA DÍAZ-STEVENS is currently Associate Professor of Church and Society at Union Theological Seminary. Her research has focused on the religious experiences of Puerto Ricans and Latinos in the United States. Her book *Oxcart Catholicism on Fifth Avenue: The Impact of the Puerto Rican Migration upon the Archdiocese of New York* was recently published by the University of Notre Dame Press.

JUAN FLORES is widely regarded for his work on Latino identity, popular culture, and the intellectual history of Puerto Rico. A number of his most important essays were recently collected in a volume entitled *Divided Borders: Essays on Puerto Rican Identity.* Professor Flores is currently the Director of the Center for Puerto Rican Studies at Hunter College, the City University of New York.

GABRIEL HASLIP-VIERA is currently chair of the Department of Latin American and Hispanic Caribbean Studies at the City College of the City University of New York. A specialist in the history of colonial Mexico, his publications include "Criminal Justice and the Poor in Late Colonial Mexico City" and "The Urban 'Underclass' in Colonial Latin America."

José Hernández is widely known for his work on migration and labor issues. He is the author of *Return Migration to Puerto Rico* and *Puerto Rican Youth Employment*, and he is currently Professor in the Department of Black and Puerto Rican Studies at Hunter College, the City University of New York.

Ramona Hernández teaches in the Social Sciences Department at La Guardia Community College and also does research at the CUNY Dominican Studies Institute at the City College of the City University of New York. She is the co-editor of *Punto 7 Review: A Journal of Marginal Discourse* and co-author of the recently published "Dominican New Yorkers: A Socio-Economic Profile."

Edwin Meléndez is the Director of the Mauricio Gaston Institute for Latino Community Development and Public Policy at the University of Massachusetts at Boston. His publications have focused on the economic crisis in Puerto Rico, the inequality of Latinos in the U.S. labor market, and the development of employment strategies for Latino workers. He is the co-author of *In the Shadows of the Sun: Caribbean Development Alternatives and U.S. Policies* and is co-editor of *Hispanics in the U.S. Labor Force* and *Colonial Dilemma: Critical Perspectives on Contemporary Puerto Rico*.

Clara E. Rodríguez has written extensively on the status of Puerto Ricans in the United States. She is the author of *Puerto Ricans: Born in the U.S.A.* and numerous essays which focus on issues of employment, race, and ethnicity among Puerto Ricans and other Latinos in U.S. society. She teaches at Fordham University, where she is a professor in the Department of Social Sciences.

José R. Sánchez teaches political science at the Brooklyn campus of Long Island University, where he chairs the Urban Studies Program. A specialist in politics and urban issues, his essays include "Housing from the Past, Puerto Ricans and the 'Door' of Participation in U.S. Politics," and "Residual Work and Residential Shelter: Housing Puerto Rican Labor from World War II to 1983."

Robert C. Smith is a specialist in Mexican immigration and the study of trans-national communities. He is currently an assistant

Professor in the Department of Sociology at Barnard College, Columbia University. His essays include "Mixteca in New York; New York in Mixteca," "Race and Social Location in the Incorporation of Mexican Immigrants in New York City," and "Post-Industrial Employment and Third World Immigration: Their Impact on Immigrant Employment" (as co-author).

SILVIO TORRRES-SAILLANT teaches English at Hostos Community College and is Director of the CUNY Dominican Studies Institute at the City College of the City University of New York. He has written extensively on issues of importance to the Dominican and Latino communities of New York. He has contributed to *A History of Literature in the Caribbean* and has published "Western Discourse and the Curriculum (The Uniting of Multicultural America)."

JESSE M. VÁZQUEZ is a specialist in counselor education and has written numerous articles on ethnic studies and multiculturalism. His most recent essays include "The Public Debate over Multicultural Education: Language and Ideology," "The Basic Principles of Ethnic Studies vs. Multiculturalism," and "Arthur M. Schlesinger's Vision of America and the Multicultural Debate." Professor Vázquez is currently the Director of the Puerto Rican Studies Program at Queens College, the City University of New York.

Introduction

GABRIEL HASLIP-VIERA AND SHERRIE L. BAVER

This collection of essays has its origins in the need to develop teaching materials for courses on the Latino experience in the New York area. Since the early 1980s, a number of important edited volumes and monographs have been published that focus on the issues affecting Hispanics throughout the United States.* In general, these works can be divided into three types. The first type continues an earlier tradition of studies that focused on particular nationality groups, such as Mexican-Americans, Puerto Ricans, and Cubans in specific localities or regions of the country, such as Chicago, Los Angeles, New York, southern Florida, the Southwest, or in the nation as a whole.[1] A second category, of more recent vintage, examines various aspects of the overall Latino ethnic experience in particular localities or regions, but these are much fewer in number.[2] The third type, which is also of recent vintage, tries to assess national trends and realities affecting Latinos as a whole by interpreting or bringing together essays or studies that deal with specific regions or nationality groups.[3]

This volume of essays is of the second category in that it evaluates issues affecting all Hispanics in a particular locality. The chapters that follow emphasize what is unique about the Latino experience in New York; however, the authors also intend that the essays will be of relevance to Latinos, policy analysts, and students of the Latino experience throughout the United States.

In comparison to other localities and regions, the history of immigration from Latin America to New York has been different in terms of its chronology and the configuration of its nationality

---

*The editors have used the words "Hispanic" and "Latino" interchangeably throughout this essay since no agreement could be reached even among the contributors to this volume on whether one of the two terms was preferable.

groups. For example, "Spanish," Hispanics, and Hispanicized Native Americans were already settled in southern California, Arizona, New Mexico, and Texas before those areas were ceded to the United States after the Mexican War of 1848. Small groups of Spaniards and Latinos were also found in Florida when that region was ceded to the United States by Spain in 1819. By contrast, the Hispanic presence in New York and other eastern and midwestern urban areas such as Philadelphia and Chicago became significant only in the early part of the twentieth century, although the origins of the migration, especially to New York and its environs, can be traced to the early nineteenth century.[4]

Local and regional differences can also be seen in the configuration and socioeconomic background of Hispanic nationality groups. Mexicans and other immigrants from Central America, for example, have become the predominant groups in the Southwest, while balanced but separate communities of Mexicans and Puerto Ricans have become foremost in Chicago. Cubans have been the most important group in southern Florida since at least the early 1960s, while Puerto Ricans, Dominicans, Cubans, Colombians, Ecuadoreans, and Peruvians have been the key Spanish-speaking participants in the migration to metropolitan New York and to other communities in the Northeast.[5]

In terms of socioeconomic background, many immigrants and migrants have come from impoverished working-class, rural, or mixed rural and urban backgrounds, such as the Mexicans who have settled in the Southwest or the Puerto Ricans who came to New York between the late 1940s and the early 1970s. Others have come from predominantly middle-class, professional, semiprofessional, and urban backgrounds such as the Cubans, Puerto Ricans, and Spaniards who settled in New York between the 1860s and 1910; the Cuban refugees who settled in South Florida in the 1960s, and subgroups among Dominicans, Nicaraguans, Colombians, Ecuadoreans, Peruvians, Argentinians, Uruguayans, Chileans and others who have settled in New York, Miami, and other localities in the eastern and southern parts of the United States since the late 1960s.

The New York metropolitan area (along with other large urban centers of the Northeast and Midwest) differs from other parts of the country in terms of the overall mix of its ethnic, racial, and nationality groups. As a "minority" group in New York, the Hispanic population is second in size to the African-American community. By contrast, Cubans are the predominant minority group in southern and central Florida, while the configuration in the Southwest reveals Mexicans constituting an absolute majority of the population in urban centers such as San Antonio, El Paso, Albuquerque, and Tucson.

Differences in demographics have also had an impact on the cultural and political issues affecting Latinos in each of the major regions or localities where Hispanics have settled. The evolving culture and politics of Latino groups in the southwestern United States, for instance, have been influenced by Mexico and Central America, reflecting the dominant position of the nationality groups that originated in that region. By contrast, a Cuban variant of Hispanic Caribbean culture and politics has been foremost in southern Florida since the early 1960s, although the influx of Nicaraguans and others from Central and South America has complicated the reality in that area since the early 1980s. In New York, the evolution of Latino culture and politics has also been influenced by the configuration of nationality groups and the particulars of the migration process. Cuban, Puerto Rican, and Spanish influences were foremost from the late 1860s to the early 1920s. Puerto Rican culture and politics became dominant between the early 1920s and the early 1970s because of the emergence of Puerto Ricans as the largest single Hispanic nationality group in the New York area during that period. Since the early 1980s, however, the evolving amalgam of Latino culture and politics has become increasingly more complex reflecting the increasing influx of Dominicans, Colombians, Ecuadoreans, and other persons from Central and South America.

The essays that follow are divided into two broad categories, "Historical and Sociological Perspectives" and "Policy Issues." In chapter 1, Gabriel Haslip-Viera offers a historical perspective on the evolution of the Latino community in New York from the early nineteenth century to the present day. The author divides the migration and settlement process into four chronological periods: the late nineteenth century, the years between 1900 and 1945, the period between 1946 and 1965, and the years from 1965 to the present. According to the author this chronological segmentation reflects the relative importance of certain Hispanic subgroups at various points in the migration process. It also reflects the differences in the socioeconomic and political factors that contributed to Hispanic migration at various stages of the historical chronology. These included the factors that propelled Latino emigration: variations in the socioeconomic characteristics of the migrants, alterations in the transportation networks that facilitated migration, changes in the immigration laws and granting of refuge status, and modifications in the socioeconomic factors that facilitated the incorporation of Hispanics into the New York labor market.

The essay by Ramona Hernández and Silvio Torres-Saillant appraises the conflicting signals of economic prosperity and social stagnation simultaneously exhibited by Dominican immigrants in New York. They argue that the overall progress of this community is endangered by several obstacles. These obstacles, however, are bound to lose significance with the passage of time and the advent of the first generation of American-born Dominicans. Somewhat less clear is the difference between gender relations in the Republic and in New York. The authors discuss the sociohistorical dynamics that will help Dominicans recognize the permanence of their settlement in the United States. This, in turn, will heighten their sense of identity as members of a minority community and help them see the need for alliances with other minorities in the States.

Political sociologist Robert Smith examines the growing presence of Mexicans in the New York area. He focuses on the historical, sociological, and economic reasons for the increasing Mexican migration, particularly from the southern region, Mixteca Sur. A theoretical issue central to this chapter is the transnational nature of this Mexican diaspora, not only the impact of the increased Mexican presence upon New York but also how money and values acquired in New York are affecting society, politics, and economics in the Mixteca Sur.

In chapter 4, sociologist Clara Rodríguez discusses the "racial" status of Hispanics in New York City and the United States. The author examines the difference between the North American and Latin American racial classification systems and the nebulous or fluctuating racial position of Latinos within North American society. She also traces the racial themes that have developed in the social science literature on New York's Puerto Ricans and offers predictions on Puerto Rican assimilation, the relationship between Puerto

Ricans, other Latinos and African Americans, and the role of "racial intermediates" within the Puerto Rican and Hispanic community. Professor Rodríguez concludes her essay by suggesting that Puerto Ricans, Latinos, and other groups with a "multiracial" orientation will challenge the predominant black/white notion of race in the United States.

In chapter 5 José Hernández presents a methodologically innovative piece using content analysis to examine Latino college students' attitudes about themselves and their community. The research adds support to the findings of other social scientists that Hispanics first identify by national group.[6] Nevertheless, Hernández found that the students also identified as Latino when describing themselves vis-à-vis the Anglo-American world. These 1980s students differed from young Puerto Ricans who came of age in the 1960s in that they saw the revitalization of their communities coming primarily from within rather than from government aid and generally had a pragmatic approach to politics. They did resemble students of the 1960s, however, in their willingness to work for community empowerment and willingness to adopt militant tactics if necessary.

The following chapter, written by sociologist Ana María Díaz-Stevens, highlights the Puerto Rican religious experience especially as it has unfolded in the New York setting. Roman Catholicism is at the core of the survey, but the author stresses that Catholicism for Latinos, and Puerto Ricans in particular, has been a religion of the home and community. The practice of faith has not been tied to the ecclesiastical institution, nor has it depended purely on the services of the clergy. In addition, Díaz-Stevens makes clear the other strands of spiritual practice that contribute to a full understanding of religion in the Puerto Rican context. Those other strands are African beliefs, the remnants of Taíno religion (usually subsumed under African-based religious practices), French spiritism, Protestantism and Pentecostalism from the United States, and, most recently, Cuban Santería.

The more policy-focused pieces begin with Edwin Meléndez's chapter examining Hispanic wage inequality in New York City. Meléndez, an economist, notes that low earnings have proven to be one of the most important underlying causes of Latino socioeconomic disadvantage. Wage differentials between Hispanics and non-Hispanic whites are attributed to lower educational levels, lack of skills, immigrant status, segmentation within the job market, and, importantly, discrimination based on race or ethnicity. These factors suggest that the "supply-side" economic policies of the 1980s have been unsuccessful in correcting the problem of Hispanic wage inequality in the absence of the strong enforcement of antidiscrimination laws and other labor-oriented regulations.

Dr. José Sánchez provides a theoretically innovative approach to the study of mainland Puerto Rican politics in chapter 9. He argues that the social-science frameworks that are usually employed to study Puerto Rican politics in New York, such as the pluralist, elitist, or political-economic, are flawed in trying to capture the political and social reality of the group's experience. The author advocates using a "social power" approach that describes power as located in existing social structures and demonstrates that social power, which Puerto Ricans do not have, is often a prerequisite for political power. Consequently, political power is not something the Puerto Rican community can get simply by striving for it.

Professor Jesse Vázquez provides an overview of problems facing young Puerto Ricans in the school system. While he focuses on issues facing students in New York City, much of his essay has implications for a discussion of the educational crisis apparent throughout the nation and especially in those schools serving Latino youth. Vázquez attempts to place the school experience of Latinos into a broad framework by identifying the key social, political, economic, and cultural processes shaping the schools in Puerto Rican communities. He also examines specific needs of Latino students in the effort to stem their high dropout rate, such as more resources for bilingual and multicultural education, maintaining potential involvement in the schools, and better teacher training for multicultural school populations. Vázquez notes, however, that these represent only a small sample of the problems hindering quality education in most Latino neighborhoods in the City and throughout the country.

The piece by Sherrie Baver focuses on the new Latino immigration to New York City. Specifically, she examines the effects of the 1986 Immigration Reform and Control Act with its key features of amnesty and employer sanctions on the Latino community, especially among Dominicans, since Dominicans had the largest number of amnesty applicants in the region. Although the article looks at the mechanics of the immigration law and has undocumented workers as its primary focus, Baver points out that little difference exists between legal and illegal workers in New York; typically, *indocumentados* are members of the same family and live in the same households as legal residents and citizens.

Finally, Juan Flores offers a brief overview of the present state of Puerto Rican or, more precisely, "Nuyorican" culture and art at the beginning of the 1990s. Flores maintains that, for Puerto Ricans, re-creating Caribbean cultural and artistic traditions on the mainland is not merely an act of nostalgia but rather "an indispensable source of self-affirmation" in the face of poverty and discrimination. Furthermore, he is careful to note that other Latino immigrants from the Caribbean are contributing to the *sabor trópico* we sense around us in New York today.

Together these essays reveal a great deal about the past and present condition of Latinos in metropolitan New York, especially that of Puerto Ricans, since Puerto Ricans remain the largest Hispanic national-origin group and, in fact, one of the largest of all national-origin groups in the city. The authors have also suggested that many of their findings and policy recommendations can be generalized to the national level. While understanding that real behavioral and attitudinal differences exist among the several Latino national-origin groups and that the Spanish-speaking population of the United States identifies first by national-origin group and only secondly as "Hispanic" or "Latino," areas of convergence exist in which the Latino or Spanish-speaking community shares common interests and goals.[7] Despite their distinctive histories, the life situations of Hispanics are similar in that (a) they are overwhelmingly urban and poor; (b) intermarriage is increasing between different Spanish-speaking groups, for example, between Puerto Ricans and Dominicans in New York; and (c) since U.S. society, in general, and the federal government (through program funding) perceive Latinos as one group, the national-origin groups are working together to struggle for perceived common goals.[8] Furthermore, given this perspective, the authors believe that Puerto Rican New Yorkers, who have been the prime focus of this volume, should not be seen as "exceptional" among Latinos.[9] The continuing high rate of poverty is not the result of culture or particular cultural characteristics. Rather it is a consequence of the structural constraints that Puerto Ricans and other Latinos have to face, which seem to be more extreme in New York, where most Puerto Ricans live, than it is in other parts of the country, such as Florida, where most Puerto Ricans appear to be better off.[10]

A final issue for students of the Latino experience not directly addressed in these essays but important for future research is whether Puerto Ricans and other Spanish-speaking groups will maintain a distinct and dynamic cultural identity or will "melt" as the symbolism suggests into the large pot that is American society. The answer depends on whether or not the nation has the tolerance and commitment to see itself as a multicultural society. Most importantly, the way Spanish-speaking groups, either individually or collectively, continue to shape their identity will reveal much about the image of the United States in the twenty-first century.

NOTES

1. Such studies include Arnaldo de Leon, *Ethnicity in the Sunbelt: A History of Mexican-Americans in Houston* (Houston: University of Houston, 1989); Richard R. Fagen, Richard A. Brody and Thomas O'Leary, *Cubans in Exile: Disaffection and the Revolution* (Stanford: Stanford University Press, 1968); Joseph P. Fitzpatrick, *Puerto Rican Americans: The Meaning of Migration to the Mainland*, 2nd ed. (Englewood Cliffs, N.J.: Prentice-Hall, 1987); Sherri Grasmuck and Patricia R. Pessar, *Between Two Islands: Dominican International Migration* (Berkeley: University of California Press, 1991); Leo Greber, Joan Moore, and Ralph C. Guzman, *The Mexican-American People: The Nation's Second Largest Minority* (New York: the Free Press, 1970); Glenn Hendricks, *The Dominican Diaspora: From the Dominican Republic to New York—Villagers in Transition* (New York: Teachers College Press, 1974); Adalberto López, ed., *The Puerto Ricans: Their History, Culture, and Society* (Cambridge, Mass.: Schenkman Publishing, 1980); Matt S. Meier and Feliciano Ribera, *Mexican Americans/American Mexicans: From Conquistadors to Chicanos* (New York: Hill and Wang, 1992); Felix M. Padilla, *Puerto Rican Chicago* (Notre Dame: University of Notre Dame Press, 1987); Alejandro Portes and Robert L. Bach, *Latin Journey: Cuban and Mexican Immigrants in the United*

States (Berkeley: University of California Press, 1985); Clara E. Rodríguez, *Puerto Ricans: Born in the U.S.A.* (Boulder, Colo.: Westview Press, 1989); and Eleanor Meyer Rogg and Rosemary Santana Cooney, *(Adaptation and Adjustment of Cubans: West New York, New Jersey* (New York: Hispanic Research Center, 1980) among others.

2. These studies include Archdiocese of New York: Office of Pastoral Research, *Hispanics in New York: Religious, Cultural and Social Experiences* (New York: Office of Pastoral Research, 1982); Angelo Falcón, "Black and Latino Politics in New York City: Race and Ethnicity in a Changing Urban Context" in F. Chris Garciá, ed. *Latinos and the Political System* (Notre Dame: University of Notre Dame Press, 1988), pp. 171–94; Joseph P. Fitzpatrick and Douglas T. Gurak, "New York Hispanics: A Demographic Overview," in Edna Acosta Belén and Barbara R. Sjostrom, eds. *The Hispanic Experience in the United States: Contemporary Issues and Perspectives* (New York: Praeger, 1988), pp. 57–78; Felix M. Padilla, *Latino Ethnic Consciousness: The Case of Mexican Americans and Puerto Ricans in Chicago* (Notre Dame: University of Notre Dame Press, 1985); Saskia Sassen-Koob, "Changing Composition and Labor Market Location of Hispanic Immigrants in New York City, 1960–1980" in George J. Borjas and Marta Tienda, eds. *Hispanics in the U.S. Economy* (Orlando, Fla.: Academic Press, 1985), pp. 299–322.

3. The third category includes, among others, Acosta Belén and Sjostrom, *The Hispanic Experience in the United States* (note 2, above); Frank Bean and Marta Tienda, *The Hispanic Population of the United States* (New York: Russell Sage, 1987); Borjas and Tienda, *Hispanics in the U.S. Economy* (note 2, above); Pastora San Juan Cafferty and William C. McCready, *Hispanics in the United States: A New Social Agenda* (New Brunswick, N.J.: Transaction Books, 1985); L. H. Gann and Peter J. Duignan, *The Hispanics in the United States: A History* (Boulder, Colo.: Westview Press, 1986); F. Chris García, *Latinos and the Political System* (note 2, above); Stephen Thernstrom, ed. *Harvard Encyclopedia of American Ethnic Groups* (Cambridge, Mass.: The Belknap Press of Harvard University, 1980); Joan Moore and Harry Pachon, *Hispanics in the United States* (Englewood Cliffs, N.J.: Prentice-Hall, 1985); Earl Shorris, *Latinos: A Biography of the People* (New York: W.W. Norton, 1992); and Thomas Weyr, *Hispanic U.S.A.* (New York: Harper and Row, 1988).

4. See the beginning of chapter 1.

5. See the works listed in note 2, above.

6. For example, Marta Tienda and Vilma Ortiz, "Hispanicity and the 1980 Census," *Social Science Quarterly* 67 (1986): 3–20.

7. As indicated in the initial results of the "Latino National Political Survey." Early findings were summarized in the *Chronicle of Higher Education,* September 11, 1991, p. A12.

8. Joan Moore and Harry Pachon, *Hispanics in the United States* (note 2, above).

9. Conservative author Linda Chavez argues that Puerto Ricans are "exceptional" in their lack of socioeconomic progress in *Out of the Barrio: Toward a New Politics of Hispanic Assimilation* (New York: Basic Books, 1991).

10. See Larry Rohter, "A Puerto Rican Boom for Florida," *New York Times,* January 31, 1994, p. A10.

Part One

HISTORICAL AND SOCIOLOGICAL PERSPECTIVES

1

The Evolution of the Latino Community in New York City: Early Nineteenth Century to the Present

GABRIEL HASLIP-VIERA

Phase One, 1810–1900

It is perhaps accurate to say that interest in the issues affecting Latinos in New York has intensified steadily in recent years. With greater frequency, journalists, academics, and government policymakers have discussed the growth of a diverse Hispanic population and its impact on employment, education, housing, crime, social services, and politics. In general, the increased scrutiny has focused attention on Latinos as a contemporary phenomenon associated with the "recent wave" of immigrants to the city; however, the origins and the evolution of New York's Hispanic community can actually be traced as far back as the early nineteenth century and possibly even earlier.[1]

Perhaps the first reference to a group that in the twentieth century would be called Latino or Hispanic was made in 1810, when Timothy Dwight, the president of Yale University, compiled a list of inhabitants or "classes" in New York, which he included in a memoir of his travels through the northeastern United States. This list made reference to "a few . . . Spaniards and West Indians," who were probably merchants or other persons associated with the small, but growing commerce between New York and Spain's possessions in the Caribbean and Latin America.[2] This was also probably true of most of the "508 persons from Mexico and South America" who were counted during the federal census of 1845; however, it also appears that there might have been a substantial undercount of Latinos in New York by federal census enumerators during this first phase of the migration process that ended around

3

1900 and that this undercount may have continued in the decades which followed.[3]

For example, the Puerto Rican activist Bernardo Vega refers in his memoirs to the large political gatherings that were frequently organized by advocates of Cuban and Puerto Rican independence. He also makes reference to the 3,000 cigar factories that employed "many Puerto Ricans and Cubans" during the early 1890s. However, it appears that these claims are not confirmed by the official statistics of the period (see table 1). According to the census of 1890, the city had a Latino population of just under 6,000, which included 218 Mexicans, 1,421 Spaniards, 907 persons from Central and South America, and only 3,448 persons from Cuba, Puerto Rico, the Dominican Republic and other parts of the Caribbean.[4]

In contrast to what developed later, Latino migration to New York was relatively modest in the years prior to 1900. Hispanic emigration to the United States was generally discouraged by the socioeconomic conditions that were prevalent in Latin America throughout the nineteenth century. Most of the Central and South American republics and colonial possessions were underpopulated or were going through the first stages of economic modernization or industrialization. In Cuba, Puerto Rico, and Brazil the importation of African slave labor continued into the 1850s and 1860s because of labor shortages in the expanding plantation sectors. As the economy of the Hispanic Caribbean changed during the late nineteenth century, slave labor was increasingly replaced by Chinese contract labor and by an increased flow of European immigrants who were attracted by the growth of the Caribbean sugar, coffee, and tobacco sectors. In the rest of Latin America, economic modernization and industrialization contributed to a significant increase in European immigration. As was the case in North America during this same period, Argentina, Brazil, Chile, and a number of other countries or regions absorbed large numbers of immigrants from Spain, Italy, France, Germany, Portugal, Great Britain, Ireland, Eastern Europe, and also from Lebanon and Syria in the Middle East.[5]

Most of the immigrants who came to New York from Latin America in the late nineteenth century were business people, professionals, white-collar workers, specialized artisans, and their dependents. It appears that a network of merchants and their subordinates were the predominant group during the early nineteenth century;

Table 1
The Latin American and Caribbean Population
of New York City, 1870–1890*

	1870	%	1880	%	1890	%
Central America	22	0.6	29	0.5	184	3.1
Cuba & West Indies**	2508	69.6	3480	65.7	3448	57.5
Cuba	1565	43.4	2073	39.1		
Mexico	86	2.3	170	3.2	218	3.6
South America	307	8.5	570	10.7	723	12.1
Spain	682	18.9	1048	19.8	1421	23.7
Total	3605	100.0	5294	100.0	5994	100.0

*Total "foreign-born population." Includes Brooklyn, Bronx, and Manhattan for the 1870 and 1880 census. For the 1890 census also includes "Long Island City" (for all countries), Queens County and Staten Island (for Spain, South America, Cuba, and the West Indies only).

**Probably includes many persons of Spanish origin or background who lived in Cuba and Puerto Rico, which were Spanish colonies throughout this period.

SOURCE: U.S. Department of Interior, Census Office, *Compendium of the Ninth Census* (June 1, 1870) (Washington, D.C.: Government Printing Office, 1872), pp. 387–91, 449. *Compendium of the Tenth Census*, Part 1 (June 1, 1880) (Washington, D.C.: Government Printing Office, 1882), pp. 547, 551. *Census of 1890* (Washington, D.C.: Government Printing Office, 1892), pp. 645–47, 670, 672, 674, 676.

however, after 1860, the Latino community became much more diversified and included the owners and employees of factories, artisan shops, grocery stores, pharmacies, barbershops, rooming houses, restaurants and other enterprises. Skilled and semiskilled artisans and laborers came to New York in increased numbers during the final decades of the nineteenth century. The majority of artisans and laborers were employed in tobacco manufacturing which expanded in the years between 1880 and 1920; however, in time, the artisans were also supplemented by a growing number of semiskilled and unskilled industrial laborers who came to New York in search of employment in factories and in services.[6]

Political exiles also came to New York during the late nineteenth century. They included disaffected liberals, socialists and anarcho-syndicalists from Spain and Latin America. They also included alienated labor leaders, writers, poets, artists, teachers, and intellectuals. In fact, New York became the headquarters for the exiled leaders and supporters of Cuban and Puerto Rican independence during this period. The Cuban patriots, José Martí, Tomás

Estrada Palma, and Dr. Julio Henna, an advocate of Puerto Rican independence, became residents of New York during the 1870s and 1880s. For a time, Martí worked for Joseph Pulitzer's New York World, which was one of the city's major newspapers, while Henna, a practicing physician, became one of the founders of Flower Fifth Avenue Hospital in upper Manhattan.

The importance of New York as a center for nationalist and revolutionary sentiment was reflected in the successful efforts to raise funds, publish newspapers, and hold political rallies. It was also reflected in the frequent visits by important political and cultural leaders who came to New York to participate in various activities but who were not residents of the city. These persons included Cuban revolutionary leaders such as Antonio Maceo and Máximo Gómez, who was actually a native of the Dominican Republic. They also included Spaniards, such as the labor leader, Santiago Iglesias; other Dominicans, such as Enrique Trujillo, the author of the epic "El Enriquillo;" and educational and revolutionary leaders from Puerto Rico, such as Eugenio María de Hostoes and Ramón Betances.[7]

The political exiles who lived in New York, at least temporarily during the late nineteenth century, became part of a small, vibrant, and growing community. In general, Latinos lived in scattered concentrations throughout Manhattan and downtown Brooklyn. Bernardo Vega suggests that there was relatively little housing discrimination against Hispanics during this period; however, he also acknowledges that the darker or more "African" looking Latinos were compelled to live in neighborhoods where African-Americans predominated. Arturo Alfonso Schomburg, a Puerto Rican activist who later achieved fame as a Black bibliophile in the Harlem community, established his first family residence in an African-American neighborhood called "San Juan Hill," which was located in Manhattan, west of Amsterdam Avenue, between 60th and 70th Streets. Despite this and other instances of racial segregation and discrimination in housing, Hispanics were generally found in most working-class neighborhoods of the city during this period.[8]

Concentrations of working-class Latinos were found in Harlem, Chelsea, Yorkville, the West Side, and the Lower East Side of Manhattan. They were also found in the Columbia Street and "Navy Yard" districts of Brooklyn. In general, most Hispanics lived in the midst of larger immigrant communities, where Germans, Irish,

Italians, Jews, Hungarians, and other groups from central and eastern Europe predominated. Bernardo Vega states that affluent Cubans lived in the largely middle-class section of south-central Harlem, north of Cathedral Parkway. He also notes that less affluent Latinos were found in the midst of a working-class Jewish community, along Madison and Park Avenues, between 100th and 110th Streets. These last two concentrations were the nucleus of what later became known as Spanish Harlem or El Barrio.[9]

Phase Two, 1900–1945

In the final decades of the nineteenth century, Cubans, Puerto Ricans, and Spaniards were the predominant groups within the Latino population of New York City. This trend continued during the next phase of the migratory process which began in 1900 and ended around 1945. Puerto Ricans, in particular, became the largest Hispanic subgroup by the early 1930s, despite an island population that was very small when compared to Latin America as a whole. According to the estimates that were compiled at that time, the Latino population of New York had reached 22,000 by 1916, 41,094 by 1920, 110,223 by 1930, and 134,000 by 1940.[10] Of the 110,223 Hispanics enumerated by the census bureau in 1930, 44,908 (40.7%) were Puerto Ricans, 22,501 (20.4%) were Spaniards, 19,774 (17.9%) were Cubans and Dominicans, 4,653 (3.5%) were Mexicans, and 18,748 (17.0%) were persons from Central and South America (see table 2).

The Antillean orientation of New York's Latino community between 1900 and 1945 reflected the socioeconomic and political changes that gripped Cuba, Puerto Rico, and the rest of the Caribbean during this period. Cuba and Puerto Rico were annexed by the United States as a result of the military victory over Spain in the War of 1898. Cuba was granted its independence in 1904, but Puerto Rico remained an unincorporated territory of the United States until 1952. Direct political involvement by the United States had an impact on emigration from Cuba and Puerto Rico in the years after 1900, but it was the relative geographical proximity to New York and the dramatic infusion of United States investment capital in the economies of both islands that had the greatest impact.

The United States also intervened actively in the internal affairs

Table 2
The Latino Population of New York City, 1920–1940*

	1920	%	1930	%	1940	%
Cuba & West Indies	8,722	21.2	19,774	17.9	23,124	17.2
Mexico	2,572	6.3	4,292	3.9	4,653	3.5
Puerto Rico	7,364	17.9	44,908	40.7	61,463	45.8
Central &						
South America	7,777	18.9	18,748	17.0	19,727	14.7
Spain	14,659	35.7	22,501	20.4	25,283	18.8
Total	41,094	100.0	110,223	100.0	134,252	100.0

*Includes "foreign-born population" (except for Puerto Ricans) for the 1920 census, the "foreign-born white population" for Cuba and the West Indies in the 1920 census, "foreign-born white" and "native white of foreign or mixed parentage" (except for Mexicans and Puerto Ricans) for the 1930 census, and "foreign-born white" and "nativity and parentage of foreign white stock" (except for Puerto Ricans) for the 1940 census.

SOURCE: U.S. Department of Commerce, Bureau of the Census, *Fourteenth Census of the United States . . . 1920*, vol. 3, table 6, p. 679; table 12, pp. 702 and 704. *Fifteenth Census of the United States: 1930*, vol. 3, part 2, table 17, p. 297; table 18, p. 301; table 19, p. 303. *Sixteenth Census of the United States: 1940*, vol. 2, Characteristics of the Population, part 5, table 24, pp. 63–64; and Special Bulletin, table 7, p. 74. Walter Laidlaw, *Population of the City of New York, 1890–1930* (New York: Cities Census Committee, Inc., 1932), table 40, p. 247; table 51, p. 253. Ira Rosenwaike, *Population History of New York City* (Syracuse: Syracuse University Press, 1972), pp. 101, 121, 203.

of the Dominican Republic during this period. The economy of the Dominican Republic experienced substantial growth during the United States military occupation of 1916 to 1924; however, regarding Dominican migration, the impact of U.S.-sponsored modernization was relatively less dramatic because the island economy was less developed than that of Cuba or even Puerto Rico. Economic growth continued with the establishment of the Trujillo dictatorship after 1930, but the movement of Dominicans to the United States or elsewhere was kept to a minimum because of the nature of the development process and the restrictive policies that were placed on emigration from that country from 1930 to 1961.[11]

In Cuba, United States investment capital further strengthened a sugar sector that was already dominant in the late nineteenth century. It also reinforced Cuba's economic dependence on the United States, which was its principle market. The expansion of the Cuban sugar sector created opportunities for some of its citizens, but it also led to economic and social misfortune for other segments of the population. Cubans were increasingly subject to the often dramatic and unpredictable effects of the volatile sugar market. Between 1900 and 1945 the Cuban economy experienced dramatic boom and bust periods that had a detrimental effect on many Cubans at each stage of the economic cycle. The result was increased Cuban emigration to southern Florida and the New York City area in the years after 1900. Cuban emigration to the United States rose because of economic dislocation and monetary inflation during periods of prosperity and growth. It also rose because of high unemployment, decreased wages, a decline in living standards, and increased political instability during periods of economic crisis and decline.[12]

Puerto Rico also experienced the detrimental effects of United States economic investment during the same period, but in contrast to Cuba, the consequences for the island population appear to have been much more devastating. As was the case in Cuba, United States economic investment in Puerto Rico was directed toward the sugar sector. There was also some investment in urban-oriented manufacturing; however, in contrast to Cuba, United States investment in Puerto Rico had a disastrous impact on the traditional, more labor-intensive coffee and tobacco sectors. The coffee industry, in particular, was extremely important to Puerto Rico's economy during this period. In the late nineteenth century it had been the dominant sector, providing most of the wealth and most of the employment for the island's population—especially in the mountainous interior region.[13]

As a result of the dramatic change in the investment climate and the shift in emphasis toward the sugar sector after the United States takeover, the Puerto Rican coffee industry experienced a prolonged and steady decline in the years between 1898 and 1930. The tobacco industry also began to wither away after an initial period of prosperity came to an end in the early 1920s. By the early 1930s, the labor-intensive coffee and tobacco sectors had ceased to be vital or even important components of the Puerto Rican economy. Thousands of rural and working-class Puerto Ricans were compelled to migrate from the coffee and tobacco growing regions of the island's interior to the coastal areas and the cities in search of employment in the sugar, manufacturing, and service sectors of the economy. The migration from the interior regions created enormous hardships for the populations that already lived in the cities and along the coast. Overall, wages fell, living standards deteriorated, and unemployment increased in the years between 1898 and 1930.[14]

This was only the beginning of a long and difficult period for the Puerto Rican economy.

Commercial treaties between the United States and Cuba and the effects of the worldwide economic depression of the 1930s initiated a period of crisis and decline for the Puerto Rican sugar industry. By 1935 the Puerto Rican economy had virtually collapsed, largely as a result of the crisis in the sugar sector and the impact that this had on manufacturing, services, and other sectors of the economy.[15] The increased migration of Puerto Ricans to New York in the years between 1900 and 1945 reflected the deepening economic and social crisis that gripped the island throughout this period. It also reflected the ease of travel to New York, the relative prosperity to be found in the United States, and the fact that Puerto Ricans were granted United States citizenship in 1917.[16]

Net migration from Puerto Rico to New York rose rather dramatically during the economic boom years of 1914–1915, 1917–1920, and 1923–1930. After 1930, the pace of migration slowed considerably as a result of the global economic depression and the impact that World War II was to have on both Puerto Rico and the United States. Most of the Puerto Ricans and Latinos who came to New York in the years between 1900 and 1945 were urban-oriented, working-class men and women. In contrast to the late nineteenth century, there were proportionally fewer individuals who were business oriented, well educated or middle class. Most of the newcomers were generally skilled or semiskilled factory operatives, artisans, white-collar workers, and service-sector employees who found similar kinds of work in the New York labor market.[17] A considerable number were skilled and semiskilled working-class women. By the late 1920s, large numbers of Hispanic women were employed in the labor-intensive service and industrial sectors. Many worked in the garment factories or performed piece work for entrepreneurs in that industry. Based on the figures compiled for Spanish Harlem in 1925, which are biased in favor of its mostly working-class population, 62 percent of all Latinos were employed in the industrial sector, 18 percent were employed in services, 16 percent were engaged in commerce, and 4 percent were listed as "owners" and "supervisors."[19]

In the years between 1900 and 1945, the burgeoning Latino population became identified with certain areas or neighborhoods of the city. According to Vega, the "barrio Latino" in East Harlem had already reached a mature stage of development by the late 1920s. Immigrants from Spain and their descendants were associated with the West 14th Street and Chelsea areas of Manhattan. At the same time, other neighborhoods, such as parts of the Lower East Side of Manhattan, South Brooklyn ("Red Hook" and the Columbia Street area), the "Navy Yard" and the Williamsburg section of Brooklyn, also became identified with the Latino community by the late 1920s or early 1930s.

For the most part, Hispanics coexisted with the earlier immigrant populations, or they eventually displaced the earlier groups after a period of time. From 1900 to 1945, the Latino population of South Brooklyn more or less coexisted with the largely Italian-American residents of that neighborhood. In East Harlem, by contrast, the Hispanic population eventually replaced the predominantly Jewish population west of Park Avenue by the Depression years of the early 1930s.[20]

The housing stock that was available to working-class Latinos was among the worst that could be found in New York City during this period. The dwelling spaces were primarily "furnished rooms," "cold-water flats," and "railroad apartments" in the "Old" and "New Law" tenements and row houses that were found in most of the neighborhoods where Latinos lived. Most of this housing stock was already considered substandard soon after it was built between the 1860s and the 1890s. Overcrowding and the lack of maintenance had already turned many of these structures and their neighborhoods into what outsiders called "slums" by the time that they were populated by Hispanics.[21]

Despite the inadequacies of the housing stock and other serious problems, Latinos had a generally optimistic view of life in the city. This appeared to be the case even during the 1930s, when the community was forced to endure the hardships of high unemployment, decreased wages, and the diminished living standards associated with the Great Depression. Latinos worked hard, got married, gave birth to children, attended church, and participated in the rich social and cultural life that they created in their communities. They patronized grocery stores, barbershops, restaurants, tailoring establishments, and other businesses owned by Hispanics and non-Hispanics. They also organized social clubs, self-help groups, and political associations, and the debated the complex social, cultural, and political issues of the day. For the most part, Latino political concerns during this period were largely oriented toward the homelands that most of them still hoped to return to at some point in the future. At this stage in the evolution of the Hispanic community, a real commitment to life in the New York area had not as yet emerged.[22]

Phase Three, 1945–1965/1970

The demographic composition and orientation of the Hispanic community underwent a significant change during the next phase of the migration process. In effect, the Puerto Rican community became synonymous with the Latino community in the years between 1945 and 1970. Thousands of Puerto Ricans began to leave the island for New York City during the early part of the postwar period because of economic and social policies that were instituted at this time. After earlier efforts to revive the Puerto Rican economy had failed during the late 1930s and early 1940s, the United States government developed an ambitious program for the industrialization of Puerto Rico in the postwar period. With the cooperation of Puerto Rico's political leaders, the government promoted the establishment of labor-intensive enterprises in an effort to reduce the island's rate of unemployment and underemployment. North American investors received tax benefits, free land, low-interest loans and other incentives in an attempt to expand the number of enterprises, but all of this was considered insufficient to overcome the perceived problem of "overpopulation" and the negative effects of the economic collapse that gripped the traditional agrarian sectors. The result was the implementation of policies designed to encourage the unemployed and the underemployed to leave Puerto Rico for the United States.[23]

Puerto Ricans were advised by government bureaucrats to leave the island for New York, where it was claimed that better employment opportunities could be found. Shipping companies, charter airlines, regular air-travel service and reduced fares were established to facilitate the flow of migrants from Puerto Rico to New York.[24] The result was a dramatic increase in the number of Puerto Ricans in New York City and its environs in the years after 1945 (see tables 2 and 3). The Puerto Rican population of New York rose from 61,463 in 1940 to 612,574 in 1960, and it continued to increase during the next decade, reaching 811,843 in 1970. There was also a rise in the number of other Latinos who came to New York during this period, but in contrast to the Puerto Ricans, the increase of other Hispanics was proportionally less dramatic. In the years between 1940 and 1970, the Cuban population rose from about 23,000 to 84,179, the Dominican population rose from an unknown figure to at least 66,914, and the population of persons from Central and South America increased from 19,727 to at least 216,120 (see tables 2 and 3).

Overall, the Latinos who came to New York during this period were overwhelmingly of the working class, and this was especially true of the Puerto Ricans. Most Puerto Ricans found employment in the labor-intensive manufacturing and service sectors of the New York economy. A significant number, mostly from the rural areas, also found employment on potato and vegetable farms in the surrounding suburban and rural areas. These individuals were brought to New York under a special agricultural contract labor program specifically created for this purpose. Normally the Puerto Rican farm workers traveled back and forth from their homes on the island to their jobs in the New York–New Jersey area; however, with the passage of time, many of these individuals settled in the city, where employment in the manufacturing and service sectors of the economy was considered somewhat more lucrative.[25]

The other Latinos who came to New York in the years between 1945 and 1970 were somewhat different in terms of their socioeconomic backgrounds than the Puerto Ricans who came during the same period. For the most part, the other Hispanics were similar to the earlier group of Latinos and Puerto Ricans who came between 1900 and 1945. Many of the other Latinos were unskilled and semi-skilled workers, but in contrast to the Puerto Ricans, they included a much larger group of persons who were well educated, urban oriented, and middle class. Overall, the Puerto Ricans who came between 1945 and 1970 were impoverished, unemployed, or under-employed persons from rural and urban areas of the island, with minimal education and few skills. However, there were also some (but fewer) Puerto Ricans who were better educated, business oriented, and middle class.[26]

A major transformation in the composition of the New York labor force enabled the city's economy to absorb enormous numbers of Puerto Ricans and other Latinos in the years after 1945. Returning

Table 3
The Latino Population of New York City, 1960–1990*

	1960	%	1970	%	1980	%	1990	%
Cuba	42,694	5.6	84,179	7.0	63,189	4.5	56,041	3.1
Dom. Rep.	13,293	1.7	66,914	5.6	125,380	8.9	332,713	18.7
Puerto Rico	612,574	80.9	811,843	67.5	860,552	61.2	896,763	50.3
Total Span. Caribbean	668,561	88.2	962,936	80.1	1,049,121	74.6	1,285,517	72.1
Costa Rica	1,761		4,429				6,920	
El Salvador	480		1,022		6,300		23,926	
Guatemala	1,019		2,036		6,323		15,873	
Honduras	2,516		6,785		14,100		22,167	
Mexico	8,260		7,893		25,577		61,772	
Nicaragua	1,300		2,014				9,660	
Panama	8,377		15,225		17,700		22,707	
Argentina	7,789		13,327		14,009		13,934	
Bolivia	558		1,218				3,465	
Chile	2,516		3,328				6,721	
Colombia	6,782		27,657		45,160		84,454	
Ecuador	4,077		20,326		40,320		78,444	
Paraguay	127							
Peru	2,297		5,438		11,640		23,257	
Uruguay	696		1,220				3,233	
Venezuela	3,478		3,410				4,752	

"Other S. Am."	9,199		13,630		18,974		
Spain	27,438		23,225		11,825		20,148
Other Hisp.	87,162		144,975		144,975		96,561
Total/Non-Carib. Hisp.	88,670	11.8	239,345	19.9	356,903	25.4	497,994	27.9
Grand Total	757,231	100.0	1,202,281	100.0	1,406,024	100.0	1,783,511	100.0

*Figures include the total number of Puerto Ricans and total "foreign-born" and "native of foreign or mixed parentage" for other nationalities in the 1960 census; total number of Cubans, Mexicans, Puerto Ricans, and total number of "foreign-born" and "native of foreign or mixed parentage" for other nationalities in the 1970 census; total number of Cubans, Mexicans, Puerto Ricans and total number of "foreign-born" only for other nationalities in the 1980 census; total number of Cubans, Mexicans, Puerto Ricans, and the total number of persons of "Hispanic origin" by nationality for other groups in the 1990 census.

SOURCE: U.S. Department of Commerce, Bureau of the Census, Census of Population: 1960, vol. 1, Characteristics of the Population, New York, part 34, table 99, p. 34/434. 1970 Census of Population, vol. 1, Characteristics of the Population, New York, part 34, table 119, pp. 34/607–34/611. 1970 Census of Population, vol. 1, Detailed Characteristics, New York, part 34, table 141, p. 34/720. 1980 Census of Population, vol. 1, Characteristics of the Population, chapter C, General Social and Economic Characteristics, New York, part 34, table 59, pp. 34/100–34/101. 1980 Census of Population, vol. 1, Characteristics of the Population, chapter D, Detailed Population Characteristics, New York, part 34, table 195, p. 34/14, 1990 Census of Population, General Population Characteristics, New York, section 1, table 5, pp. 47, 49–51. 1990 Census of Population, Social and Economic Characteristics, New York, section 1, table 6, pp. 45, 47–49. John I. Griffin and Jean Namias, eds., New York Metropolitan Regional Fact Book (New York: New York Council on Economic Education, 1965), table T2.12. Population Division, New York City Department of City Planning, Puerto Rican New Yorkers in 1990 (New York: Department of City Planning, 1993), tables A and B, pp. 13–14.

veterans of mostly European extraction were able to take advantage of new programs that were established by the federal government to promote upward economic and social mobility in the early years of the postwar period. For example, special education programs enabled returning veterans to leave their jobs in the factories and the low-grade services to become white-collar workers, managers, professionals, and entrepreneurs. At the same time, the federal housing programs of the early postwar period enabled veterans and their families to leave the congested inner city for the greener, more open spaces of the suburbs. The movement of the earlier immigrant groups and their descendants from the city to the sub-urbs was continuous in the years between 1945 and 1970. It was also reinforced by the exodus of corporations and small businesses and the establishment of new enterprises in the communities that proliferated in the suburbs and in other parts of the country.

The upward mobility of the earlier immigrant groups and the movement of people from New York to the suburbs created a vac-uum in the manufacturing and service sectors of the urban economy. In fact, many enterprises in these sectors actually experienced labor shortages in the early postwar period and developed recruitment programs to attract workers from outside the city. The result was the complete transformation of labor in manufacturing and in ser-vices in the years after 1950. Persons of European extraction, such as the Irish, Jews, Italians, and Greeks, were increasingly replaced by Puerto Ricans, other Latinos, and by African-Americans who came from the southern states.

Overall, Puerto Ricans and other Latinos worked in the garment industry, in paper box factories, in enterprises that manufactured dolls or plastic products, in restaurants, in grocery stores, in hotels, in office buildings, in residential structures, as cooks, dishwashers, "bus boys," messengers, elevator operators, custodians, and building superintendents. A smaller number were also employed in sales or as white-collar workers or lower-level managers in corporations or in public and private agencies and institutions.[27]

The massive influx of Puerto Ricans and other Latinos and the movement of the earlier immigrant groups and their descen-dants from the city to the suburbs permitted the growth and expan-sion of neighborhoods that were associated with the Hispanic population in the years after 1945. "El Barrio" or Spanish Harlem expanded eastward from Park Avenue to the East River between 1948 and 1955. A huge new concentration of mostly Puerto Rican Latinos also emerged in the South Bronx during the same period. In the Lower East Side, Puerto Ricans continued to displace the earlier, mostly Jewish residents, and they also established themselves in new concentrations in the West Side and Upper West Side of Manhattan. The Puerto Rican–Latino neighborhoods of Brooklyn and Queens also experienced growth during this period. The Puerto Rican enclave in the Navy Yard district of Brooklyn expanded northward and eastward into parts of Williamsburg, Greenpoint, and Bushwick. At the same time, the South Brooklyn enclave around Columbia Street expanded southward to include parts of Park Slope and Sunset Park.[28]

To some degree, the quality of the housing stock available to Latinos improved during this period, but overcrowding was a very serious problem, especially in the late 1940s and early 1950s, when severe housing shortages developed. In Spanish Harlem and the Lower East Side of Manhattan, the mostly Puerto Rican Latinos continued to occupy the same cold-water flats, furnished rooms, and railroad apartments that were considered substandard in the 1920s and even earlier. The same was also true of the housing stock in Red Hook, the Columbia Street area, and the Williamsburg section of Brooklyn; however in other neighborhoods, such as the South Bronx, the West Side of Manhattan, and the Sunset Park, Bushwick, Brownsville, and East New York sections of Brooklyn, the housing situation was somewhat more complex. To be sure, tenement buildings were to be found in all of these neighborhoods, but there were also roomier multiple-family dwellings, row houses, brownstones, and the larger apartment buildings that were originally built for middle-class residents. There were also the low- and high-rise housing projects that were built by the city and the state with increased frequency between 1935 and 1970. In general, apartments or accommodations in the privately owned buildings were more spacious, with larger rooms and full-sized kitchens and bathrooms; however, in most cases, the landlords merely collected the rents and allowed their properties to deteriorate soon after they were occupied by Puerto Ricans and other Latinos. By contrast, the publicly owned housing projects were initially established and administered as ideal communities. In time, however, these structures were overwhelmed by the introduction of "problem," "negligent," or "welfare families" and allowed to deteriorate through disinterest or neglect.[29]

Phase Four, 1965–Present

The composition of New York's Latino population and the population of the city as a whole was profoundly transformed during the most recent stage of the migration process which began in the first years of the 1960s. Starting as early as 1959, people from Cuba, the Dominican Republic, Colombia, Ecuador, Peru, and other countries in Central and South America began to arrive in New York in increasing numbers, and many of them came illegally. Cubans fleeing Castro's revolution were the first major group to settle in the New York area during this period, and they were soon followed by the Dominicans, who came in substantial numbers after the 1965 civil war. Most of the Cubans came as political refugees under a special program that was established by the federal government as part of its anti-Castro or anticommunist policies. The influx of Dominicans was made possible by a complex of factors which included the aftereffects of political turmoil and civil war, the never-ending search for cheaper labor in New York, and the relaxation of Trujillo-era restrictions on emigration. Some of these factors as well as other circumstances set the stage for increased immigration from Central and South America during this same period. In the years after 1965, Colombians, Ecuadoreans, Peruvians, Salvadorans, and others arrived in New York in substantial numbers. New York's Latino population increased 135.5 percent from 757,231 in 1960 to 1,783,511 in 1990 (See table 3), and non-Puerto Rican Hispanics accounted for a substantial proportion of this increase. Although the Latino population was 80.9% Puerto Rican in 1960, Puerto Ricans accounted for only 50.3% of the Latino population by 1990.[30]

Economic and social forces were the most powerful contributors to Hispanic migration in the years after 1960. Overall the peoples of Latin America and the Caribbean were profoundly affected by an accelerated process of development that, in most places, had its origins in the early postwar period. Economic modernization, industrialization, rapid population growth, and increased corporate investment from the United States and other industrial countries created economic, social, and political instability in most of the countries of Latin America during this period. As was the case in Cuba and Puerto Rico between 1900 and the 1940s, rapid economic change produced economic and social opportunities for some groups and social dislocation or crisis for other groups. By the late 1950s and early 1960s large numbers of persons in countries such as Mexico, Colombia, Peru, and Ecuador, began to migrate from the rural areas to the urban centers because of unequal regional development or modernization. At the same time the economies of the urban centers in most of these countries were not expanding rapidly enough to accommodate the mass of migrants that came to the cities from the countryside. The result was increased economic, social, and political insecurity for both rural and urban populations. Thousands of persons were uprooted in the countryside by rapid growth, economic reorganization, and monetary inflation. These same forces often had a detrimental effect on significant sectors of the urban populations as well, and this was especially true during periods when development was intense and migration from the countryside was substantial. Economic retrenchment, periods of high unemployment, government austerity programs, and high birthrates also had a negative impact on both rural and urban populations. These same forces were also frequently associated with the rise of political instability, interpersonal violence, rebellions, and civil wars. The result was increased migration to the United States from the increasingly troubled societies of Latin America in the years after 1960.[31]

In contrast to the largely rural and impoverished Puerto Ricans who migrated between 1945 and 1970, the Latinos who came after 1960 were generally urban, better educated, had more skills, and many came from middle-class, professional, or business-oriented backgrounds. In this sense, the new immigrants were comparable to the earlier group of Puerto Ricans and other Hispanics who came to New York in the years between 1900 and 1945. Of course, the proportion of middle-class individuals varied from one Latino sub-group to another. Immigrants from Argentina, Chile, and Uruguay, as well as the Cubans who came in the early 1960s, were more likely to be of the middle class than were the Dominicans, Colombians, Hondurans, or the Mexicans who began to arrive in substantial

numbers at the end of the 1980s; however, as was the case in the
earlier period, middle-class orientation did not guarantee an easier
transition to life in the city. Many of the better-educated persons,
including quite a number with middle-class, professional, or semiprofessional backgrounds, experienced downward economic and
social mobility upon their arrival in New York. Some were fortunate
enough to find white-collar employment if they had an adequate
command of English. Others started their own businesses in the
neighborhoods where they settled, but most were compelled to
accept working-class employment in the services and in manufacturing. As a result, Latinos with working-class and middle-class
backgrounds were employed in factories, restaurants, hotels, small
businesses, and other enterprises, and to a significant degree they
replaced the largely Puerto Rican and African-American labor force
that was traditionally employed in these sectors.[32]

The neighborhoods traditionally associated with the Latino
communities continued to expand rather dramatically in the years
after 1960. At the same time new enclaves were established throughout the city and older ones were devastated as a result of increased
problems with housing that involved the continued flight of earlier
immigrant groups and their descendants, a dramatic slowdown in
the construction of residential buildings for lower-income people,
and the new phenomena of housing abandonment, vandalism,
arson, and rising homelessness.[33]

Certain neighborhoods also became associated with particular
Hispanic subgroups or conglomerations of subgroups. For example,
the Upper West Side and the Washington Heights section of Manhattan became increasingly associated with the Dominican community.
For a time a Cuban community emerged in this area as well; however,
most Cubans eventually settled in other places, such as Astoria, the
Elmhurst section of Queens, and especially Union City, Jersey City,
and West New York, New Jersey. Colombians, Ecuadoreans, Peruvians, Dominicans, and other subgroups became identified with new
enclaves that emerged in the Jackson Heights, Woodside, Elmhurst,
East Elmhurst, and the Corona sections of Queens. Conversely, it
appeared that Mexicans and other persons from Central America
were beginning to displace Puerto Ricans and other Latinos from their
traditional enclaves in "El Barrio" at the end of the 1980s.[34]

Conclusion

This brief historical survey of New York's Latino population begins to reveal the differences that exist among the numerous Hispanic communities that have migrated to the region and to other parts of the United States since the middle of the nineteenth century. In one respect, dissimilarities can be seen in the composition of the Latino communities when these are broken down by national origin. Puerto Ricans, Dominicans, Cubans, Colombians, Ecuadoreans and other persons from South America have been the most important sub-groups in the evolution of New York's Latino community, with Puerto Ricans having played the dominant role. In differing combinations these same groups have been important to the evolution of other Hispanic communities throughout the Northeast and Midwest. By contrast, Mexicans and, more recently, Salvadorans and other persons from Central America have been predominant in the Latino communities of Texas, California, and the Southwest. In southern Florida, Cubans and other expatriate groups such as the Nicaraguans have played the most significant role, while in Chicago separate Mexican and Puerto Rican communities have developed in coexistence at different times since the early part of the century. In fact, up until the late 1970s, a line could have been drawn separating the Northeast, the Middle Atlantic states and Florida from the rest of the country. Although there was some overlap in the Middle West, Puerto Ricans, Cubans, Dominicans, and other nationals from South America and the Caribbean were the predominant groups east of the line, while Mexicans and people from Central America were the most important groups in the communities west of the line.[35]

The chronology of Latino migration and settlement also differentiates the various communities that have evolved across the country. Mexicans, "Spanish Americans," and Hispanicized Indians already occupied various parts of Texas, California, and the Southwest prior to the takeover of these areas by the United States between 1836 and 1848. Florida also had a small Spanish-oriented population prior to the United States occupation in 1819, but in the Northeast and the Middle West, most of the Hispanic communities emerged in the late nineteenth or early twentieth centuries and even later. Although the emergence of New York's Latino community can be traced to at least the early 1800s, significant expansion did not begin until the later part of the nineteenth century. The development of Chicago's Hispanic community also began in the late nineteenth century, but it was not until the World War I period that Latinos became a significant factor in the demography of that city. In contrast to what transpired in Chicago and New York, most of the Hispanic communities in the Northeast and Middle West began to evolve in earnest only after the Second World War. This was the case in Philadelphia, Boston, Cleveland, and in Bridgeport and Hartford, Connecticut.

The geographical breakdown of Latino communities can be differentiated in other ways besides chronologically and by country of origin. For example, the Hispanic populations of Texas, California, and the Southwest have been traditionally much more rural in their orientation than the Latino communities of the Northeast, Southeast, or Middle West. At the same time, the communities in southern Florida have attracted or absorbed proportionally larger numbers of the affluent from Latin America than the other Hispanic communities of the United States. At certain times, New York's Latino community has also been somewhat mixed in terms of its economic and social configuration; however, overwhelming poverty and working-class backgrounds have been the rule in Texas, California, and most parts of the Southwest.

By the mid 1990s it was not clear which direction the Hispanic community would take in the future. Economic, geographic, and social diversification will probably continue, but there also may be a trend toward cultural homogenization within the Latino community as a whole. At this point, assimilation into U.S. society over the long term does not seem very probable because assimilation has failed as a social reality and social policy for most immigrant and minority groups during the past forty years. There has also been a growing acceptance of cultural pluralism and diversity within U.S. society. This is reflected in the promotion of educational programs that emphasize multiculturalism and the positive acceptance of terms such as "African American," "Asian American," "Chicano," "Hispanic," "Latino," and "Native American" in the lexicon of educators, bureaucrats, journalists, politicians, policymakers, and the public as a whole. What seems to be certain is that New York will probably continue to function as a major entry point for Latin Americans, Asians, Africans, and other immigrant and migrant groups in the foreseeable future. At the same time, it also appears that no constitutionally acceptable policy or program will be able to completely stop or even significantly reduce the increased flow of foreigners from other parts of the world in the foreseeable future. Recent calls for a halt to the immigration of "pre-modern," "unskilled people from Third World countries" may have an impact, but if the legislative experience of the 1980s is any guide, compromises will be made.[36] Powerful economic interests, especially in the agricultural and service sectors, are committed to immigration as a means of reducing labor costs. They were successful in their campaigns to weaken the Immigration Reform and Control Act of 1986, and they will probably lobby very hard to stop or weaken any legislation that would significantly reduce the flow of foreigners into this country.

NOTES

1. The terms "Latino" and "Hispanic," used interchangeably in this chapter, refer to all persons living in the United States whose origins can be traced to Spain and the Spanish-speaking countries of Latin America and the Caribbean. Included in this category are all U.S. immigrants who have come from these countries and their descendants who live in the United States, whether they are Spanish-speaking or not.

2. Ira Rosenwaike, *Population History of New York City* (Syracuse, N.Y.: Syracuse University Press, 1972), pp. 22–23. Reference to the trade between the Hispanic Caribbean and New York during the nineteenth century is made in César Andreu Iglesias, ed., *Memoirs of Bernardo Vega: A Contribution to the History of the Puerto Rican Community in New York*, trans. Juan Flores (New York: Monthly Review Press, 1984), p. 46, and Virginia Sánchez-Korrol, *From Colonia to Community: The History of Puerto Ricans in New York City, 1917–1948* (Berkeley: University of California Press, 1994), pp. 11–12. See also Franklin W. Knight, *The Caribbean: The Genesis of a Fragmented Nationalism*, 2nd ed. (New York: Oxford University Press, 1990), pp. 116–17; Louis Pérez, Jr., *Cuba: Between Reform and Revolution* (New York: Oxford University Press, 1988), pp. 82–85, 107, 138, 149–52.

3. Rosenwaike, *Population History of New York City*, p. 40. Historically, most undercounts in the census have been attributed to the existence of a significant number of poor or working-class people within a given population. It is said that such persons are generally reluctant to enter into any kind of contact with government institutions because

of the perception that such contact will lead to obligations or future difficulties with the authorities.

In recent years, the urban census enumerations have become increasingly controversial because of the Census Bureau's inability to accurately count or estimate the urban foreign or impoverished population. This has led to congressional hearings, recounts, lawsuits, and other problems.

For comments regarding the accuracy of the population estimates for New York City for the years prior to 1930 see Sánchez-Korrol, *From Colonia to Community*, pp. 57–58, 59, 62, 107. Also see Iglesias, *Memoirs of Bernardo Vega*, pp. 12, 46, 102, and 146–47 for other estimates on the size of the Latino population during this same period.

4. *Census of 1890* (Washington, D.C.: Government Printing Office, 1892), pp. 645–47, 670, 672, 674, 676, and Iglesias, *Memoirs of Bernardo Vega*, p. 73, also pp. 63–79 and passim.

5. For a general discussion of economic development in Latin America during the nineteenth century see Leslie Bethell, ed., *The Cambridge History of Latin America, vols. 4 and 5: 1870–1930* (Cambridge: Cambridge University Press, 1985); David Bushnell and Neil Macaulay, *The Emergence of Latin America in the Nineteenth Century* (New York: Oxford University Press, 1988). For case studies that discuss labor shortages and immigration as they relate to economic development in nineteenth-century Latin America see David Rock, *Argentina: 1516–1987: From Spanish Colonization to Alfonsín* (Berkeley: University of California Press, 1987), chapters 4, 5, and passim; Hermanus Hoetink, *The Dominican People, 1850–1900: Notes for a Historical Sociology* (Baltimore: John Hopkins University Press, 1982), chapters 2, 4, and passim; Laird Bergad, *Coffee and the Growth of Agrarian Capitalism in Nineteenth-Century Puerto Rico* (Princeton: Princeton University Press, 1983); Rebecca J. Scott, *Slave Emancipation in Cuba: The Transition to Free Labor, 1860–1899* (Princeton: Princeton University Press, 1985); Manuel Moreno-Fraginals, *The Sugarmill: The Socioeconomic Complex of Sugar in Cuba, 1760–1860*, trans. Cedric Belfage (New York: Monthly Review Press, 1976), pp. 20, 60, 83, 89, 119, 133, 141, and passim; and Pérez, *Cuba*, pp. 114–16, 201–2, and passim.

6. Iglesias, *Memoirs of Bernardo Vega*, pp. 45–46, 53, 57–58, 64, 73, and passim; Sánchez-Korrol, *From Colonia to Community*, pp. 11–17. During the late nineteenth century, the price of sugar produced in Cuba, Puerto Rico, and the Dominican Republic was increasingly determined by refiners, importers, brokers, and bankers based in New York City. One of the most important brokers of this period was Manuel Rionda, a New York based Cuban. In the early years of the twentieth

century, Rionda merged his successful company with Czarnikow Ltd., a London-based firm, to create the Czarnikow-Rionda Company. Within a few years this company came to dominate the Caribbean sugar market to such an extent that it could act as sole broker for the entire Cuban sugar industry and for some 80 percent of the sugar produced in Puerto Rico and the Dominican Republic. See Manuel Moreno-Fraginals, "Plantations in the Caribbean: Cuba, Puerto Rico and the Dominican Republic in the Late Nineteenth Century" in Manuel Moreno-Fraginals, Frank Moya Pons, and Stanley L. Engerman, eds., *Between Slavery and Free Labor: The Spanish-Speaking Caribbean in the Nineteenth Century* (Baltimore: John Hopkins University Press, 1985), pp. 10–13, 20, and passim.

7. Iglesias, *Memoirs of Bernardo Vega*, pp. 39–79; Sánchez-Korrol, *From Colonia to Community*, pp. 11, 13, 167–72; Angelo Falcón, "A History of Puerto Rican Politics in New York City: 1860s to 1945" in James Jennings and Monte Rivera, eds., *Puerto Rican Politics in Urban America* (Westport, Conn.: Greenwood Press, 1984), pp. 18–20.

8. Iglesias, *Memoirs of Bernardo Vega* pp. 12, 85–86; Elinor Des Verney Sinnette, *Arthur Alfonso Schomburg: Black Bibliophile and Collector* (New York and Detroit: New York Public Library and Wayne State University Press, 1989), p. 23.

9. Iglesias, *Memoirs of Bernardo Vega*, pp. 7, 9, 12, 16, 33, 46, 74. Also, see Sánchez-Korrol, *From Colonia to Community*, pp. 51–62 and passim, and Lawrence R. Chenault, *The Puerto Rican Migrant in New York City* (New York: Columbia University Press, 1938), pp. 89–109 and passim.

10. Iglesias, Memoirs of Bernardo Vega, p. 12. For the 1920, 1930, and 1940 estimates, see the sources listed in table 2.

11. For a discussion of economic development in Cuba, Puerto Rico, and the Dominican Republic during the first half of the twentieth century, see the relevant sections in Knight, *The Caribbean*; Pérez, *Cuba*; Louis Pérez, *Cuba under the Platt Amendment, 1902–1934* (Pittsburgh: University of Pittsburgh Press, 1986); Julio Le Riverend, *Historia económica de Cuba* (Barcelona: Ediciones Ariel, 1972); James L. Dietz, *Economic History of Puerto Rico: Institutional Change and Capitalist Development* (Princeton: Princeton University Press, 1986); Marlin D. Clausner, *Rural Santo Domingo: Settled, Unsettled, and Resettled* (Philadelphia: Temple University Press, 1973); and Frank Moya Pons, *Manuel de historia Dominicana* (Santiago, R.D.: Universidad Católica Madre y Maestra, 1978), pp. 427–525. Also, see Sánchez-Korrol, *From Colonia to Community*, pp. 17–28 for another discussion of Puerto Rican economic development and its relationship to migration during the period 1900 to 1940.

12. Pérez, *Cuba*, pp. 189–288; Le Riverend, *Historia económica de Cuba*, pp. 187–250.

13. The importance of the nineteenth century Puerto Rican coffee and tobacco sectors is discussed in Dietz, *Economic History of Puerto Rico*, pp. 4–78.

14. Dietz, *Economic History of Puerto Rico*, pp. 79–135 and Sánchez-Korrol, *From Colonia to Community*, pp. 17–28.

15. Dietz, *Economic History of Puerto Rico*, pp. 135–81.

16. For a discussion on economic opportunities for Puerto Ricans in New York, the relative ease of travel, and the role played by the 1917 citizenship legislation in the migration process, see Sánchez-Korrol, *From Colonia to Community*, pp. 28–46.

17. Ibid., pp. 28–29, 30, 32–34, 57 and passim.

18. Ibid., pp. 89–96, 107–12, and passim.

19. Ibid., pp. 29, 30.

20. Iglesias, *Memoirs of Bernardo Vega*, pp. 7, 9–12, 16, 28, 85–86, 91, 98, 103, 105, 151, 155; Sánchez-Korrol, *From Colonia to Community*, pp. 53–62.

21. Iglesias, *Memoirs of Bernardo Vega*, pp. 119–20, 155, 184; Sánchez-Korrol, *From Colonia to Community*, p. 57; and Chenault, *The Puerto Rican Migrant*, pp. 97–100, 106–7. Housing conditions in New York between 1900 and 1945 are also discussed in Anthony Jackson, *A Place Called Home: A History of Low-Cost Housing in Manhattan* (Cambridge, Mass.: MIT Press, 1976) and Richard Plunz, *A History of Housing in New York City* (New York: Columbia University Press, 1990).

22. Sánchez-Korrol, *From Colonia to Community*, pp. 135–66, 172–203; Falcón, "A History of Puerto Rican Politics in New York City," pp. 20–42; Rosa Estades, *Patterns of Political Participation of Puerto Ricans in New York City* (San Juan: Editorial Universitaria, Universidad de Puerto Rico, 1978), pp. 29–36. For additional comments, see Iglesias, *Memoirs of Bernardo Vega*, passim.

23. Dietz, *Economic History of Puerto Rico*, pp. 182–310; see especially pp. 206–21, 226–28, 247–55, 282–88. A number of general studies have been written on Puerto Rican migration and the Puerto Rican experience on the United States mainland in the years between 1945 and 1970 or the present. The most current or recent of these include Joseph P. Fitzpatrick, *Puerto Rican Americans: The Meaning of Migration to the Mainland*, 2nd ed. (Englewood Cliffs, N.J.: Prentice Hall, 1987); History Task Force, Centro de Estudios Puertorriqueños, ed. *Labor Migration under Capitalism: The Puerto Rican Experience* (New York: Monthly Review Press, 1979); Adalberto López, ed., *The Puerto Ricans: Their History, Culture and Society* (Cambridge, Mass.: Schenkman Pub-

lishing, 1980), pp. 313–466; and Clara E. Rodríguez, *Puerto Ricans: Born in the U.S.A.* (New York: Unwin and Hyman, 1989).

24. Fitzpatrick, *Puerto Rican Americans,* pp. 18–20; Adalberto López, "The Puerto Rican Diaspora: A Survey," in López, *The Puerto Ricans,* pp. 314–19. Rodríguez, *Puerto Ricans,* pp. 6–8 and passim.

25. United States Department of Labor, Bureau of Labor Statistics, *A Socio-Economic Profile of Puerto Rican New Yorkers,* Regional Report # 46 (New York: U.S. Department of Labor, Middle Atlantic Regional Office, 1975); Fitzpatrick, *Puerto Rican Americans,* pp. 24–25; Rodríguez, *Puerto Ricans,* pp. 4–6, 26–48, and passim; and Tom Seidl, Janet Shenk, and Adrian DeWind, "The San Juan Shuttle: Puerto Ricans on Contract" in López, *The Puerto Ricans,* pp. 417–32.

26. Evidence that demonstrates the differences in socioeconomic background between Puerto Ricans and other Latinos is quite sparse for this period. Two examples of Hispanic subgroups that were clearly more middle-class in their orientation during the period 1958 to 1970 were Cubans and Colombians. See Eleanor Meyer Rogg and Rosemary Santana Cooney, *Adaptation and Adjustment of Cubans: West New York, New Jersey* (New York: Hispanic Research Center, Fordham University, 1980), pp. 35–40 and passim; and Fernando Urrea Giraldo, "Life Strategies and the Labor Market: Colombians in New York in the 1970s," *Occasional Papers,* no. 34 (New York: Center for Latin American Studies, New York University, 1982), pp. 8–10 and passim.

27. On the transformation of the New York economy during the period from 1945 to 1970 and the role played by Puerto Ricans in this change, see Fitzpatrick, *Puerto Rican Americans,* pp. 11–13, 92–103, and passim; Rodríguez, *Puerto Ricans,* pp. 31–35, 37–42, 44–45, and passim; Clara E. Rodríguez, "Economic Factors Affecting Puerto Ricans in New York" in History Task Force, *Labor Migration Under Capitalism,* pp. 214–15; U.S. Department of Labor, *A Socio-Economic Profile of Puerto Rican New Yorkers* (1975), pp. 78–104 and passim, and Michael N. Danielson and James W. Doig, *New York: The Politics of Urban Regional Development* (Berkeley: University of California Press, 1982), pp. 50–64 and passim. Also, see the pamphlets and reports that were distributed during this period, such as Commonwealth of Puerto Rico, Department of Labor, Migration Division, "The Jobs We Do," 1953; Joseph Monserrat, "Industry and Community—A Profitable Partnership," 1953; New York City, Department of Commerce, "Puerto Ricans: A Key Source of Labor," 1956; and others.

28. The expansion of Puerto Rican neighborhoods in the period 1945–1970 is discussed in Nathan Kantrowitz, *Negro and Puerto Rican Populations of New York City in the Twentieth Century* (Washington, D.C.:

American Geographical Society, 1969); Morris Eagle, "Puerto Ricans in New York City" in Nathan Glazer and David McEntire, eds., *Studies in Housing and Minority Groups* (Berkeley: University of California Press, 1960); and U.S. Department of Labor, *A Socio-Economic Profile of Puerto Rican New Yorkers*, pp. 30–41. Also, see the relevant pages in Jackson, *A Place Called Home* and Plunz, *A History of Housing in New York City*.

29. See Eagle, "Puerto Ricans in New York City;" Rodríguez, *Puerto Ricans*, pp. 106–19; and the relevant pages in Jackson, *A Place Called Home* and Plunz, *A History of Housing in New York City*.

30. For a discussion of Cuban and Dominican migration to the United States and New York in the years after 1960, see Richard R. Fagen, Richard A. Brody, and Thomas J. O'Leary, *Cubans in Exile: Disaffection and the Revolution* (Stanford: Stanford University Press, 1968); the relevant sections of Alejandro Portes and Robert L. Bach, *Latin Journey: Cuban and Mexican Immigrants in the United States* (Berkeley: University of California Press, 1985); Rogg and Santana Cooney, *The Adaptation and Adjustment of Cubans*; José del Castillo and Christopher Mitchell, eds., *La inmigración Dominicana en los Estados Unidos* (Santo Domingo: Editorial CENAPEC, 1987); and Sherrie Grasmuck and Patricia R. Pessar, *Between Two Islands: Dominican International Migration* (Berkeley: University of California Press, 1991).

31. The relationship between investment capital, economic development, social change, and international migration from developing to industrialized societies has been discussed recently in Saskia Sassen, *The Mobility of Labor and Capital: A Study in International Investment and Labor Flow* (New York: Cambridge University Press, 1988). In addition, specific examples from Latin America and elsewhere are found in June Nash and María Patricia Fernández-Kelly, eds., *Women, Men, and the International Division of Labor* (Albany: State University of New York Press, 1983) and Steven E. Sanderson, ed., *The Americas in the New International Division of labor* (New York: Holmes and Meier, 1985).

32. For a discussion of middle-class orientation and downward social mobility among specific Latino subgroups, see Rogg and Cooney, *Adaptation and Adjustment of Cubans*, pp. 35–46, and Urrea Giraldo, "Life Strategies and the Labor Market: Colombians in New York." Discussions or essays dealing with Hispanic immigration to the New York metropolitan area in the years after 1965 are also found in Elizabeth Bogen, *Immigration in New York* (New York: Praeger, 1987); del Castillo and Mitchell, *La inmigración Dominicana*; Grasmuck and Pessar, *Between Two Islands*; Evelyn S. Mann and Joseph J. Salvo, *Characteristics of New Hispanic Immigrants to New York City: A Comparison of Puerto Rican and Non-Puerto Rican Hispanics* (New York: Department of City

Planning, 1984); Nancy Foner, ed., *New Immigrants in New York* (New York: Columbia University Press, 1987); Constance R. Sutton and Elsa M. Chaney, eds., *Caribbean Life in New York City: Sociocultural Dimensions* (New York: Center for Migration Studies, 1987); Roger D. Waldinger, *Through the Eye of the Needle: Immigrants and Enterprise in New York's Garment Trades* (New York: New York University Press, 1986).

33. Kantrowitz, *Negro and Puerto Rican Populations of New York City*; Jackson, *A Place Called Home*, pp. 254–308, Plunz, *A History of Housing in New York City*, pp. 313–40 and especially pp. 323–24, and *Report of the Mayor's Commission on Hispanic Concerns* (New York: 1986), pp. S15–S18, 54–88; Market Research Department of WADO Radio, *Facts: The New York Hispanic Market Report* (New York, 1988).

34. Market Research Department of WADO Radio, *Facts: The New York Hispanic Market Report*, 1988. Clay F. Richards, "Jobs Top Latinos' List of Concerns," *New York Newsday*, October 13, 1991, p. 28.

35. A number of studies have been written on Latino communities or specific Latino subgroups in various parts of the country outside of New York City or the northeastern part of the United States. These include Fagen, Brody, and O'Leary, *Cubans in Exile*; Portes and Bach, *Latin Journey*; Matt S. Meier and Feliciano Ribera, *Mexican Americans/ American Mexicans: From Conquistadors to Chicanos* (New York: Vintage Books/Random House, 1989); Felix M. Padilla, *Puerto Rican Chicago* (Notre Dame, Ind.: University of Notre Dame Press, 1987); and Julian Samora and Patricia Vandel Simon, *A History of the Mexican-American People* (Notre Dame, Ind.: University of Notre Dame Press, 1976; rev. ed. 1993) among others.

For a general overview of the Latino experience in the United States, see Earl Shorris, *Latinos: A Biography of the People* (New York: W. W. Norton, 1992); Joan Moore and Harry Pachon, *Hispanics in the United States* (Englewood Cliffs, N.J.: Prentice Hall, 1985); and L. H. Gann and Peter J. Duignan, *The Hispanics in the United States: A History* (Boulder, Colo.: Westview Press and the Hoover Institution on War, Peace and Revolution, 1986).

In the opinion of this writer, Duignan and Gann present a distorted, self-serving, and ultraconservative view of the Latino experience which reflects the politics of the Hoover Institute more than it does any attempt at an objective analysis of Latinos and their history.

36. The calls for a halt to immigration by "unskilled," "pre-modern people from Third World countries" have been articulated by Peter Brimelow, among others. See Peter Brimelow, *Alien Nation* (New York: Random House, 1995) and especially Peter Brimelow, "Time to Rethink Immigration?" *National Review* 44, no. 12 (June 22, 1992): 30–46.

2

Dominicans in New York: Men, Women, and Prospects

RAMONA HERNÁNDEZ AND SILVIO TORRES-SAILLANT

Beginning with an assessment of a number of prevalent scholarly claims concerning Dominican migration, we hope to arrive at an understanding of the Dominican experience in the United States, using New York City as a focal point. Dominican immigrants, of course, defy monolithic portrayals; while many Dominicans are poor or even destitute, other enjoy prosperity. In attempting to define the Dominican community one must avoid drawing exclusively from the extremes. Since the human experience of a people cannot be appropriately fathomed in such a brief discussion as we have undertaken here, we will limit the focus of this essay to class, gender, international relations, and social marginality as issues pertinent for understanding the prospects of the Dominican people for becoming a strong and stable New York community. In tackling this inquiry we have tried to keep in mind its complexity and amplitude, seeking to account for the gradations between the polarities.

People from the Dominican Republic have been living in New York in large numbers for only three decades. Their presence can be seen as a consequence of nearly 150 years of economic and political relations between their homeland and the United States. Decades ago an American diplomat amply documented the longevity of the ties between the two countries (Tansill 1938). Among the crucial milestones of those ties, one may recall that during the nineteenth century both Dominican and American government representatives sought passionately to annex the small Antillean nation to the then expanding United States territory.

This monograph was prepared under the auspices of the CUNY Dominican Studies Institute at The City College of New York and benefited from the financial support of the Aaron Diamond Foundation.

By 1907 America was so involved in Dominican affairs that both states signed an agreement whereby for more than three decades thenceforward Washington would exercise control over the collection and application of customs revenues and all fiscal transactions in the Dominican Republic. Not unconnected with the logic of that arrangement, in 1916 the United States installed an American military government that ruled Dominicans directly until 1924. By the time American soldiers left, a new leader, Rafael Léonidas Trujillo, was emerging in the country's armed forces. He had received his training in the National Guard, the military institution created by the government of the occupying forces.

Trujillo came to power six years later, and the grip of his iron-fisted dictatorship held Dominicans in check until his violent death in 1961. American soldiers landed on Dominican soil again in 1965 to crush a popular uprising that had sought to restore President Juan Bosch, the democratically elected chief of state who had suffered a coup d'état by the reactionary faction of the military. The occupying American forces paved the way for the rise of Joaquín Balaguer, a right-wing politician who had served under Trujillo throughout his tyrannous regime (Torres-Saillant 1993:64). Supported by the United States, from 1966 to 1978 Balaguer's government implemented economic policies and development strategies that privileged industrialization to the detriment of agricultural production. This led to massive unemployment, high rates of inflation, and increasing external debt (Alemany, Alvarez, and Feria 1981).

Over the last three decades, as the Dominican economy has deteriorated, leaving home has become an exceedingly frequent option for people to secure their material survival. A year-by-year account of the number of Dominican immigrants legally admitted into the United States shows a rapid increase since 1965 (see table 1). Precisely how many Dominicans now live in the United States, however, cannot be reported with any degree of accuracy. A sizeable portion of these immigrants come into this country through other than official channels. As a result, scholars of Dominican migration can only guess at the actual size of this immigrant population (Larson and Sullivan 1988). Larson and Sullivan have shown the often great disparity between the various estimates, varying anywhere from 300,000 to 1,000,000

Table 1
Dominican Immigrants Legally Admitted to the United States

1961	3,045	1974	15,680
1962	4,603	1975	14,066
1963	10,683	1976	15,088
1964	7,537	1977	11,655
1965	9,504	1978	19,458
1966	16,503	1979	17,519
1967	11,514	1980	17,245
1968	9,250	1981	18,220
1969	10,670	1982	17,451
1970	10,807	1983	22,058
1971	12,624	1984	23,147
1972	10,670	1985	23,787
1973	13,858	1986	26,175

SOURCE: Grasmuck and Pessar, *Between Two Islands* 1991: 20, table 1.

immigrants, depending on the emphasis of the author and the sources consulted (Larson and Sullivan 1989: 70).

While we cannot claim knowledge of the exact number of Dominicans living in the United States, we can safely affirm that New York City houses the largest portion of that number. From 1980 to 1986, 60 percent of all Dominican immigrants legally admitted to the United States settled in New York. Current data show that one in every six immigrants who settle in New York City belongs to the Dominican community, thus making it the largest immigrant group in the city and its fastest-growing ethnic minority. Washington Heights and Inwood in northern Manhattan have become predominantly Dominican neighborhoods. From 1983 to 1989 Dominicans constituted over 80 percent of all immigrants who settled in Washington Heights (Dept. Of City Planning 1992a).

Beyond Dichotomous Profiles

Most studies of Dominican migration to the United States have presented dichotomous profiles of the socioeconomic backgrounds of the migrants. These studies portray Dominican immigrants as either urban, middle-class, educated individuals who held jobs before migration (Ugalde, Bean, and Cárdenas 1979; Ugalde and Langham 1982; Bray 1984, 1987; Baéz Evertz and Ramírez D'Oleo

1985; Portes and Guarnizo 1991; Grasmuck and Pessar 1991) or as rural, poor, illiterate people who had scarcely maintained jobs prior to migration (Gonzalez 1970, 1973, 1976; Hendricks 1974; Vicioso 1976). Similarly while some scholars have seen Dominicans as industrious builders of "vibrant communities" in their American space or as shrewd investors who have fueled the economy of their homeland, others perceive them as a transient, unsettled group whose yearning to return home hampers their business possibilities in the receiving society. Women have invariably been seen through the prism of a feminist approach that associates migration with liberation. Formerly passive and socially subordinate, Dominican women have presumably managed to escape the bondage of a patriarchal society, having drastically changed their social behavior in the U.S.

Empirical observation of the socioeconomic development of the Dominican community leads to a mixture of conflicting signals. The community appears to be flourishing economically, as one can gather from a look at the northern part of Manhattan, where the majority of grocery stores, travel agencies, gypsy-cabs, clothing and shoe stores, restaurants, many pharmacies, beauty salons, barbershops, and liquor stores are owned and operated by Dominicans, whose economic presence extends also to small factories, bars, a finance sector, large supermarkets, and the immeasurable informal sector.

The apparent prosperity of Dominicans has been noted by various authors for whom this community has developed an enclave economy in New York that contributes to the development of an entrepreneurial sector in the Dominican Republic (Portes and Guarnizo 1990). Portes and Guarnizo note that in New York, "approximately 20,000 businesses are owned by Dominicans ... [that] Dominicans own around 70% of all Hispanic *bodegas* (grocery stores), which generates a sale of 1.8 billion dollars per year ... [that] Dominicans operate 90% of the gypsy-cabs, three supermarket chains, and two television channels" (Portes and Guarnizo 1990:61). Linda Chavez has described the Dominican haven of Manhattan as a "vibrant commercial" area where "even the manner in which people moved on the street, attested to [its]...vitality" (Chavez 1991:152). To stress the ability of Dominicans to prosper in New York, despite formidable odds, Chavez points out that although only 30 percent of all adult Dominicans have completed high school, they somehow manage to own 70 percent of all Hispanic small businesses in New York (Chavez 1991:150).

Concomitant with their presumed prosperity, however, Dominican neighborhoods show the following contrasting conditions: dilapidated housing, abandoned cars, piles of garbage on street corners, public facilities such as parks, playgrounds, and subway elevators which are unfit for human use. Dominicans live predominantly in Washington Heights, the most densely populated area of the city. Muggings, drug abuse, drug trafficking, and drug-related crimes have become common in the area. By mid-September of 1993 as many as sixty-four Dominican taxi drivers and bodega workers had lost their lives violently during that year alone (*El Nacional* 23 Sept. 1993:3). The Thirty-fourth Police Precinct, which serves a predominantly Dominican area, proved unable to address the volume of crime in the area and in 1993 had to be split into two precincts. There is perhaps no weightier sign of the precarious circumstances of Dominicans in Washington Heights than the large number of strong, potentially productive young men one finds standing on street corners whiling away their time.

Even apart from empirical observation, the available data hardly confirm the view of the New York Dominican community as the prosperous enclave that some scholars have seen. In 1980, for instance, one-fourth of all families in Washington Heights were living well below the poverty level. By the 1990s their socioeconomic status had not improved, for 32.4 percent of the population depended on public assistance (Dept. of City Planning 1991: 277). By the same token, the number of female heads of households increased from 21.5 percent in 1980 to 26.0 percent in 1990 (Dept. of City Planning 1992b:211). From 1987 to 1989, of all the health districts in Manhattan, Washington Heights exhibited the third highest percentage in infant mortality, low birth weight, and births out of wedlock (DeCamp 1991: 7, table 3).

Some have argued that the future of an immigrant group lies in its ability to accumulate knowledge through education (Carnoy, Daley, and Hinojosa Ojeda 1993:47–50). If that is so, the prospects for Dominicans appear grim. This community has the highest rate of high school dropouts and the lowest on-grade reading scores. The area's schools are characterized by overcrowded classrooms and facilities are clearly in a state of disrepair. Children in some schools are exposed to gas leaks and other health hazards (Dept. of City Planning, 1991:291).

From Transience to Permanence

Michael Piore's notion of "birds of passage," a metaphor for immigrants with a transient mentality who see themselves always as temporary workers, is evident in the thinking of many scholars who have focused on Dominicans in the United States (Waldinger 1986; Hendricks 1974). The transience observed by scholars refers to the immigrant workers' desire to return home, to regain their native land. That desire is seen by some as preventing Dominicans from properly settling as a permanent community in the receiving society. The underlying contention is that success and progress in American society, no matter how insignificant, lie in the immigrants' realization of their permanence, their psychological separation from the native land, and their adoption of the receiving soil as their home. A 1986 study which compared Dominican and Chinese owners in the garment industry ascribed a greater degree of success to the Chinese than to their Dominican counterparts. To explain the lesser economic achievement of Dominicans, the author appealed, among other things, to their transient mentality. The author identified a Dominican reticence to settle which translated into a lack of real efforts to diversity, expand, or modernize their businesses (Waldinger 1986: 177, 181–82).

The high rate of return migration among Dominicans and their direct involvement in the economic or political life of their native country has provided further evidence of their impermanence. Ugalde interprets return migration among Dominicans, particularly males, as a direct result of their inability to adapt to the receiving society (cited by Castillo and Mitchell 1987:45). Many Dominican parents living outside the homeland dream of seeing their children return to the native land, where they would use the skills they learned abroad for the betterment of their home country (Pessar 1987:124). Upon leaving their country, a good many had the clear intention of returning home some day to build a house of their own or to open a small business (Grasmuck, 1987:130).

Consistent with their mental detachment from the receiving society, the involvement of emigrants in the economic life of their homeland may have led to the development and financing of an entrepreneurial sector in the Dominican Republic (Portes and Guarnizo 1991:187). Similarly, many argue that Dominicans have little participation in American politics and that their political behavior is more in response to events taking place back home than to local agendas (Dwyer 1991:68). Clearly, as some have in effect shown, Dominicans do exhibit a strong attachment to their native land to the point of perhaps undermining, complicating, or delaying their adaptation to the receiving society. However, one should avoid viewing that trend monolithically. Dominicans have also established social structures that are convincing indicators of permanence in and adaptability to their new environment.

In the political realm, the community has had a Dominican Advisory Board to the Governor. The National Council of Dominican-Americans, an organization formed with the expressed purpose of fostering political leadership and encouraging Dominicans to pursue public office, has already achieved some visibility. Dominican leaders have joined forces with other minority spokespersons in the design of local political agendas, particularly as regards the municipal government. The 1993 mayoral elections witnessed a great deal of Dominican participation. In addition to the election of a Dominican to the City Council in 1991, Dominicans have run for a seat in the State Assembly, have held a number of district leadership positions, and have led the fight for the modification of the city's political map so as to assign a separate congressional district to Washington Heights, thus opening the possibility for a Dominican to reach the nation's Capitol.

Dominicans have also become active agents in community development. They have joined the School Board No. 6 and the Community Planning Board No. 12 in Manhattan, showing significant interest in the local institutions which are important to their daily lives in New York. They have also formed myriad organizations with the purpose of enhancing the quality of life locally through improving the rapport of the community with the Police Department as well as other city agencies and institutions. The Dominican Parade is over a decade old. Washington Heights houses at least three strong direct-service agencies that have effectively

vied for public funds: the Community Association of Progressive
Dominicans, the Alianza Dominicana, the Dominican Women's
Development Center. Sports, cultural, and youth organizations
abound in most Dominican neighborhoods. Affluent Dominicans,
particularly physicians and other highly paid professionals, have
increasingly purchased condominiums, cooperative apartments,
and houses throughout New York.

Dominican educators have begun to make their presence felt
at various levels. At least two pertinent organizations have emerged
since 1989 with the idea of representing the interests of Dominican
students, teachers, and staff in the public systems: the Council of
Dominican Educators, dealing with higher education primarily at
the City University of New York, and the Dominican Association
of Education Professionals, dealing with the New York City Board
of Education. A graphic indication of Dominican participation in
school matters is their militant campaign to have schools named
after major figures from Dominican history. Their lobbying in this
regard has thus far resulted in the naming of the Juan Pablo Duarte
School, after the founding father of the Dominican Republic, the
Salomé Ureña de Henríquez School, after a nineteenth-century
Dominican poet laureate, and the Gregorio Luperon High School,
after the esteemed patriot who fought to liberate the country from
annexation to foreign territories in the nineteenth century. The three
schools are in northern Manhattan.

If the rate of naturalization can be seen as an indication of the
level of permanence of a given group in the receiving society, as
Robert Warren has contended (1989:41), current data would support
the notion that Dominicans have gradually come to terms with
their immigrant home. The 1990 census shows that Dominicans are,
indeed, becoming United States citizens. In the city of New York
they outnumbered all other immigrants who pursued the citizenship in the period 1982 through 1989 (Dept. of City Planning
1992a:131). Further evidence indicates that during recent years
Dominicans have been naturalizing at a higher rate than in previous
years. While by 1980 only 7.8 percent of all Dominican permanent
residents who entered since 1960 had become naturalized (Warren
1989:41), by 1989 as many as 18.1 percent of a cohort admitted in
1977 had done so (Dept. of City Planning 1992a:137).

However, there is no denying that for Dominicans the decision to stay in the United States for good causes considerable stress. Their apparent reluctance to accept the United States as their home once and for all has to do with the nature of their migratory process and the history of both countries. Most Dominicans did not leave their home country voluntarily. They were impelled by complex political and socioeconomic forces created by the power structures of both the United States and the Dominican Republic. In fact, most recent massive migration to the United States has been associated with political and economic activities spurred by the American involvement in the sending societies (Portes and Guarnizo 1991:32; Portes and Walton 1981; Ricketts 1987; Sassen 1981, 1988). Scholars have argued, for instance, that recent developmental policies imple-mented in Caribbean societies in response to American investments have led to massive out-migration from the region (History Task Force: Centro 1979; Bonilla and Campos 1982, 1986; Hernández, 1990).

The United States and Dominican Migration

Scholars tend to explain the large wave of Dominican migration to the United States as resulting from at least two major factors. First, the Dominican Republic needed to quell the element of dissent following the revolution of 1965, which had brought about a U.S. military invasion and the subsequent installment of a U.S.-spon-sored right-wing government. Both governments saw benefit in encouraging out-migration from the Dominican Republic as a safety valve to expel political discontent (Grasmuck and Pessar 1991:31; Portes and Guarnizo 1991:32). American visas were granted to those identified as revolutionaries or potentially so. The second factor has to do with North American economic activity in the country which has arguably brought about emigration. Erol Ricketts (1987) holds that massive direct or indirect foreign capital investment in the Dominican Republic during the last decades has affected the entire social fabric by creating unemployment through the use of capital-intensive production processes and by destabilizing local production, thereby causing loss of public revenues and unemploy-ment. American enterprise in the country—which includes invest-ment in trade, Free Zones, U.S. aid and private loans—has been

examined by Dominican scholars from the point of view of its effect
on the labor market and the quality of life of the masses of the
people (Castillo et al. 1974; Serrulle and Boin 1981, 1983; Vicens
1982; Gómez 1984; Lozano 1985; 1987).

As noted earlier, the Dominican Republic is hardly the only
society where scholars see a link between massive out-migration
and the direct intervention of a foreign power. The relationship
between foreign investment and Caribbean migration pointed out
by Ricketts had been noted earlier by Campos and Bonilla in
explaining Puerto Rican massive migration to the United States.
They argued that the increase in foreign capital in Puerto Rico,
while generating wealth and new jobs, also accentuated joblessness
and poverty (Bonilla and Campos 1982). They describe the phenomenon as an inherent feature of capitalist accumulation. In their
words: "the structured intermingling of multinational workforces
at many sites becomes as central to continued capitalist expansion
as the freedom of capital to range at will among nations in search
of usable pools of labor" (Bonilla and Campos 1986:68).

During the 1960s the desire of American capitalists to further
reduce the cost of production via a cheaper labor force and infra-
structure led to considerable capital flow from the United States
into the Dominican Republic, a country that at the time promised
and delivered those advantages (see table 2). Penetration of foreign
capital into the country was facilitated by Joaquin Balaguer's administration. While not impeding capitalist accumulation at home, the
government passed laws that were favorable to foreign accumulation. Balaguer's regime embraced economic policies that were dictated by the declared compulsion to develop. The country adopted
a new economic model that emphasized the expansion of the industrial sector using foreign investment. Industrial production
increased mainly via the Export Processing Zones (EPZ), and new
industrial jobs were created (see table 3). During the period from
1970 to 1975 over 80 percent of the firms established in the EPZ
came from the United States. By 1988 American firms faced competition from other industrialized nations such as Japan, but they still
controlled more than 63 percent of investments in the EPZ industries, with native Dominican capital accounting for a mere 10 percent
(Abreu et al. 1989: 76).

From 1970 to 1980 the number of Export Processing industries

Table 2
Foreign Investment in the Dominican Republic

Year	In Millions of Dollars
1964	154
1965	153
1966	168
1967	172
1968	175
1969	184
1970	245
	In Dominican Pesos
1970	22,671,400
1980	239,250,600

SOURCES: For 1964–70: Castillo et al., *La Gulf & Western en República Dominicana*, 1974: 183. For 1970 and 1980: Serrulle Ramia and Boin, *La inversión de capitales imperialistas*, 1981: 21.

in the Dominican Republic increased from two to seventy-six (Moya Pons 1992:388). Concomitantly, unemployment increased from 20 percent to 27 percent during the same period (Serrulle and Boin 1981:121). The expansion of industrial production and opening of a certain job market did not reduce the pool of unemployed workers in the country (see table 4). Rather, as Sassen (1988) has argued, although the development of the Export Processing Zones in the Dominican Republic generated new jobs, it tended to increase unemployment, since segments of the population formerly alien to the labor force were now recruited into production. In effect, over 70 percent of the new jobs developed by the expansion of the new industrial production went to women (Abreu et al. 1989:116).

At the same time that Dominican society faced the challenges of economic transformation, the United States was undergoing internally a trying process of adjustment. The country had to deal with a relative labor shortage as a result of a number of variables that had led to the expulsion from the labor market of certain categories of workers such as blacks, Puerto Ricans, and unionized workers. The expulsion of such workers came about through a combination of technological changes and discriminatory hiring practices (Bonilla and Campos 1986). In other cases, the need to reduce the cost of production and maximize capital accumulation motivated the rejection of workers from large unionized centers of

Table 3
Industrial Jobs in the Dominican Republic*

	La Romana		S. P. Macorís		Santiago		Puerto Plata	
Year	No. of Indus.	No. of Jobs	No. of Indus.	No. of Jobs	No. of Indus.	No. of Jobs	No. of Indus.	No. of Jobs
1969	1	—	—	—	—	—	—	—
1970	2	126	—	—	—	—	—	—
1971	5	362	—	—	—	—	—	—
1972	9	1,281	1	—	—	—	—	—
1973	14	1,432	5	394	3	—	—	—
1974	17	2,106	5	1,138	7	—	—	—
1975	17	2,780	7	1,189	10	1,175	—	—
1976	16	3,594	10	1,549	12	1,530	—	—
1977	17	4,483	14	2,367	15	2,125	—	—
1978	19	5,839	17	2,646	25	3,060	—	—
1979	19	6,802	23	2,758	30	4,600	—	—
1980	18	7,659	25	3,344	33	5,401	—	—
1981	19	9,231	31	3,402	39	6,764	—	—
1982	18	7,250	33	3,465	38	7,360	—	—
1983	22	7,421	36	5,148	37	7,704	5	419
1984	22	8,718	41	6,510	42	9,827	5	471

*Industrial jobs in the Free Trade Zones.
SOURCE: Moya Pons, *Empresarios en conflicto*, 1992: 388, table 18.

production. The process exemplified here, consistent with capitalist dynamics, simultaneously rejects some workers and attracts others to the centers of production, generating a constant movement of the factors of production (Bonilla and Campos 1986:68; Marx 1967). From the recognition of this relative labor shortage and its harmful effect on the process of production came the Family Reunification legislation which, in turn, stimulated Dominican migration.

Intent on providing an answer to labor-market problems, the proponents of the 1965 Family Reunification legislation operated under the assumption that the new law would attract mostly Western European immigrants. Brooklyn Democrat Congressman Emanuel Celler, a key proponent of the bill, clearly stated that the new legislation would not draw many people from Third World countries: "There will not be, comparatively, many Asians or Africans entering the country since the people of Africa and Asia have very few relatives here; comparatively few could immigrate from those countries because they have no family ties to the United States"

Table 4
Unemployment in the Dominican Republic

Year	%
1970	24.1
1980	22.2
1981	20.7
1982	21.3
1983	22.1
1984	24.2
1985	27.2
1986	28.7
1987	26.3
1988	20.8
1989	19.6
1990	23.3

SOURCES: For 1970: Ceara-Hatton, *Crecimiento económico y acumulación* 1990: 60. For 1980–1990: Ceara-Hatton, *Gasto público social y su impacto* 1992: 5, Table 1.

(cited by Briggs 1992:111). Consequently, few Dominicans were expected to come to these shores. With only a negligible number of Dominicans living in the United States before 1965, they too had scarcely any family ties here. In fact, the legislation, in establishing a quota on migration from the Western Hemisphere, seems to have sought to control the influx of people from the region. The Congress assumed that the large population growth of Latin American countries, which legislators viewed as a problem, could have a harmful impact on American society (Briggs 1992:108; Bogen 1987:22). As a preventive measure, therefore, Congress decreed that the number of immigrants coming from the Americas would not exceed 120,000 per year, thus marking the very first time in American history that a limit was placed on migration from Latin America and the Caribbean.

In light of this background, it seems fair to say that Dominican migration has occurred largely as a reaction to forces put in motion by geopolitical and economic transactions initiated and controlled by the United States. Paradoxically, the receiving society was ill-prepared to welcome the new immigrants or to make their settlement here easy. Their adjustment to American society has, therefore, been necessarily problematic. Nevertheless, they have, generally speaking, acknowledged that they are here to stay. They have come to an understanding of the irreversibility of their migration due to

the influence of their American-born children, their gradual attainment of the life-style of their new abode, and the continued deterioration of the economic and political situation in the Dominican
Republic which makes the prospects of a return highly improbable.

Life, Liberty, and Women's Pursuit of Happiness

Some feminist social scientists have argued that migration to the
United States has generated psychological and material benefits for
Dominican women workers. They argue, for instance, that female
workers, insofar as they share income and authority, have built
egalitarian households, drastically transforming the role they held
prior to migration (Grasmuck and Pessar 1991:148). They contend
that a salary enables women workers to create a new dynamics in the
household, and as a result the women see themselves as decision-
making agents and they now reject the absolute authority of their
mates in the home (Pessar 1987:120). Their renegotiation of the
household space and their self-affirmation have brought social
awareness to most Dominican women (Grasmuck and Pessar 1991:
195; Hernández-Angueira 1990:81, 86). Employment in the receiving
society has given rise to more equitable households, empowering
women in the family structure, often to the chagrin of their men,
who are likely to pose serious resistance. Consequently, these
women tend to hesitate before considering a return to their native
land, for fear of losing their gains in American society (Pessar
1987:123).

Clearly, the idea that Dominican women develop self-esteem
and social awareness after migration derives from the scholars'
particular readings of the two societies involved. A common interpretation, unstated but perceptible in comparisons of the two countries, would seem to assume that the lack of modernization,
economic diversification, and technological progress in the Dominican society go hand in hand with women's subordination. Women
are thus portrayed as passive recipients of the cultural myths of
an essentially traditional and patriarchal Dominican society. This
reading equates economic underdevelopment with a lack of social
awareness, insinuating that back home women fail to challenge the
authority of their male partners and obediently adhere to the norms

of a male-centered society. Such is the reasoning adduced by Pessar to explain Dominican women's reticence to return home, for there "they might well end up cloistered in the home since the sexual division of labor in the Dominican economy militates against productive employment for women of their training and class background" (1987:123). Furthermore, these women act under the compulsion of a "housewife ideology," which, among other things, limits their physical movements, possibility of employment, and sexual behavior (Georges 1990:130–35).

The opposite assumption becomes perceptible in readings of the receiving society. In the United States, a modern and technologically advanced society, women presumably have access to a greater degree of economic progress. The society's high level of development facilitates women's social awareness and the establishment of an egalitarian household, allowing women the control of their resources. Interestingly, the work of feminist scholars who have looked at American society critically would seem to challenge such a placid picture of gender relations. A glance at the works of authors like Barbara R. Bergman (1986), Jane Humphries (1988), Marilyn Power (1988), and Marie Richmond-Abbot (1992), would reveal that American society can hardly be deemed free of gender oppression and inequity. We should say that the favorable interpretation of the active role of women in American society is not declared openly by the scholars who have written on Dominican migration with a focus on gender relations. Rather, it becomes evident in many of their passing remarks and in their usual manner of reporting on the ideological transformation of their female informants upon coming to America. We thus learn of a Dominican couple living in New York who rearranged their household structure in order to emulate the egalitarian division of labor of the receiving society. "Now that we are in the United States, we should adopt American ways," they are reported as saying (Grasmuck and Pessar 1991:152). An author examining the causes of women's social subordination in a Dominican town feels she has reason to hope that "patterns described for Piñera women may begin to change when they migrate to the United States" (Georges 1990:246).

Dominican scholars and observers, however, would challenge the view that construes Dominican women before migration as subordinated objects, passively responding to the demands of a patriarchal social order. A field study conducted in the summer of 1993 in the Dominican Republic looked at women who had traveled illegally to Puerto Rico in small, dangerous wooden boats called *yolas*. Most women interviewed claimed that they would not give in to the will of their men. They generally asserted that no men or family could stop them from embarking in a shabby dinghy bound for Puerto Rico or any other island in the Caribbean when they felt the need to secure their livelihood (Hernández and López 1993:15). Similarly, in *Sueños Atrapados* (Dreams Ensnared), a film documentary by Sonia Fritz we get a sense that women in the Dominican Republic see themselves as either equal or superior to men when it comes to showing responsibility, courage, and emotional strength (Fritz 1994).

Hernández and López similarly posit that Dominican women's awareness of their power to rule their own lives, though living in a male-centered society, derives from a peculiar historical experience. In the Dominican Republic, they claim, female/male relationships transcend verbal negotiations. Nor do women assume openly defiant attitudes in the household or the rest of society, as may be the case in societies that boast of a more seemingly egalitarian structure. Their resistance assumes subtler or less public manifestations. While men in the Dominican Republic, as in any patriarchal society, enjoy control over the mechanisms used in the forging of public opinion, women have tended to circumvent men's power in the sphere of action. Women have created their own vehicles to resist social subordination. They appear to have concerned themselves more with the deeds than with the words. While men openly write laws and dictate the norms that control women's social behavior, women have rarely waited for approval before taking action. Not only have they played an active role in revolutionary or nationalist movements in their country, but on the whole they have outnumbered their male counterparts in the traumatic decision to leave home to secure their material survival abroad when need has so dictated.

That women have been actively combating social subordination in the Dominican Republic has been sustained by Carmen Julia Gómez (1990), who states that women have fought male domination through a form of resistance she calls "insubordination." She traces the legacy of women's insubordination and finds it manifested in the subversive actions of such women as the Mirabal sisters, Abigail Majía, and Evangelina Rodríguez, as well as the collective acts of women who have defied accepted social practices and rules of conduct.

Women's collective "insubordination" is reflected today in their tendency to maintain single households, dispensing with the presence of males, in a Catholic society that recognizes matrimony as the only appropriate form of conjugal relationship and of bringing up children (Gómez 1990:16). Gómez contends that Dominican women's historical insubordination has enabled them to expand their space in a male-centered society and has weakened social barriers based on gender division (p.15). The process has been a long and painful one. The open struggle for equality can be traced at least to the turn of the century, with the 1920s marking a pivotal moment with the rise of an organized feminist movement.

The ideas and social behavior of Dominican women should be seen as evolving from the complex historical formation of the Dominican people, whose culture and outlook are not obliterated in the single act of migration or the paid employment that presumably ensues. This is not to say, however, that migration to the United States may not have further accentuated their sense of themselves as social and political beings. Migration may very well have opened possibilities for empowerment that were previously nonexistent for them without necessarily insinuating an ideological renaissance.

The Space of Marginality

In New York, most Dominicans, women as well as men, occupy marginal social spaces, the less prosperous side, that is, of what many have referred to as the "dual city," a city divided into the haves and have-nots, two flanks separated by an ever larger gap (Mollenkopf and Castells 1991). They have yet to produce solid institutions with the power of transmitting social values, practices, and norms aimed at ensuring the protection and preservation of the community. Despite the many individual instances of achievement in business or the professions, the community is still ill-equipped to address its social problems collectively. Acute school dropout rates, street violence, drug use, and teenage pregnancy are all rampant conditions in predominantly Dominican neighborhoods like Washington Heights, gravely besetting the future prospects of the community's youth. Nor is the New York experience of most Dominican adults—marked by scarce housing, the lack of appropriate health services, extreme population density, and severe unemployment—particularly promising. Vital municipal institutions such as the Department of Sanitation and the Police Department seem to work less efficiently in Washington Heights than they do elsewhere in the city, causing many to feel that municipal authorities care little for how Dominicans live.

The perception that the norms that operate in the mainstream society are less formally applied to Dominican neighborhoods either in the provision of services or in the enforcement of the law leads to an understanding of the community's space as one of social isolation, which, as William Wilson would contend, can cause serious damage. In his study of poverty in some African-American communities, Wilson has ascribed a meaningful role to social isolation and disconnection from mainstream society. Among other things, isolation may lead to undesirable social behavior among the poor, nourishing an element of self-destruction in the community (Wilson 1987:60). Much of the discomfort that many hard-working and law-abiding Dominicans experience in Washington Heights, for instance, may derive from their sense of living in an unregulated space where law enforcement can see no difference between devils and saints and where no city agency rushes to fix a damaged street light.

The Community's Prospects

Dominican migrants in New York form a large and growing ethnic minority community, enclaved in a society whose present economy seems to have little need for new, unskilled, immigrant hands. The continued influx of new migrants from the Dominican Republic, the varying levels of adaptability exhibited by sectors of the community with different lengths of residence in the immigrant space, and their dissimilar degrees of acceptance of the new abode as a permanent home make it exceedingly difficult to grasp conceptually their current stage of development as an ethnic minority in American society.

As long as the present state of affairs continues, all monolithic claims made by commentators on the situation of Dominicans in the United States will remain simultaneously true and false.

If one should ask whether Dominicans in New York can appropriately be called permanent residents or temporary visitors (Spalding 1989), one may find enough of both as to be able to make a case for either alternative. Dominicans show serious involvement in local politics, but at the same time one can argue that electoral concerns in the native land detract from their effective immersion in their immediate political reality. While children of Dominican parents have outnumbered all other ethnic groups in New York City's public schools over the last few years, licensed Dominican teachers are still a rarity in the system. Despite the numerical significance of Dominican children in the city's schools, Dominicans have yet to reach a position in which they can influence policy-making or the design of curriculum in their school districts (Stevens-Acevedo 1993:14). The community has not yet provided its children the benefit of positive role model teachers who look and sound like themselves or appropriate exposure in the classroom to the history and culture of their people so that they may recognize themselves as legitimate components of the human experience.

One may justifiably find it hopeful that the City University of New York (CUNY) reports a rapid growth in Dominican enrollment, with members of this community constituting the second largest segment of the immigrant student body among those admitted in the fall of 1992 (OIRA 1993). The presence of numerous Dominican students in the university system may induce a rosy interpretation of the community's prospects, particularly in light of a prevailing belief that links education with upward mobility. Yet those students belong to at-risk pools, since they tend to be enrolled in the CUNY colleges with the lowest retention and graduation rates. By the same token, while Dominicans outnumber other Latinos in the student bodies of many CUNY colleges, chances are very slim of their ever coming across a faculty member of Dominican descent, even in the courses offered by Ethnic Studies and Latin American and Caribbean Studies departments.

Clearly, any close look at Dominicans in New York will reveal symbols of misfortune that compete with whatever evidence of prosperity one might perceive. The community's vulnerability is most convincingly manifest in its inability to shape its own image within the larger society. In terms of scholarly portrayals of Dominican immigrants, the present endeavor is probably one of the first texts in this country's academic sphere whose authors represent the group under study. The few Dominican authors most frequently cited in bibliographies on this topic (Vicioso 1976; Castillo and Mitchell 1987; Baéz Evertz and Ramírez D'Oleo 1985) produced their work in the Dominican Republic; only one of them has lived in New York for a considerable time. The bulk of the literature on Dominicans in the United States has come from scholars who have no stake in the survival of the community. From an assessment of some of the earliest studies (Hendricks 1974; Kayal 1978), one may even speculate on the extent to which some of those scholars have construed an image of Dominicans that, by relegating them to the realm of otherness, denormalizes and, in so doing, dehumanizes them (Torres-Saillant 1989). The community is a long way intellectually from influencing the larger society's perception of Dominican immigrants in the United States.

One may hope that the recent establishment at the City University of New York of a Dominican Studies Institute for sponsoring research and disseminating knowledge on the Dominican experience will serve to create networks of Dominican scholars throughout the United States. Should it succeed, the community will empower itself intellectually by having its own spokespersons to interact in defining Dominicans' sociohistorical experience. By participating in the scholarly production on Dominican migration and the various facets of Dominican life in the United States, the community will attain a measure of control over the manner in which Dominicans are presented to the rest of society.

Also, in due time, Dominicans in New York will reach a point at which they can ward off vilification from the local media. For some years now news stories on Washington Heights and its inhabitants in the city's press have been concerned almost exclusively with drugs and violent crime. The *New York Post* has frequently lent its pages to news articles that speak of Dominicans as "a community where three of the biggest sources of income are drugs, loan sharking, and money laundering" (McAlary 1991:21). Defamatory portrayals of the community, which date back less than ten years, have increased in frequency and virulence since the summer of 1992, when the death of José "Kiko" García at the hands of an officer from the Thirty-fourth Precinct sparked three days of upheaval in Washington Heights.

Mike McAlary, a city journalist who seems intent on denouncing Dominican depravity, has painted the community thus: "The Dominican Republic has always exported talent to the United States. The sports pages are filled with statistics of Dominican baseball heroes in the Major Leagues. But for every George Bell and Pedro Guerrero, Stan Javier and Julio Franco thrilling American audiences, there are now a dozen lethal drug dealers from San Francisco de Macorís terrorizing neighborhoods in upper Manhattan (McAlary 1992:3). With the backing of the *New York Post*, McAlary made a four-day trip to the Dominican Republic in order to get at the roots of the crime problem among Dominicans. In San Francisco de Macorís, the city chosen for his sojourn, the journalist assessed the prevailing moral climate this way: "There is a hint of dark evil in every gold-toothed smile, and the sound of sinister laughter in the pock-marked streets" (McAlary 1992:3).

In addition to the print media, the journalist's report from his trip to the Dominican Republic reached the airwaves through a broadcast of "Inside Edition" on CBS. Dominican wrongdoing in New York subsequently became the subject of an NBC News report entitled "Immigration: The Good, the Bad, and the Illegal," which was broadcast nationally on Sunday, March 28, 1993. These examples suffice to illustrate what we have termed the vulnerability of Dominicans in this country. For the time being they have no means of challenging their detractors. The turning point will come, one may hope, when the Dominican community has accrued enough economic and political power to command respect. By then perhaps members of the community will have penetrated the media, and Dominicans with access to the columns of English-speaking newspapers and the cameras of mainstream television may have a say in the construction of their public image.

Such, then, is the situation found by contemporary scholars on Dominican migration. The visible elements of that drama admit equally of either an optimistic or a pessimistic view regarding future prospects of the community. Thus, one-dimensional analyses inevitably fail to encompass the complexity of the situation. As a rule, then, the scholar on Dominican migration ought to resist the temptation to generalize.

However, even if the evidence at hand only partially supports our option, the present essay will close positively. Since we, as Dominicans, have a stake in the well-being of the community under study, we feel compelled to share the optimism of baseball great Felipe Rojas Alou, the Dominican-born Montreal Expos manager. Attributing extraordinary prowess to his compatriots he sees no obstacles that Dominicans cannot conquer and proudly declares that his people "don't know fear," recalling how often they dare "to cross the Atlantic in boats to get to the United States. The only thing on their mind is to give it all they've got" (Rains 1992:37). In concurrence we believe that in the fierce struggle for survival, Dominicans have shown they have the mettle. A community many of whose members have successfully crossed treacherous waters and defied the fury of sharks deserves the benefit of the doubt.

WORKS CITED

Abreu, Alfonso, et al. 1989. *Las zonas francas industriales: El éxito de una política económica*. Santo Domingo: Editora Corripio.

Alemany, Wilfredo, Alexis Alvarez, and Rafael Feria. 1981. "La expansión del capitalismo 1966–1978 (El papel de la industria)." Centro de Estudios de la Realidad Social Dominicana, Universidad Autónoma de Santo Domingo. *CERESD* 11:1–211.

Baéz Everstz, Franc, and Frank Ramírez D'Oleo. 1985. *La emigración de dominicanos a los Estados Unidos*. Santo Domingo: Fundación Friedrich Ebert.

Bergman, Barbara R. 1986. *The Economic Emergence of Women*. New York: Basic Books.

Bogen, Elizabeth. 1987. *Immigration in New York*. New York: Praeger Press.

Bonilla, Frank, and Ricardo Campos. 1982 "Bootstraps and Enterprise Zones: The Underside of Late Capitalism in Puerto Rico." *Review* 5.4:556–90.

———. 1986. *Industry and Idleness*. New York: Centro de Estudios Puertorriqueños, The City University of New York.

Bray, David. 1984. "Economic Development: The Middle Class and International Migration in the Dominican Republic." *International Migration Review* 18(2):217–36.

———. 1987. "The Dominican Exodus: Origins, Problems, Solutions,"
    In *Caribbean Exodus*, ed. Barry B. Levine, pp. 152–70. New York:
    Praeger.
Briggs, Vernon. 1992. *Mass Immigration and the National Interest*. New
    York: M.E. Sharpe, Inc.
Carnoy, Martin, Hugh Daley, and Raul Hinojosa Hojeda. 1993. "The
    Changing Economic Position of Latinos in the U.S. Labor Market
    since 1939." In *Latinos in a Changing U.S. Economy: Comparative
    Perspectives on Growing Inequality*, ed. Rebecca Morales and Frank
    Bonilla, pp. 28–54. New York: Sage Publications.
Castillo, José del, and Christopher Mitchell, eds. 1987. *La migración
    dominicana en los Estados Unidos*. Santo Domingo: CENAPEC.
Castillo, José del, et al. 1974. *La Gulf & Western en República Dominicana*.
    Santo Domingo: Editora de la UASD.
Ceara Hatton, Miguel. 1990. *Crecimiento económico y acumulación de
    capital: Consideraciones teóricas en la República Dominicana*. Santo
    Domingo: Centro de Investigación Económica, Inc. (CIECA).
———. 1992. *Gasto público social y su impacto en la distribución del ingreso:
    Principales tendencias en la República Dominicana*. Santo Domingo:
    Centro de Investigación Económica, Inc. (CIECA).
Chavez, Linda. 1991. *Out of the Barrio: Towards a New Politics of Hispanic
    Assimilation*. New York: Basic Books.
Cordero, Margarita. 1985. *Mujeres de abril*. Santo Domingo: Centro para
    la Acción Femenina.
DeCamp, Suzanne, 1991. *Selected New York City Public School Data*. New
    York: Community Service Society.
Department of City Planning. 1992a. *The Newest New Yorkers: An Analy-
    sis of Immigration into New York City during the 1980s*. New York:
    Department of City Planning.
———. 1992b. *Demographic Profiles*. New York: Department of City Plan-
    ning.
———. 1991. *Community District Needs, Manhattan: Fiscal Year 1993*. New
    York: Department of City Planning.
Dwyer, Christopher. 1991. *The Dominican Americans*. The Peoples of
    North America Series. New York: Chelsea House Publishers.
Fritz, Sonia. 1994. *Sueños atrapados*.
Georges, Eugenia. 1990. *The Making of a Transnational Community: Migra-
    tion, Development, and Cultural Change in the Dominican Republic*.
    New York: Columbia University Press.
Gómez, Carmen Julia. 1990. *La problemática de las jefas de hogar: Evidencia
    de la insubordinación social de las mujeres*. Colección Teoría. Santo
    Domingo: CIPAF.

Gómez, Luis. 1984. *Relaciones de producción dominantes en la sociedad dominicana: 1875–1975*. Santo Domingo: Editora Alfa y Omega.

Gonzalez, Nancie L. 1970. "Peasants' Progress: Dominicans in New York." *Caribbean Studies* 10(3):154–71.

———. 1972. "Patron-Client Relationships at the International Level." In *Structure and Process in Latin America*, ed. Arnold Strickon and Sidney M. Greenfield, pp. 179–209. Alburquerque: University of New Mexico Press.

———. 1976. "Multiple Migratory Experiences of Dominican Women." *Anthropological Quarterly* 49(1):36–44.

Grasmuck, Sherri. 1987. "Las consecuencias de la migración internacional de origen urbano para el desarrollo nacional: El caso de Santiago." In *La inmigración dominicana en lost Estados Unidos*, ed. José del Castillo and Christopher Mitchell, pp. 111–50. Santo Domingo: CENAPEC.

Grasmuck, Sherri, and Patricia Pessar. 1991. *Between Two Islands: Dominican International Migration*. Berkeley: University of California Press.

Hendricks, Glen. 1974. *The Dominican Diaspora: From the Dominican Republic to New York City—Villagers in Transition*. New York: Teachers College Press.

Hernández, Ramona. 1990. "Comentarios." In *Los dominicanos en Puerto Rico: Migración en la semi-periferia*, ed. Jorge Duany, pp. 122–27. Río Piedras, Puerto Rico: Ediciones Huracán.

Hernández, Ramona, and Nancy López. 1993. "Las Mojadas: Dominican Women Yola Migrants." New York: unpublished manuscript.

Hernández-Angueira, Luisa. 1990. "La migración de mujeres dominicanas hacia Puerto Rico." In *Los dominicanos en Puerto Rico: Migración en la semi-periferia*, ed. Jorge Duany, pp. 73–88. San Juan, Puerto Rico: Ediciones Huracán.

History Task Force: Centro de Estudios Puertorriqueños. 1979. *Labor Migración Under Capitalism: The Puerto Rican Experience*. New York: Monthly Review Press.

Humphries, Jane. 1988. "Women's Employment in Restructuring America: The Changing Experience of Women in Three Recessions." In *Women and Recession*, ed. Jill Rubery, pp. 20–47. New York: Routledge and Kegan Paul, Ltd.

Kayal, Philip M. 1978. "The Dominicans in New York," Parts 1 & 2. *Migration Today* 6 (3):16–23; 6 (4):10–15.

Larson, Eric M., and Teressa A. Sullivan. 1987. "Conventional Numbers in Immigration Research: The Case of the Missing Dominicans." *International Migration Review* 21(4):1474–97.

————. 1989. "'Cifras convencionales' en las investigaciones sobre migración: El caso de los 'dominicanos desparecidos.'" In *Dominicanos ausentes: Cifras, políticas, condiciones sociales*, ed. Joachim Koop and Frank Moya Pons, pp. 67–114. Santo Domingo: Fundación Friedrich Ebert-Fondo Para el Avance de las Ciencias Sociales.

Lozano, Wilfredo. 1985. *El reformismo dependiente*. Santo Domingo: Ediciones Taller.

————. 1987. *Desempleo estructural, dinámica económica y fragmentación de los mercados de trabajo urbanos: el caso dominicano*. Santo Domingo: Fundación Friedrich Ebert.

Marx, Karl. 1967. *Capital*, vol. 1. New York: International Publishers.

McAlary, Mike. 1991. "The Framing of a Cop." *New York Post*, 9 Oct., 2.

————. 1992. "Washington Heights' Deadly Dominican Connection." *New York Post*, 16 Sept., 3.

Mollenkopf, John Hull, and Manuel Castells, eds. 1991. *Dual City: Restructuring New York*. New York: Russell Sage Foundation.

Moya Pons, Frank. 1992. *Empresarios en conflicto: Política de industrialización y sustitución de importaciones en la República Dominicana*. Santo Domingo: Fondo para el Avance de las Ciencias Sociales.

Necos, Belkis. 1993. "Profile of the Dominican Community in New York City." Preliminary Report presented at the Conference on Dominican Research Issues, the City College of New York, under the auspices of the CUNY Dominican Studies Institute, June 5.

OIRA [Office of Institutional Research and Analysis]. 1993. Preliminary Report on Caribbean students admitted in the Fall 1992 by National Origen. New York: The City University of New York.

Paulino Ramos, Alejandro. 1987. *Vida y obra de Ercilia Pepín*. Santo Domingo: Editora Universitaria UASD.

Pessar, Patricia. 1987. "The Dominicans: Women in the Household and the Garment Industry." In *New Immigrants in New York*, ed. Nancy Foner, pp. 103–29. New York: Columbia University Press.

Portes, Alejandro, and Luis E. Guarnizo. 1991. *Capitalistas del trópico: La inmigración en los Estados Unidos y el desarrollo de la pequeña empresa en la República Dominicana*. Santo Domingo: Facultad Latinoamericana de Ciencias Sociales/Proyecto República Dominicana. Original English edition: *Tropical Capitalists: U.S.-Bound Immigration and Small Enterprise Development in the Dominican Republic*. Washington, D.C.: Commission for the Study of International Migration and Cooperative Economic Development, 1990.

Portes, Alejandro, and John Walton. 1981. *Labor, Class, and the International System*. New York: Academic Press.

Power, Marilyn. 1988. "Women, the State, and the Family in the U.S.: Reaganomics and the Experience of Women." In *Women and Recession*, ed. Jill Rubery, pp. 140–62. New York: Routledge and Kegan Paul, Ltd.

Rains, Bob. 1992. "A Contender is Exposed." *USA Today Baseball Weekly*, 12–18 Aug., 36–37.

Richmond-Abbott, Marie. 1992. *Masculine and Feminine: Sex Roles over the Life Cycle*. New York: McGraw Hill.

Ricketts, Erol. 1987. "The Relationship between U.S. Investment and Immigration from the Caribbean: Prospects for the Regan Administration's Caribbean Basin Initiative." Paper presented at the Socialist Scholars Conference, Borough of Manhattan Community College, April.

Sassen, Saskia. 1981. *Exporting Capital and Importing Labor: The Role of Caribbean Migration to New York City*. Occasional Papers No. 28. Center for Latin American and Caribbean Studies. New York: New York University.

———. 1988. *The Mobility of Labor and Capital: A Study in International Investment and Capital Flow*. Cambridge: Cambridge University Press.

Serrulle Ramia, José, and Jacqueline Boin. 1981. *La inversión de capitales imperialistas en la República Dominicana*. Santo Domingo: Ediciones Gramil.

———. 1983. *Fondo Monetario Internacional: Capital financiero, crisis mundial*. Santo Domingo: Ediciones Gramil.

Spalding, Hobart A. 1989. "Dominican Migration to New York City: Permanent Residents or Temporary Visitors?" *Migration Today* 5:47–68.

Stevens-Acevedo, Anthony. 1993. "Una junta escolor más conservadora." *El Nacional* 25 May, 14.

Tansill, Charles Callan. 1938. *The United States and Santo Domingo 1798–1873: A Chapter in Caribbean Diplomacy*. Baltimore: The John Hopkins Press.

Torres-Saillant, Silvio. 1989. "The Construction of the Other in Studies of Dominican Migration." Paper presented at the XV International Congress of the Latin American Studies Association, Miami, Florida, December.

———. 1993. "Dominicans & the U.S. Go Way, Way Back." *New York Newsday*, 28 June, 64.

Uglade, Antonio, Frank Bean, and Gilbert Cárdenas. 1979. "Interna-

tional Migration from the Dominican Republic: Findings from a
National Survey." *International Migration Review* 13 (2):235–54.

Ugalde, Antonio and Thomas C. Langham. 1982. "International Return
Migration: Socio-Demographic Determinants of Return Migration
to the Dominican Republic." In *Return Migration and Remittances:
Developing a Caribbean Perspective*, ed. William F. Stinner, Klaus de
Alburquerque, and Roy S. Brice-Laporte, pp. 73–95. Washington,
D.C.: Research Institute on Immigration and Ethnic Studies-
Smithsonian Institute.

Vicens, Lucas. 1982. *Crisis económica: 1978–1982*. Santo Domingo: Editora Alfa y Omega.

Vicioso, Sherezada (Chiqui). 1976. "Dominican Migration to the United
States." *Migration Today* 20:59–72.

———. 1993. "A cien años: Salomé Ureña o la praxis entre poesía y
feminismo." In *The Women of Hispaniola: Moving Towards Tomor-
row*, ed. Daisy Cocco de Filippis, pp. 61–67. Selected Proceedings
of the 1993 Conference. New York: York College of the City University of New York.

Waldinger, Roger D. 1986. *Through the Eye of the Needle: Immigrants and
Enterprise in New York's Garment Trades*. New York: New York
University Press.

Warren, Robert. 1989. "Datos sobre legalización y otra información
estadística acerca de la inmigración dominicana a los Estados
Unidos." In *Dominicanos ausentes: Cifras, politicas, condiciones sociales*, ed. Joachim Knoop and Frank Moya Pons, pp. 39–65. Santo
Domingo: Fundación Friedrich Ebert-Fondo para el Avance de
las Ciencias Sociales.

Wilson, William Julius. 1987. *The Truly Disadvantaged: The Inner City,
the Underclass, and Public Policy*. Chicago: University of Chicago
Press.

Zaglul, Antonio. 1980. *Despreciada en la vida y olvidada en la muerte:
Biografía de Evangelina Rodríguz, la primera médica dominicana*. Santo
Domingo: Editora Taller.

3

Mexicans in New York: Membership and Incorporation in a New Immigrant Community

ROBERT C. SMITH

Mexicans have emerged as one of the newest and fastest-growing immigrant groups in New York City, yet relatively little is known about them. In this chapter I will examine some aspects of the migration and incorporation of Mexicans into the life and social structures of New York City. In brief, I will argue that the incorporation of Mexicans in New York does not conform with either the model of the immigrant "melting pot" or the ethnic pluralist model that attempts to move "beyond the melting pot." It fits more closely, although not completely, with a third sociological model of "segmented assimilation" proposed by Portes and Zhou (1993). Mexican incorporation into New York City is best described as a contradictory set of processes characterized by the development of simultaneous, partial, and sometimes contradictory memberships in their communities and their states of origin and destination. How these memberships are developed relates to the ways in which Mexican immigrants negotiate the myriad of social structures they confront in U.S. society, including racial and ethnic discrimination, patterns of employment, and a changing relationship with the American and Mexican states. I will develop this argument through an analysis of the history of Mexican migration to New York City; and by looking at Mexican immigrants' relationship to work, the state, and the labor market; their social and political organization; and the problems of undocumented and second-generation Mexican immigrants. The theoretical arguments and insights developed are not necessarily exclusive to the Mexican case, and where possible I will attempt to compare the Mexican case in New York to Caribbean cases in New York and Mexicans in California.

I will draw on varied data sources, including ethnographic

fieldwork I have done in New York and Mexico, volunteer service work in the Mexican community, and interviews with employers of Mexicans for an ongoing project that has only been partially completed.[1] I do not intend to offer a comprehensive analysis of the Mexican community in New York but rather to provide an introduction as well as material for classroom discussion.

I. The Theoretical Problem: Simultaneous and Partial Memberships and the Process of Immigrant Incorporation

The assimilationist paradigm—with its central image of a "melting pot"—was dominant in studies of immigrant incorporation from the 1920s, when the paradigm first took shape, until the late 1960s. Assimilationist theory posited a unilinear process through which immigrants would conform to an idealized white, Anglo-Saxon Protestant model of "American-ness." Accordingly, a main theoretical task under assimilationism was to explain why certain groups assimilated to this model at different rates. It was presumed that all groups would eventually do so, or at least try to do so. Under this paradigm, race and ethnicity figure as factors which retard or enhance the rate and extent of assimilation, a position espoused with unusual directness in Warner and Srole's 1945 study of assimilation. It draws explicitly on racial and ethnic criteria in evaluating the prospects for and rapidity of assimilation. Later assimilationists acknowledge that racism among the dominant groups in society can itself inhibit assimilation, but the underlying premise is that assimilation is the normative and theoretical goal (Gordon 1964).

The ethnic pluralism paradigm attempts to move "beyond the melting pot," in Moynihan and Glazer's (1968) words, to explain the persistence of ethnic and racial identities of immigrants. This perspective employs what Omi and Winant call the "immigrant analogy," which posits that the experiences of earlier white immigrants will or should be repeated by more recent black immigrants from the American South and by contemporary non-white immigrants. This perspective presumes that the new immigrants will become "ethnics" through upward mobility, just as the old immigrants did. (Kristol 1966 and Lauria 1992.) In this model, racial and ethnic differences are seen as facilitating integration, as immigrants are assimilated as hyphenated Americans: Italian-Americans, Irish-Americans, and so forth. One implication is that groups who do not experience upward mobility—particularly blacks—have not upheld their part of America's bargain with its immigrants: work hard and suffer for a generation or two, and your children and their children will enjoy America's bounty. Such a position denies four hundred years of racial discrimination against blacks, as well as the importance of whiteness in the upward mobility of European immigrants (Lieberson 1980; Lauria 1992; Roediger 1991; Frankenberg 1993; Kershberg 1981). Theoretically, the important point to keep in mind is that such a position still posits assimilation as the road to upward mobility.

Portes and Zhou (1993) draw on their own and others' work to turn this logic on its head and posit a model of upward mobility through "segmented assimilation." For example, both Portes' studies of Cubans and Gibson's (1988) study of Sikhs in California subvert the reasoning that upward mobility comes mainly through integration, as the assimilationists would have it. Rather, in these cases, Sikhs and Cubans did better by "assimilating" as Sikhs and Cubans. These theorists argue that maintaining their own separate communities in the U.S. facilitates the creation of social networks and the accumulation of social and cultural capital (Portes and Sessenbrenner 1993; Waldinger and Bailey 1991b). "Separatism" allowed them to rise. Assimilation not only fails to provide advantages, it poses dangers, according to Stepick and Portes (1994). Hence Stepick reports that Haitians in Liberty City have assimilated into an inner-city black culture, which in our society virtually ensures that the second generation of Haitians in the U.S. will be poor. The difference lies in the articulation of these cultural traits with the structural conditions of the larger society. Within the context of a discriminatory society, their blackness decreases Haitians' life chances (Waters 1994).

My analysis begins with the concept of segmented assimilation, but uses it in tandem with the concept of membership. I will argue that Mexican incorporation into New York is characterized by simultaneous memberships and attachments to villages and towns in Mexico and to New York City, to Mexico and the United States. Put within the language of Portes and Zhou (1993). Mexicans' "assimilation" is segmented in large part by the on-going connection with their villages in Mexico and with their Mexican state, through its consular offices in the U.S., as well as through its interaction with New York's ethnic mosaic and racial structure. In this way, Mexicans' simultaneous memberships in their communities in New York and Mexico bind their solidarity and segment their assimilation. Throughout this analysis, "membership" is understood as a graduated concept, containing degrees, and not as an all or nothing enterprise in conception or in practice. One can be a marginal member of a community, with some rights of memberships and not others. As we will see later, such is the case with the partial membership of undocumented immigrants in American society. As an antecedent to developing these arguments through an analysis of four aspects of life in the Mexican community in New York, we now turn to examining the history of Mexican migration to New York (Goldring 1992).

II. A Brief History of Mexican Immigration to and Settlement in New York City

"We crossed the border on July 6, 1942," says Don Pedro, describing how he and his brother Fermin were the first ones to go to New York from the Mixteca Baja, the region in south-central Mexico from which comes the majority of Mexican immigrants to the New York metropolitan area. The Mixteca Baja includes the southernmost part of the state of Puebla, the northernmost part of the state of Oaxaca, and the easternmost part of the state of Guererro (see Smith, 1995). This region provides 64 percent of the Mexican immigrants to New York, of which 47 percent come from the state of Puebla alone. (Váldes and Smith 1994). Don Pedro is from a place I will call Ticuani, which is probably the first municipio in the Mixteca Baja to send immigrants to New York City.

According to Don Pedro, this Mexican migration to New York City began almost by accident. Don Pedro and his brother were working in Mexico City, attempting to get contracts for the Bracero Program, through which the U.S. government brought Mexicans to the United States to work in agriculture on contracts of several weeks' or several months' duration. Then, a friend of Don Pedro's put him in touch with Alberto Montesinos, an Italian-American from New York who vacationed in Mexico City every summer. Montesinos gave the two young Ticuanenses (people from Ticuani) a ride to New York, put them up in a hotel, and found them jobs within two days. "There was a war on, so they were happy to have us working," Don Pedro told me in 1993. "We opened the road," he said, looking back on the fifty years of migration to New York from Puebla that began with his own trip.

We can separate Mixteca migration to New York into three periods. The first runs from 1942 to the late 1960s, say about 1968. During this period, the few Mexicans who migrated to New York were part of several small networks of families from several municipios in southern Puebla. Beginning in the late 1960s and early 1970s, more municipios began to send migrants, and an increasing percentage of their inhabitants became involved in the migration process. The extent of migration grew steadily until the mid- to late 1980s, when Mexican migration to New York exploded.

A constellation of factors combined in this third period to cause this increase in New York–bound migration from Mexico. First, Mexico was in the midst of the decade-long economic crisis that caused the 1980s to become known in Mexico as the *"década perdida"* or "lost decade." The state of Puebla actually experienced a net contraction of its economy in the 1981–85 period (Cornelius 1992), and the Mixteca Baja region, marginal to begin with (Presidencia de la República 1982), was hit especially hard. Other factors within New York had related effects. A second set of factors behind this explosion related to the identification of Mexicans as a "preferred labor source" (Cornelius 1992) in certain industrial sectors of New York, including restaurants, light manufacturing, and other services. This identification is ethnically defined, as will be discussed in the next section. It also came about as Mexicans themselves began to constitute a certain critical mass of immigrants in New York, such that migration for newcomers was greatly facilitated by such changes as a ready supply of Mexican products and foods, and the emergence of certain Mexican *barrios* or neighborhoods.

The Immigration Reform and Control Act (IRCA) of 1986 was the final cause of this surge in Mexican migration. Mexicans ranked second only behind Dominicans in the number of applications filed to legalize their status through IRCA's amnesty program in New York City, with about 9,000 and 11,000, respectively (Vardy 1990).

The effect of the amnesty program was manifold. First, migration increased in anticipation of the amnesty program, and then again after 1988 in the hopes of a second amnesty program. Second, it served to catalyze the process of extended-family reunification. With the legalization of migrants in New York and the permanence that implied, wives, children, and other family members began coming to the United States to be with their families, regardless of their legal status. With the "myth of return" shattered by legalization, the inhibitions against reuniting in the U.S. were greatly lowered. (See Gonzáles de la Rocha 1993 for an analysis of this with respect to *viudas migrantes* or "migrant widows.") Moreover, the newly legalized people in New York provided the nuclei through which migrant networks were suddenly expanded in the late 1980s and early 1990s.[2]

These factors resulted in the surge in the numbers of Mexicans in New York and, correspondingly, a virtual emptying of parts of the Mixteca Sur, especially in Puebla. For example, the municipio of Ticuani lost about 38 percent of its population between 1980 and 1990, most through New York–bound migration. According to a survey done in 1993, 41 percent of Ticuanenses live in New York City, 48 percent in Ticuani itself, and the other 11 percent in different parts of the U.S. and Mexico (Smith 1994, chapter 4). Ticuani is not atypical in this respect. A group of municipios from the same region experienced population growth of –8.6 percent over the same period, again mainly due to New York–bound migration (Valdés and Smith 1994).

Estimates of the size of the Mexican population in New York vary significantly, in large part because a sizeable portion of it is undocumented. If many sources disagree on its actual size, most agree that the Mexican population in New York is growing very rapidly. One indication of this comes from the New York City "Emergency Immigrants Education Census" taken in public schools annually since 1989 to count the number of new immigrants in the schools. Mexico ranked sixth in the number of new immigrant children, behind such large senders as the Dominican Republic, China, and Jamaica.

The 1990 Census counted 61,722 persons who listed their ethnic heritage as Mexican, as opposed to 22,577 in 1980, for an annual growth rate of 10.5 percent (Valdés and Smith 1994). Using Census

Number of Mexican Immigrant Children Enrolled in the
New York City Public Schools, 1989–93

School Year	Number
1989–90	996
1990–91	1492
1991–92	1777
1992–93	1785
Total	5850

SOURCE: New York City "Emergency Immigrants Education Census," New York Board of Education, 1993 and 1992 versions.

estimates of the undercount of Mexicans (Mahler and Domínguez 1991), adjusted to take account of certain conditions that would tend to exaggerate the undercount even further, I estimated there were about 100,000 Mexicans in New York in 1990 (Smith 1992).

Population Concentrations and the Socioeconomic Location of Mexicans in New York City

A distinctive characteristic of the Mexican population in New York is its lack of concentration in one particular area. There is no "East L.A." or Pilsin District in New York. This dispersion is reflected in the table below, which lists the numbers of Mexican-origin population in each borough as reported by the U.S. Census of 1980 and of 1990, and the annual growth rate in that population over the decade of the 1980s. The wide dispersal of Mexicans is not random; rather, it reflects certain idiosyncracies in the networks through which Mexicans come to New York, as well as their relationship to the larger social and economic structures in the city. Each concentration or settlement has its own peculiar story; however, an important part of every story involves a process that most immigrants have experienced: namely, entrance and temporary settlement in marginal areas of Manhattan, then a move out to cheaper and more spacious accommodations in Queens, the Bronx, and Brooklyn (Katznelson 1988). This has been an important pattern for Mexicans. Several of the largest Mexican concentrations in Manhattan are in areas where there are Single-Room Occupancy (SRO) hotels or other such transient lodging. In one case, immigrants

Mexican Origin Population by County in New York City,
with Annual Growth Rates, 1980–90

Counties	1980	1990	Growth Rate
Brooklyn	7,364	21,623	11.3
Queens	4,285	13,342	11.3
Manhattan	6,438	12,800	6.9
Bronx	4,017	12,481	11.3
Staten Island	473	1,476	11.4
Total	22,577	61,722	10.5

SOURCE: 1980 and 1990 U.S. Census; estimates derived by Valdés in Valdés and Smith 1994.

from one municipio in Mexico maintained a virtual monopoly over several SROs in Manhattan—for example, by never officially moving out but replacing one *paisano* with another—and then, as a group, they moved into particular neighborhoods in Queens and the Bronx.

Mexican residence in SROs is functional for the new immigrants: they pay cheap rent and they can walk to the service jobs that they hold, for example, on the Upper West Side of Manhattan. Their residence is also symbolic of their position *and* mobility within the larger society. That is, they begin by occupying the same physical space as the mentally ill, welfare recipients, and transients in these SROs—living invisibly in Manhattan, the center of cultural power— but end up moving out to live among other immigrants in their own "middle-class" space in the "outer boroughs" (see Katznelson 1988). East Harlem and Manhattan Valley have served similar functions for many Mexican immigrants, providing entry into an invisible social location outside the fray of racial and class antagonisms, making it possible for immigrants to work hard and keep most of their life contained within the orbit between work and sleeping quarters. Mexican immigrants are in many ways, to use Rouse's (1990) diction, "perfect proletarians."[3]

There is another reason recent immigrants have had such an easy time finding housing in a generally tight housing market in New York. They are ideal tenants for slumlords looking to make money: they cram otherwise nearly unrentable apartments (which may include crack dens on the same floor) with large numbers of immigrants paying, typically, $25 per head per week. In many cases the landlord receives a higher rent than if he had rented the apartment on the open market. For example, if ten men rent a one-bedroom apartment and all pay $100 per month, that is $1000 in cash, off the books, for the landlord, for an apartment that might rent for $500 to $600 per month on the market. Many other building superintendents rent basement rooms without toilets or showers to undocumented immigrants and other low-income New Yorkers, including students and people employed at minimum-wage jobs. In one case, I came to know a family of four (and the wife was again pregnant) living in a noisy, humid room that separated the boiler room from the rest of the basement. By reaching out both hands I could nearly touch the walls on either side of the room. It was so loud we had to go outside to talk.

Other concentrations of population in Brooklyn and Queens are adjacent to subway lines which offer ready access to the restaurant and garment districts and other jobs in downtown Manhattan. Still other concentrations are in areas where there are many small light-manufacturing firms, such as the Brooklyn neighborhood of Sunset Park.

A final discernible pattern is the settlement of Mexicans among other Spanish-speaking populations, especially Puerto Ricans and other Latin immigrants in El Barrio (Spanish Harlem) and Washington Heights in Manhattan, in certain immigrant neighborhoods in Queens and Brooklyn and in the south Bronx. This has become especially important since the late 1980s, when Mexicans became a visible minority group within these neighborhoods.

III. The Social and Political Organization of Public Life in the Mexican Community in New York City

The forms that Mexican political and social organization have assumed in New York result from the marriage of the molecular form of immigrant social organization—the social network—with larger organizational forms "imported" from Mexico. The first of these larger forms is what Wolf (1957) called the "closed corporate peasant community" (see also Kearney 1993a). The second form presumes to encompass the entire Mexican population of the New

York area and to represent "the Mexican community." The Mexican consulate is at the center of this second form of incorporation, which draws its character from the ubiquity of the peculiar party-state organization that is the ruling party in Mexico, the *Partido Revolucionario Institucional* (Institutional Revolutionary Party), or PRI. More concretely stated, the importance of the consulate in organizing the Mexican community in New York has underlined the *Mexican* identity fostered through the incorporation of Mexicans into New York, hence reinforcing their simultaneous memberships in the communities of Mexico and the U.S. Recently, forms of activity more independent from the consulate and more fully based on issues related to life in New York have begun to spring up. In most cases, these organizations still must develop some relationship with the consulate as they negotiate the development of the Mexican community in New York.

This pattern of the consulate being the center of public life in the Mexican community in New York resembles the pattern of Mexican consulates elsewhere in the United States in earlier times (González 1993) and other groups, such as Koreans in New York fifteen years earlier. Kim (1981) argues that the Korean consulate pervaded every sphere of public life in the Korean community in New York and made it a virtual "colony" of the consulate. While there are differences, the Mexican and Korean cases offer an interesting comparison to each other and to the Dominican case. In the Dominican case, the party divisions from home were imported to the U.S. and then served as structures in organizing the social and political life of Dominicans in the city. The Dominican community has, however, moved beyond this form of organization and begun assertively developing its own leadership centered on issues within New York (see Hernández and Torres-Saillant in this volume and Ricourt 1994).

Transnational Communities as Structures of Incorporation

A first step in analyzing the role played by transnational communities in the incorporation of Mexicans in New York City is to examine what a transnational community is. In this section I draw on my fieldwork in New York and in Mexico on the village of Ticuani in the southern Mexican state of Puebla. Transnational communities are locally oriented communities whose social and political practices are carried on by members who have migrated to different locations (Smith 1995). As noted above, 41 percent of the Ticuani community lives in New York while 48 percent live in Ticuani, with the remainder sprinkled throughout Mexico and the U.S. Over the course of fifty years of migration, the Ticuanenses living in New York have come to play an increasingly important role in the social and political life of their home town in Mexico, in part because of their greater economic resources and in part because of changes in technology that allow them to participate simultaneously in their lives in New York and in Mexico. For example, the leaders of the community in New York regularly hold "town meetings" with those in Ticuani by use of a conference call. They have also flown to Ticuani on weekends to oversee the progress of projects that they have funded (Smith 1995).

Many of the transnational communities in New York grew out of a form of political and social organization described by Wolf (1957; 1986) as a "closed corporate peasant community." Such communities were "step-children of the Spanish conquest," according to Wolf, and were held together by practices which privileged the collective over the individual through a religious cargo system. In such a system, religious and political power were largely fused, and authority was gained through the fulfillment of one's duty as the *mayordomo*, or marshall, of the town's feast of their patron saint. This feast involved the expenditure of a great amount of the mayordomo's wealth to put on a good celebration. After the successful fulfillment of the mayordomo's obligations he ascended to a position of authority among the council of elders who ran the town. Ascent into this council of elders is frequently determined by one's kinship relations, both real and fictive; of particular importance are one's relations of *compadrazgo*, or "godfathership." Another practice is the donation of one's *faenas*, or communal labor obligations, to the town as a sort of communal "dues" or "taxes."

Several of the practices used by Ticuanenses today to gather donations are adapted versions of social forms derived from the closed corporate peasant community. A most important example involves the gathering of funds for public works projects in Ticuani. Since the early 1970s the Ticuani Solidarity Committee in New York has funded the construction of two schools, the installation of lights, repairs to the church and municipal palace. Most recently, they gathered more than $100,000 to install a potable water system in Ticuani, a sum greater than the Mexican local, state, and federal contributions combined. The committee's ability to gather such a great amount of money among Ticuanenses in New York—$300 per head of household—results from their trustworthy reputation among Ticuanenses in New York and the practice's consonance with the older custom of *faenas*. The Ticuanenses in New York dispense with their communal obligations by providing their *faenas* as *cooperaciones* (cooperations) in the form of money donated in New York for projects in Ticuani.

Such practices provide a form for the continuation and reinforcement of a communal public life among Ticuanenses even though they are dispersed throughout the city. This is true even among New York-born, second-generation Ticuani immigrants. The Ticuani youth group, for example, continues the ethic of privileging the communal over the individual through its activities dedicated to the completion of public works projects in Ticuani. Through a series of volleyball tournaments held in Brooklyn and attended mainly by Ticuanenses, they have renovated a kindergarten and are currently at work raising funds for the renovation of an old chapel dedicated to Padre Jésus. In another example, Ticuanense youth in New York collect money to stage an annual "Torch Run" (*Antorcha*) for Padre Jésus, and many of the youth return to Ticuani to participate. Hence, second-generation Ticuanenses reinforce their identities as members of a transnational community.

This transnational membership acquires meaning not only in the context of the relationship with Ticuani, but also with respect to the larger society in New York. One important aspect of this process involves the relationship, actual and potential, of Ticuanense youth to what is known in popular parlance as the "underclass." While the term is often ill-used and potentially dangerous in policy debates because of what it obfuscates (Gans 1992; Fainstein 1994), we can usefully employ the word "underclass" in describing a *belief* among many Americans that there exists a group of the "underserving poor" (Katz 1989) who are poor because of their shoddy culture and values or bad work habits (Lewis 1968; Murray 1984; Mead 1987). Hence, the "underclass" can be understood as a "social fact," as Durkheim understood this term.

The social fact of a belief in an underclass is being reproduced by the Ticuanenses in New York. In practice this means that the Ticuanenses engage in activities meant to distinguish their children from the other youth, usually believed to be African-American or Puerto Rican, whom they see as falling prey to a variety of urban vices associated with New York. One example of this was the making of a video, "Ticuani in History," by a group of New York and Ticuani-residing Ticuanenses. The video depicts scenes of Ticuani's indigenous past, recalling its role as a *lugar de paso* (point of passage) in pre-Columbian Mexico. One of the video makers told me that they had made the video in order to teach their youth about where they had come from, so that they would know that they had not come from New York and the vices that they associated with it. Waters (1994) describes similar practices among West Indian parents, who fear that their children will see themselves and will be seen as black Americans, and attempt to inculcate a reinforced ethnicity among the second generation.

Another example of the bonding of Ticuanense identity in response to the racial and ethnic structures in New York involves the meaning given to the volleyball tournaments organized by the Ticuani Youth Group. This other meaning was made clear to me during a conversation with the group's president at one of the volleyball tournaments. Pointing to the assembled crowd of Ticuani players and spectators, the president defined the group's purpose to me with constant reference to the alleged cultural inferiority and lack of motivation of American blacks and Puerto Ricans. "Look at the blacks and Puerto Ricans," he told me, "they have all kinds of problems: drugs, crime, teen pregnancy, disobedience to their parents, girls walking alone at nght. . . Look at this group," he said, pointing to the assembled Mexicans. "Do you think the Puerto Ricans and blacks have this kind of community? this kind of culture? No," he answered, "they do not, and this is the problem." He told me that groups such as the Ticuani Youth Group and events such as the tournament were what enabled Mexicans to live in the same neighborhoods as blacks and Puerto Ricans but still turn out alright. According to the president, such events are evidence of the "better culture" which Mexicans bring with them and which enables them to resist the bad influences that the blacks and Puerto Ricans apparently cannot. Preventing such outcomes by preserving their Mexican culture and Ticuanense practices was the mission that the president saw in holding the tournament, whose proximate, formal goal was to raise money to fix the chapel to Padre Jésus. In this context, a religious activity takes on a new meaning—Padre Jésus, the patron saint of Ticuani, is seen to protect Ticuanenses even as they reside in or are native to New York. Thus, the forms of public life imported from Mexico have been used in adapting to—and, ironically, also in reproducing—social structures, including ethnic and racial hierarchies that immigrants encounter in New York.

The Mexican Consulate and the Emergence of "the Mexican Community" in New York

The Mexican consulate has played a central role in the emergence of an organized Mexican community in New York. Indeed, it has provided the larger organizational structure within which the various social networks and sports and civic clubs have come to connect with each other and to create an emerging, truly "Mexican" consciousness and community in New York. The most important ways that the consulate has done this has been by linking up the various isolated examples of community-building among Mexicans in New York, by providing material support for them to increase the scope of their activities, and by offering them a new symbolic resource of organizing under the aegis of the Mexican state. Linking these social networks and sports and civic clubs is important because these have been identified by many scholars as the "microstructures" of migration (Portes and Walton 1981; Massey et al. 1987; Lomnitz 1977).

This emergence of a "Mexican community" must be understood within the context of two of its larger constituent processes. On the one hand, Mexican immigrants in New York have undergone a process of settlement in New York through which they have bought houses, raised children, and established their private and communal lives in the new environment (Massey et al. 1987; Lourdes de Villar 1989). This process has led Mexicans in creating an emerging community. On the other hand, the Mexican consulate and Mexican state have changed their stance toward the Mexican community in New York and the U.S. Two main factors spurred this awakening of the Mexican state to the massive Mexican population in the United States. The first was the legalization of almost two million Mexicans through the amnesty provisions of the 1986 Immigration Reform and Control Act. This legalization shattered the "myth of return" both among migrants and among Mexico's elite (González-Gutiérrez 1993; García y Griego 1993). Mexico's elite had previously assumed that this large population in the U.S. was largely made up of temporary migrant workers who would return to Mexico eventually. The legalization of two million workers made this assumption untenable. If the amnesty program hinted at how many Mexicans had settled in the U.S., then the strong support for Cuauhtémoc Cardenas, evidenced by the large crowds he drew in Los Angeles and elsewhere, signaled the potential political importance of this large expatriate community (see Smith 1993b; Alarcón 1993). For these and other reasons, the Mexican government created the Program for Mexican Communities Abroad in 1990, directed by Dr Díaz de Cossio, an American-trained engineer. Through this endeavor the program and the consular offices began an intensive outreach campaign and were charged with implementing the International Solidarity Program, the counterpart of former President Salinas's major domestic policy initiative, the Solidarity Program.

In New York the Program for Mexican Communities Abroad and the International Solidarity Program have helped create a Mexican community in a number of ways. One of the most important steps has been the creation of the FEDEMENEU, or Federación Deportivo Mexicano del Noroeste de los Estados Unidos (Mexican Sports Federation of the Northeastern United States). Sports leagues form out of the social networks of small groups of friends from the same towns or villages and are a basic structure in the formation of immigrant communities (Massey et al. 1987; Portes and Walton 1981; Lomnitz 1977). On the soccer field one encounters old friends from the village and renews those ties. This is an essential function in constituting an immigrant community.

In creating the FEDEMENEU the Program for Mexican Communities Abroad and the Mexican consulate were able to broaden the organizational scope of the league and also to deepen the connections of these groups to their communities of origin and to parts of the Mexican state. According to its only president, the league began in 1972 when "eight people met to practice soccer." By 1976 they had organized an end-of-season tournament in which four of the six member teams played. By 1980 there were fourteen teams, and by 1987 there were thirty teams. The count in 1994 was forty-seven teams. Many of these teams are organized on the basis of origin in a common village in Mexico. In the 1990s this original soccer league has served as the organization around which the larger Mexican community is constructed. Newer independent leagues have been incorporated into the FEDEMENEU, as were the long-standing baseball and basketball leagues, and running and karate clubs. The steep increase in the numbers of teams and leagues reflects the steeply growing population of Mexicans in New York and their increasing settlement here.

The FEDEMENEU is the Mexican state's way of incorporating these new Mexican immigrants into its "Mexican community" in New York. This is part of a larger project by the Program for Mexican Communities Abroad, which organizes sports leagues by region in the United States and sponsors competitions between the U.S. teams and counterparts in Mexico, including return trips to Mexico for the U.S.-based Mexican competitors. The result has been the formation of a regional organization that links leaders of various sports leagues from different geographic locations in the greater New York area. They hold annual banquets honoring the winners of their tournaments and a large event that unites all the members of the FEDEMENEU in the tristate region.

It is interesting that the federation is organized both on the basis of its Mexican-ness and on the basis of its regional location in the northeastern United States. Hence, its activities convey the message that the organization is both of and for Mexicans, specifically for those in a particular place in the United States. These simultaneous memberships are reflected in many small details in the federation's activities. For example, to qualify as a Mexican for any of the federation's competitions, one need not be born in Mexico, but only to have Mexican ancestry. Such simultaneous memberships are manifest in the anomalous situation I observed at a federation dance. A woman who has lived in New York for many years stood as a contestant in the race for queen of the federation's annual banquet. As part of her competition, she stood in front of a Solidarity banner in a church hall in Manhattan and thanked "their" president, Carlos Salinas de Gortari, for making this whole program possible for the development of Mexican youth. On another occasion the president of the Mexican Baseball League handed me a card after his league had joined the federation. While previously his card had only the imprint of the Mexican Baseball League of New York on it, this emblem now shared space with the symbol for the (Mexican) National Commission on Sports. The league's president wished to make known his affiliation with this Mexican national organization and to show his linkages both with the Mexican community in New York and with the organs of the Mexican state.

The organization of the federation and other such large organizations has fostered the creation of links with various levels of the state in New York, especially its bureaucratic administrative incarnations in such agencies as the police department and parks department. That these links have been deepened could be clearly seen in the large, crowded ceremony inaugurating the Mexican Soccer League season of 1992. First, Consul General Manuel Alonso thanked Julio Sierra, the president of the Soccer League, for his more than 20 years of service. He went on to thank, "in the name of our country(men) (*patria*) in New York," Elizabeth Aivars, of the City's Department of Immigrant Affairs and (absent) Mayor David Dinkins for their support of Mexicans in New York. Raúl Cárdenas, the Mexican soccer star, had also been brought in by the Program for Mexican Communities Abroad. He spoke to both the Mexicans present and to Elizabeth Aivars and the mayor for their warm welcome of Mexicans in New York. Elizabeth Aivars celebrated the role of Mexicans in "revitalizing the spirit of New York" and said she "joined eight million other New Yorkers" in welcoming them. Several others spoke similarly, including the dedicated and well-loved Assistant Chancellor of the Consulate in New York, Lic. José Antonio Lagunas. Finally, Manuel Alonso, Elizabeth Aivars, and Raúl Cárdenas together chose and awarded a prize for the best team, judged on the basis of their uniforms and banners, and tightness of their line-up.

These examples put into relief the transnational arena which immigration is creating.

IV. Mexican Immigrants, Work, and Prospects for the Future in New York City

We turn now from examining the social and political forms of organization in the Mexican community to economic modes of incorporation. As with other aspects of incorporation, this one also admits of degrees and kinds. There are four main questions for this discussion: (1) In what jobs do Mexicans work? (2) How do they get these jobs? (3) What led to the rapid hiring of Mexicans in New York City in the late 1980s? And (4) What are the prospects for the second-generation Mexican immigrants in New York? This final question in particular leads to issues of membership and its degrees within the United States.

Mexican Employment Patterns in New York City

Figures from two different research projects are available regarding the kinds of jobs Mexicans hold. The first is a study of 346 immigrants interviewed through the Mexican consulate in New York. Most were recently arrived immigrants who were returning to Mexico mostly for visits. They came to the consulate seeking documents that would enable them to get back into Mexico. There was also a minority with U.S. visas who were going to Mexico for a visit.[4] The table below shows the occupations and educational levels of this sample in Mexico and in New York for these document seekers.

This table shows that 80 of 138 immigrants in the "service workers" category in New York had some kind of education beyond secondary school, which equates roughly to ninth grade in the U.S. (Note: "hours worked per week" refers to hours worked in New York; "educational level" refers to Mexico.) This conforms to the profile described by Cornelius, among others. This educational level represents a significant loss to Mexico in terms of investment, because these well-educated workers are leaving Mexico to work in service industries in the United States. Only five of the ninety-nine respondents who were students in Mexico were also students in the U.S. A large portion of these former students went into the service occupations in New York, meaning primarily working in restaurants and delivery services and the like.

The number of hours worked is suggestive of the worker's legal status and overall working conditions. The service occupations, in which the undocumented are most likely to work, also show the largest number of people—seventy-six—working more than fifty hours per week, versus forty-two people working forty hours per week and thirty people working forty-one to fifty hours

Mexican Immigrants by Occupation in Mexico Prior to Migration,
Current Job in the U.S., Educational Level, and Hours Worked per Week

Occupation[a]	Mexico	New York	Edu.[b]	W/H/W[c] 40	41–50	50+
1. Managers	1	1	1	—	1	
2. Professionals	6	1	1	—	—	1
3. Technicians and associate professionals	9	5	4	2	2	1
4. Clerks	3	5	4	4	1	
5. Service workers and shop and market sales workers	15	138	80	42	20	76
6. Skilled agricultural and fishery workers	8	16	7	9	1	6
7. Craft and related trade workers	37	26	12	13	7	6
8. Plant and machine operators and assemblers	20	34	23	19	4	11
9. Elementary occupations	121	94	53	42	20	32
10. Armed Forces	6					
Students	99	5				
Homemakers	21	21				
Total	346	346				

[a] Categories taken from the International Classification of Labor, United Nations.
[b] Edu.: People with studies higher than secondary education.
[c] W/H/W: Working hours per week
SOURCE: Valdés and Smith 1994; table compiled by Valdés.

per week. "Plant operators" and "elementary occupations" also show more people working more than fifty hours per week than working forty-one to fifty, though more work forty hours than work more than fifty hours. That more people work more than fifty hours than work forty-one to fifty seems to reflect the ethnographic observation that undocumented immigrants are made to work many more hours than immigrants with visas.

A second measure of Mexican occupation structure is presented below. This table draws on data from a survey I did in Ticuani in 1992 and has the advantage of sampling long-term as well as recent immigrants to New York.

Occupations of Ticuanenses Currently Residing in New York City

Occupation	Frequency	Percent
Businessman	1	1.0
Student or preschool age	9	9.6
Homemaker	12	12.8
N.Y. restaurant	25	26.6
N.Y. service or factory	47	50.0
Total	94	100.0

Total: 111   Valid cases: 94   Missing cases: 17

SOURCE: Author's survey, February 1992.

This table confirms the profile of Mexican incorporation described by Portes and Borocz (1989) that Mexicans are primarily in the secondary labor market.[5] It shows that a full 26.6 percent of all Ticuanenses work in the restaurant industry in New York, while 50.0 percent work in one of the service industries or a factory. This category includes domestic workers, factory operatives, messengers, greengrocery workers, and others.

Parallel Immigrant Social Networks and Mexican Employment in New York City

Providing this profile of Mexican employment in New York does not answer the question of how Mexicans get jobs, and how and why they emerged as a "preferred labor source" (Cornelius 1992) in New York in the late-1980s and 1990s. In investigating these questions, I chose to focus on groups of immigrant employers, especially Greeks and Koreans, who hire Mexicans in high numbers. We can begin to investigate the question of how Mexicans get jobs by turning it over to ask why non-Mexican immigrant employers were hiring Mexicans instead of coethnics. At least two reasons suggest themselves. First, immigration from certain source countries such as Greece seems to have decreased in recent years, leading to a shortage of coethnic labor (Karpathakis 1993). This shortage has changed the relationship between coethnic employers and employees. A steady stream of new coethnic arrivals would be needed since only these new arrivals are willing to do the most unpleasant jobs (Bailey 1987). One Greek restauranteur described the situation this way: "There are no good Greek workers any more. . . . First of all, they don't come—they do better in Europe. And you tell them to do something, and they say 'F—— you.' They don't want to do it."

Another dimension of the shortage in coethnic supply is the high rate of self-employment among such groups as Greeks and Koreans combined with the labor-intensive nature of their businesses. Koreans, for example, were much more likely than white or Hispanic business owners to employ those who were not coethnics, for just these reasons: Not only are so many Koreans self-employed, but they also require a relatively large number of workers for a small business (Waldinger 1990). These factors help explain why there was a demand for non-coethnic labor.

A related factor regards the kind of relationship between a coethnic and a non-coethnic employer and employee. Employers reported that Mexicans were highly desirable as employees because they were cheaper to hire, and hiring them did not entail the same kind of reciprocal obligations as hiring a coethnic. Both Korean and Greek employers stressed these aspects of the relationship with Mexicans. One Korean employer explained his preference for hiring Mexicans by comparing the relative merits of Korean and Mexican employees. While Korean employees would work "spontaneously" and speak the same language, Mexicans only do the work they are told to do. However, Koreans also "tend to consider themselves as members of the employer's family as time goes by" and this is "rather burdensome" to the employer.[6] (See also Kim 1994.)

Korean employees also frequently ask for a raise. Indeed, the Korean employees cost much more to hire than the Mexicans. One Korean employer paid $500 per week to hire a Korean, but hired two Mexicans for $230 and $270 per week. When his business slowed down the employer fired the Korean and one of the Mexicans, hiring another Mexican for $170 per week. This was roughly equal to the going rate of $180 a week for seventy hours of work, as discovered by informal surveys Smith did with Mexicans employed in Korean greengroceries in 1990 and 1992. In the interview, the employer reported that he preferred to hire two or three Mexican workers for the same money as hiring one Korean worker. Presumably, the employer is constrained from hiring Koreans for a cheaper wage not only because there are fewer Koreans for hire but also because he would be breaking a coethnic social expectation that he pay the going wage of $500 per week to Korean workers.

A final factor involves the ethno-racial rhetoric in which the hiring decisions of employers were couched. The hiring of Mexican workers takes place within an ethno-racialized framework—that is, one that uses race and ethnicity as an important if tacit boundary or marker for evaluating potential workers (Waldinger and Bailey 1991a). This use of race and ethnicity as a parameter for hiring is expressed in the "immigrant analogy" (Omi and Winant 1986) and its imputation of moral and economic failure on the part of blacks and Puerto Ricans. This dual dynamic was clearly articulated to me in one of the interviews I had with a Greek restauranteur. After explaining to him that the purpose of the interview was to learn more about his experiences with different kinds of workers, and in particular with Mexicans, this restauranteur began by identifying with the Mexicans as immigrants: "Why do Greeks hire Mexicans to work? Very good—working-wise—compared to the others. . . . As an immigrant myself, moving up as I did, it's easier to teach them [Mexicans]. They're willing to follow . . . [and] step by step they become cooks." When I asked about his experiences with other groups, and in particular blacks and Puerto Ricans, he said: "I have never had any experience with blacks" as workers, so I cannot evaluate them. Yet he went on almost immediately to express his dissatisfaction with the appearance of blacks in general. Several times he offered the example of a black man who works in a bagel place nearby who, he said, smelled bad, had an earring (a point he mentioned several times) and "looked like a homeless guy."

In the rest of the interview, the restauranteur returned repeatedly to this dual project of affirming the sameness of the Mexican immigrants he hires and himself and their fundamental difference with blacks. This position is perhaps most succinctly expressed in his statement: "We came from the same background . . . not from welfare." Later in the interview his identification became more intense. He raised his voice, and his eyes began to tear slightly as he described his own history of coming to the U.S. "When I came to this country," he said, I worked "fourteen hours a day, seven days a week. . . . I know what it means to work," he said. He expressed this identification most clearly when he declared, emotionally, that when he came to this country, "I was a Mexican. I was a good Mexican." This identification is strongly related to another belief regarding the strong work ethic and high productivity among Mexicans and the presumed lack thereof in other groups. Referring to blacks and Puerto Ricans, he said "One Mexican is good for five of them."

It is important that we consider such remarks within their structural context. First, undocumented Mexican workers *are* cheaper to hire and willing to work longer hours than natives, and also, as we have seen, than many coethnic immigrants, in this case Greeks and Koreans. Yet the Mexicans preferred status is not inherent in being Mexican, even though it comes to be understood this way by employers and employees, natives and immigrants alike. Rather, it is the result of their particularly weak bargaining position vis à vis employers—they are non-coethnic, undocumented, and do not speak English—combined with their more positive view of the low wages they receive. For many such recent immigrants, they think of their earnings relative to what they will buy back home and less with respect to what others earn in the U.S. Second, the preference for Mexicans (or other immigrant groups) over natives, and in particular over African Americans and, in New York, over Puerto Ricans as well, reaffirms James Baldwin's oft-quoted and critical observation (paraphrased here): You always know where the bottom is because that's where the Black folks are. Indeed, the preference for immigrants is constructed using African Americans, and here also Puerto Ricans, as an "other" against which the former's virtues are defined. Immigrants, in turn, learn this American lesson, and benefit from it, as part of their process of "Americanization" (Morrison 1994; Roediger 1991; Smith 1994). Stated in terms of the concept of membership central to this article, defining themselves in opposition to the "other" of African Americans and Puerto Ricans becomes part of their taking possession of their membership in certain contexts in American life.

Alternative Scenarios for Second-Generation Mexicans in New York City

The final question involves what will happen to the second generation of Mexicans in New York. Stated perhaps too starkly, the question is this: Will second-generation Mexican immigrants in New York experience the "second-generation decline" feared by Gans (1992), or the upward mobility through "segmented assimilation" celebrated by Portes and Zhou (1993) or will they experience some other mode of incorporation? While no definitive answer can be given now, evidence suggests the outcomes are highly contingent and will vary significantly. Analyzing who within the Mexican population (and other populations) winds up in one category versus another is an important theoretical task that can only be addressed in a cursory fashion here. Below I offer both positive and negative scenarios. The future will likely manifest elements of both. The well-being of second-generation Mexicans in New York can be judged by the balance of such scenarios.

A positive scenario would be realized through at least two possible routes, both highlighting the importance of social networks and the social capital they create (Coleman 1988; Portes and Sesen-brener 1993; Fernández-Kelly 1993; Granovetter 1985; others) and the uplifting effects of an ethnic, immigrant economy (Light and Bonacich 1988; Waldinger and Bailey 1991c). One route would be through the creation of a critical mass of Mexican entrepreneurs serving both the needs of the Mexican population and those of the larger society. Given that Mexicans as a group possess relatively fewer resources in the financial and educational (human capital) realms than Cubans and Koreans or Greeks, the relationships that they develop or do not with their non-coethnic employers may serve as one way in which Mexican immigrants gain access to training and the financial and social capital that they need to become entrepreneurs on their own. (See Waldinger and Bailey 1991c.) In several cases, Mexican entrepreneurs have told me that they began their enterprises through the sponsorship of non-coethnics, especially Greeks and Dominicans in the restaurant industry (Smith 1992d; Hermann 1994).

In these cases, the relationship seems to begin as one of exploitation, but over time becomes reciprocal to a point where it approaches a coethnic relationship. This nearly coethnic reciprocity grows out of the personal friendship between the employer and the worker, and can be understood as a kind of "co-immigrant" reciprocity. In one case, a Mexican worker was offered $10,000 by his Dominican employer when he sold his interest in the restaurant in which the Mexican worked. The Dominican employer had always said: One day I will do something good for you because you are a good worker. The Mexican worker asked his former boss to recast the offer: What is $10,000? he said. Once it is spent, it's spent. Teach me to run a restaurant instead. The Dominican employer agreed, and worked for his former Mexican employee for two months for free to teach him how to run a restaurant. The Mexican is running a successful restaurant in Manhattan several years later. The empirical and theoretical question—which can only be posed here—is to what extent such a non-coethnic "hand up" will extend outward within the Mexican community and replicate the upward mobility that Greeks, Koreans, and Dominicans have experienced through their social networks. One must also note that becoming an entrepreneur is not the only possible positive outcome here. Mexicans as a group could become involved in long-standing, perhaps intergenerational, relationships with non-coethnic employers that could offer them middle-class jobs (e.g., as waiters or cooks) that require large investments in training and are better than the jobs they would get in most of the service industries.

A second route to upward mobility could come through similar mechanisms developed through the Mexican community and the consulate in New York. In connection with the Program for Mexican Communities Abroad, several entrepreneurs created the Mexican Chamber of Small and Medium-Sized Business in 1991, which provides business advice and logistical support, and intends to help promote Mexican small businesses in New York. These businesses are directed both at the local market and at creating links between Mexico and the U.S.—"Smith to Sánchez to Sánchez" as one Mexican official put it, referring to the links between American, Chicano, and Mexican-based businesses that they hope to foster. This project is another example of the Mexican state attempting to develop the Mexican community in the United States. These efforts echo those of the Korean consulate in New York in the 1970s and 1980s, during which time much of the capital and logistical links between, for example, Korean-based producers and Korean businessmen in New York, were controlled by the Korean consulate (Kim 1981).

A third route to upward mobility could be through a "middle-class, segmented assimilation strategy." This refers to the relatively large proportion of second-generation Ticuanenses who are attending college and preparing for jobs as nurses, social workers, accountants, and other professional positions. Parental expectations and the high prestige of having someone graduate from college have contributed to this inclination toward college among second-generation Ticuanenses. It is possible that college could provide upward mobility for the immigrants.

It is not certain that it will do so, however, nor that it will help all Ticuanenses equally. Ticuanense women are much more likely to enter and complete college in New York than are men. The men tend to move toward blue-collar jobs in their teens and do not pursue college. It seems that this difference is connected to the understandings of gender by these second-generation immigrants. Masculinity seems to be associated with working early in one's teens and earning money, and in dropping out of school. Staying in school and attending college are seen to be more acceptable for women. While these observations are preliminary, important areas to investigate will be the relationship between the social construction of gender and social success. How does gender relate to the "push out" rate, as opposed to the drop-out rate, which presumes to measure how many people "choose" to leave school? We need to study what factors create a situation where students, especially young men, feel they have no real choice except to leave school, and hence are "pushed out" (Cordero-Guzmán 1994; Willis 1977; López 1994).

Connected with this "push out" rate, we come to the hard question that Gans (1992) grimly poses: What will happen to the large number of non-white second-generation immigrants, especially men, who do not receive an education that prepares them for well-paying jobs in the service sector but are (presumably, due to "Americanization") not willing to take the same entry-level jobs as their parents? Gans fears that these young men will join the ranks of the unemployed and socially deviant, and not find a place in American society. The quick money of drug sales poses a particularly dangerous alternative in this situation (Bourgois 1991 and 1995). This scenario conforms with the implications of Stepick's analysis of negative assimilation: downward mobility and marginalization through assimilation. It also resonates with the worst fears of West Indian parents for their children (Waters 1994). Such a possibility is all too plausible for at least some of the second-generation Mexicans in New York and must be entertained seriously by community leaders and others concerned with this issue. This issue cuts directly to the value of the membership held by second-genera-tion Mexican immigrants in New York.

In the final section, we turn to another aspect of Mexican incorporation into New York City that addresses the issue of mem-bership and will have implications for the future—the impact of legal status on the lives of undocumented immigrants.

V. The Plight of Undocumented Immigrants: Exploitation within Contradictory State Projects of Inclusion and Exclusion

Undocumented workers constitute the most vulnerable sector of workers in the Mexican community, as in most immigrant commu-nities. This vulnerability emerges not just in the sphere of work, but also in the legal and personal spheres. The consequences of this vulnerability range from simple exploitation in low or unpaid wages or dangerous working conditions, to physical abuse, deprivation of freedom, violent attack, and even death. I have seen such things in my fieldwork in New York over the last seven years and believe that undocumented status plays a role in producing such outcomes by making undocumented immigrants vulnerable.

The vulnerability of undocumented workers must be "con-structed." In other words, it is not a "natural" condition, but rather results, at least in part, from the structural conditions in which the immigrants find themselves. Bosniak (1987) has analyzed the vulnerability of undocumented immigrants with unusual clarity. She argues that undocumented immigrants are caught between contradictory "inclusionary" and "exclusionary" projects of the American state. The inclusionary project stems from the Constitu-tion, which extends the protection of law to all "persons" living within the United States, not to all "citizens." Hence, the Supreme Court ruled in *Plyler v. Doe* that the children of undocumented immigrants had the same constitutional right to education as the children of native-born Americans. Labor law provides another example. Minimum-wage laws protect all workers, not all citizens. The exclusionary project of the American state is embodied in its efforts to keep out unauthorized entrants such as undocumented immigrants. This project stems from the principle of sovereignty on which is based a nation state's right to control its own territory, including the right to refuse entry to all non-citizens.

The conflict between these two projects is nowhere more clearly expressed than in the vulnerability of undocumented immigrants in employment. Under the inclusionary project, these workers have the right to the same wage and hour protections as citizen workers. Yet their very presence in the United States is unauthorized, and hence they may be subject to deportation if discovered by the Immigration and Naturalization Service. In this context, undocumented people often fear that any contact with official agents of the state—the police, hospital or school authorities, or Legal Aid lawyers—may subject them to deportation. Hence, in reality, undocumented immigrants are often prevented from exercising their legal rights under the inclusionary project because of their fear of deportation under the exclusionary project. This fear is justified in many cases, though not in New York City, which has an Executive Order/City Council Resolution prohibiting the sharing of information regarding someone's immigration status except in connection with a criminal investigation.[8] In this section we will discuss three different arenas in which immigrants experienced vulnerability and exploitation because of their undocumented status.

Esquineros: *Day-Labor Markets and Exploitation of Undocumented Construction Workers*

The first case was reported to me by undocumented construction workers who had not been paid their wages. In the mid- to late-1980s, day-labor markets began to spring up in and around New York City, as they had previously in California and elsewhere. One observer calls these day-laborers *esquineros* (Mines 1992) after *esquina* or "corner." Day-labor markets result from a situation of excess labor which gives the workers very little power in negotiating with employers. The workers present themselves at the corner and wait for an employer to offer them work for the day. If the wage offered is not enough, the only option for the worker is to walk away from the job, for which other *esquineros* wait. This situation approaches the neo-classical ideal of a perfectly competitive labor market with very little state regulation.

Yet even after a wage for the day's or week's work is set, the workers are not assured of payment. Many workers are dropped off at the end of the day and paid less than they had agreed upon; others are not paid at all. In response to this problem, the Center for Immigrants Rights initiated a project in which they informed workers of their right to be paid and gave advice regarding how to increase the chance of being paid or recovering their money.

One case related to me involved a crew of Mexican workers who had been recruited as day laborers and offered an extended contract. Their employer paid them at the end of the first week, but at the end of the second week he said that they would have to wait to be paid because the employer was short on cash. When the employer repeated the same pattern the third week, the Mexican crew quit. One of the crew members told me that he later learned that the contractor had pulled the same trick on other crews of Mexicans at other construction sites. He seemed to be simply using the workers as disposable labor, tricking them to work and when they refused simply getting another crew.

I advised one of the crew members that despite his undocumented status, he still had a right to recover the money, which for the crew as a whole came to between $8,000 and $10,000. In a series of conversations, he indicated to me that he did not want to pursue the case legally. It was too great a risk, he thought, and the chances of success were too small. It was better to lose a few hundred dollars than to take the chance that he would get deported and leave his wife and children stranded in El Barrio with no means of support. The theoretically important point here is that even when he had knowledge of his rights under the inclusionary project of the state in his standing as a worker, and had legal representation and support, the vulnerability of this worker made exercising his rights dangerous in his eyes. His seemingly pessimistic calculus was based on his lived experience: he knew that if he pursued the case, neither I nor the people at the Center for Immigrants Rights would be the ones who could end up being deported. And even if the chance of his deportation was slim, the price for himself and his family was still too great to contemplate for the uncertain recompense of a few hundred dollars and the exercise of his rights. It was the exclusionary project that proved decisive in this case.

Mexican Flower Vendors: Exclusion and Vulnerability to Violence and Economic Loss

A second case involves the highly vulnerable position of the Mexican flower vendors in New York, most extremely illustrated in the death of an undocumented flower vendor in Washington Heights on Father's Day, 1991. Don Sixto Santiago Morales rose early that day to take advantage of the extra sales that he hoped to make on the holiday. Three youths robbed him as he walked down Amsterdam Ave. that morning. Having been robbed before, he fought back, suffered a heart attack, and died. The case attracted brief but intense media attention and spurred political action by the vendors themselves, as well as attempts by the Police Department and local community groups to ameliorate the plight of the vendors.

However, the fundamental parameters of the vendors' vulnerability lay largely, though not completely, beyond the reach of these earnest efforts. One reason was that the vulnerability of the vendors was not just to violence but to economic loss as well. Because they are not documented, they are ineligible in New York City to get permits to sell flowers. Even if they had permits, they would be unlikely to get them because of the legislative cap on the numbers of permits. The vendors were subjected to sudden financial loss when the police confiscated their flowers. The loss of a full cart of flowers can set a worker back between $200 and $300 dollars, which is a considerable sum for someone making between $150 and $200 per week on average. The efforts of the police—notably Assistant Police Commissioner Yolanda Jiménez—and of political, religious, and civic leaders to include the vendors in the community and relieve their plight bumped up squarely against the legislative exclusion of the vendors because of their undocumented status. The exclusionary project of the state triumphed—but not completely—over the attempts of these other leaders to include the vendors in the community and offer them the same protection.

A clear example of this vulnerability can be seen in the way the vendors negotiated their relations with the police. Many of the vendors complained that they had been harassed by the police, had their flowers destroyed in front of them in fits of pique by the police, had been subjected to racial and ethnic slurs by the police, had been refused protection by the police, had been threatened with deportation if they continued selling flowers,[9] and had been threatened with being "beaten by blacks" if they kept selling, among other complaints. Moreover, the vendors believed that they were being targeted for enforcement of the vending laws while other unlicensed vendors went unharrassed. Finally, the vendors could not fathom why the police were enforcing the vending law against them while they permitted full-scale, open air drug bazaars to operate in the neighborhoods where the vendors lived. It defied all logic and made them feel they were being treated unjustly and with a lack of *respeto* (respect).[10]

In a series of meetings between the police and the Mexican Flower Vendors Organization, which was formed in response to Don Sixto's death, Assistant Police Commissioner Yolanda Jiménez and several detectives and a captain informed the vendors of what constitutes improper conduct for a police officer, and how to file a complaint against a police officer. None of the vendors in the organization ever filled out complaints against a police officer. One pregnant vendor, who showed bruises on her wrists and arms, alleged that an officer had used excessive force in arresting her for selling flowers and had targeted her specifically—arresting her several times. However she refused to file a complaint even after verbally telling the commissioner her story. She refused, she said, because she thought it would make things worse: maybe the officer would get disciplined, but probably not. And no matter what, a complaint would make the officer more angry and, like a bee, more likely to sting. She also feared that a complaint would make other officers angry and thus would bring down the wrath of the Police Department on the heads of flower vendors whose ability to sell depends in large part on the officers' willingness to look the other way. In this case, the undocumented immigrants were effectively deprived of police protection and of protection from police abuse. This shows again how the exclusionary project of the state renders meaningless their rights under the inclusionary project.

Undocumented Domestic Workers: Isolation, Fear and Exploitation

The vulnerability of undocumented workers is compounded in the case of domestic workers by isolation, gender, and the all-encompassing nature of the work. In this context, the exclusionary project of the state almost completely obscures its inclusionary project and greatly increases the vulnerability of the domestic workers. The following discussion takes up two cases, the first of which draws on the following passages from a taped interview with a Mexican domestic worker in New York. In the interview, the woman speaking, whom I will call "Micaela," describes how an acquaintance of hers was, for all intents and purposes, held against her will in her job on Staten Island. The words in brackets are mine and have been added for clarity; the words in parentheses are in the original Spanish.

> Micaela: This woman is from Oaxaca, she was working with a *patrona* the first time (she came to New York). The second time, she came to Staten Island with a . . . tourist visa. And the *Señora* (the employer) went to get her at the airport. With her complete trust (*toda la confianza*) she (the employer) asked her for her visa, to safeguard it for her. And during six months that she was with her, she did not want to pay her. She paid nothing, every week. We, we (the other domestic workers). . . told her that this Señora was treating her unjustly, and all of us domestic workers met there, so that she could talk to her employer and tell her to pay up. But when we went to the house, they told us that she had gone back to Mexico.
> RS: The *muchacha* that worked there?
> Micaela: That *muchacha*.
> RS: Did you all talk with her?
> Micaela: The *muchacha*? Yes. We talked with her on two occasions . . . in Staten Island. We ran into her in the street because she was going to leave the girl (employer's daughter) at school. And we said to her that we wanted to help her, that we wanted to talk to the *Señora* so that she would not be treating her that way. But it looked like she was afraid.
> RS: Why?
> Micaela: I don't know. That the woman would send her back to Mexico. I don't know.
>
>   . . .
>
> We listened to a program on *Univisión* (Spanish language cable channel from Mexico), the program is called *Cristina*. . . . In this program they had people who helped the illegal persons who do domestic work (*trabajan en casas*). There were telephone numbers.

And through these things on television, we were not afraid, then, to ask for a raise, or for I don't know what else. . . .
RS: To ask for a raise . . . or for what else?
Micaela: That when they speak badly to you, you can say to them that it's not OK for them to speak badly to you. That they can—well—without, without screaming. For example, when they fire you. . . .But we do not have the telephone numbers of the persons that can help us, and always the same thing keeps happening.
RS: That you're afraid?
Micaela: Well, I am not afraid because, if, if they fire me from my job, I can look for another job. . . .(The same thing happens that) many *muchachas* are fired. Or like this *muchacha* that went, that they sent back to Mexico with just her ticket and $200 in her hand.
RS: She never went to get help?
Micaela: No. She was afraid. She was afraid of —I don't know! That the *Señora*—now I remember on one occasion that she told me that the *Señora*, the *Señora* had hit her.
RS: Really?
Micaela: She hit her in the face. . . . I believe, I think, but I'm not sure, that probably this *Señora* had threatened her.
RS: Have other domestic workers had such problems?
Micaela: My cousin, for example. (Micaela went on to relate a similar story about her cousin.)

This conversation offers much to discuss. Regarding the actual conditions of the domestic workers, we should note that the resolution of the case of the woman whose passport had been held points to the powerlessness of domestic workers and the potential to change that situation. The worker was "sent to Mexico" by her employer at the end of her time on her tourist visa with only the price of her ticket and "$200 in her hand" after six months of work. Such meager compensation smacks of peonage and violates minimum wage and other laws. Moreover, that these domestic workers learned of their rights first through a television program indicates their degree of isolation—they were not in contact with any organization which offered such information. (The Center for Immigrants Rights began a program to help domestic workers, about which Micaela was later given information.) Finally, Micaela notes that even after they have this information, they are unable to effectively demand just treatment for their friend—she ends up being "sent" back to Mexico before they have a chance to help her.

We should note that the women did not hesitate out of a sense that they did not know whether her treatment was unjust or not. Even before seeing the television program, the women knew that this was an injustice. However, even with this information, Micaela notes that "the same thing keeps happening" in that people are still unjustly treated and fired. The hopeful aspect of the situation is that even without the legal and other support that they might have had, the workers united to demand that their compatriot be treated fairly. This points to the possibility for organized resistance to such exploitation. Adapting an idea from James Scott (1976), the treatment of this woman from Oaxaca violated the "moral economy" of the domestic workers.

Gender and violence, and the threat of it, played important roles in this case. The extreme isolation of the domestic worker from Oaxaca on Staten Island—where public transportation is more limited than in the rest of the city, where there is a much smaller Mexican community, and where information about the rights of immigrants seems to be less publicly available—added to the woman's vulnerability to coercion and abuse. It is also directly linked to the gendered division of labor that defines domestic work as "women's work." That Micaela and the other domestic workers "ran into her on the street" while she was dropping off one of her employer's children at school suggests that this woman did not interact much with the other domestic workers. Moreover, the way in which Micaela talks about going to the employer's house indicates that the group of domestic workers went there after making a conscious decision to do so. This suggests that they did not see this woman regularly.

Micaela stated repeatedly that the woman from Oaxaca was "afraid" of her employer: that her employer would have her sent back to Mexico, that she had "hit her in the face," and that she may have been subjected to other unrevealed threats. Micaela says repeatedly that she "does not know" why the woman was afraid, just that she knows that she was afraid. Micaela relates a story in which she was told that the woman had been physically abused by her employer. She also suspects that the woman's fear indicates she had been threatened in other ways as well. That the employer had her passport and visa—the woman's only documents proving who she was—suggests that this is another way the woman was controlled by her employer. Perhaps she believed that she would not be able to return to Mexico and her family without her passport? This is a fear which I have heard repeated several times by other undocumented workers: that they will be arrested and imprisoned in the United States in connection with their undocumented status and not be able to return to see their families in Mexico. While such a fear seems unfounded in fact, it can easily be imagined as real by someone so isolated and uninformed about her rights.

This case was "resolved" with the domestic worker returning to Mexico. At the end of six months, the employer dropped her off at the airport with $200. It was the only pay she received for this six months of work. Despite having others who were also badly treated, the other domestic workers never followed up by calling the numbers they had seen on television, because they were afraid of the consequences. The isolation, fear, and legal vulnerability of the domestic worker was combined with the greedy, obscene cruelty of her employer: thus, the domestic worker was robbed of her simple human dignity.

The story related by Micaela is not unique. In another case, Flor (not her real name) was working in a wealthy beach community in New Jersey, a job which she took through a referral agency in Brooklyn. She had to agree to forfeit a portion of her wages as a fee for being placed in the job. Yet even after working off this fee, she was not paid the wages she had been promised. When she demanded her pay, they refused. She felt intimidated in the house and told her employers that she wanted to leave, but they would not drop her off where she could get back to New York, and, not knowing anything about New Jersey and not speaking English, she had to wait several days for her brothers to come from the Bronx and pick her up in New Jersey. Her employers owed her between $500 and $600 dollars. She was never paid, despite the intervention of immigrants rights advocates. In one conversation, both the husband and wife of the house (Flor's employers) told me that United States law did not require one to pay an employee "if the person is illegal." I responded by saying that a person cannot be "illegal," but can be in a country without a visa, and hence be "undocumented." I also corrected them by informing them that United States labor law does require them to pay people like Flor, even if they are in the country illegally. Still, Flor was never paid, in part because she was afraid that her employers would come after her if she pursued her case. Again, the exclusionary project rendered null the inclusionary project.

Conclusion: Simultaneous and Partial Memberships in the Incorporation of Mexican Immigrants into New York City

We have looked at several aspects of the incorporation of Mexicans into New York City and have viewed various realms of social existence with respect to the kinds and quality of membership that Mexicans coming to New York are likely to experience. In concluding, I would like to discuss some of the implications of these arenas for theory, particularly our conceptualizations of degrees and kinds of membership held by immigrants. These three realms—those of social and political organization, of work and future, and the legal status of undocumented immigrants—each present practices and structures inconsistent with both the melting pot and ethnic pluralist assimilation models. The melting pot assumes assimilation to a white, Christian model; ethnic pluralism assumes assimilation to a harmonious world of cultural difference practiced on level political, social, and economic fields. In both of these models, membership is clearly marked and fully held by all members. Ethnicity is a "clean" marker, denoting only cultural difference and having no meaning beyond this.

The history of Mexican immigration to New York and its political, social, and economic development are not easily understandable using the melting pot or ethnic pluralist models. The transnationalism I analyzed took two separate forms: the local level organizing of the Ticuanenses in New York City and Puebla; and the macro level organizing of the Mexican state through the activities of the Program for Mexican Communities Abroad. These two sets of activities underline the importance of simultaneous memberships in more than one political, cultural, and ethnic community in the contemporary period. Local level transnational community membership, such as that held by the Ticuanenses in New York, supports second-generation Mexican immigrants as they confront racial and ethnic discrimination and economic marginalization in the process of immigrant incorporation. The Mexican state, through the consulate and the Program, plays a surprisingly important role in creating a "Mexican community" in New York. The significance of the activities of the Mexican state or of the Ticuanenses is not clear under the melting pot or ethnic pluralist paradigms. By positing as a goal the analysis of degrees of membership, taking explicit note of the practical and simultaneous membership of immigrants, we can make sense of these outcomes. The framework of simultaneous membership provides us with a way of looking at these developments. It also allows us to see how they relate and does not require us to classify them as anomalous.

The analysis of work and its future for Mexicans in New York shows the contingency of their future prospects here, as well as those of other immigrants. This section has attempted to get beyond the aphorism that "immigrants get ahead because they work harder" (which is true to a certain degree) to analyze the mechanisms by which opportunities are created and constrained. Though much of the research is preliminary, this analysis has emphasized the importance of examining the articulation between micro-level structures such as immigration networks and macro-level social processes such as ethno-racial discrimination and their micro-level manifestations. The future for Mexican immigrants in New York and their second-generation children is uncertain and contingent. What is certain is that this future will not conform neatly with either the melting-pot or the simple ethnic-pluralist models.

I have also attempted to analyze the substance of membership for immigrants and to talk of the differences in degrees and kinds of memberships. This line of analysis stands in contrast to the melting-pot and ethnic-pluralist models, which posit sometimes tacitly full, inclusive and unique membership for immigrants (see Smith 1994; Brubaker 1989 and 1991). Undocumented immigrants are clearly the most vulnerable in this regard, caught as they are between the state's inclusionary and exclusionary projects. Yet second-generation Ticuanenses and other Mexicans also have only uncertain substantive membership. For example, what does the future hold for second-generation, noncollege (or nonhigh-school) educated Mexican young men? As Gans rightly fears, they too are vulnerable despite their "full" membership as United States citizens.

This is an exciting and important time in which we as a society are renegotiating the kinds of "social contracts" we make with newcomers. It is imperative that a good analysis of the lived experience of immigrants be brought into public debates. This means that we must take account of the changing economic and social conditions that immigrants face, and must vigorously confront those who would deny the importance of marginalizing forces, including ethno-racial discrimination, in the incorporation and ultimate fate of all immigrants. We must also take a long, hard look at the human cost incurred by those living in the margins of American society, be they immigrants or their children, or the native-born Americans.

NOTES

1. I would like to thank the following organizations and people for the financial and other support for the research and analysis on which this chapter draws: the Social Science Research Council Dissertation Fellowship Program on the Urban Underclass, 1991–92, with funds provided by the Rockefeller Foundation; Dr. Jorge Bustamante for my appointment as a Visiting Research Scholar at El Colegio de la Frontera Norte during the fall of 1992 through the fall of 1993, with funds provided by the Tinker Foundation; Dr. Douglas Chalmers, the Institute for Latin American and Iberian Studies and the Department of Political Science at Columbia University for a Write-Up Fellowship and Research support for the fall of 1993; and a National Science Foundation Grant to improve Doctoral Dissertation Research (Program in Sociology) for the academic year 1993–94.

2. See Smith 1994a, chapter 4, for an analysis of how these factors played out for the municipality of Ticuani.

3. See Rouse, "Men in Space," for an interesting analysis of this relationship in another context.

4. Many undocumented immigrants do not bring any documentation at all when they come to New York, and hence must go to the Mexican Consulate when they wish to return to Mexico to get some kind of document demonstrating their Mexican citizenship.

5. The occupational structure of the Ticuanenses in New York is mirrored by the occupational structure of those living in Ticuani, as can be seen in the table below. Whereas almost all of the Ticuanenses in New York are working in factories or restaurants, those living in Ticuani primarily work as homemakers or are students or preschool

children. Homemakers and children account for 67.7 percent of Ticu-ani's population, while they account for only 21.7 percent of the population of Ticuanenses living in New York.

Occupations of Ticuanenses Currently Living in Ticuani

Occupation	Frequency	Percent
Campesino	17	13.4
Professional in Mexico	15	11.8
Businessman	2	1.6
Student or Preschool Age	54	42.5
Homemaker	32	25.2
Wage Worker in Ticuani	7	5.5
Total	128	100.0

Total cases: 128, valid cases: 127, missing cases: 1

SOURCE: Author's survey, February 1992.

6. Notes from a formal interview by Dong Wan Joo, a Korean graduate student at the City University of New York, Graduate Center, who also heads the Korean Research Institute in the Flushing section of Queens, New York.

7. This position was also expressed by Professor Pyong Gap Min of Queens College (CUNY), who recently authored a report on the ethnic basis of economic solidarity in the Korean community in New York. Professor Min stressed the importance of social sanctions against exploiting other Koreans. By exploiting Mexicans, Koreans are able to experience upward mobility within the group and get around the sticky issue of coethnic exploitation. He noted that this interethnic behavior turns the traditional wisdom regarding immigrant exploitation on its head: in this case, immigrants do not get ahead by "exploiting their own" but by exploiting some other group, in this instance Mexicans. Professor Min also noted that Koreans are using Mexican employees all over the country and in unexpected places such as Atlanta, where there is not a large Mexican population. The employment of large numbers of Mexicans by Koreans highlights the importance of parallel immigration networks of Koreans and Mexicans. See Min 1994; also Smith 1990 and 1992d; Waldinger and Smith 1990.

8. This policy was passed during the last administration of former mayor Edward I. Koch. However, a school principal on Staten Island, responding to the influx of Mexican, Polish, and other immigrant chil-

dren into his school, demanded that Mayor David Dinkins direct the police to help the INS deport undocumented aliens. Mayor Dinkins refused. No such ordinance exists in New Jersey or on Long Island, where the police have assisted the INS in carrying out raids to deport undocumented workers. See Mahler 1992.

9. If true, such behavior constituted a clear violation of the City's Executive Order forbidding the sharing of information about the immigrant's legal status except in connection with a criminal investigation. Selling flowers without a permit is a misdemeanor, not a felony, and hence would not constitute a criminal investigation.

10. See Bourgois 1991 and 1995; Fernández-Kelly 1993.

WORKS CITED OR CONSULTED

Alarcón, Rafael. 1993. Personal Communications.
Bailey, Thomas. 1987. *Immigrant and Native Workers: Contrasts and Competition*. Boulder, Colo.: Westview Press.
Bosniak, Linda. 1988. "The Dual Identity of the Undocumented Worker under United States Law." *Wisconsin Law Review*.
Bourdieu, Pierre, and Loic Waquant. 1992. *An Invitation to Reflexive Sociology*. Chicago: University of Chicago Press.
Bourgois, Philippe. 1995. *In Search of Respect: Selling Crack in El Barrio*. New York: Cambridge University Press.
———. 1991. "In Search of Respect: The Crack Alternative in Spanish Harlem." Working paper. New York: Russell Sage Foundation.
Brubaker, W. Rogers, ed. 1989. *Immigration and the Politics of Citizenship in Europe and North America*. Washington, D.C.: German Marshall Fund of the United States and University Press of America.
Coleman, James. 1988. "Social Capital in the Creation of Human Capital." *American Journal of Sociology* 94, Supplement, pp. 95–120.
Cornelius, Wayne. 1990. "Labor Migration to the U.S.: Development Outcomes and Alternatives in Mexican Sending Communities." Final Report to the Commission on the Study of International Migration and Cooperative Economic Development. Center for U.S. Mexican Studies, University of California, San Diego. March.
———. 1992. "From Sojourners to Settlers." In Reynolds and Hinojosa, eds., *U.S.-Mexico Relations: Labor Market Interdependence*. Stanford: Stanford University Press.
Chavez, Linda. 1991. *Out of the Barrio: Toward a New Politics of Hispanic Assimilation*. New York: Basic Books.
Cordero-Guzmán, Hector. 1994. "The Structure of Inequality and the

Status of Puerto Rican Youth" *Centro de Estudios Puertorriqueños, Boletín* 5 (1).

Durkheim, Emile. 1895. *The Rules of Sociological Method.* Trans. 1968. W. D. Halls. New York: Free Press, 1982.

Fainstein, Norman. 1986–87. "The Underclass—Mismatch Hypothesis as an Explanation for Black Economic Deprivation." *Politics and Society* 15 (4): 403–52.

———. 1994. "Lecture on the Urban Crisis." City College of New York, March.

Fernández Kelly, María Patricia. 1993. "Towanda's Triumph: Unfolding the Disputed Meanings of Adolescent Pregnancy in a Baltimore Ghetto." Draft working paper. New York: Russell Sage Foundation.

Frankenberg, Ruth. 1993. *White Women, Race Matters: The Social Construction of Whiteness.* Minneapolis: University of Minnesota Press.

Gans, Herbert J. 1979. "'Symbolic Ethnicity': The Future of Ethnic Groups and Cultures in America." *Ethnic and Racial Studies* 2, (1): 1–20.

———. 1990. "Deconstructing the Underclass: The Term's Dangers as a Planning Concept." *Journal of the American Planning Association* 177: 271–77.

———. 1992. "Second Generation Decline: Scenarios for the Economic and Ethnic Futures of the Post-1965 American immigrants." *Ethnic and Racial Studies* 15 (2).

García y Griego, Manuel. 1993. "Comments on Smith." In Robert Smith, "Deterritorialized Nation Building." New York University, Spring.

Gibson, Margaret. 1988. *Accommodation without Assimilation: Sikh Immigrants in an American High School.* Ithaca, N.Y.: Cornell University Press.

———. 1991a. "Ethnicity, Gender, and Social Class: The School Adaptation Patterns of West Indian Youths." In Gibson and Ogbu, eds., *Minority Status and Schooling: A Comparative Study of Immigrant and Involuntary Minorities.* New York: Garland Publishing.

———. 1991b. "Minorities and Schooling: Some Implications." In Gibson and Ogbu, eds. *Minority Status and Schooling: A Comparative Study of Immigrant and Involuntary Minorities.* New York: Garland Publishing.

Goldring, Luin. 1992. "Diversity in Transnational Migration." Ph.D. dissertation, Cornell University.

González de la Rocha, Mercedes. 1993. "El Poder de la Ausencia: Mujeres y Migración en una Comunidad de los Altos de Jalisco." In Jesús Tapia Santamaria, ed., *Las Realidades Regionales de la Crisis Nacional*. Zamora, Michoacán: El Colegio de Michoacán.

González Gutiérrez, Carlos. 1993. "The Mexican Diaspora in California: The Limits and Possibilities of the Mexican Government." In A. Lowenthal and K. Burgess, eds., *The California-Mexico Connection*. Stanford: Stanford University Press.

Gordon, Milton. 1964. *Assimilation in American Life: The Role of Race, Religion and National Origin*. New York: Oxford University Press.

Granovetter, Mark. 1985. "Economic Action and Social Structure: The Problem of Embeddedness." *American Journal of Sociology* 91: 481–510.

Guarnizo, Luis. 1994. "'Los Domincanyorks': The Making of a Binational Society." *Annals of the American Academy of Political and Social Science*, May.

Hermann, Pauline. 1994. Ph.D. dissertation proposal, City University of New York, Graduate Center, Summer.

Hershberg, Theodore, et al. 1981. "A Tale of Three Cities: Blacks, Immigrants, and Opportunity in Philadelphia: 1850–1880, 1930, 1970." In T. Hershberg, ed., *Philadelphia*, pp. 462–64. New York: Oxford University Press.

Jencks, Christopher. 1992. *Rethinking Social Policy*. Cambridge, Mass.: Harvard University Press.

Karpathakis, Anna. 1993. "Sojourners and Settlers: Greek Immigrants to Astoria, New York." Ph.D. dissertation, Department of Sociology, Columbia University.

Kasinitz, Philip. 1988. "Facing Up to the Underclass." *Telos* 76: Summer.
———. 1992. *Caribbean New York*. Ithaca, N.Y.: Cornell University Press.
———, and Jan Rosenberg. 1994. "Missing the Connection: Social Isolation and Employment on Brooklyn Waterfront." *Working Papers: Michael Harrington Center for Democratic Values and Social Change*. Queens College, CUNY.

Katz, Michael. 1989. *The Underserving Poor: From the War on Poverty to the War on Welfare*. Princeton, N.J.: Princeton University Press.
———. 1993. *The Underclass Debate: Views from History*. Princeton, N.J.: Princeton University Press.

Katznelson, Ira. 1988. "Reflections on "Space and the City." In John H. Mollenkopf, ed., *Power, Culture and Place: Essays on New York City*. New York: Russell Sage Foundation.

Kearney, Michael. 1991. "Borders and Boundaries of State and Self at the End of Empire." *Journal of Historical Sociology* 4 March.
———. 1993a. Lecture, New York Academy of Sciences. March 22.

―――. 1993b. Personal Communications.

Kim, Dae Young. 1994. "Beyond Coethnicity: Mexican Employees and Korean Employers." Sociology Department, City University of New York, Graduate Center.

Kim, Ilsoo. 1981. *New Urban Immigrants: The Korean Community in New York* Princeton, N.J.: Princeton University Press.

Kirschenman, Joleen, and K. Neckerman. 1991. "'We'd love to hire them, but . . .' The Meaning of Race for Employers." In Christopher Jencks and Paul E. Peterson, eds., *The Urban Underclass*. Washington, D.C.: Brookings Institution.

Kristol, Irving. 1966. "The Negro of Today Is Like the Immigrant of Yesterday." *New York Times Magazine*, September 11: 50–51; 124–42.

Lauria, Antonio. 1992. "Towards a Transnational Perspective on Migration: Closing Remarks." In Nina Glick Schiller et al., eds., *Towards a Transnational Perspective on Migration*. New York: Annals of the New York Academy of Sciences, vol. 645.

Lewis, Oscar. 1968. "Culture of Poverty." In Daniel Patrick Moynihan, ed., *On Understanding Poverty: Perspectives from the Social Sciences*. New York: Basic Books.

Lieberson, Stanley. 1980. *A Piece of the Pie: Blacks and White Immigrants since 1880*. Berkeley: University of California Press.

Light, Ivan. 1972. *Ethnic Enterprise in America: Business and Welfare among Chinese, Japanese and Blacks*. Berkeley: University of California Press.

―――, and Edna Bonacich. 1988. *Immigrant Entrepreneurs*. Berkeley: University of California Press.

Lomnitz, Larissa Adler de. 1977. *Networks and Marginality: Life in a Mexican Shantytown*. New York: Academic Press.

Lourdes de Villar, María. 1989. "From Sojourners to Settlers: The Experience of Mexican Undocumented Migrants in Chicago." Ph.D. dissertation, Department of Anthropology, Indiana University, Bloomington.

Mahler, Sarah. 1992. "'Tres Veces Mojado': Undocumented Central and South American Migration to Suburban Long Island." Ph.D. dissertation, Department of Anthropology, Columbia University.

―――, and B. Domínguez. 1990. "Preliminary Undercount Estimation of Mexicans in New York City." Bureau of the Census.

Massey, Douglas, and Luin Goldring. 1992. "Continuities in Transnational Migration: An Analysis of 13 Mexican Communities." Paper presented at the Conference on New Perspectives on Mexico-U.S. Migration, University of Chicago, October 23–24.

————, R. Alarcon, J. Durand, and H. Gonzalez. 1987. *Return to Aztlan: The Social Process of International Migration From Western Mexico.* Berkeley: University of California Press.

————, Kathryn Donato, and Zai Liang. "The Long Term Consequences of a Temporary Worker Program: The U.S. Bracero Experience." *Population Research and Policy Review.*

Matute-Bianchi, María Eugenia. 1994. "Ethnic Identities and Patterns of School Success and Failure among Mexican-Descent and Japanese-American Students in a California High School: An Ethnographic Analysis." *American Journal of Eduation* 95 (1).

Mead, Lawrence. 1986. *Beyond Entitlement: The Social Obligations of Citizenship.* New York: Free Press.

Min, Pyong Gap. 1994. Report to the National Science Foundation on Korean Immigrants in New York.

Mines, Richard. 1981. "Developing a Community Tradition of Migration: A Field Study of Rural Zacatecas, Mexico, and California Settlement Areas." *Monograph #3* San Diego: Center for US-Mexico Studies.

————. 1992, 1993 and 1994. Personal Communications.

Morrison, Toni. 1994. "On the Backs of Blacks." In N. Nills, ed., *Arguing Immigration.* New York: Touchstone Books.

Moynihan, Daniel P., and Nathan Glazer. 1968. *Beyond the Melting Pot: The Negroes, Puerto Ricans, Jews, Italians and Irish of New York City.* Cambridge: MIT Press.

Murray, Charles. 1984. *Losing Ground: American Social Policy, 1950–1980.* New York: Basic Books.

Ogbu, J. U. 1987. "Variability in Minority School Performance: A Problem in Search of an Explanation." *Anthropology & Education Quarterly* 18 (4): 312–34.

Omi, Michael, and Howard Winant. 1986. *Racial Formation in the United States.* London and New York: Routledge.

Portes, Alejandro, and R. Bach. 1985. *Latin Journey: Cuban and Mexican Immigrants in the United States.* Berkeley: University of California Press.

————, and Jozsef Borocz. 1989. "Contemporary Immigration: Theoretical Perspectives on Its Determinants and Modes of Incorporation." *International Migration Review* 23 (3).

———— and Min Zhou. 1992. "Gaining the Upper Hand: Economic Mobility Among Immigrant and Domestic Minorities." *Ethnic and Racial Studies* 15 October: 495–522.

———— and Min Zhou. 1993. "The New Second Generation: Segmented Assimilation and Its Variants." *Annals of the American Academy of*

Political and Social Science, no. 530 (November). Philadelphia: Sage Publications.

——— and Rubén Rumbaut. 1990. *Immigrant America: A Portrait*. Berkeley: University of California Press.

——— and Julia Sesenbrenner. 1993. "Embeddedness and Immigration: Notes on the Social Determinants of Economic Action." *American Journal of Sociology* 98: 1320–50.

——— and Alex Stepick. 1993. *City on the Edge: The Transformation of Miami*. Berkeley: University of California Press.

Presidencia de la República. 1982. *Geografía de la Marginalización en México*. Coordinación General del Plan Nacional de Zonas Deprimidas y Grupos Marginados, México, D.F.

Ricourt, Milagros. 1994. "Political Organizing among Dominican Women in New York." Presentation to Ph.D. Working Group on Immigration, City University of New York, Graduate Center, July.

Rodríguez, Clara, and Hector Cordero-Guzmán. 1992. "Placing Race in Context." *Ethnic and Racial Studies* 15 (4).

Roediger, David. 1991. *The Wages of Whiteness: Race and the Making of the American Working Class* New York: Verso.

Rouse, Roger. 1990. "Men in Space: Power and the Appropriation of Urban Form among Mexican Migrants in the U.S." Paper presented at Residential College, University of Michigan, March.

———. 1991. "Mexican Migration and the Social Space of Postmodernism." *Diaspora* vol 1.

Rumbaut, Rubén. 1990. "Immigrant Students in California Public Schools: A Summary of Current Knowledge." Baltimore: John Hopkins University, Center for Research on Effective Schooling for Disadvantaged Students. *Report No. 11*.

Scott, James. 1976. *The Moral Economy of the Peasant: Rebellion and Subsistence in Southeast Asia*. New Haven: Yale University Press.

Smith, Robert C. 1992a. "Mexicanos en Nueva York." Distrito Federal: Revista de NEXOS, March.

———. 1992b. "Mixteca in New York; New York in Mixteca." New York: NACLA Magazine, August.

———. 1992c. "Una Región Transnacional: La Mixteca Neorquina." Ojarasca México, D.F., November.

———. 1992d. "Social Networks, Immigration and the Underclass: An Analysis of the Formation of Labor Market Niches for Recently Arrived Undocumented Mexican Immigrants in New York City." Proposal to the National Science Foundation, Grants to Improve Dissertations, Program in Sociology (earlier version submitted to the Social Science Research Council, 1990).

————. 1992e. "A Preliminary Estimation of the Census Undercount of Mexicans in New York." Draft paper.

————. 1993a. "Deterritorialized National Building: Transnational Migrants and the Re-Imagination of Political Community by Sending States." Seminar on Migration, the State and International Relations, Occasional Papers Series, New York University, Center for Latin American and Caribbean Studies, spring.

————. 1993b. "Los Ausentes Siempre Presentes: The Imagining, Making and Politics of a Transnational Community between Ticuani, Puebla, Mexico, and New York City." *Working Papers on Latin America*, Institute for Latin American and Iberian Studies, Columbia University, October.

————. 1994a. "Race and Social Location in the Incorporation of Mexican Immigrants into New York City." Paper presented at the Conference of Fellows: Research on the Urban Underclass, Social Science Research Council, Ann Arbor, Michigan, June.

————. 1994b. "Upward Mobility or Social Marginalization?: The Contingent Futures of Second Generation Mexican Immigrants in New York City." Proposal to the Russell Sage Foundation, September.

————. 1995. "Los Ausentes Siempre Presentes: The Imagining, Making and Politics of a Transnational Community between Ticuani, Puebla, Mexico and New York City." Ph.D. dissertation, Department of Political Science, Columbia University.

————. Forthcoming. "The Social Structure of Accumulation, Immigration Pathways and the Immigration Reform and Control Act of 1986: The Construction of Labor Market in the Pennsylvania Mushroom Industry, 1969-89." In W. Cornelius, eds., *Sectoral Perspectives on the Use of Mexican Labor in the U.S.* Center for U.S.-Mexican Studies, La Jolla, Calif.

————, and Saskia Sassen. 1992. "Post-Industrial Employment and Third World Immigration: Their Impact on Immigrant Employment." In C. Reynolds and R. Hinojosa, eds., *Labor Market Interdependence between the U.S. and Mexico.* Stanford: Stanford University Press.

Stack, Carol. 1974. *All Our Kin.* New York: Harper and Row.

Sullivan, Mercer. 1989. *"Getting Paid": Youth, Crime and Work in the Inner City.* Ithaca, N.Y.: Cornell University Press.

Valdés de Montano. Luz María, and Robert Smith. 1994. "Mexicans in New York." Final Report to the Tinker Foundation, February.

Vardy, Frank. 1990. Official with New York City Population Department. Interview by author. April.

Waldinger, Roger. 1986. *Through the Eye of the Needle: Immigrants and Enterprise in New York's Garment Trade.* New York: New York University Press.

―――. 1990. "Korean, Hispanics and White Ethnic Employers in New York." Unpublished manuscript.

―――, and Thomas Bailey. 1991a. "The Changing Ethnic /Racial Division of Labor." In Castells and Mollenkopf, eds., *Dual City: Restructuring New York.* New York: Russell Sage.

―――, and Thomas Bailey. 1991b. "The Continuing Significance of Race: Racial Conflict and Racial Discrimination in Construction." *Politics and Society* 19 (3).

―――, and Thomas Bailey. 1991c. "Primary, Secondary, and Enclave Labor Markets: A Training Systems Approach." *American Sociological Review* 56 (4): 432–45.

Warner, W. Lloyd, and Leo Srole. 1945. *The Social Systems of American Ethnic Groups.* New Haven: Yale University Press.

Waters, Mary C. 1994. "Ethnic and Racial Identities of Second Generation Black Immigrants in New York City." *International Migration Review*, vol. 28 (Winter).

Willis, Paul. 1977. *Learning to Labour: How Working Class Kids Get Working Class Jobs.* New York: Columbia University Press.

Wolf, Eric. 1957. "Closed Corporate Peasant Communities in Meso-America and Java." *Southwestern Journal of Anthropology* 13: 1–18.

―――. 1959. *Sons of the Shaking Earth.* Chicago: University of Chicago Press.

―――. 1986. "The Vicissitudes of the Closed Corporate Peasant Community." *American Ethnologist* 13 (2): 325–30.

4

Racial Themes in the Literature: Puerto Ricans and Other Latinos

CLARA E. RODRÍGUEZ

As we examine the experiences of recent Caribbean and Latin American immigrants to the United States, we see that they—like many previous immigrants—bring in their own perspectives on race and ethnicity. These perspectives may sometimes be at variance with the perspectives which prevail in the United States. We also see that there is an interest in issues of race and ethnicity that continues, indeed sometimes surfaces, well beyond the first generation. As more recent immigrants begin to contend with the racial structure and dynamics of the United States, the earlier experiences of Puerto Ricans with regard to race hold important lessons for other and/or newer immigrant groups. Of particular relevance are the views of scholars who early examined the experiences of Puerto Ricans. For, it is this type of academic writing that often forges the broader lens through which groups come to be understood in the United States—and through which groups come to understand or reinterpret themselves. It is these writings that often give impetus to revisionist, oppositional, or more integrative works by others.

I will begin by examining the difference between the Latin American and the North American racial classification systems and the anomalous and/or fluctuating racial position that Latinos have held in the United States. I then proceed to a discussion of the racial themes in the literature on Puerto Ricans. The methodology of the major works reviewed is analyzed and six themes in this literature are discussed. These are: (1) the question of whether Puerto Ricans are a race or not; (2) the continuum of racial types among Puerto Ricans and a corresponding nomenclature for these types; (3) the generally more "benign" quality of race relations in Puerto Rico; (4) the harsher racial climate in the United States; (5) the hypersensitivity to color of Puerto Ricans; and (6) the theme of "mistaken identity."

The last section reviews the perspectives taken by the authors in the major works and highlights three areas that are also germane to the issue of race. One is the authors' expectations or predictions about Puerto Rican assimilation in the U.S.; another is their preoccupation with the relationship between African Americans and Puerto Ricans; and, the third is the focus on racial "intermediates" within the Puerto Rican community. I conclude by suggesting that the presence of Puerto Ricans and the increasing numbers of other similar multiracial groups challenge the black/white notion of race in the United States.

The Clash of Race Orders

The Puerto Rican racial experience in the U.S. illuminates many of the difficulties experienced when a group migrates from one racial environment to another. Puerto Ricans arrived in the United States with different perceptions of race, and different racial mixtures. They entered a U.S. society that had a biologically based, biracial structure and that had tended to accommodate multiracial cultural groups into this structure. The U.S. racial structure assumed a white-notwhite division of the world. Euroamerican whites were at one end of this polarity and African blacks were at the other. Groups, such as Asians and Native-American Indians, who had also been in the U.S. since its earliest beginnings, occupied ambiguous "grey" positions within this dichotomy. They were not white, they were not black. Historical events and the geographic distribution and isolation of these groups made their racial position less salient in the public mind than the basic white-black dichotomy.

Similarly, the racial status of Latinos, as a group, was not prominent. In many regards it was ambiguous,[1] as is reflected in the changing racial classifications used for Hispanics in the U.S. census. According to Omi and Winant (1983:56), in 1930 Hispanics (more specifically, Mexicans) were included in the census as a racial category. In 1950 and 1960 they surfaced as "Persons of Spanish

Mother Tongue." In 1970 they were "Persons of Both Spanish Sur-
name and Spanish Mother Tongue." Finally, by 1980 a specific
Hispanic identifier was added.[2] Identification of race was asked in
a separate question. In planning for the 1990 census, the suggestion
that perhaps Latinos should be counted as a separate racial group
was defeated through strenuous community opposition.[3] In essence,
Latinos rejected the idea that they should be counted as a separate
race group. Thus, historically, it appears that in terms of categoriza-
tions Latinos have straddled the white–notwhite race order in the
U.S.

Race in Latin America

There is another dimension to be taken into account in analyzing
the question of race among Latinos in the U.S. This is that the racial
perceptions and ambiences of Latin America differ from those which
evolved in the United States. Although each country in Latin
America has evolved its own racial context because of its unique
history, a number of authors argue that Latinos, as a whole, have
a different conception of race. Ginorio (1986:20) articulates the distinction well:

> As a result of all the extensive racial mixture and the fluidity of
> racial definitions, the conception of race in Latin America is one
> of a continuum with no clear demarcation between categories. In
> contrast to this racial system, in the U.S. race is seen as a dichoto-
> mous variable of white or black. Not only does the U.S. racial
> system differ from the Latin American one in recognizing discrete
> as opposed to continuous groups, it also limits racial distinctions
> to a very small number of categories—four or perhaps five, if in
> addition to white, black and yellow, red and "brown" are seen
> as distinct racial categories. The basis for such distinctions in the
> U.S. is genealogical. If an arbitrary set amount of black blood can
> be determined to exist, the individual is classified as black. Thus,
> an individual is racially defined at birth and can change that
> identity only by "passing."

Thus, race in Latin America is often seen as a continuum of "social
races" (Wagley 1965) or a "black-white" continuum (Ginorio 1979;
Wade 1985).

Others argue that race for Latinos is as much cultural or social as it is racial (Ginorio 1979; Pitt-Rivers 1975; Wagley 1965; Petrullo, 1947:16; Padilla 1958:75; Wade 1985; Harris 1970). For example, Pitt-Rivers (1975:90) argues that race in Latin America "refers to a group of people who are felt to be somehow similar in their essential nature." This more "ambiguous" concept of race has been a strong theme in Latin American literature and political thought (Muñoz 1982; Vazconcelos 1966). Yet it is not often alluded to in North American discussions of Latin America. This conception of race may have had its antecedents in Spain, been redefined in the colonial context, and may now again be in the process of redefinition in the United States.

The fact that race may be seen differently in Latin America, or that it may be less discussed, does not mean it is an issue that has been effectively resolved. (Wade 1985; Betances 1972; Rodríguez 1989: ch. 3) Race has always been an important, not always commendable part, of the evolution and development of Latin America. The enslavement of both Africans and indigenous peoples was widespread, and it was often accompanied by cruelty and harsh treatment. Neither Puerto Rico nor other parts of Latin America have been racial paradises. The emphasis on the racial superiority of white Europeans during Spain's colonization period became an inherent part of Spain's legacy to Latin America. Moreover, traces of these earlier historical antecedents can be found in the present-day cultures of Latin America. This legacy is evident today and is often subtlety manifested, e.g., in common parlance, kinky hair is referred to as *pelo malo* (bad hair) and standards of beauty seldom deviate from the European model—as a glance at the models in popular Latin American publications will attest.

Nonetheless, the race orders are different in the north and in the south. The Puerto Rican racial experience points up these differences and the difficulties that result when a multiracial cultural group migrates to an essentially biracial country. The literature to be reviewed reflects the conflict of racial classification systems and the problems that flow from this conflict. For purposes of clarity, the review will emphasize major works on Puerto Ricans written during the early period of the migration, when Puerto Ricans were relative newcomers and when issues of race were not yet affected by the subsequent and substantial changes introduced by the Black

Power movement.[4] But first a word on the studies examined and their methodologies.

Methodology of the Major Works

With the exception of Padilla's (1958) and Gosnell's (1945) community studies, most of the works reviewed were done by North American social scientists using a variety of descriptive, ethnographic, and survey research methods. For example, Mills et al. (1950) and Tumin and Feldman (1961) used a fairly structured survey approach, with Mills emphasizing participant observation as well. Both of these survey studies involved over 1,000 respondents. Padilla (1958) and Gosnell (1945) also used structured interviews, participant observation, and had considerable numbers in their samples. But they appear to have also investigated more qualitative sources than Mills et al. (1950) and Tumin and Feldman (1961). Padilla (1958), for example, included the diaries and personal experiences of the interviewers and workers; and Gosnell (1945) made many references to the literature and popular culture of Puerto Ricans. Chenault (1970), the earliest recorder of the Puerto Rican community cited here, used a mixture of secondary sources, e.g., census reports, data from the Puerto Rico Department of Labor, the Emergency Relief Bureau of New York City, the New York City Housing Authority, the Department of Health, and newspapers. He also interviewed social workers and those in close contact with the group; finally he indicates he also had "experiences of life" in Puerto Rico and in New York. Handlin (1959) also approached his study of Puerto Ricans (and African Americans) in a similar multifaceted manner.

Petrullo (1947) and Rand (1958), on the other hand, present rather journalistic accounts. Indeed, Petrullo says, "To make it readable I have avoided full documentation and detailed discussion of minutiae" (preface, p. v). While Rand calls his study a "sociologist's objective view," he cites no methodology or other significant documentation. A working journalist, his narrative weaves in and out of what he's heard or read about Puerto Ricans from others. There are a number of works that stand somewhere between these two extremes. They combine a variety of sources and make reference to information derived from surveys and questionnaires that others have gathered (e.g., Senior 1961; Glazer and Moynihan 1970), or they present logically thought-out essays (e.g., G. Lewis 1963; López 1973). Lastly, there are the fieldwork and community studies, which were mainly done in Puerto Rico and which also range from the life history approaches taken by O. Lewis (1966) and Mintz (1960) to the more extensive fieldwork studies of La Ruffa (1971), Landy (1959) and Steward et al. (1956).

Racial Themes in the Literature

A reading of these works yields a series of common themes that speak to the issue of race among Puerto Ricans. (1) One theme has been the question of whether Puerto Ricans are a race or a multiracial society. Although this has been a constant question, it has not yielded a definitive answer. There are other themes that have elicited more general agreement. These are: (2) that there exists a continuum of racial types and corresponding nomenclature for these types among Puerto Ricans; (3) that there is a generally more "benign" quality of race relations in Puerto Rico; and (4) that darker Puerto Ricans experience negative social and economic consequences upon migrating to the U.S. There are also areas and themes where there has been disagreement. For example, (5) despite the general consensus on the insignificance of race in institutional treatment in Puerto Rico, there has been some disagreement on how salient or significant race is on other more personal levels, while one author has asked whether Puerto Ricans have a hypersensitivity to color. (6) The last theme, found most often in the fictional literature, is that of "mistaken identity," i.e., being identified racially instead of culturally. Each of these themes is discussed below.

The Puerto Rican Race?

Although some of the themes speak to the situation of race in Puerto Rico and others are relevant to race in New York or the U.S., one theme that has spanned both the island and the States has been the debate about whether Puerto Ricans are a race or a multiracial society. Gosnell (1945:180 ff.) in her early study of Puerto Ricans

in New York noted the persistent (and by then historical) debate
that existed in Puerto Rico concerning the racial composition of
Puerto Ricans in Puerto Rico. Petrullo (1947) in his study of Puerto
Rico devotes a chapter to the question of "The Puerto Rican 'Race.' "
He concludes, "There is no Puerto Rican race, but there are white
and black Puerto Ricans and all sorts of mixtures in between" (p.
14). This issue of the percentage distribution of whites and blacks
among Puerto Ricans has also been touched upon by most social
scientists researching Puerto Ricans. This debate continues today.
It is fueled by the tendency to view Puerto Rico and Puerto Ricans
from the North American racial perspective—where one is white
or notwhite—and not from the Latin American racial classification
system.

Continuum of Racial Types

The racial classification system in Puerto Rico has more in common
with the Latin American conception of race than with the U.S.
conception. Thus, in Puerto Rico there is a continuum of racial
types. On this, i.e., the continuum of racial types and corresponding
nomenclature for them, there has been general agreement (Gosnell
1945; Padilla 1958; Steward et al. 1956; Landy 1959; La Ruffa 1971;
Mills et al. 1950; Fitzpatrick 1971; Glazer and Moynihan 1970; Mintz
1960). The general categories noted in Puerto Rico are "blanca/o"
(white), "india/o" (similar to the U.S. conception of Asian Indians,
i.e., dark-skinned and straight-haired), "morena/o" (dark-skinned
with a variety of Negroid or Caucasian features), "negra/o" (equivalent to very black, black Americans in the U.S.) and "triguña/
o," a term that can be applied to each of the foregoing groups
except very blond, European-type blancos. The term "negra/o" is
also commonly used as a term of endearment without any racial
connotation. Where each of these categories ends and another begins
is vague and there is not always complete agreement on this (Ginorio and Berry, 1972).[5]

The Quality of Race Relations in Puerto Rico

In the literature, there has also been general agreement that the
quality of race relations in Puerto Rico is superior to that in the

United States. The majority of North American social scientists who have studied the island have found race relations within the body politick to be rather "benign" and somewhat unimportant (Chenault 1970; Glazer and Moynihan 1970; Petrullo 1947; Mintz 1960; Steward et al. 1956 and Giles et al 1979). Some authors have argued that color is also less important to Puerto Ricans in social and family relations than is the case in the United States (Chenault 1070; Glazer and Moynihan 1970:142). Despite this general consensus on the *insignificance* of race in institutional treatment, there has been some disagreement on how salient or significant race is on other more personal levels. Steward et al. (1956:291), Landy (1959), G. Lewis (1963:424), and Tumin and Feldman (1961:228) argue that Puerto Ricans in Puerto Rico are very conscious of race, especially skin color, while La Ruffa (1971) argues there is covert racism on the island especially toward "Africanisms," and Padilla (1958:74) states that it is to your advantage to look white in Puerto Rico. Thus, there is agreement on the relatively more benign nature of race relations in Puerto Rico as compared with the U.S. There is less agreement on whether race for Puerto Ricans is important or unimportant on more personal levels.

Prejudice in Puerto Rico

Given what has been generally agreed to be a more benign racial climate in Puerto Rico, the issue of whether prejudice exists has been greatly debated. Some authors have argued that "Puerto Ricans seem to have developed a Creole ethos tolerant of the mulatto group . . . but scornful of the black sector . . ." (Duany 1985:30, see also Zenon Cruz 1975; and Longres 1974:68 ff.), while Betances (1972) has argued that there is a "prejudice of no prejudice" in Puerto Rico and that this in itself constitutes a prejudicial act. Zenon Cruz (1975) has argued that there are specific prejudices against Africanisms in Puerto Rico and that there is a depreciation of negritude.

Other rather complex and still debated questions have been raised concerning the question of prejudice in Puerto Rico. For example: Have Indian and African elements been destroyed or integrated into Puerto Rican society? Is the race issue in Puerto Rico dealt with by ignoring it, or is it really not an issue? Is it necessary for harmonious "race" relations that all Puerto Ricans have some African ancestry? Are the prejudices against Africanisms in Puerto Rico an American import (Movimiento Pro Independencia, 1963)? Is there an unrecognized color gradient as one moves up the income scale in Puerto Rico (Picó de Hernández 1975)? If so, is this due to Puerto Rican preferential policies for light Puerto Ricans, discriminatory policies against blacks, inequalities inherited from slavery days, or the result of American imperialism? Is the whole debate over whether there is prejudice in Puerto Rico the result of a colonialized mentality? These questions indicate the complexity of the race issue in Puerto Rico, but they are questions that can also be asked of other Latin American countries.

Hypersensitivity to Color

An interesting perspective is presented by G. Lewis (1963), who sees the racial mixture as having produced a massive complex of color psychology "with serious results both for the quality of self-esteem and of social life" (p.225). He agrees there is no overt racism but says there is a very real sense of color snobbishness based on the awareness of "shades." The whitening or bleaching phenomena that some attributed to racial transformation in Latin America is seen by Lewis as a problem, for it implies that self appraisal revolves around whether or not individuals are able to garner the recognition necessary to be whitened. If this is the case, then migrants to New York may be bringing (or may have brought) a heightened sensitivity to color and race that became all the more acute with the sharp, biologically based segregation existent in the States and with the significant changes wrought by the Black Power movement. Fitzpatrick (1971) alluded to this when he said that the Puerto Rican's problem with color in New York was a concern which was already present but in a much different context in Puerto Rico.

Racial Consequences in the United States

What happened when Puerto Ricans came to the States? The literature of Puerto Ricans in the United States takes note of the many difficulties that resulted because of race. Chenault (1970:92), speaking of the pre–World War II community said that instances of difficulty on account of color were so frequent that numerous examples could be given. While Steward et al. (1956:127) said "An outsider cannot easily tell how the color line works in Puerto Rico but there seems no doubt that dark skin is a worse handicap in New York than there, and that realization of this can shock the dark-skinned migrant." The negative *economic* consequences for dark Puerto Ricans in New York were noted by a number of authors. Mills (1950:72–74) found that in the late 1940s "colored" or intermediate men, i.e., those who would be defined as "indios" and "grifos" in Puerto Rico, earned less than white men and experienced less mobility.[6] Senior (1961) also found somewhat later that in New York the "colored" Puerto Ricans had a problem getting jobs. While Katzman (1968), using 1950 census data, found Negro Puerto Ricans to be more underemployed and underpaid than white Puerto Ricans but to have few differences with regard to white-collar employment.[7]

According to the literature, early on there seemed to be an awareness of the harshness of the U.S. race order particularly on darker Puerto Ricans. A number of authors make reference to what they perceive to be selective migration patterns—that is to say, a tendency for more white Puerto Ricans to migrate to New York than dark Puerto Ricans (Chenault 1970:60–61; Senior 1961:28; Petrullo 1947:23). They also took note of a tendency among the "colored," i.e., the intermediate and Negro Puerto Ricans, to want to return to Puerto Rico and to be more cautious about staying in New York (Mills et al. 1950:48; Senior 1961:28). Chenault (1970:24) observed early on that "the colored" find less discrimination on the island than in the U.S.

In the housing area, there was also note made of the difficulties experienced because of race. As Senior (1961:28) observed: "When he comes to the States, the Puerto Rican newcomer who is colored may experience his first difficulty getting a job or finding a place to live because of his color." He became, according to Senior (1961), a minority within a minority. Earlier indications of residential patterning according to race had also been noted by Chenault (1970:127), who observed a tendency in the pre–World War II period for "colored Puerto Ricans" to live in East Harlem and for color to be an important determinant of whether they could move into the more white area of Washington Heights (p. 92). Similarly, in the

1940s Gosnell (1945:313) noted some residential patterning according to the race of Puerto Ricans and a tendency for some Puerto Ricans to "pass for white" in white areas. Thus, residence early on was significantly affected by "race."

Less visible but, nonetheless, just as significant were the social and psychological changes experienced as a result of race. These too were duly noted in the early literature on the Puerto Rican community in the U.S. Gosnell (1945:310–11), for example, noted that in New York City the "traditional pride in white descent" was intensified. Padilla (1958:75 ff.)—looking at the Puerto Rican in New York a decade later and through a similar ethnographic study— found that while in Puerto Rico social race was subordinate to social class, in New York, social race was central to Hispanic life and important in mobility. She also noted the use of whiteness for upward mobility in New York. Mills et al. (1950:7) also noted the concern of the migrants with proving that they were white, while López (1973) was to argue later that Puerto Ricans had internalized race prejudice toward others and themselves.

Psychological Impact

Some speculation about the impact of race on mental health is also to be found in the literature. For example, Berle (1958) noted that black Puerto Ricans seemed to predominate among Puerto Rican drug addicts. Malzberg (1967) noted that more Puerto Rican blacks were admitted to New York state psychiatric hospitals than non-black Puerto Ricans. Teichner and Berry (1981:281) made reference to the need to address the racial problems of Puerto Ricans in the treatment of psychiatric illness, while Longres (1974:67) said "Psychologically, the most damaging experience encountered by a Puerto Rican continental is an encounter with racist attitudes." He argued that this undermined "the sense of autonomy and initiative brought by the migrating Puerto Rican" and left "a residue of self-doubt and inadequacy" (p. 67). He saw this as a collective problem affecting all Puerto Ricans; a problem that was detrimental to individual mental health as well as to social cohesion. At the base of the problem was the experience of being forced to identify according to the socially defined racial standards of the U.S. and thereby confronting and questioning their own racial identity.

Being classified according to U.S. racial standards has meant being identified racially instead of culturally; this has meant for many being reclassified into a different culture. This reclassification experience and its consequences have been a persistent theme in the literature. It is an experience that has affected Puerto Ricans of all colors. It is found in the memoirs and literary works of the Puerto Rican migration, e.g., in the *Memorias de Bernardo Vega*, Colón's *A Puerto Rican in New York*, and Thomas's *Down These Mean Streets* and Rivera's *Family Installments*. The experience most often cited in the works is that of the darker Puerto Rican who is taken to be Negro, colored, or black,

However, the perplexing situation of the Puerto Rican who is viewed as white similarly yields confusion, anger, and a clear aware-ness of group divisions. For example, there are the stories retold by Colón (1961), where the white-looking daughter cannot meet her darker mother at her work place because the people she works for don't like colored people; or when only the white Puerto Ricans in an extended family will be served at a segregated restaurant in the pre-sixties period; or the case in which an apartment is rented to a white-looking member of the family, and when the others arrive, they all become the object of discrimination (Iglesias 1984).

If such reclassifications did not have real consequences, they might be seen as trivial aberrations in the stream of life. However, this has not been the case; identification as African American or even as Hispanic/Puerto Rican or Latino has had economic, residential, social, and even political consequences. Although the political con-sequences of race have been less well documented, it is clear that gerrymandering and voting prohibitions have been used to sup-press racial minorities. On an individual level, political conse-quences are also often a consequence of other forms of discrimination, e.g., housing, income. The real consequences to such classifications in the U.S.—regardless of phenotype—were made quite explicit by a respondent in Oscar Lewis's *La Vida*; he said: "I'm so white that they've even taken me for a Jew, but when they see my Spanish name, they back right off" (1966:180–81).

The respondent in the Oscar Lewis study was faced with the historical choice that many ethnic Americans met, i.e., whether to change their name and pass for nonethnic or whether to keep their ethnic name and pay the consequences. For Puerto Ricans the process was more complicated. Another choice had to be made, i.e., whether to be of the "white" race or of the "black" race. It appears that when Puerto Ricans first came they perceived that there were two paths, to the white world and to the not-white world. Two realities seemed to be evident: choice of path was dependent on racial classification according to U.S. standards, and race influenced the rewards to be gained from the system (i.e., housing, jobs, income). It seems that use of these standards would divide the group, negate the cultural existence of Puerto Ricans, and ignore their expectation that they be treated, irrespective of race, as a culturally intact group (Rodríguez 1989c, 1991).

Researcher's Perspectives

That the literature provides evidence of greater racial discrimination in the U.S. does not come as a great surprise, although it is always of interest to see such patterns documented. What is more curious are the perspectives or the assessments of social scientists with regard to race and Puerto Ricans. For example, there are: (a) the scholars' expectations about Puerto Rican assimilation in the U.S.; (b) the preoccupation with the relationship between African Americans and Puerto Ricans; and (c) the focus on racial "intermediates" within the Puerto Rican community. Each of these will be discussed in turn.

Anticipated Assimilation Paths

The assumption or conclusion of many of the authors reviewed was that with greater time in the U.S., Puerto Rican racial attitudes would become more like those in the U.S. This point had early been made by Chenault (1970:151), who noted that "the attitude of Puerto Ricans with regard to color seems to be affected by the length of residence in this country. It is the opinion of those who have studied the group for many years that the white Puerto Rican, after he has lived in New York for several years, takes up what is described as the 'American attitude' on the question of color." Fitzpatrick (1971) also speculated about whether Puerto Rican openness on race would change in the U.S. and make for a division of the community into

white and black. In other words, whether the race order in the U.S.
would make for separate assimilation paths. The expectation was
that this would eventually happen and that those who could not
assimilate into the white communities and who would not assimilate into the black communities would remain as the standard bear-
ers of the Puerto Rican community.

Handlin (1959:60 ff.) also articulated this possibility but added
that another possibility existed. This was that there would be a decline
in color-consciousness and that white and "colored" Puerto Ricans
might "develop a coherent community to which newcomers would
be added" through immigration. However, he pointed out that this
possibility would depend not just on a decline in color-consciousness
but "in some part on the reactions of the larger community. . . . As far
as the Puerto Ricans were concerned, there seems to be a growing
consciousness of, and pride in, their group identity. That may reflect
their preference for the second alternative, if the penalties of following it do not become too great." Thus, it was anticipated that Puerto
Ricans would become white or black with greater time in the U.S.
Alternatively, if Puerto Ricans were to retain a "coherent," i.e., an
integrated, community they would have to pay a price and it would
ultimately depend on the reactions of the larger community and on
a decline in color-consciousness. Whether this has occurred is discussed elsewhere (see Rodríguez 1990).

Blacks and Puerto Ricans

There are various references in the early literature on the desire of
Puerto Ricans to distinguish themselves from African Americans.
Chenault (1970:150) says, for example, "Probably the outstanding
fact about the racial attitude of the Puerto Rican in Harlem is that
he insists upon being distinguished from the American Negro."
Making general reference to other studies (on West Indians in Harlem), he suggests that there appears to be an interesting correlation
between color and the desire to be distinguished from the American
Negro. It seems that the darker the person is, "the more intense is
his desire to speak only Spanish and to do so in a louder voice" (p.
150). Similar observations are also noted by Glazer and Moynihan
(1970:11), Handlin (1962:60, 114) and Rand (1958). Indeed, Rand
(1958:128–29) notes, "When the dark migrants learn about the color

line, they react by differentiating themselves from the Negroes as much as they can. If they go to one of the city's hospitals, for instance, they object if the attendants write them down as 'Negro' on the admission forms. . . . They cling to their Spanish as a badge of distinction, and often they speak it with loud voices in public places, like subway trains. . . . I have heard from various sources that some Negroes in Harlem are learning Spanish too, as a way of ceasing to be Negroes."

What is puzzling about these observations is that the observers should be so surprised that any group would be reluctant to identify with a group that was not just culturally and linguistically quite different, but that was also a stigmatized group within the society. It raises the question of why they would expect darker Puerto Ricans to identify with blacks.[8] It appears that the surprise is the result of applying the North American racial classification standards; thus, because you look black, you must be black and to be black is to be just like American blacks, not to have a different culture or language. Although it is possible and easy to distinguish between Italians, Greeks, and Germans, it is not possible, or perhaps desirable, to distinguish between African blacks, West Indian blacks and American blacks. Culture becomes subordinate to race, and perhaps in the case of blacks, it ceases to exist altogether in this conception.

Intermediates

The focus on intermediates is also in some ways curious. Given the biracial nature of the U.S., one would expect that Puerto Ricans would be seen as just white or black. This more traditional classification has been evident in some studies (see, for example, Katzman 1968) and in the earlier census treatment of Puerto Ricans. In the decennial censuses of 1950, 1960, and 1970 Puerto Ricans were classified as white or Negro/black. However, other studies have focused on intermediates. Mills et al. (1950:152 ff.), for example, defined intermediates as those who in Puerto Rico might be seen as "indios" or "grifos."[9] In this study, intermediates were found to be the least adapted as compared with white and Negro Puerto Ricans. The authors state: "The facts of migration present problems to them that the whites or Negroes do not have to face so crucially. About three times as many of the men in the intermediate racial group score low on adaptation as do the white or Negro men." The study argued that intermediates were lacking a model of adaptation within the city; thus, it was "harder for the intermediate groups" because there were no "standards with which to conform."

Mills et al. (1950) argued that intermediates were not accepted by American whites and that they were reluctant to enter the American Negro community. This same study also found intermediate (and Negro) migrants to be "more cautious than the whites about planning unreservedly to stay in N.Y." (p. 48) and perceived themselves as less liked, inferior, and less adapted to the New York situation. The conception of an intermediate category is noted in other studies. Padilla (1958), for example, noted the difficulty of intermediates, their ambiguous feelings, and their tendency to heighten Puerto Rican identification for fear of being taken as anything else. Glazer and Moynihan (1970:134), citing the earlier Mills et al. (1950) work, echoed the same theme that intermediates were the least assimilated and the most passionately attached to whatever identified them as Puerto Rican. However, they added that the anxiety of the intermediates with regard to their color was greater than any objective differences in treatment would warrant.

What is curious about the use of the intermediate category is why it exists within a country with an essentially biracial, genetically based racial classification system. It is possible that the conception of the intermediate group had its roots in the Puerto Rican racial context and that this was transported via respondents or researchers to the research done in the U.S. However, it is also possible that the existence of a multiracial group, a group that is neither clearly white nor black, yields (within a biracial context) the conception of a third alternative. Thus, we see the brown category for Chicanos or Mexican Americans, or the general reference to Latinos as tan, Spanish, or Spanish white. The racial implications that some attribute to the terms "Hispanic" or "Latino"—as when the police describe a suspect as a "young Hispanic male"—might also be seen as examples of this phenomenon.

A Reflection on the Researchers' Perspectives

In the literature, a common perception of the researchers is that this intermediate group was afraid of being seen as black and of not being accepted as white. The comments on intermediates also imply the existence of a polarized racial structure wherein individuals and groups have to be accommodated. The last inference that can be made from the literature is that individuals who did not accommodate to the biracial structure would have to pay a price. The assumption was that you must be white or black—there could be no in-betweens. The assumption was also made that Puerto Ricans chose the intermediate categories as (1) a way of avoiding being seen as black and because (2) they would not be accepted as white.

However, other possibilities must be calculated when considering why individuals would use intermediate classifications. It may have been that some who would not be classified as racial intermediates might nonetheless have chosen to see themselves as intermediates, even though phenotypically they were white. It may also have been that intermediates "preferred" to be intermediates and this might have had little to do with *not* wanting to be black or *not* being able to be white. For example, they might have found that an intermediate classification was more representative of who they were physically or racially. Or, it might have allowed or affirmed a cultural identity that was subsumed or lost in the identification as white or black American. Others might have felt that such a classification was also a more accurate reflection of who they weren't, i.e., they were not white Americans and they were not black Americans and they did not care to be either. They may have opted to be intermediates because they had a personal attraction for intermediates, found greater personal or political identification with intermediates, or perceived greater freedom of class movement as intermediates.

This is not to say that there were not some who typified the pattern described in the literature. The power structure of the society cannot be denied, and identifying with whites was identifying with the more powerful, while identifying with blacks was identifying with the less powerful. However, to assume that this was the only pattern or preference is a large assumption. The assumption also implies that people accepted and wanted to be a part of a biracial structure. But, these assumptions are perhaps better understood in hindsight. Writers of the time had not yet experienced the racial transformations that were to follow in the late sixties and seventies. The perspective encompassed in the "Black is beautiful" movement had a major impact on the racial and cultural identities of many who were of African, European, Asian, and Latin American heritage. Consequently, alternatives to traditional modes were more readily understood and expected. Recent census data also confirms Latinos' tendency to respond to race in ways that differ from those expected in the U.S. In 1990, when asked what their race was, 43.5 percent of all Latinos in the country responded they were "other" and wrote in a Spanish descriptor; 52.1 percent said they were "white"; and 3.0 percent said they were "black" (U.S. Bureau of the Census, 1990).

Conclusion

In analyzing both the fictional and nonfictional literature on Puerto Ricans we have found a number of racial themes and perspectives that illustrate the difficulty that North Americans have had in coming to terms with Puerto Ricans as a multiracial group. These difficulties have undoubtedly also been experienced by other earlier groups that were, or became, multiracial cultural groups, e.g., Native-American Indians, and Cape Verdeans. The research suggests that Puerto Ricans and other similar groups present a challenge—by their mere presence—to the demise of the biracial system in the United States.

NOTES

The author gratefully acknowledges the assistance of Karen Carrillo and Janet Guerrero as research assistants.
 1. Race is in many ways similar to gender. It is socially constructed and it is basic to identity and therefore to society. Ambiguity about one's "race" is in many societies like ambiguity about one's gender. It leads to confusion, sometimes rejection, anger, and intolerance. The fully androgenous individual must be very consciously or purposely androgenous or they will not be able to deal with the societal consequence, i.e., the often negative or ambivalent reactions their androgyny elicits among others in the society who are more clearly gender defined and who seek to define others according to strict gender definitions.
 2. The 1980 Census question asked if the person was "His-

panic" or of Spanish origin and allowed individuals to indicate whether they were Mexican, Puerto Rican, Cuban, or to write in something in the "other" category. A separate item was asked to determine race for the total U.S. population.

3. The proposal was strongly opposed "through the most aggressive campaign ever seen by the Bureau of the Census." The census agency officials decided to abandon the proposal, fearing it would cause a withdrawal of much-needed community support. (Quote from N. McKenney, Census Bureau official, cited in *Hispanic Link Weekly Report*, vol 4, no. 21 (May 26, 1986).

4. See Omi and Winant (1983) for an excellent analysis of how social relations were transformed through political struggle over racial meanings.

5. An interesting conception of this continuum was advanced early on by Padilla (1958:74), who argued that in Puerto Rico there was a biracial continuum, with the two poles being white and black. Although her premise was that there was an overarching biracial structure, she maintained that, contrary to the situation in the United States, the categories in the middle of the continuum were not castelike and that one could experience mobility within one's lifetime from one group to the next.

6. Mills et al. (1950:72–74) also found white men to experience greater upward and downward mobility than the intermediate group, who tended to stay in semiskilled and unskilled jobs both in New York and in Puerto Rico.

7. Katzman, 1968:373 also found black Puerto Ricans to be "more successful in obtaining white-collar jobs" than black Anglos.

8. Would the comments have been made of Italians, Greeks, or Germans who insisted on being identified as Greeks, etc., or on speaking their language?

9. However, in the text, intermediates and Negroes are often lumped together and this combined group is referred to as "the colored."

BIBLIOGRAPHY

Berle, B. 1958. *Eighty Puerto Rican families in New York City*. New York: Columbia University Press.

Betances, Samuel. 1972. "The prejudice of having no prejudice," *The Rican* 1:41–54.

Chenault, L. 1938c, 1970. *The Puerto Rican migrant in New York City.* New York: Columbia University Press.

Colón, J. 1982. *A Puerto Rican in New York and other sketches.* New York: International Publishers.

Duany, Jorge. 1985. "Ethnicity in the Spanish Caribbean: Notes on the consolidation of Creole identity in Cuba and Puerto Rico, 1762–1868." *Ethnic Groups* 6:99–123.

Fitzpatrick, J. P., Rev. 1971. *Puerto Rican Americans.* Englewood Cliffs, N.J.: Prentice-Hall.

Ginorio, Angela. 1979. "A comparison of Puerto Ricans in New York with native Puerto Ricans and Native Americans on two measures of acculturation: Gender role and racial identification." Ph.D. diss., Fordham University, New York City.

———. 1986. "Puerto Ricans and interethnic conflict." In *International Perspectives on Ethnic Conflict: Antecedents and Dynamics,* ed. Jerry O. Boucher, Dan Landis, and Karen Arnold. Sage Press.

——— and Paul C. Berry. 1972. "Measuring Puerto Ricans' perceptions of racial characteristics." (Summary.) Proceedings of the 80th Annual Convention of the American Psychological Association, 7:287–88.

Glazer, N., and D. P. Moynihan. 1970. *Beyond the melting pot.* 2nd ed. Cambridge, Mass.: MIT Press.

Gosnell Aran, Patria. 1945. "The Puerto Ricans in New York City." Ph.D. diss., New York University.

Handlin, O. 1959. *The newcomers: Negroes and Puerto Ricans in a changing metropolis.* Cambridge, Mass.: Harvard University Press.

Harris, Marvin. 1970. "Referential ambiguity in the calculus of Brazilian racial identity." In *Afro-American Anthology,* eds. Norman Whitten, Jr., and John F. Szwed. New York: The Free Press.

Iglesias, C.A., ed. 1984. *Memoirs of Bernardo Vega.* New York: Monthly Review Press.

Katzman, Martin. 1968. "Discrimination, subculture and the economic performance of Negroes, Puerto Ricans and Mexican-Americans." *American Journal of Economics and Society* 27, no. 4: 371–75.

La Ruffa, A. 1971. *San Cipriano: Life in a Puerto Rican community.* New York: Gordon and Breach Science Publishers.

Landy, D. 1959. *Tropical childhood.* Chapel Hill. University of North Carolina.

Lewis, G. K. 1963. *Puerto Rico: Freedom and power in the Caribbean.* New York: Monthly Review Press.

Lewis, O. 1966. *La Vida: A Puerto Rican family in the culture of poverty—San Juan and New York.* New York: Random House.

Longres, John F. 1974. "Racism and its effects on Puerto Rican continentals." *Social Casework*, February, pp. 67–99.

López, A. 1973. *The Puerto Rican papers.* New York: Bobbs-Merrill.

Malzberg, B. 1956. "Mental disease among the Puerto Ricans in New York City, 1949–1951." *Journal of Nervous and Mental Disease*, 123, no. 3: 262–69.

————. 1965. *Mental disease among the Puerto Ricans in New York City, 1960–1961.* Albany, N.Y.: Research Foundation for Mental Hygiene, Inc.

————. 1967. "Internal migration and mental disease among the white population in New York State, 1960–61." *International Journal of Social Psychiatry* 13, no. 3: 184–91.

Mills, C. W., C. Senior, and R. Goldsen. 1950. *The Puerto Rican journey: New York's newest migrants.* New York: Harper & Bros.

Mintz, S. W. 1960. *Worker in the cane: a Puerto Rican life history.* New Haven, Conn.: Yale University Press.

Movimiento Pro Independencia. 1963. *Tesis Política: La hora de la independencia.* San Juan, P.R.: Movimiento Pro Independencia.

Muñoz, Braulio. 1982. *Sons of the wind: The search for identity in Spanish American Indian literature.* New Brunswick, N.J.: Rutgers University Press.

Omi, M., and H. Winant. 1983. "By the rivers of Babylon: Race in the United States," Parts I and II. *Socialist Review* 71:31–66 and 72:35–68.

Padilla, E. 1958. *Up from Puerto Rico.* New York: Columbia University Press.

Petrullo, V. 1947. *Puerto Rican paradox.* Philadelphia: University of Pennsylvania Press.

Picó de Hernández, I. 1975. "The quest for race, sex, and ethnic equality in Puerto Rico." *Caribbean Studies* 14: no. 4: 127–41.

Pitt-Rivers, J. 1975. "Race, color and class in Central America and the Andes." In N. R. Yetman, and C. H. Steele, eds., *Majority and minority*, Boston: Allyn and Bacon.

Rand, C. 1958. *The Puerto Ricans.* New York: Oxford University Press.

Rivera, E. 1983. *Family installments: Memories of growing up Hispanic.* New York: Penguin.

Rodríguez, C. E. 1989. *Puerto Ricans: Born in the USA.* Boston: Unwin & Hyman. (Reissued by Westview Press in Boulder, Colo., in 1991.)

————. 1990. "Racial classification among Puerto Rican men and women in New York." *Hispanic Journal of Behavioral Sciences* 12, no. 4: (November): 366–79.

Senior, C. 1961. *The Puerto Ricans: Strangers—Then Neighbors.* New York: Freedom Books.

Steward, J. H., R. A. Manners, E. R. Wolff, E. Padilla Seda, S. W. Mintz, R. L. Scheele. 1956. *The people of Puerto Rico: A study in social anthropology.* Chicago-Urbana: University of Illinois Press.

Teichner, V. J., and F. W. Berry. 1981. "The Puerto Rican patient: Some historical and psychological aspects." *Journal of the American Academy of Psychoanalysis* 9, no. 2: 277–89,

Thomas, P. 1967. *Down these mean streets.* New York: A. Knopf.

Tumin, M., and A. Feldman. 1961. *Social class and social change in Puerto Rico.* 2nd ed. Princeton, N.J.: Princeton University Press.

U.S. Bureau of the Census. 1990. Public Use Microdata tapes (1 percent sample of the population).

Vazconcelos, J. 1966. *La raza cósmica.* 3rd ed. Mexico: Espasa-Calpe.

Wade, P. 1985. "Race and class: The case of South American Blacks." *Ethnic and Racial Studies* 8, no. 2: 233–49.

Wagley, C. 1965. "On the concept of social race in the Americas." In *Contemporary cultures and societies of Latin America and the Caribbean*, ed. D. B. Heath and R. N. Adams. New York: Random House.

Zenon Cruz, I. 1975. *Narciso descubre su trasero.* Humancao, P.R.: Editorial Furidi.

5

The Identity and Culture of Latino College Students

JOSÉ HERNÁNDEZ

For many years Latino college students have been leaders in the advancement of our communities in New York. Having survived an often hostile school environment, they reach a level of study which provides access to professional careers. The prospect of a good job after graduation means a decent income, security, and work that will be satisfying to themselves and gain them prestige among others. College graduates have greater potential for influencing the improvement of living conditions, especially if employed in crucial positions as teachers, administrators, or human service providers.

Latino college students also tend to acquire a critical view of society as their exposure to community problems helps them to analyze situations and question authority when necessary. Their responses intensify when their communities become the subject in courses on the history, culture, and life conditions of Latino people. Student activism comes about from an awareness of social issues and the urge to do something to improve society. A sense of mission frequently inspires college students to select careers in which they see the chance to contribute to solutions, as agents of change.

Those of us concerned about the future of Latino people often wonder how college students of the present generation respond to the identity question of "who (or what) am I and are we?" Our concern goes beyond such labels as "Latino," or "Spanish," or nationality names like Puerto Rican, Dominican, or Colombian, to the topic of "what does it mean to be a Latino?" So much has happened since an initial answer was given by the founders of Latino Studies, years ago. Moreover, social pressure to assimilate to an Anglo-American way of life intensified during the period when today's students grew up. They entered a world in which negative images of Latinos were taken for granted, along with public disregard for diversity and the need to correct for inequalities built into "the system."

Although culture includes all aspects of human behavior (such as food, music, clothing, and language) a people's future is most determined by the values governing their lives. Values are ideas about good and bad that define ways in which people act, expect others to act, and relate to one another on a daily basis. Latino values come from American Indian, African, and Spanish traditions that differ markedly from Anglo values. The conflict inspired by Anglo dominance encourages the retention of Latino values as an ideal. But, in practice, people tend to reconcile these differences in various ways that usually weaken their traditional values.

Origins of This Study

Since one's identity is expressed in culture, the main goal of my study was to discover and describe the values of Latino college students. By determining how they felt life should be lived, their inner selves would become visible. In social research, values are best studied while people are solving a problem they define as important. Usually, a problem is planned to happen in a laboratory or field experiment. I obtained data on student values by using the final examinations of a course on Puerto Ricans in the United States, at Hunter College, City University of New York. By the end of the fall 1986 semester, the class understood the subject and wanted to learn more about the new generation of youth. Because I had almost no published information regarding this, I decided to ask the students to write a final problem-solution essay as research material.

Research Methods

The content analysis presented here resulted from coding the key words and meaning of 3,819 sentences, averaging twelve words each and ninety-three per essay. Words or phrases were sorted into categories of identity, problems, and solutions, and then matched by similarity of expression. The Nota Bene text-base computer program was used for this purpose, and totals resulting from matching became data for statistical analysis with the SPSS program language.[1] The distributions elaborated here were correlated with student grades from A+ to C− in order to determine whether the findings related to my judgment of quality in a systematic way. These tests proved not significant within standard limits for the null hypothesis.

Of the forty-one students twenty-eight were Puerto Rican, and the rest were Dominicans, Colombians, Ecuadorans, Haitians, West Indians, and Americans of African and European origins. The content of their essays mainly concerned Puerto Ricans, which was the subject of the examination. Statements about other Latinos were not enough for a separate analysis, but the results proved to be of general significance, evoking questions for further research. The transcription and coding of the student expressions were checked for accuracy, as in a photocopy. Quotations later presented are shown exactly as written (including mistakes in spelling and grammar)—except for words added in brackets to clarify the meaning.

In the spring 1989 semester a Dominican student completing an independent study project on youth became a leader in the protest and occupation of the Hunter College administration building. The student kept a copious journal of experiences as the activities developed and reached a successful completion. This provided a basis for a report which I used as a source of information on college student values, as observed in an actual crisis situation. My observation of the student movement was also based on my witnessing of events. The new information served to validate the analysis of examinations.

Identity

The sense of peoplehood shared by members of a racial-ethnic group identifies their culture as a distinct experience and way of life, commonly expressed in a collective name. This answer to the question "who are we?" may change, as the peoplehood changes, because of major events such as migration or inclusion in another society by war, occupation, and dominance. It can be expected that college students will be among the first people in such a group to think about and express these changes in ways that influence others to keep the previous names or adopt a new one.

Puerto Rico has been a U.S. possession for almost a hundred years, and Puerto Ricans have lived in the continental United States for several decades. Their experience provides a valuable case in the study of Latino identity, as widely affected by inclusion in the American population. If traditional identity has changed, college students would use different names in reference to this group.

Figure A shows that a large majority (83 percent) of actions and attributes about Puerto Ricans in the student essays referred exclusively to "Puerto Rican" as an identity. This provides clear evidence that peoplehood is still strong. However, the references were almost totally limited to Puerto Ricans in the U.S. Only a small fraction linked the Puerto Rican identity to the island and people of Puerto Rico. The indigenous name of "Boricua" appeared only once, and was misspelled. This indicates that a strong sense of

A. Puerto Rican Identity

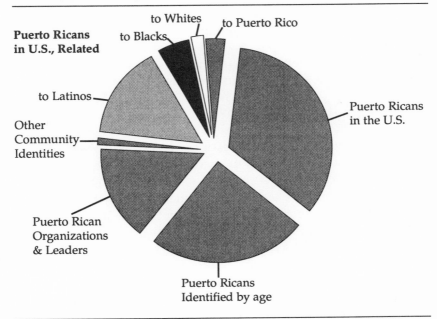

Puerto Rican identity was perceived, but clearly separate from Puerto Rico. The students saw Puerto Ricans as a group having a distinct identity among other groups in the United States.

Since the late 1960s, many immigrants from Latin America have come to live in the same cities as Puerto Ricans. For convenience in relating to the Anglo world, generic identifiers have arisen, such as "Latino, Hispanic, and Spanish." Studies have shown that these names are not ordinarily used instead of national identity when people talk about themselves within the Latino world. But the repeated experience of being treated by society as if "all of you are the same" seems to be influencing our people to express a unified sense of Latino identity, when facing the Anglo world.[2]

Some evidence for these conclusions was found in the student essays. Among all references to Puerto Ricans, 12 percent were in relation to other Latino groups, the most common identity next to "Puerto Rican." The connection was more common among students who were not Puerto Rican, which means that they saw Puerto Ricans as part of the larger Latino group more often than the Puerto Rican students saw themselves. The difference may be that Puerto Ricans were alone as a large Latino group in New York before the recent immigration. Now, there are Dominicans, Colombians, Ecuadorans, and several other groups—and many institutions, such as television and newspapers, that are Latino in identity. Also, Puerto Ricans have sometimes felt as outsiders to Latin America, thinking that as U.S. citizens they are considered outsiders by other Latinos.

An even stronger sense of Puerto Rican isolation was evident in a small number of references to the rest of American society. Less than 1 percent of the expressions spoke about Puerto Ricans in relation to whites and about 4 percent related them to blacks or African Americans. The results tell us of continuing segregation from Anglo Americans and of some contact with blacks in working and lower-class neighborhoods. Such figures are obviously much lower than expected from the many years that Puerto Ricans have lived in New York City. The social isolation is especially impressive, considering that most of the references were written by Anglo- and African-American students—not by Puerto Ricans—and the course was given by the Department of Black and Puerto Rican Studies.

Feeling alien both to Puerto Rico and American society was

a recurrent theme in classroom discussions. Other Latino students who felt rejection similar to that of Puerto Ricans also voiced concern about being "left-out in a dead-end world." The data from the final examinations made it clear that a general attachment to community filled this social void. About half of the statements about Puerto Ricans specified part of the population or a certain aspect of community life—features of life in New York society that all students had experienced to some extent.

The largest community category (28 percent of all references) consisted of age designations, such as "children, youth, parents, old people." Considered in relation to the meaning of statements, a heavy emphasis on generation gaps was evident. The students saw their world as very different from that of Puerto Ricans who came from Puerto Rico in large numbers in the 1950s and who currently are the grandparents. They also felt different from their parents, who reached adulthood in the 1965–75 period, years in which many Puerto Ricans were involved in political movements of protest and demand for government action to improve life conditions.

A closely related finding was the student's frequent mention of a lack of political awareness and participation among Puerto Rican youth. Next to age, the most frequent community references were to organizations and leaders, sometimes called "successful" Puerto Ricans. In general, the students' attitudes combined both positive feelings—respect for the accomplishments of the parent generation—and a sense of ignorance and inadequacy in regard to the militancy of the Civil Rights era and its products. Students generally felt that organizations such as ASPIRA, the Young Lords, the Institute for Puerto Rican Policy, and the National Congress for Puerto Rican Rights were remarkable achievements, but actions that stood beyond capabilities for use as models.

Feelings of social distance from the parent generation were also motivated by what the students perceived to be changes in behavior and lifestyle among young adults. Today's youth (it was repeatedly stated) had to live and find their way in a different world, one in which the government and society were not receptive to militancy, nor even to a quiet affirmation of a group's distinct identity. Individual responsibility and group cooperation had to be encouraged more than hopes of improvement from resources outside the Puerto Rican community. Thus, the sense of peoplehood remained strong but was expressed in defensive and introverted values.

Positive Attributes of Puerto Ricans

The statements made by students regarding Puerto Ricans were coded to indicate specific behavioral patterns that can be used to compose a stereotype or mental image. Students generally admit that taking a course on Puerto Ricans helps to change their ideas of how these people should be pictured. The students in the study certainly had a more positive vision of Puerto Ricans than the negative images prevailing in New York City. But their personal experiences strongly influenced their pictures of Puerto Ricans, as did the assigned readings and classwork. Nevertheless, certain attributes that were taught were hardly mentioned; for example, the values of personal dignity and social respect, machismo and the need for change in gender roles, expressiveness, stoicism, and familism. Other attributes (especially those about youth) were much more strongly emphasized in the examination than in readings and classwork. (See figure B.)

The three positive attributes most frequently mentioned were that Puerto Ricans:

1. *have aspirations*. Many said that they "want to get ahead," "have dreams," "are looking for a better life," "can do it" and are "hardworking," "motivated," "willing to sacrifice themselves," and that "they're going to prove themselves."
2. *struggle*. They "fight back when challenged," "respond to discrimination by their struggle." They are "fighters" and "very political" in orientation. Often it was said that "they've struggled for many years," and "paid their dues."
3. *have great pride*: They "have love for their people," "show strong feelings about their identity," "feel good about being Puerto Ricans," and simply, "have lots of pride!"

These three attributes appeared in almost all the examinations. Puerto Ricans, however, mentioned aspirations and struggle more often than others, and other students mentioned pride more often

B. Positive Attributes about Puerto Ricans

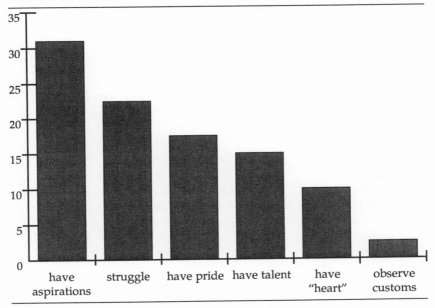

than the Puerto Ricans. This difference shows that Puerto Rican students had a somewhat stronger vision of their motivation for success in society, and of their struggle to overcome obstacles to achievement. Other students tended more to admire the strength of the Puerto Ricans' national identity, their sense of ethnic responsibility, and their cultural alternative to Anglo assimilation.

The students generally agreed on attributes less frequently mentioned, that Puerto Ricans:

4. *have talent.* Many said that they have a great potential for accomplishment. Some statements were more specific: "very musical," "great poets and entertainers." No one mentioned, however, abilities for science, technology, and careers that are currently well paid and in high demand—as was taught.
5. *have "heart."* They "participate," "form close groups," "do anything to help each other," "are kind and cooperative,"

"feel sorry for others in trouble," "reach out to others," "are warm and affectionate," and "have lots of love."
6. *observe customs*. The least mentioned category included a variety of such statements as they are "family oriented," "religious people," and "maintain friendship ties." Only one student said that they want to preserve and transmit their culture and historical traditions of Puerto Rican society.

Cultural continuity with the society of origin was quite evident, however, since most of these attributes are strongly traditional to the Puerto Rican national character, especially the struggle, pride, and having heart. This shows that students who considered themselves as separate from the island were still Puerto Rican in certain values. Nonetheless, their emphasis on having aspirations and talent were clearly a product of the United States experience and showed equally strong desires to reach success and acceptance in American society. Thus, the students' vision of Puerto Ricans blended both tradition and a response to the environment in which they live and have to develop to mature adulthood.

Perception of Problems

A more detailed picture of the new culture was obtained from statements on what is wrong in the life of Puerto Ricans. About two-thirds of these statements referred to the social environment in which Puerto Ricans live. The rest were attributed to Puerto Ricans themselves—the negative part of the students' stereotype. The negative remarks about Puerto Ricans were more frequent than would have been expected from students during the 1965–75 period, those who militated for the establishment of Puerto Rican Studies and attributed all the problems to an oppressive social order, in an ideological manner. Although the students studied did mention the institutions most criticized in the literature embodying the original viewpoint, their vision of reality showed less tendency to condemn the social system and was more candid in its self-criticism.

As shown in figure C, the students saw discrimination as the fundamental cause of problems in the social environment. This was

C. Perception of Problems

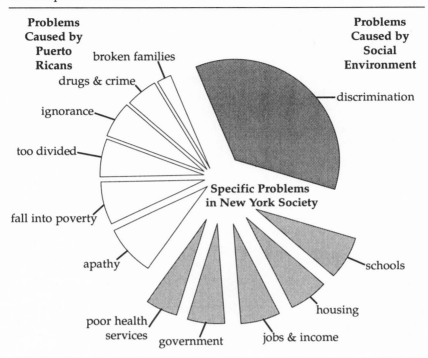

Problems Caused by Puerto Ricans

broken families

drugs & crime

ignorance

too divided

fall into poverty

apathy

poor health services

government

jobs & income

Problems Caused by Social Environment

discrimination

Specific Problems in New York Society

schools

housing

mentioned in 27 percent of the problem statements in a variety of ways: "low public image, unfair treatment, given a bad deal." The students saw Puerto Ricans as severely deprived of opportunities and benefits available to other Americans, because of a negative evaluation in prejudice, and this negativity as an influence in exclusionary actions, neglect, and deliberate barriers to success. For example, one student said:

> Hopefully some day we Puerto Ricans will be what we always wanted to be—another simple human being—and able to perform the jobs and have the opportunity we deserved as American citizens without any sort of discrimination whatsoever.

Many students saw discrimination at present as a long-term result of a history of inferiority as a domestic dependent or internally colonized people, whose poverty in Puerto Rico was brought about by the American invasion and occupation. According to this view, Puerto Ricans were forced by their dependency and poverty to move to the United States. In effect, the migrants were pushed out in order to be used in low-paid factory jobs, as was needed in America.

Regarding life conditions in New York, the students generally saw Puerto Ricans as assigned to an "end-of-the-line" position in a competitive, greedy, and materialistic society. Puerto Ricans became "welfare problems" when cheap factory work was exported to poor nations and when people from these nations were brought to New York to do cheap service work as replacements for Puerto Ricans; blacks, and other citizens of color. Another student said:

> Discrimination has contributed to the fact that we are on welfare, since there is no work, and without money you cannot dress well, have a better home and an adequate education. I wonder why, after they made us such useless beings, they don't want to help us out of the trap they put us in.

The students mentioned schools, housing, neighborhoods, political participation, jobs, income, and health as specific ways in which discrimination becomes a problem for Puerto Ricans. The poor quality of these vital aspects of life was expressed as follows:

> Education should be geared toward creating an aware community that is ready for the world—not crippled in its integration into the larger community, ready to drop-out, sell drugs, and stand on welfare lines, waiting for some hand-out.

In sum, the students showed a conviction that New York society has failed to understand and adequately respond to people coming as displaced American citizens—recruited on false promises for manufacturing when this was about to decline—and then forgotten when the city itself declined in the wake of economic changes.

Anger and despair were expressed in statements about Puerto Ricans as a source of problems. The problem people were typically seen as apathetic, lacking a positive self-vision, and divided among themselves into rival groups that blame each other for the Puerto Rican situation. A student summarized this as follows:

> Very often the middle class Puerto Ricans blame the poor people for their problems. They say that if the poor had moved up, being

a Puerto Rican would not be seen as negative. The poor on the other side blame themselves, when society is what they should blame. They give in too easily and give up.

Replacing a negative image of themselves with a determination to have a better future was seen as essential to avoid "falling into the same trap—in school being tracked as a slow-learner, getting a menial job, being confined to poor housing, etc., etc."

Ignorance and feelings of helplessness were typically seen as causes of escapist and self-destructive behavior. A student said:

Since our problems started [when we were seen] as racially stig-matized, second-rate citizens at the bottom of American society, we have been told . . . that we do not have nothing much to say because of our culture. Now, without any rights or hope, many of our youth have thrown themselves into the world of drugs and crime.

Some students saw Puerto Ricans as people who had to awake from a bad dream and take action to correct family situations in which:

homes either are very poor and unsuitable environments or are broken homes, where teaching and educating the young becomes very difficult. I am not saying [it is] impossible, but the success stories do not come near to out-weighing the failures.

This kind of frank admission of problems created by Puerto Ricans themselves had not surfaced during the course, which followed the approach of attributing problems to the environment, as developed by the writers who created the current literature on the topic.

Proposed Solutions

During the Civil Rights era and in the literature it created, one finds a predominant emphasis on government action in solving social problems such as those just described. According to this view, if progressive laws were passed, and sufficient money and enough attention were given to the improvement of life conditions, disad-vantaged groups like the Puerto Ricans could emerge from their situation to enjoy the benefits of citizenship in equality with other Americans. No longer would they have to worry about discrimination, low-quality public services, and deteriorated housing. The right public policy would enable everyone to have some prosperity and happiness, and planned opportunities for personal ambition would help develop talent previously wasted.

The most important result of this study was that the students did not see this as the best way to solve the problems. Instead, they proposed a set of values that placed responsibility for the solutions mainly on the Puerto Rican community. Government action was mentioned in only a small percentage of statements and was one of the least mentioned among solutions to be developed by others. In general, the students saw a revolutionary change in community life as essential to achieve the goals set forth by the leaders of the Civil Rights movement. Most of this had to do with policy internal to the community, as a foundation for steps to be taken in relation to other cultural groups in New York society.

The details are illustrated in figure D, which shows unity as the item considered most important for community change. Students were also concerned with developing an awareness of the identity and culture of Puerto Ricans, in order to bring about empowerment, which I defined as the process of gaining strength to be self-determining and to influence others in American society. One student stated:

> You got to know who you are, where you come from and where you [are] going to. And, then you got to know what you want, and how you [are] going to get it. If Puerto Ricans do this and stick together, there's no problem that they can't solve.

The general idea was that the time had come for Puerto Ricans to put aside their internal differences and begin to care for their own people in a much more effective way. This meant helping youth to change their minds away from defeatism and toward a confident, self-directing mentality that would solve problems on their own terms. If that was gained, Puerto Ricans would change the minds of other New Yorkers toward having a more positive stereotype, and chances for improving life conditions would be strengthened. In sum, this approach was called empowerment or self-determination, with unity.

The students proposed nine major goals for practical action in the empowerment of the Puerto Rican community:

1. *organize the people.* "We need leadership," "people must be made aware," "an answer is mobilization for change," "must find ways of coping," "Puerto Ricans must work together."
2. *advocacy.* "We must stand up for our rights!" "They have to learn how to put pressure on the rich," "get a strong protest started," "avoid exploitation, by lobby actions."
3. *networking.* "To communicate with, understand other Puerto Ricans," "help people know what is out there." "We really need more peer counseling, we can learn from each other."
4. *voting and involvement in government.* "Every Puerto Rican should register to vote," They "need representation," "to elect people who are in it for others, not for the money."

D. Proposed Solutions

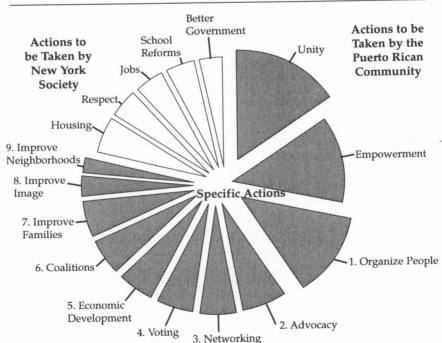

5. *better use of economic system.* They must "learn business," "gain skills," "invest and get others to invest," "set up companies that hire other Puerto Ricans," and "make it!"

6. *coalitions with other groups.* They should "strengthen ties with Hispanic communities," "join with Latinos and Blacks" and "remove obstacles to unity with the oppressed people."

7. *improve family life.* Adults should "be motivated to educate their kids," "be made to see reality," "stop setting a bad example." "Kids shouldn't pay for their parents mistakes."

8. *improve public image.* "Should show others we can do it," "work to get more recognition," "Middle class could come out and be known as Puerto Ricans who are successful."

9. *volunteer neighborhood action.* We need "a patrol to stop drugs," "a watch group for crime," "tenants associations," "fundraising," "a one-on-one to get people off welfare."

The students studied saw these as the most effective ways of answering the question posed in the final examination: "Make up an agenda for improving life conditions (30%), and explain how these goals could be reached within five to ten years from now (70%)." Their responses, presented here in a collective manner, indicate that the new generation strongly felt that a redirection of values and empowerment through community revitalization is the answer to the social and economic problems experienced by Puerto Ricans in the United States.

Secondarily, the students called for certain changes in the New York environment. The need most frequently mentioned was for improved public provision for housing and neighborhoods. This was often related to the problem statements that have been described, and the students' personal experiences. Many mentioned the need for others to have sensitivity and respect for Puerto Ricans. For Anglos to "be nice" was a desire typically expressed by migrants from the island, years ago. During the conservative times of the 1980s it returned as a solution for the discrimination which the students saw as the major cause of problems. Solutions presented as very important in the text materials and class were mentioned in the student essays— improved public provisions for jobs and income, schools, government, and health programs—but these were seen as less important than self-determination, with unity.

Student Solutions Applied to C.U.N.Y. Budget Cutbacks in 1989

Except for their lack of faith in government, the students' values resembled those which inspired the parent generation to establish Puerto Rican Studies and the community organizations previously mentioned. Considering the solutions proposed, their sense of ignorance and inadequacy about activist involvement and abilities to develop collective measures seemed a contradiction. Perhaps it reflected the rebellious attitude typical of people at their life stage, and a lack of experience in being positioned in adult leadership by real conditions calling for action.[3] Three years later, it became clear that an increase in tuition proposed by the New York State government would prevent many students from continuing their education. Budget cuts reducing the availability of teachers and coursework would limit the chances of obtaining a college education, even if they continued. The prospect persuaded students like those studied to become militant and create actions that showed how effectively they could make the transition from empowerment values to activism and community organization.

The 1989 protest was begun and led mainly by Latino students, Dominicans, Colombians, and Puerto Ricans. A basic observation was that the value of freedom, so deeply rooted in the Dominican way of life from the struggle for independence and democracy, was a source of strong motivation. The Dominican migration to New York is generally believed to have been set in motion by the American occupation in 1965. Economic intervention followed the military invasion and political changes—a new order that brought about scarcity of employment and rapid increases in the cost of living. Dominicans arrived when New York was in a sharp economic decline, accompanied by a deterioration of social and political life. This background has inspired a critical view of American life and the disposition to struggle for advancement against unfavorable odds.

The Colombian community is said to have begun when people who fled from the civil violence in the 1950s moved to New York. More recent immigrants left unsettled political conditions and limited chances for economic advancement. Colombians favor peace in their respect for law and order, success in business through hard work, and respectability from civic responsibility. They have a strong sense of loyalty both to their people and the United States, and deeply resent the public stereotype of being involved in dealing drugs. Colombian students in public colleges like Hunter tend to be more liberal than their parents, but they typically follow the traditional sense of struggle against injustice and for human rights which was a major motive for immigration. They tend to be critical when faced with unfulfilled expectations, especially in regard to limited opportunities for education and employment.

Although quite different in origin and nature, the Dominican and Colombian community backgrounds both predispose young people to use empowerment for solving problems in their world. Sustained determination and energetic effort contributed to the success of the occupation of the Hunter College administration building for eight days. In contrast with the diverse political causes pursued by student protesters from 1965 to 1975, their sharply targeted goals showed remarkable self-determination. From the occupation of City College on April 23, 1989, until Governor Cuomo vetoed the tuition increase eleven days later, the student effort at all of the City University campuses was effective in influencing public opinion to change from condemning to supporting the protest.

"The Students United Will Never be Defeated" was written in big letters on the banners and cardboard signs carried by those who marched in the streets, calling attention to their protest. Those words expressed the reality of an unusually close relation among the thousands of protesters. Latinos coalesced with Asians, Arabs, and African and Anglo Americans in a harmonious way, seldom before seen in New York. In the report mentioned at the beginning of this chapter, the student stated: "we were all in it together, mainly working-class people of color, many of us adults supporting their own children; we were older than students just out of high school." Unity was all the more important, because it was said that the occupation was not planned. It evolved out of a casual student sit-in and a meeting to consider the budget cutbacks.

The student report on the 1989 protest was studied to see if the plan proposed by students in the final examination was found in this instance of actual problem solving. If their values were typical of the new generation's culture, the same approach would be taken in an instance of direct involvement in the improvement of life conditions. The student's report and my own observations confirmed this supposition, since we both found evidence that:

1. *People were organized.* Effective leadership guided a vast, complex effort by many people, performing the tasks needed for the occupation, acting and living together in harmony.
2. *Advocacy was done.* A media committee contacted television, newspaper, and radio outlets with persuasive information on student demands and succeeded in changing public opinion.
3. *Networking took place.* Communication circuits made "news spread so fast" among students in various groups, those in other colleges, and the many persons who became involved.
4. *A Political process was followed.* Internal consensus among students resulted from meetings. Dealings with the police, college officials, legislators, and the governor were orderly.
5. *Economic support was gained.* Students set up a collection and dispensing system to manage money needed for expenses in the occupation and such things as buttons and banners.
6. *Coalitions strengthened the protest.* College faculty and non-student workers were recruited and involved. Students reached out to high schools and young people in general.
7. *Family interests were attended.* Students informed parents and older people in radio and television shows in Spanish and group visits to churches and community organizations.
8. *Public images were improved.* What the media began calling "spring fever" and "rowdy" was gradually taken seriously as "we kept calm" and reason prevailed over emotions.
9. *The college environment was protected.* After victory at the state level, the protest went on until local demands were met with promises by the college administration. Buildings were returned, clean and functional.

In summary, the student activists used the same empowerment and unity plan as found in our study of the final examination. Their cheer, "Education is our right, fight! fight! fight!" reaffirmed the self-determination which had brought them to college—in most cases, the first in their families. It symbolized a drive to gain equality in a society which entitles its citizens to opportunity through public schooling. The need to influence others required a dramatic display of anger and a hostile confrontation, after many peaceful efforts (massive letter-writing campaigns and lobbying) had failed. A close, harmonious relation among students was the key to their eventual victory, which shows how effectively unity works as a means to improve community life conditions.

Conclusions

Our study of the final examination in a Puerto Rican Studies class (fall 1986) revealed that the students saw the Puerto Rican identity as a living and influential factor, especially regarding family, friends, and community. What it means to be a Puerto Rican was spelled out in expectations about attributes and actions, the way to define community problems, and how solutions can be put into practice. The general result was that their values belong to a culture blended from tradition and the experience of life in the United States. Added to values from Puerto Rico, the students showed ways of thinking typical of the parent generation, people reaching mature adulthood during the 1965–75 period of awakening.

Faced with similar problems, the new generation's response resembled that of the pioneers who founded the national activist organizations. However, the experience of growing up during more conservative times and with inertia, austerity and neglect in government has influenced youth to reject public money and programs as a solution. Instead, they wanted to revitalize the community, empowering people to solve the problems. Social isolation has strengthened the Puerto Rican identity and brought about a desire to join with others having similar backgrounds. A Latino presence in immigrant communities has facilitated a relation with people who share some of their traditional culture, and the same problems of life in New York during the "post-industrial" period.

The 1989 protest made clear that the political direction of the Latino college student culture was shared by various groups of young people who belong to new immigrant communities. A common basis for the development of empowerment and unity was found in political dependence on the United States in the nations of origin, cultural differences from Anglo Americans, and a sense of alienation from the majority way of life in New York. Like the American experience in the 1965–75 period, these factors inspired an outlook that combined an awareness of discrimination, distrust of the regular means of obtaining success, and self-determination as the effective way of improving life conditions. To struggle in overcoming obstacles in an energetic but peaceful way was seen as the strategy to get whatever could be obtained in a society based on greed and scarcity. Unity was sought, especially as a means to influence others to make room for a new and different generation.

Among Central American students, for example, life conditions in New York are often viewed as a struggle between the privileged rich and the masses of poor people. They generally saw the United States as intervening in the life of ordinary people through the Central American aristocracy and promoting an environment of alienation and distrust. This outlook motivated the students' desire for freedom and democracy on their own terms. But the system of greed and scarcity was taken for granted, which meant that the struggle had to be waged by personal education and group awareness in overcoming obstacles to the improvement of common people. Students hoped to somehow influence Anglo Americans to change their negative stereotype of "smallness and ignorance" toward a positive picture of the Central American people. Their orientation resembled that of other Latinos and disposed them to solidarity with students of African, Arab, and Asian origins.

The Puerto Rican experience has served as a prototype of what living in New York means to immigrants from culturally different and politically dependent nations. The immigrant Latinos find the same discrimination and barriers to opportunity, problems of low-quality services and deteriorated neighborhoods. One response has been a continued identity by nationality. But a general plan for improvement is also developing—based on empowerment and unity, instead of public money and programs. The struggle against the obstacles of Latino aspirations includes such means as organizing people, advocacy, networking, the use of government and economic systems, coalitions uniting groups for action, improvement of a group's public image and family life, and care for neighborhood living conditions. These were found both in a study of college student values and the 1989 student protest, which gave evidence of a larger trend in changing cultural patterns during New York's transition to a post-industrial economy, from 1965 onward.

NOTES

1. I wish to thank the students in BLPR 244 for their help in providing the material for research. Permission to use the final examinations for this purpose was granted by the Hunter College Committee for the Protection of Human Subjects on May 26, 1987. Nota Bene is produced by Dragonfly Software, a division of Equal Access Systems, Inc., New York, N.Y. Version 2.0, 1987, was used to count the frequency of words and the codes for meaning. Those selected for research were tabulated as input data with a fixed format for 41 cases of essays, using the *Statistical Package for the Social Sciences*, by Hadlai Hull and Norman Nie (Hightstown, N.J.: McGraw-Hill, 1981).

2. This summarizes the complexity studied by Felix M. Padilla, *Latino Ethnic Consciousness: The Case of Mexican Americans and Puerto Ricans in Chicago* (Notre Dame, Ind.: University of Notre Dame Press, 1985). I wish to thank Dr. Padilla and Prof. Clara E. Rodríguez for their suggestions in developing this chapter.

3. This idea was influenced by Jesse M. Vázquez, "Accounting for ethnicity in the counseling relationship: a study of Puerto Rican college students," *Ethnic Groups* 1 (1977): 297–318, in which attitudes toward older Puerto Ricans are analyzed. Also important was Jesse M. Vázquez, "The ethnic matrix: implications for human service practitioners," *Explorations in Ethnic Studies*, 9, no. 2 (July 1986): 1–18, in which the student tendency to accept the values of the older generation (despite their rebellion) can be understood in terms of the intensity of feelings of identity.

6

Aspects of Puerto Rican Religious Experience: A Sociohistorical Overview

ANA MARÍA DÍAZ-STEVENS

Although the 1511 papal decree *Romanus Pontifex*, issued by Julius II created three dioceses[1] in the so-called New World, the first ranking Christian prelate on American soil was the Roman Catholic Bishop Alonso Manso, who on Christmas day 1513, arrived at the newly instituted Apostolic See in Puerto Rico with ecclesiastical jurisdiction over all the Spanish colonies. Based on this fact, Puerto Rico can claim the distinction of being the door through which the institution of Christianity officially enters the newly "discovered" territories. The significance of Puerto Rico as the first site for the initial institutionalization of Christianity in the New World becomes evident when one considers the strong relationship that existed between three basic institutions instrumental in the colonization of the New World: the Church, the Audiencia, and the military. Given the geographic distance and the isolation in which the island of Puerto Rico was kept, especially during this first colonization period, it is important to note the geographic separation of the first official Apostolic See and the Audiencia (established in Santo Domingo). The establishment of the first Apostolic See in Puerto Rico was perhaps one of the few events that gave the often-forgotten island some recognition and preeminence, as was the naming of Manso official inquisitor, a "privilege" many of us would rather forget. But if the importance of this event eludes us, at the very least it should be recognized that by the time the Pilgrims landed at Plymouth Rock on the North American continent, the Christian faith had approximately a century to take root and grow in what was then a Spanish colony and is now a Caribbean territory under the U.S. flag. But Catholicism is not Puerto Rico's only religion. African beliefs, the remnants of the religion of the indigenous Tainos (usually now subsumed under African-based religious practices), French Spiritism (from the teaching of Allan Kardec), and Protestantism and Pentecostalism from the United States also have deep roots among the Puerto Rican people. More recently, after the Cuban Revolution, the introduction of Afro-Cuban religion Santería has made an impact, especially among the Puerto Ricans living on the U.S. mainland.

In Latin America, which served both as a field for expansion and laboratory for experimentation, Christianity underwent a transformative process, acquiring new characteristics depending on regional and cultural particularities. The transformative process in Puerto Rican religious expression is still operative and, rather than dwindling, is given new vigor in the migration of Puerto Ricans to the U.S. Thus, while a Protestant theologian in the 1960s proclaimed in England the death of God, in Spanish Harlem, Puerto Ricans sang: "Oh! Señor a tí venimos,/la comunidad hispania,/padres, hijos y familia,/ todos uno, sólo un alma." Thus, the disenchantment with the religious establishment and basic disbelief in the importance of religion among the erudite community of the modern world is not true among the poor, the working class, the common people of the barrios.[2]

Religion has not fallen by the wayside because it is deeply woven into Puerto Rican culture. Tested by the crises of modern society in the most complex contemporary metropolitan area as well as by harsh deprivations imposed by a far-from-voluntary migration, the Puerto Rican migrants' faith in themselves and in their basic religious beliefs have survived with remarkable vitality. As part of their legacy, the Puerto Rican people in migration offer a new spirituality and religious mode. Church leaders have recognized that the Puerto Ricans, along with the other Latinos, are indeed "a breath of fresh air in the Church."[3] However, it remains to be seen if this new mode of religion will be maintained, lost, or further transformed as the Puerto Rican population disperses throughout the different regions and states of the union.

It has become clear that if the Catholic Church is to maintain clout in New York City it must also keep the fealty of the Puerto Rican and Latino communities. The Latino population is one of the fastest-growing ethno-minority groups in terms of demographics and is the fastest-growing group within the Catholic Church. The

United States is the home of the fifth largest Spanish-speaking population in the world. Nationwide, Latinos are the most numerous American ethnic Catholics, thus surpassing the Italians, who until recently claimed that distinction. Worldwide, the Latino communities of this country, along with Spanish-speaking European, Caribbean, and South American nations, constitute the largest language group of Catholics. Catholicism, as practiced by the Latinos in general and by Puerto Ricans in particular, historically has been a religion of the home and community. The practice of the faith has not been tied to the ecclesiastical institution, nor has it depended purely on the services of the clergy.

In an earlier study I have outlined how the condition of being identified as the "periphery" affected certain regions during Spanish colonialism and how this, in turn, affected the proximity and relationship of the people to the religious institutions (see Díaz-Stevens and Stevens-Arroyo, 1992). Here I would like to: (1) outline the historical process that has fashioned the Puerto Rican religious expression since Spanish colonial times; (2) summarize how Puerto Rican Catholicism differs not only from that of European immigrant groups but other Latinos such as the Mexicans; (3) explain what happened to Catholicism as U.S. institutions, including the Protestant churches, were implanted in Puerto Rico after 1898; (4) analyze the role of religion in the migration of Puerto Ricans to the northeast; and finally (5) describe the impact upon religion and the Church.

Historical Backdrop

The characteristics of Puerto Rican Catholicism depend upon the urban-rural dichotomy that evolved because Spanish policy neglected the island's countryside. More deeply felt during the first two and a half centuries of the colonization, this isolation continued throughout the entire process until 1898, when the U.S. marines arrived at Guánica on the southern shore of the island. Of great importance in Puerto Rico's history is its role in providing a transition from the medieval forms of conversion to the approaches implemented later on the American continents. Medieval practice favored conversion *en masse* through the acceptance of the native ruler into the Church. However, divine intervention or miraculous appearances, such as that of Our Lady of Guadalupe in Mexico, was the preferred way of legitimizing the acceptance of a *"pueblo"* to the fold. The acceptance and promulgation of conversion *en masse* was closely tied to the state recognition of power, which meant that only Christians could be lords. In Puerto Rico and the Caribbean the *encomienda* system was the legal device utilized to elevate common Spaniards to a position of "protector" over the natives, assuming for the lands and colonizers of the newly settled territories responsibilities resembling those of European feudal lords. As benign as the *encomienda* may have appeared on paper, in actual practice, rather than a voluntary trade-off of service for defense, it was denounced by such persons as Antón de Montesinos and Bartolomé de las Casas as a masked manipulation to perpetuate the exploitation of resources and the enslavement of the natives.

Spanish Policies: Basis for the Island's Isolation and Rural Neglect

The Spanish policy of concentrating resources for the fortification of San Juan and development of the urban coastal towns with easy access to the open sea, brought undue hardship and isolation to the hinterlands. The restrictions on Puerto Rico's trade throughout the seventeenth and until the first half of the eighteenth century unintentionally set the basis for contraband trade. This left the royal treasury in arrears, to the detriment of public works and roads (Figueroa 1972; 101), while concentrating economic power in the hands of a few shrewd "entrepreneurs" who saw in the need for basic commodities for the inhabitants a tremendous opportunity to satisfy their own greed. These policies and the infrequent travel between the empire and the small colony kept the island isolated from the metropolis and the interior mountain region virtually cut off from the urban coastal towns, producing a society of deep contrasts, where differences between rural and urban life-styles ran deep (Silvestrini and Sánchez 1987: 174 ff.). During these centuries Puerto Rico was little more than a military outpost for Spain valued mostly for its strategic position. Despite official pronouncements, Puerto Rico and other neighboring islands also became a center of operation for smugglers, oftentimes with the active participation and protection of the very same officials who were responsible for implementing law and order (see Figueroa 1972: 79 ff., and 101, 144).

During this period, roughly from 1539 to 1765, the foundations of a Puerto Rican society were set. It assumed the following characteristics that distinguish the Caribbean from Mexico and other continental colonies: the island's isolation from Spain; the separation and the lack of communication between the coastal urban centers and the interior; the neglect of the hinterland; the early disappearance of the native people due either to flight from the island, miscegenation, or various natural or man-made causes; the rapid depletion of gold; and dependency upon an extraofficial market and economy (bartering and contraband trade, especially in the urban centers) for basic commodities. Puerto Rico, moreover, was different from other Caribbean colonies because it had fewer slaves throughout the colonial period and a less-developed sugar plantation economy.

Racial and cultural mixing

Miscegenation, particularly among the lower class, was the norm, not the exception, for the island's population, even while Spain made laws to regularize and even prevent racial intermarriage (Figueroa 1972). But, unlike Mexico, where *mestizaje* means a mixture of Indian and Spanish blood, in Puerto Rico and other areas of the Caribbean the percentage of African blood is much higher. This is not to say that Taínian blood in the Puerto Rican population is nonexistent.[4] Culturally, however, except for some remnants in language and the names of places, Taíno culture has been extinct since the sixteenth century.

Lacking a strong Taínian impact, Puerto Rican Catholicism is strikingly different from the Mexican experience and from that of other Latin American countries where an appreciable Indian influence endures. Those Taínian influences that do persist are cloaked in the spirit and life-style of the *jíbaro* or mountain dweller, since it was to the mountains that the Indians remaining on the island fled in their desire to be freed from Spanish power and control. Other persisting remnants may be discovered in the mixing of African beliefs with Taínian mythology and practices as a result of the hybridization that took place between these two peoples in

Puerto Rico and on neighboring islands where they escaped as
cimarrones (runaway slaves).

From 1607 to 1633, only 2,240 slaves were imported to replace
the Taínos as a cheap labor force. Since there had been as many as
35,000 Indians at the Spaniards' arrival, the black population
scarcely replaced the Taínos. Nearly a century and a half later, in
1765, on the eve of the large-scale sugar cultivation effort that would
considerably expand the island's population, there were only 5,037
black slaves in Puerto Rico. This constituted 10 percent of the 39,846
inhabitants.[5] If we estimate the free blacks and mulattos at another
10 percent, that would bring the number of blacks and mulattos to
20 percent of the total population, a smaller percentage than that
in other sugar-producing Caribbean islands, such as Cuba. So while,
on the one hand, what remains of the Taínian culture is less significant than the Indian influence present in other parts of Latin
America, on the other hand, the African impact in Puerto Rico is
not as high as in other parts of the Caribbean. However, the black
presence in Puerto Rico brought with it customs and traditions
which have persisted and which added a dimension to the Caribbean experience not widely found among people of Mexican origin.
Until the reforms of the Enlightenment in the middle of the eighteenth century, these economic, social, and demographic factors
constituted the historical backdrop for Puerto Rico's development.

Development of a jíbaro *cosmovision and spirituality*

In the interior mountain region, far from the urban centers and
their activities, the *jíbaros* developed their own response to the
Spanish institutions and to their own environment. For the most
part, the response to the institutions was one of aloofness and even
disdain for the urban centers and their "upper-class *blanquitos*"
with their laws and contrived mannerisms. Ultimately what was
at stake was a means of subverting these laws, of twisting them to
the *jíbaros'* advantage, because as was commonly believed *"aquel
que hace la ley, hace la trampa."* (The person who makes the law also
knows how to circumvent it.) This mentality has persisted until the
present day and is encapsulated in phrases such as *"Yo, como soy
bruto . . ."* (Since I am a numbskull), used as a common excuse to
shun responsibility before an urban dictum or to cast suspicion

upon its applicability. In fact, it is a cunning way of manifesting contempt, not for one's own abilities, but for a way of life that is judged unfamiliar and even inferior despite its pretensions. The oblique way in which even the Puerto Rican of today looks at life's exigencies and reacts toward the unknown has been called *peleita monga* and can be roughly translated as circumventive aggressiveness (see Albizu Miranda and Marty Torres 1958).

In a rural society where former soldiers and sailors, active pirates and privateers predominated, religion had an uphill battle. Following the official policy for other institutions, parish churches were not erected in the rural settlements. At best there were some scattered *ermitas*, or shrines, cared for by lay persons who, despite their personal piety and religious commitment, had no authority or preparation to celebrate the liturgy or impart the sacraments. Infrequently visited by overworked and sometimes uninterested clergy, the *ermitas*, nonetheless, became the center of communal prayer and devotion. Where there were no *ermitas*, oftentimes one of the homes would become the place of prayerful reunion. In most cases home altars were prepared where the few statues brought by an ancestor in migration or the *santos de palo* carved by local artists had their place of honor. In the absence of an ordained clergy, lay people took on the responsibility of directing the prayers. With the passage of time such a role became invested with an aura of prestige and was accepted as a privileged position within the rural community. Because in this transformative process the person sought had to be a paragon of virtue and wisdom, oftentimes the task fell to an elderly woman, who was given the name of *rezadora*. Among the roles that assumed importance in rural society were those of the *rezadora* and of the *comadrona*, who, due to the high rate of infant mortality, added the role of baptizer to that of midwifery.

Close to the cycle of nature and committed to an often difficult struggle for subsistence, the people of the rural areas fashioned a religious expression around the two things without which their existence would not be possible—land and family. And since family went far beyond the father-mother-siblings nucleus to include grandparents, uncles, aunts, cousins, in-laws, etc., the religious expression that emerged was ultimately communal in nature. These traditions are so rooted in a communal identity and ethnic origins that at times they operate more as culture than as a faith commitment. This is not to deny religious meaning to such traditions, since they form the core of what is today known as "popular religiosity," projecting the unarticulated premises of faith and religious commitment. These early roots of Puerto Rican Christianity, greatly influenced by medieval traditions, were molded by the Puerto Rican personality and environment to become for us today a unique and autochthonous expression of the Catholic faith.[6]

A livelihood based on subsistence farming also meant that people were very dependent on nature's goodness and on divine benevolence. Thus religious practices and nature's cycles were very closely tied together. The planting and pasturage season, for example, usually began in early February and was initiated by the Feasts of the Purification of Mary (*Nuestra Señora de la Candelaria*) and of St. Blaise. These two feasts coincided with the clearing of the land for planting and the spring mating of the herds. Bonfires were set ablaze at dusk amidst the shouts of "*¡Qué vivan San Blás y La Candelaria!*"; each family trying to outdo the other in joyful clamors and the size of the bonfires. When these died down the community met for prayers. Those who could go to town that day would have their throats blessed by the priests; if not, a blessing in the home by the oldest person of the family would suffice. As in Spain and much of Europe, fire and light are associated with Candlemas and blessing with candles for St. Blaise, but coincided with the old Roman feast of Lupercalia, which celebrated the fertility of flocks of sheep.

Easter brought springtime feasts, with special attention to vicarious identification with the sufferings of Christ. Good Friday, with its emphasis upon fasting and pain, sometimes supplanted Easter Sunday in the focus of Christian celebration. The springtime feast of the Finding of the Holy Cross (May 3) coincides with the month dedicated to the Blessed Virgin Mary and both allowed for the introduction of femininity into festivals of spring. These included various processions, often with young women assuming important roles, in which a statue of Mary is crowned with flowers or a home altar is erected with a prominent cross amidst flowers and candles, and before which people from the community come to sing a special rosary called *rosario de cruz*.

Among the summertime feasts were those of St. John the Baptist (June 24) and Our Lady of Mount Carmel (July 16), which were of relevance to the maritime settlements, and included various forms of bathing and the blessing of waters. The Feast of St. James the Apostle (July 25) has rich roots in Iberian practice, where he is referred to as Matamoros and was used to reenact symbolically the centuries-long wars between Christians and Moors. In Puerto Rico, La Fiesta de Santiago was celebrated by donning costumes reminiscent of a Spanish past. Loiza Aldea in Puerto Rico, where a heavy concentration of people of African descent live today, is famous for the celebration of this fiesta and for the *vejigantes* masks made of papier maché or coconut husks. Curiously, this very Spanish feast has acquired a new Puertoricanized meaning (see Ricardo Alegría 1983).

The harvest season was marked by celebrations of prominent feasts such as St. Michael the Archangel (September 29), St. Francis of Assisi (October 4), Our Lady of the Rosary (October 7) and St. Raphael Archangel (October 24). These liturgical feasts would often be matched with particular harvest or other autumn agricultural practices. The feasts of All Saints (November 1) and All Souls (November 2) carried resonances of pre-Christian rites that communicated with the dead. Every household would secure its supply of candles which were lighted immediately after dusk in memory of the dead members of that family and community. It was believed that if an offer of candles and prayers for the repose of the departed souls was not made, this would provoke the souls' restlessness, forcing them to visit the neglectful families or individuals to remind them of their responsibilities. A favorite prank was to wait until dark to dress up in black so as to be unnoticed and go to the neighboring houses assuming the identity of a recently departed relative to *asustarlos* or "haunt" them. People usually did not like to go out that night for fear that they would encounter some apparition of *ánimas en pena*, that is, unsatisfied or suffering departed souls.

Even today, the most important cycle is that of Christmas which begins around the Feast of the Immaculate Conception (December 8) and ends the second Sunday of January, called "Bethlehem's Octave." Sometimes people like to begin celebrating at the end of November and prolong the festivities another week, referred to as *la octavita*. The nine consecutive days before Christmas are celebrated with masses at dawn, called *Misas de Aguinaldo* (sometimes, *Misas de la Aurora*), ending with *la Misa del Gallo*, on Christmas eve. The *aguinaldo* meaning "gift," has also become a musical form of particular creativity, allowing native instruments and improvised versification in a popular style. It is this type of music which is utilized as neighbors go from house to house giving *asaltos* or *parrandas*, partaking of drink, food, good conversation, and merry-making along the way, until all the houses in the neighborhood have been visited and members from the different households have joined in the group.

In addition each town has its patron saint, so that the village would often add a week of festivities not unlike medieval feasts that symbolically united the different classes in a common Christian belief and practice. Civic, religious, and even ribald elements of parades, processions, and carousing were put into stark conjuncture that celebrated the community as much as the saint's life and works.[7]

In mid-nineteenth-century Spain and Latin America, the anti-clerical movements distanced the upper classes still further from traditional expressions of Catholicism. With such antagonism toward the Church, especially among those agitating for governmental reforms, these expressions of the common people were sometimes targeted for attack and eradication. In Puerto Rico, agitation for separation from Spain and the island's independence formed the basis for a nationalist sentiment that endured until the United States' invasion of 1898. With the Catholic Church's identification with Spanish rule, Puerto Rican nationalism was generally held to be incompatible with Catholicism. However, the deep roots of traditional religious practice among the common people permitted a turnabout of this nationalist vs. Catholicism dichotomy. Both in New Mexico, where Father Antonia José Martínez (1793–1867) articulated a prophetic form of Catholic practice identified with the common people and in Puerto Rico where leaders like José de Diego (1866–1918) and Pedro Albizu Campos (1891–1965) advocated independence and Catholicism, popular religiosity acquired a powerful political significance. In the case of Puerto Rico, even when deep nationalistic feelings have been registered, Puerto Rican anticlericalism has not been as strong as in some Latin American nations or Spain.

The North American Connection

To understand the Puerto Ricans' religious reality today it becomes necessary to first understand the processes of Americanization and

Protestantization among them. The two terms describe a process of change in values and in patterns of social behavior. The first term refers to the political and legal aspects of this change, including the adoption of the English language, while the latter is the remaking of religious organization and expression into the general mold of the Reformation. In relationship to the religious institution, this means an egalitarian choice of church leaders, emphasis upon individual revelation through the reading of the Scriptures rather than a dependency upon tradition for discernment of the divine, exclusion of devotion to Mary and the saints, a paucity of religious symbols, such as statues, medals, candles, etc.

So much of popular culture in the U.S. reflects values deriving from the Protestant matrix that it is difficult to avoid the conclusion, frequently expressed in tabloids and scholarly presentations alike, that the dominant culture of the U.S. is Protestant. Tying together North American political economic power with Protestantism, some intellectuals consider Protestantism more "modern" and "enlightened." Thus, the nineteenth-century educator-sociologist Eugenio María de Hostos theorized that the Catholic religion represented mankind in its infancy, Protestantism its adolescence, and agnosticism its adulthood. His thought echoes some of the premises of his contemporary Max Weber.

It was such an assumption that persuaded many to propose the elimination, or at least the subordination, of Catholicism and the Spanish language and culture in Puerto Rico as a means toward the implantation of a Protestantism accompanied by the acquisition of the Anglo-Saxon language and U.S. values and culture. In 1903, for example, the Protestant missionary publication *El defensor cristiano* printed an article in which a warning was issued concerning the threat of "Romanism," which is described as a hindrance "to any democratic system and to those who seek freedom but continue to support the Romanist system. . . ." *El defensor cristiano* declared that the Puerto Rican Catholics were like blind people "seeking an unrealizable dream," because Catholicism "is opposed to" and "flees from" education and "looks upon public schools as its enemies," while Protestantism "accepts" education and "looks upon public schools as their friends."[8]

Since the supremacy of U.S. values and religion was held as a valid assumption, the Protestant religion was used to legitimize the military invasion in the nineteenth century as something necessary and beneficial to the people and their island, just as the Catholic religion had in the sixteenth and seventeenth. In fact people such as Commander George G. Groff established a close relationship between military and religious enterprises, viewing the U.S. intervention in Puerto Rico as a commitment both civil and divine. Thus, he called upon "good men, who can see in others, and understand even Latins. . .to spy out the land and to establish pioneer churches, and specialty schools."[9] The same sentiment was echoed by David W. Creane when the George O. Robinson Orphanage Building in San Juan was being erected:

> It is no slight task laid upon our Government by Divine Providence to bring the people of Porto Rico to the highest standard of American citizenship—and nothing short of that will satisfy God. . . . We stand professed witness to Gospel power to save, regenerate, and inspire men to godly service.[10]

Rather than a mere personal view of individual inclination, this way of thinking was reflected in much of the Protestant missionary literature of the day published on both the island and the mainland. The 1906 Annual Report of the Board of Missions of the Presbyterian Church in the U.S.A. used language which linked the work of U.S. religious and government institutions in Puerto Rico and described that work as a mandate:

> Under the influence of our commerce and schools and religious philanthropic agencies the character of the people is being transformed. But if the great masses of these are to be lifted out of darkness into the light and prepared for the exercise of the prerogatives and privileges of American citizenship, then must the work of education and Christian evangelization not only be maintained, but enlarged and persecuted with new vigor and earnestness.[11]

Thus, despite more complex and controlled ways of subjugation, the basic attitude of the English-speaking Protestant North Americans toward Puerto Ricans was scarcely different from that of the Spanish Catholics who centuries before had done the same with the Taíno and other aboriginal populations.[12]

Considered as inferior to Protestantism and English, the religion of the people, Catholicism, and their language, Spanish, were marked for destruction. It is difficult, then, to adequately understand the shape religion has taken among Puerto Ricans during this century without first accepting the complicity of the U.S. in this process. On the premise that everything funded by the Spanish government was public property, U.S. rule brought claims that parish schools, rectories, cemeteries, hospitals, convents, and even church buildings were town properties. The Church was humiliated to the point of being forced to appeal to the Supreme Court of the U.S. in 1908 to reclaim some of its material resources. Ultimately these claims and counterclaims by Church leadership were settled out of court, but the Spanish clergy were denied the usual salary paid by the state. With no other means of support many were forced to return to Spain. Those who stayed had to declare their citizenship at the end of three years or return to Spain. Those wanting to come in for the first time or those wanting to return to the island had to petition for a visa.[13] Emphasizing the denial of financial sustenance from the state as the cause for departure, while downplaying Spanish national pride and patriotic sentiment, U.S. Protestant and Catholic leadership alike equated the Spanish priests' departure from the island with a supposed lack of zeal for the apostolate. Such an assessment of the situation led persons such as Father Thomas Sherman, chaplain to the American army of occupation in Puerto Rico and son of General William Tecumseh Sherman, to describe institutional Catholicism in Puerto Rico as virtually bankrupt.

> Puerto Rico is a Catholic country without religion whatever. The clergy do not seem to have any firm hold on the native people, nor do they have any lively sympathy with the Puerto Ricans or Puerto Rico. . . . Now that the priests are deprived of government aid, many are leaving the country. The Church was so united with the State and so identified with it in the eyes of the people that it must share the odium with which the Spanish rule is commonly regarded. . . . Religion is dead on the island.[14]

Control of the school system and its manipulation for the twin goals of Protestantization and Americanization was another powerful tool to disestablish Catholicism.

> That this education should be in English we are clearly of the opinion. . . . Porto Rico is now and is henceforth to be a part of the American possessions and its people are to be Americans. . . . The Question of good citizenship and education can be more easily settled through the public schools than by any

> other method . . . put an American schoolhouse in every valley
> and upon every hilltop in Porto Rico, and in these places the
> well-fitted and accomplished American school-teachers, and the
> cloud of ignorance will disappear as the fog flies before the
> morning sun.[15]

These "young men and young women of ability and discretion"
are seen as "true patriots . . . worthy [of] the highest commendation"
since their work is perceived as a commitment requiring "solemn
and sacred sacrifice for the Americanizing of the people of Puerto
Rico."[16] This was evident in the active collaboration of the state in
promoting and hiring of U.S. (first) and (later on) island missionaries
as teachers. On the other hand, hiring Puerto Rican teachers who
had in any way demonstrated preference for the Spanish language
and Puerto Rican independence was not only avoided but actively
militated against.[17] Furthermore, in many of the public schools the
position of principal fell to Protestant ministers' wives, who on
account of their proselytizing and Americanizing interests were
keen on the use of English as the principal medium of instruction,
even when knowledge of this language among native Puerto Rican
faculty and school administrators was, to say the least, rudimen-
tary.[18] Until 1948 the post of secretary of education was appointed
by the governor. In this overwhelmingly Catholic country, these
appointees were with few exceptions from the U.S., but even when
they were Puerto Ricans, they were always Protestants.

As a further measure to do away with Catholicism as speedily
and thoroughly as possible, in a meeting held at Riverside Church
in New York, the diverse Protestant denominations agreed to divide
up the island into portions, with each denomination concentrating
its efforts in a particular region, so as not to compete with one
another.[19] The attack upon Catholicism did not stop at the institutional level, however. U.S. officials and missionaries alike actively
engaged in the actual elimination of Puerto Rican cultural symbols.
Targeted for destruction were the most popular feast, La Fiesta de
Reyes, and the wooden *santos*,[20] objects of Puerto Rican popular
devotion and religiosity. Numerous centuries-old wooden statues,
valuable not only because they represented the people's religious
expression but because they were gems of folkart, were thus burned
in bonfires pretty much in the same way that Bishop Landa had

burnt native Mayan manuscripts centuries before in the Yucatan peninsula of southeastern Mexico.

The Development of Protestantism in Puerto Rico

The advocacy role played by the state in Puerto Rico in the introduction and spread of Protestantism explains its success only in part. The zeal and commitment of the missionaries was, of course, another important ingredient. The failure of the Catholic Church to truly educate the masses in the faith, the historical neglect of the rural areas, the diminished resources in terms both of finances and personnel wrought by the U.S. invasion and subsequent policy may be given as further explanation. The financial backing of the Protestant missionary effort by their missionary boards or headquarters in the U.S. cannot be overlooked. Neither can we ignore the role of the new converts, oftentimes resigned Catholic priests. In many instances, although subordinates to the English-speaking ministers, these ex-priests have been viewed as the apostles of Puerto Rican Protestantism.[21]

Because both material resources and top leadership positions came from and were administered by agents extraneous to the local community, this meant that power also rested in the hands of outsiders. Since the local native missionaries shared the language and culture of the people, they also had the task of preaching and recruiting new members. However, they were not allowed any policy-making decisions. What this meant for the Puerto Rican native ministers was a trade-off somewhat familiar to them; that is, less structural power, but greater freedom of action and expression at the local level among the members of his congregation.

At the beginning, a very important characteristic of Puerto Rican Protestantism was the adherence of certain areas of the island to a particular Protestant denomination, a direct consequence of the Comity Agreements signed in New York in 1898 and 1900 by which Puerto Rico was divided into missionary districts. But according to one of Puerto Rico's writers, "Puerto Ricans are a people in search of religion."[22] It was not long until frequent movements of members from one denomination to the other were registered, especially as people began to shift geographically as a result of greater industrialization of the island.

Among the non-Catholic Christians on the island, Pentecostalism claims the highest numbers today. Founded in Puerto Rico in 1916 by Salomón Feliciano Quiñones upon his return from Hawaii and California and spurred on by Juan Lugo, who was responsible for most of the organizational work, Pentecostalism increased dramatically, so that by 1930 half as many Puerto Ricans were Pentecostal as those who were mainline Protestant. Pentecostalism continues to grow among the Puerto Ricans both on the island and the mainland. If in fact Pentecostalism is the fastest-growing religion among all Spanish-speaking, its beginning among many of them can be traced to this Puerto Rican experience, especially since the Puerto Rican Pentecostal churches have sent missionaries to New York, Texas, California, New Mexico, and several Latin American countries.

Another Puerto Rican religious expression which distanced itself from the Catholic, Protestant, and even Pentecostal churches is La Iglesia de Mita. Its founder and first leader was Juanita García Peraza, a Catholic converted to Pentecostalism who later also became dissatisfied with her Pentecostal congregation. Charismatic and millenarian in approach, Juanita's efforts emphasized the intervention of the Holy Spirit and her representation as the Spirit's incarnation on earth. Like Pentecostalism, this church has also been brought to areas of the U.S. where there are heavy concentrations of Puerto Ricans and Latinos and to some areas of the Caribbean and Latin America, becoming in the process the first autochthonous Puerto Rican religion to be exported.

Catholicism in Puerto Rico after 1898: The Mixing of Traditions

Like the Protestant churches, the Catholic Church also sent its missionaries and was part of the Americanization impulse. Having had years of experience with Latinos in the Southwest of the United States, but not recognizing subtle differences between the two groups, the Catholic missionaries came to Puerto Rico with the notion that this was another New Mexico. Placide Chapelle, former archbishop of Sante Fe, New Mexico, was the first apostolate delegate for Cuba and Puerto Rico at a time when both were being ruled by U.S. military governments. From 1898 to 1907 the Bavarian-born U.S. citizen James Blenck served as bishop of Puerto Rico at the insistence of the U.S. episcopate. He crusaded for the maintenance of Church properties but closed the local seminary and undermined the hopes of Puerto Rican political leaders who looked at Catholicism as a cultural and social defense against Americanization. He went as far as banning *La Misa del Gallo* on Christmas eve in the San Juan Cathedral because he considered it too rowdy and offensive to U.S. culture.[23]

In an effort to counteract the Protestant inroads on the island, Bishop Ambrose Jones, Puerto Rico's bishop from 1907 to 1921, sought to increase the number of missionaries from New York and Philadelphia. In the process the local clergy were, if not directly displaced, at least relegated to a secondary role and place of importance within their own Church.[24] Lay organizations such as Catholic Daughters of America and the Knights of Columbus were organized among the wealthy;[25] and the English-speaking pastors were preferred to the few remaining native Puerto Rican priests. For all practical purposes the Catholic Church promoted statehood for Puerto Rico, so that in 1917, when the U.S. unilaterally imposed U.S. citizenship upon the Puerto Ricans, only Blenck, who now was the archbishop of New Orleans, uncharacteristically offered any opposition to this imposition. The scarcity of native Puerto Rican priests (or of Latino priests in general) cannot be laid solely at the feet of the Spanish colonization process. Nor is the result a "defeat" in Puerto Rican commitment and spirituality; not even the by-product of a culture which values family highly. The relationship of the U.S. bishops and U.S. priests in Puerto Rico with the native clergy and a prevalent negative attitude toward Puerto Rican autonomy and the maintenance of Puerto Rican culture discouraged many a would-be candidate. Thus, the scarcity of native vocations can be tied to a certain extent to the institutional Church's attachment to the Americanization effort and to the open identification of its ecclesiastical leaders with an agenda rejecting Puerto Rican self-determination.

Ultimately, however, one of the biggest challenges facing Puerto Rican Catholics, then and now, is the native clergy. To be a priest in Puerto Rico a young man had to leave not only the family but the island, and his language and culture to be educated in the United States.[26] In this process, the social distance between him and his future flock was likely to increase. Once ordained, the native priests were stationed in the urban churches away from the remote rural areas that needed their care so badly. And yet it was in these small villages and remote areas where Catholic tradition tended to thrive as they went through a process of criollization. Once again the *jíbaros*, in their isolated mountain regions, used distance between them and the urban institutions as a means of safeguarding the traditions that they had fashioned and enjoyed for centuries. They continued to go to the urban church to procure those "religious commodities" which they could not provide for themselves, but they continued believing in a spirit world with which they sought immediate communication, just as they kept the home altars and communal devotions, and the quasi-clerical roles which they had appropriated for themselves in the absence of an ordained clergy. In Puerto Rico Los Hermanos Cheos movement and the preaching of their contemporary Madre Elena,[27] are responses of the lay community both to the neglect they felt from their Church and to the challenge of the Protestant effort. In summary, the social distance which made Puerto Ricans less important to the ecclesiastical institution also made the institution less important to Puerto Ricans, as they sought and found resources within their own communities to respond to their spiritual needs.

Puerto Rican Catholicism and the New York Experience

Although there were Puerto Ricans coming to the United States before this century, a Puerto Rican migration as such is not registered until the fateful Spanish-Cuban War turned into the Spanish-American War. One of its results was the revocation of Puerto Rico's newly acquired sovereignty as Spain was forced to hand over the island to the U.S. as the spoils of war. Because migration from the island to New York City, especially during the Great Puerto Rican Migration (1946–1964), was so large, the original *barrios* had not sufficient housing to accommodate the newcomers. Overwhelmingly young and with children, Puerto Rican migrants began to move into formerly Irish, Italian, and Jewish neighborhoods. Used to the extended rather than to nuclear family arrangement, with different tastes in music, food, and clothing, speaking a different language while having U.S. citizenship, the Puerto Rican influx meant that the social complexion and type of services available in the neighborhood, indeed in the city, had to change. An added dimension to this was the racial perception of the Puerto Ricans as nonwhite. This prompted many a white person to leave the neighborhood once Puerto Ricans began to move in.

From the Puerto Rican perspective, the challenge of living in an environment, where even nature seemed different was indeed a very difficult one. Severed, oftentimes, from the extended family and from the agricultural cycle which had defined his existence, the *migrante campesino* in New York had many adjustments to make, even in terms of religion. Like the other institutions, the churches also had to respond to the newcomers. In claiming the loyalty of most of the migrants, the Catholic Church also saw itself with a far greater challenge. For the Protestant and Pentecostal churches, besides a challenge, the newcomers presented a great opportunity for conversions.

The Catholic Church the world over is divided into dioceses. In the United States each diocese is centered around a city or (in the case of New York) a group of boroughs within a city. The dioceses are composed of neighborhood parishes, often called territorial parishes.[28] Added to these were the national parishes, serving a particular ethnic or language group, most often ministered to by clergy from religious orders based on the homeland of the group. The advantage of having national parishes were many: the clergy assigned to these knew the language and customs of those they served, the diocese did not have to invest its diocesan priests, and the parishes were self-sufficient since they were financially supported by their members. Yet, it was expected that with the passage of time the national parishes would cease to exist as their members became Americanized and joined the territorial parishes. Sociologists argue that the national parishes allowed the immigrants a continuity of cultural and religious expression, while they integrated into the receiving society, without sacrificing a cohesive group identity. The idea was to provide for an Americanizing of Catholicism rather than allowing Americanization to also become Protestantization.

In 1902 of the thirty-five national parishes in the Roman Catholic Archdioceses of New York, only one was Spanish, Our Lady of Guadalupe. Gradually more Spanish-language chapels were added: La Milagrosa, La Esperanza, Holy Agony, Most Holy Crucifix, and St. Cecilia. With the massive arrivals of the Puerto Ricans, Francis Cardinal Spellman decided not to increase the number of linguistic parishes for the Spanish-speaking. By the 1950s many of the national or linguistic parishes had lost their congregations to assimilation, age, and residential mobility, and he probably felt the same would be true for the five Spanish-language parishes already established. Yet, these parishes were important in the maintenance of Catholicism in this nation.

After consultation with the clergy, Spanish-speaking leaders, and scholars, Cardinal Spellman opted for another alternative in response to the presence of the Puerto Rican migrants in the archdiocese. He turned the existing territorial parishes into integrated parishes which would minister to both the Spanish-speaking and the English-speaking congregations. As a first measure, Spanish priests, mostly from religious congregations, were invited to join the parish staff, even if on a temporary basis. The Puerto Rican faithful were invited to become members of these parishes and to contribute to its activities and maintenance by whatever means available to them. As members of the parish they were allowed the use of parish facilities. Preference, however, was invariably given to the English-speaking group in services and resources, even when the numbers of Puerto Ricans and Latinos were greater and their parish activities better organized. Without the benefit of a Puerto Rican native clergy, ultimately the archdiocese saw the need to train its own clergy in the Spanish language, and in Puerto Rican and Latino cultures, and for this the Institute of Intercultural Communications was established in Ponce, Puerto Rico in consortium with the Catholic University there. .

In terms of utilization of existing facilities and personnel, this arrangement was an improvement over the national parish approach. It had its drawbacks, however. For one thing, the Puerto Ricans and Latinos did not feel that the parish truly belonged to them, although they did identify with the parish and worked assiduously to create a Puerto Rican/Latino worshiping community there. "Toleration" rather than "ownership" marked their "belonging."

In fact, instead of being integrated into the existing parish community, they were relegated to the basement church, where they often remained "out of the sight and mind" of church officials and the English-speaking congregation. "Let's keep them in their place," was the prevailing sentiment of the other parishioners and the older clergy.

In contrast with the Puerto Ricans in New York, who were ministered to by priests from Spain or by those in the U.S. who had learned to speak Spanish, Mexican Americans in the Southwest had their national parishes attended to by priests from Mexico, if no Mexican Americans were available. Thus, they enjoyed what Puerto Ricans did not: a truly bilingual and bicultural clergy.[29] In South Florida the arrival of Cuban clergy after 1959 was a blessing not only for the Cuban community but for the Catholic community, which, in general, was suffering a chronic lack of priests. The ecclesiastical authorities acted swiftly to incardinate or officially integrate the newly arrived Cuban priests into the institutional church, "killing two birds with one stone," so to speak.

In his response to the Puerto Rican presence, Spellman decided to go beyond the local level. Using as a paradigm the Bishops' Committee on the Spanish-speaking (formed in 1948 under the auspices of the National Council of Catholic Bishops and the National Catholic Welfare Conference as a response to the needs of the Mexican and Mexican-American farm workers in the Midwest and Texas), the Archdiocese of New York founded an Office for Spanish-American Catholic Action in 1953. This office sought to work closely with Church and government agencies on the island in order to coordinate the social concerns apostolate with the resources of parishes which were primarily interested in pastoral care of Puerto Ricans. It was through this office that the Institute of Intercultural Communications was established in 1957 with the expert help of Msgr. Ivan Illich, who was also to be the Institute's first director.[30] This effort was later expanded so that a number of training centers were established in Dunwoodie Seminary and other Catholic schools in New York to give continuity to what was offered through the Institute during the summer months and even to initiate new members who, thus far, had not been able to avail themselves of the opportunity that the Institute offered in Puerto Rico. Ordained members of the clergy, as well as seminarians, men religious and women religious[31] were incorporated into the program. However, the focus was not upon lay leadership training.

While cultural awareness of Spanish-language classes were being emphasized in the training of the clergy and religious personnel, lay persons were provided with apostolic training and given participation in pastoral care with the large-scale introduction of the Cursillo Movement after 1960. These "Little Courses in Christianity" had their origin in Spain. They utilized a retreat-type environment and instruction by lay persons in order to transform a cultural Catholicism to a vital practice of the faith. There is no question that in the Cursillo, the laity remained subordinated to the clergy adhering to the hierarchical structures of Catholicism. But the Cursillo, nonetheless, allowed lay persons to assume certain functions which had traditionally been assigned to the clergy. Sociologically speaking, the factors of personal testimony and the emotional impact of group dynamics made this movement into a Catholic version of a Protestant conversion experience. In contrast to the Cursillo in Puerto Rico, where the movement was dominated by a conservative clergy and upper- and middle-class Cuban exile elite, the New York experience of the movement offered the working-class Puerto Ricans a much-needed means for self-expression and identity as faithful members of the Church. It became so popular that in New York to be a *cursillista* and a Catholic were synonymous (see Stevens-Arroyo, 1980b).

The Cursillo did much to counteract the common image of Puerto Rican Catholics as cultural Catholics. It also helped greatly in keeping Puerto Ricans loyal to the Church and limiting the exodus to Pentecostalism. Subsequent to the Cursillo, the Catholic Church has also incorporated a Pentecostal movement within its orthodoxy that has attracted many Puerto Ricans and other Latinos to reconversion as Catholics but worshiping as Pentecostals. But the non-hierarchical model of Church instilled by the Charismatic Movement clashes with the vision of Church promoted by the Cursillo. In some instances, the two groups have found a common ground and have been able to cooperate in an amiable manner, while in others, significant differences and even hostility endure. If they do have something in common, it is their competence to compete with the proselytizing efforts of the Pentecostal churches among Latino Catholics.

The 1960s: Santería, Vatican II, and Political Unrest

Cuban tobacco workers had brought to the United States as early as 1870 an Afro-Caribbean religion called Santería, where Catholic, Spiritist, and Yoruba beliefs are mixed together to call upon and influence the spirit world. But it was not until the Cuban influx of the sixties that the impact of this belief system began to make inroads among other Latino communities, particularly among Puerto Ricans in the Northeast (see Pérez y Mena 1991). Besides the exodus of Puerto Ricans to Pentecostalism, then, Santería added a new dimension to the challenges the Catholic Church had to face in its attempt to keep the loyalty of the people. While Santería was always present among Latino musicians and artists, the repercussions of Santería among the common people would go unnoticed by many until much later. It was not until the 1980s that with the arrival of the *Marielitos*—marking the third wave of Cuban migration—its greatest impact was felt.

Perhaps one reason for the rising numbers of Puerto Rican converts to Pentecostalism on the mainland relates to the question of indigenization. Most Puerto Rican Catholics encountered an institutional Church which was not only cold but at times antagonistic. In many instances it looked down on the mode of Catholicism the Puerto Ricans had brought with them. The message many Puerto Ricans received was that their religious traditions and practices were inferior to those observed by earlier immigrants. This perception perhaps was based on the fact that the religious traditions, practices and artifacts of earlier immigrants had developed in closer contact with the ecclesiastical institutions.

Few would deny that when Pope John XXIII opened the windows of the Church by calling the bishops to the Second Vatican Council (1963–1965), a breath of fresh new ideas rushed in. For one thing, the Council brought to full flower the concept of indigenization, and in the process did for the Church the world over what the ecclesiastical institution had not done in centuries.

Liturgical reforms compelled celebration of the Mass in the language of the people and urged incorporation of local musical and cultural expressions. Questions were asked about the meaning of the Church, its role in the modern world, the nature of relations between bishops, clergy, and laity, and the role of politics and social concerns within the traditional ministry of pastoral care. In the New York Spanish-speaking apostolate, however, many of these issues had been already addressed because of the particular nature of the Puerto Rican migration and the challenge it had brought before the ecclesiastical institution. What had been the exception for the Puerto Ricans because of their particular needs now became the rule for all because of the Council's mandates. Coming as it did at the end of the Great Puerto Rican Migration, then, the Council gave legitimacy to the expression of Catholicism the Puerto Ricans had brought with them and to the "experimental response" their presence had evoked within the Church in the northeastern United States.

In the late 1960s, toward the end of Msgr. Robert Fox's tenure as head of the New York Catholic Archdiocese Hispanic apostolate,[32] the social and political upheavals underway served to underline the need for further focusing on these and similar questions. In the United States, the Civil Rights movement, the War on Poverty, the Voting Rights Act of 1965, the radical changes in immigration laws, and the Vietnam War presented both responses and further challenges. Grouped with others under the new categories of "minority" and "Hispanos," the Puerto Ricans saw their numbers grow with the influx of Latin Americans. While "diluting" their presence as Puerto Ricans, these changes cast the Puerto Ricans in new roles. As citizens they would do for other Latinos what the Latinos could not do for themselves, that is, to represent the new groups before the institutions of this society until they were integrated and naturalized.

Conscious that Catholicism was capable of change and would respond positively if Church leaders were confronted with the people's needs, the director of the Archdiocesan Office for the Spanish-speaking apostolate, Father Robert L. Stern, invited Medellín theologian Edgar Beltrán to a pastoral meeting in New York on October of 1971. This meeting confirmed the direction Stern had taken toward the indigenization of the ministry in New York and the opening up of the theological process to the laity, mostly Puerto Rican, in his charge. Thus began the process that gave rise to three Hispanic National Encounters in 1972, 1977, 1985, all in Washington, D.C.

The two basic recommendations that came out of these

Encounters addressed the Church at the institutional diocesan level and at the local community level and demonstrated the progressive stance of much of the leadership. Basically they asked for greater Latino representation at power levels and the elevation of importance of diocesan offices for the Spanish-speaking apostolates, on the one hand, and, on the other, for greater commitment of resources in terms of materials and leadership, as well as the training and recognition of parish-level movements, especially among the laity.

Subsequent to the first two Encounters, in 1983, in an attempt to give an official response to the Hispanics voice within the Catholic Church, the bishops issued a pastoral letter, *The Hispanic Presence: Challenge and Commitment.* According to Father Joseph Fitzpatrick's summary,[33] the letter "outlines the challenge to the Church in terms of ministry and response to the social, economic, and political needs of the Hispanics; and it makes a firm commitment to make available whatever resources are necessary to enable the Hispanics to become a vital and creative part of the Catholic experience in the United States." (Fitzpatrick 1987:127). To clarify the needs and aid in the response, two major studies were commissioned: the first by the Archdiocese of New York and the second by the Archdiocese of Newark.[34]

Ultimately, however, the Hispanic Pastoral Encounters and these studies had a mixed effect. In some dioceses the door was opened for the recognition of a Latino presence that had been hitherto ignored. Elsewhere, especially in places like San Antonio, where the Latino population was relatively homogenous, it added impetus to an already healthy presence. There were also places where the final result was a weakening of Latino militancy.

In places like New York and Newark, where the Latino groups were many, the institutional Church opted for adopting a neutral term, "Hispano," (sometimes, "Spanish-speaking"). While this may have helped the institution in avoiding duplication of resources, the use of the term diluted the specific focus upon national and cultural identity. The biggest losers in the postconciliar reorganization were the Puerto Ricans of New York and New Jersey, although they constitute some 65 percent of the total Latino population in those states. Already transformed into a celebration for all Latinos and the urban poor, and thus diluted in importance as a Puerto Rican fiesta during Fox's term in the archdiocesan office, the San

Juan Fiesta in honor of Puerto Rico's patron saint had now to compete for funds and sponsorship with those of Cuba, the Dominican Republic, Colombia, etc. (see Díaz-Stevens 1990). Of the three native Spanish-speaking bishops that were appointed—David Arias (a Spaniard) for Newark, René Valero (a Venezuelan) for Brooklyn, and Francisco Garmendia (a Spaniard) for New York—none was taken from the largest groups, that is, Puerto Ricans, Cubans, Dominicans, and Colombians.[35] While not antagonistic to the people they served, these bishops were at a disadvantage in mobilizing the people and keeping alive the sort of militancy that produced the successes of the Encounters' recommendations in predominantly single-nationality regions such as Miami and San Antonio.

Tokenism and cooptation and the continuous lack of a representative native clergy were additional problems. While some may claim that the Church has made enormous efforts to recruit Hispanics into the priesthood, at least in the Northeast, very little concrete evidence can be found to this effect. On the other hand, of the already limited number of vocations (priests and religious) that the Church has been able to attract, it has been able to retain but a small fraction. For example, of about a dozen Hispanic priests (Puerto Rican, Dominican, Colombian, Spaniards) working with Robert Stern during the seventies, at least five have resigned the active ministry. A good number of those who have left the active ministry cite an environment which rather than celebrates, discourages their cultural values and ethnicity.[36] It should be noted that the "leadership positions" were not given to the most qualified candidates, nor were these positions invested with real power to effect policy. Furthermore, while the choices may have been relatively good ones given the commitment and influence of these leaders with the community, their accountability was redirected. Thus, these leaders spent more time and energy in convincing the people of the correctness of institutional policies than in presenting the people's real needs before the institution. Added to these problems is that of appointing a leader who in fact is antagonistic to the community. Thus, through the imposition of incompetent leadership, through the reorientation of accountability and prioritizing, through the imposition of bureaucratic hurdles and the depletion of resources, or through appeal to personal ambition or psychological "burnout," the effectiveness of Latino leadership has been limited.[37]

Conclusion

In June 20, 1992, the directors of the offices and schools of Hispanic ministry in the Northeast sponsored a one-day bilingual conference on multiculturalism in the Church, which was held at Fordham University, Rose Hill Campus, in the Bronx. Under the title "Preparing for a Multicultural Church: 500 Years of Hispanic Religious Experience in the Americas," the conference included lay and ordained leaders in the Latino Catholic community who came together to assess the present-day needs of the Church and to celebrate the accomplishment of the apostolate among the Latinos. In the plenary session, the most innovative suggestion seemed to be the establishment of a "mini-seminary" where Latino men (single and married) could be trained for the deaconate. Besides the fact that there was already an active deaconate program in New York City dating back to the seventies, it must be remembered that this position represents a step below that of priest.[38] In other words, what was being envisioned for the Latinos was the maintenance of a position as "foot soldiers," where they would be asked to do the work of keeping alive the fealty of the Latinos for the Church but would receive very little decision-making power.

In this way, the institutional Church would assure its continuity and viability while keeping the Latinos in a subordinate position in the English-speaking groups. And yet, keeping the Latino in the fold is of paramount importance for the Church because it is among them that its greatest energy and vitality is registered. Many have come to recognize that without the active participation of Puerto Ricans and other Latinos, the Church's visibility would suffer immeasurably, not only in New York but throughout the United States, where they constitute at least 25 percent of its membership.

For some at that meeting who had been working in the Spanish-speaking apostolate for decades and who knew well its history, the conference seemed to provide grounds for the sad conclusion that after so many years of planning and projects, the Catholic Archdiocese of New York had run out of new alternatives to minister effectively to the new needs of its Puerto Rican and Latino constituencies. The institutional Church today is an institution in crisis. The New York Church of the 1960s and 1970s, with its pastoral encounters, its commissions, and its inclusive philosophy of lay involvement and participation, seems indeed a thing of the past. Both the Archdiocesan Office for the Spanish-speaking Apostolate, which showed so much promise in the 1970s, and the Northeast Pastoral Center, which came about as a result of the Hispano National Encounters, seem out of touch with the needs of the local parishes and, therefore, incapable of formulating a plan of action that keeps step with that reality.[39]

Despite the bleak prospect that dwindling institutional resources and sometimes sheer ineptitude (be it governmental or ecclesiastical) may present, there is still much room for optimism and hope. Despite their limited numbers, at the local level there are still priests and members of religious life communities who continue to unselfishly dedicate their entire lives to these communities. More and more, lay leaders are assuming greater responsibilities, and, as a whole, religion and the people's faith commitments are strong. Centuries of neglect and isolation from ecclesiastical and other urban institutions in the homeland have taught Puerto Ricans and other Latinos that the answer to their needs is not to be found at the institutional level. From history and their own hard-earned experiences they have learned to be self-reliant, to look within themselves—the individual person, the family, and the local community—for inner strength and the solution of their problems.

The social distance that kept urban and rural in a dichotomized reality back home is still operative today, despite the technological advances of their new environment. We see it in the separation of the Latinos from the English-speaking in terms of resources, leadership, and even place of worship, in the distance between archdiocesan policies and local needs, in the inability of U.S. Catholic culture with all its resources to dominate the resilient Puerto Rican religious spirit and the culture that has given it shape and expression. If there is one thing the presence of the Puerto Ricans has taught the Church in New York, it is this: one need not forsake one's ethnic roots in order to be faithful to Catholicism in this country. Reluctant to change, as any other institution, the Church continues to struggle with this reality. But change it must. In the meantime, the Puerto Rican and Latino experience continue to be a challenge and an opportunity for the Church. Already it has enhanced the Church's claim to catholicity or universality, even in spite of itself, making it possible for more than one Catholic religious expression to be manifested in this country.

NOTES

1. The dioceses were Concepción de la Vega, Santo Domingo, and Puerto Rico.

2. In fact, religious values embedded in Puerto Rican cultural traditions were deemed instrumental by Msgr. Robert Fox, head of the Hispanic apostolate office (then under the name Spanish Catholic Action) and director of the anti-poverty program Summer in the City, in counterbalancing the 1967 New York riots. For more details, see Mary Cole, *Summer in the City* (New York: Kenedy, 1968); Antonio M. Stevens-Arroyo, *Prophets Denied Honor.* (Maryknoll, N.Y.: Orbis Books, 1980); Ana María Díaz-Stevens, *Oxcart Catholicism on Fifth Avenue: The Impact of the Puerto Rican Migration upon the Archdiocese of New York* (Notre Dame, Ind.: University of Notre Dame Press, 1993). The words of the hymn quoted here are from a later 1960s recording: music and direction by musicologist Angel Pérez. Pérez later was made Coordinator of Communications for the Spanish-Speaking Apostolate of the Archdiocese of New York.

3. This is the sentiment expressed time and again by the staff of the Archdiocesan Office of Pastoral Research and especially by its director, Ruth Doyle.

4. In 1515, there were 14,636 Taínos in Puerto Rico, that is, about half of the estimated number when the Spaniards began permanent settlements in 1509. By the census of 1778 only 2,302 pure Indians on the island were recorded. One can suppose that there were many more who intermarried. Eugenio Fernández Méndez, *Historia Cultural de Puerto Rico 1493–1968* (San Juan de Puerto Rico: Edicones "El Cemí," 1970), p. 80, states: "Latinos creencia tan extendida de que la población aborigen de Puerto Rico, se extinguiera totalmente está basada como veremos, en una confusión entre la asimilación cultural y la extinsión biológica. Un *reciente estudio de la biología humana de Puerto Rico,* aparte de los testimonios históricos de Abbad y Lasierra y Salvador Brau, *nos ofrece sobrado razón para creer que una parte considerable de la composicón genética de nuestra población deriva de la ascendencia indígena"* (my emphasis.) In

note 17, he gives as reference, Fred P. Thieme, *The Puerto Rican Population: A Study in Human Biology*, (Ann Arbor: University of Michigan Press, 1959). He also cites his own work, especially, *Encomiendas y Esclavitud de los Indios de Puerto Rico 1508–1550*. (Seville: Escuela de Estudios Hispanoamericanos, 1967). For more information on population counts during the Spanish colonization period see Loida Figueroa, *History of Puerto Rico* (New York: Anaya Book Co., 1972).

5. These numbers and estimates are based on demographic data reported by Blanca G. Silvestrini and María Dolores Luque de Sánchez, Loida Figueroa, and Eugenio Fernández Méndez. See Loida Figueroa, *History of Puerto Rico*, pp. 107–28. Page 83 gives the results of a 1530 census conducted under don Francisco Manuel de Lando. On page 74, note 61, Figueroa gives a table comparing the racial make-up of the population from 1771 to 1778. On p. 112, note 117, mentions that Camp Marshall Alejandro O'Reilly arrived in Puerto Rico in 1765 to obtain general information. Immediately he set out to assess the conditions of the island. Among other things he conducted a settlement-by-settlement census and found that "Of the slaves, there was a total of 3,439 men and women (no specifications of [by gender] sexes) and 1,598 children (again no specifications of [by gender] sexes). Eugenio Fernández Méndez, *Historia Cultural de Puerto Rico 1493–1968* (San Juan de Puerto Rico: Ediciones "El Cemí," 1970), on p. 168, states: "En los años de 1765 a 1794 los esclavos en Puerto Rico aumentaron en un 300 por ciento," giving as reference J. J. Acosta, "Nota en *Historial de Iñigo Abbad*, p. 362). Blanca Silvestrini and María Dolores Luque de Sánchez, *Historia de Puerto Rico: Trayectoria de un pueblo*. (San Juan de Puerto Rico: Cultural Puertorriqueña, Inc., 1987), pp. 200–3 give demographic statistics for the 1700s tracing the population growth by ethnic/racial composition. The graph on p. 202 seems to have inverted the categories "White" and "Indigenous." The information on "Slaves" corroborate the rate of growth quoted by Fernández Méndez.

6. See Jaime Vidal, "Towards an Understanding of Synthesis in Iberian and Hispanic American Popular Religiosity," in *An Enduring Flame: Studies on Latino Popular Religiosity*, ed. Anthony M. Stevens Arroyo and Ana María Díaz-Stevens (New York: Bildner Books, 1994).

7. For a summary of the nature of medieval patron feasts and how one of these *fiestas* was brought to and transformed in New York by the Puerto Rican migration, see Ana María Díaz-Stevens, "From Puerto Rican to Hispanic: The Politics of the *Fiestas Patronales* in New York," *Latino Studies Journal* 1, no. 1 (January 1990): 28–47.

8. Quoted by Emilio Pantojas García, *La iglesia protestante y la americanización de Puerto Rico* (San Juan de Puerto Rico: PRISA, n.d.), pp. 21, 22.

9. Quoted in Emilio Pantojas García, p. 14. See also Aida Negrón de Montilla, *Americanization, Puerto Rico and the Public School System, 1900–1930* (Río Piedras, Puerto Rico: Editorial Universitaria, 1975).

10. Quoted by Pantojas García, p. 14.

11. Quoted in Pantojas García, p. 23.

12. For a sample of the type of literature that was being produced and made accessible to educators and missionaries see Joseph B. Seabury, *Porto Rico: The Land of the Rich Port*, Box XII of the series The World and Its People (New York, Boston, and Chicago: Silver, Burdett and Company, 1903). See esp. pp. 45 and 46: "The people are excitable, fond of amusements, and they read very little. In these respects the Porto Rican of to-day resembles the Spaniard of four hundred years ago. The ancestors of many of the Porto Ricans came from Andalusia. This province bears a relation to the other provinces of Spain somewhat similar to that of Ireland to Great Britain. Like the Irish, the Andalusians are bright, witty, rather quick-tempered, perhaps, but never holding a grudge. A similar temperament is characteristic of the people of Porto Rico. Although the blood of different classes mingles freely in their veins, they have never been a rebellious or a warlike people. No general insurrection has ever occurred on the island. If any criticism can be brought to bear upon them, it is that they have been too submissive and long-suffering under Spanish rule. They have never shown a warlike spirit towards the people of other islands, and they are, on the whole, orderly and docile, peaceable, industrious, considerate of one another's welfare. They are anxious to become American citizens and to acquire American ways. They have long considered the United States another name for fidelity, humanity, and brotherly love. They are as Dr. Carroll says, good material of which to make steady and trusty American citizens." In 1926, however, another writer also studied

by educators and missionaries to the island, revisited the issue of the education and Americanization of Puerto Ricans. See Knowlton Mixer, *Porto Rico: History and Conditions, Social, Economic and Political* (New York: Macmillan, 1926), pp. xiv, xv. "This education [bilingual or adding English to the curriculum] is of benefit principally to the city dweller and reaches the country districts but slowly. The 'Jíbaro' will need the fostering care of a benevolent government for another generation at least. That he should be left to the exploitation of the city lawyers and politicians is the danger inherent in a too rapid extension of autonomy. Porto Rico is the natural meeting ground for Latin and Anglo-Saxon America and in this lies our opportunity to strengthen the bond between the continents, not through Americanization of the Island, but by making it the center of exchange of knowledge between the people, the binding link in the chain of good will uniting two continents."

13. Loida Figueroa, *Breve historia de Puerto Rico*, Part Two (Río Piedras: Editorial Edil, 1977), p. 272, explains that U.S. officials considered giving the inhabitants of "the new conquered territories" the same rights or recognition given to those granted to "the uncivilized tribes of Alaska." Basically, what was proposed and determined was to maintain Puerto Ricans (who were perceived as less than civilized aborigines) as wards of the United States with no citizenship and to extend to Spaniards (whom they saw as civilized Spanish citizens) an option to stay and declare U.S. citizenship at the end of three years. The United States seemed to have turned a deaf ear to the claims that Puerto Ricans, like Spaniards, were Spanish citizens. On page 384, after analyzing the disruptive impact of the new regime upon the institutional Catholic church in Puerto Rico and citing Edward J. Berbusse, S.J., *The United States in Puerto Rico* (Chapel Hill: University of North Carolina Press, 1966), pp. 107, 195, 203, Figueroa (herself a Protestant) concludes: "En consecuencia, la abrupta cancelación del subsidio eclesiástico asignado en el presupuesto insular, equivalente a 92,000 pesos anuales, dejaba a la jerarquía sin medio para sostener el culto religioso en el país." (The abrupt cancellation of the ecclesiastical subsidiary of 92,000 pesos designated annually in the insular budget, left the [Catholic] hierarchy without means to sustain religious work [worship] in this country.)

14. Quoted in Arthur James, *Thirty Years in Puerto Rico*, 1927,

pp. 32, 33. For a more detailed account of the conflicts between the Catholic Church and the U.S. colonial regime in Puerto Rico, see Elisa Julían de Nieves, *The Catholic Church in Colonial Puerto Rico, 1898–1964* (Río Piedras: Editorial Edil, 1982).

15. *Insular Affairs, Report of the U.S. Commission to the Secretary of War; Upon Investigation made into the Civil Affairs of the Island of Porto Rico with Recommendations* (Washington, D.C.: Government Printing Office, 1898), p. 53.

16. Puerto Rico, Commissioner of Education Office, *Annual Report of the Commissioner, 1900*, pp. 13, 15.

17. Paul G. Miller, appointed Commissioner of Education for Puerto Rico in 1915, wrote: "My attention has been called to the fact that a group of University students have sent a petition to the House of Representatives asking for the amendment to a Resolution to the effect that a definite demand for independence for Puerto Rico be made. Since this petition is made by American citizens at a time when the nation has been carefully scrutinizing the loyalty of all its citizens, I hereby order you to send me a list of all members of the graduating class who plan to enter the teaching profession. I will not appoint or approve any nomination by a school board in favor of any person whose loyalty to the United States of America is in doubt. Please make this list available to me." Appeared in *La Democracia*, January 18, 1919, p.1.

18. The U.S. policy of mandating the use of English in the public school system in Puerto Rico has been documented and analyzed in detail by Aida Negrón de Montilla. For a humorous interpretation of this situation, see *"Peyo Mercé enseña inglés"* by Abelardo Díaz Alfaro, in *Short Stories from Puerto Rico*, edited by Kal Wagenheim (San Juan de Puerto Rico: Institute de Cultura Puertorriqueña, 1971).

19. See Donald T. Moore, "Puerto Rico para Cristo" (Ph.D. diss. Southwest Baptist Seminary, Fort Worth, Texas, 1969). Also see CIDOC, Sondeos, N. 43. On pp. 2–3, Moore reports that at that "remarkable prayer meeting" they "knelt around the map . . . upon the table and prayed that God might help us to enter Puerto Rico in such a way that there might never be any missionary hostility of any kind in that island."

20. See Elisa Julián de Nieves, p. 246. Speaking of René Marqués, a well-known Puerto Rican playwright, author of *La car-*

reta, Julián de Nieves writes: "While he argued that the decline of peasant imagery could not be blamed exclusively on some fanatic evangelists who reportedly burned and threw hand-carved figures of saints into the river, he claimed that the Protestant campaign against this folk art 'dramatizes in concrete form the broader and more general problem posed between Hispanic, agrarian and Catholic tradition and the Protestant, industrial and Saxon influence'" (p. 246). Accounts of the destruction of these saints and other Catholic religious devotional materials were common in Puerto Rico even in the 1950s, when I was an elementary school student on the island.

21. For more detailed information concerning the various priests who left the Catholic Church and became active Protestant leaders on the island and how they were viewed, see Moore, "Puerto Rico para Cristo."

22. To Pedro Juan Soto is attributed the opinion that Puerto Ricans are not so much a religious people as a people always in search of religious experiences.

23. Quoting René Marqués, Elisa Julián de Nieves writes: "The church of San Felipe, now a Cathedral, among other ritual spectacles at different times of the years, used to present at the *aguinaldo* and *gallo* masses a pageantry of male and female pastors [shepherds and shepherdesses] in their picturesque attire, [with] their *cascabeles* and *panderetas*, singing carols and almost dancing, before the main altar, spectacles that are fascinatingly profane which the Puritan priests of the North eliminated on taking charge of the parish. They also tried to do away with the three classic processions of the Holy Week, those of the Sepulture, the Solitude and the Encounter. They were not able to go that far, but they did succeed in depriving them of their traditional beatitude, splendour and popular spontaneity" (*The Catholic Church in Colonial Puerto Rico: 1898–1964* [Rio Piedras: Editoral Edil, 1982], pp. 245, 246).

24. Elisa Julián de Nieves says that in 1897, "the Puerto Rican clerics made up 21 percent of the parochial clergy (29 out of 138); in 1960, they stood at 9 percent (29 out of 302). In sum, the parish under the American stewardship was to a much greater extent the domain of the foreign clergy than it was in Spanish times and consequently further removed from the spiritual leadership of fellow nationals. The practice since the beginning of the American episcopacy was to place whole parishes, even vicarages, under one

or other of the religious communities, or to put it more accurately, to recruit one of the congregations to take full charge of one or more parishes. The pioneering instruments in this process of denaturalization of the Puerto Rican parish were the American Redemptorists" (p. 82). Bishop Jones's episcopacy was marked by what in hindsight may be described as inconsistencies. While he sought to "Americanize" the Catholic Church in Puerto Rico, instituted a Catholic school system consistent with that of the U.S., and seemed to favor the clergy from the U.S. over those he found on the island (whether native or Spaniards), he also instituted a native seminary and many other institutions, such as hospitals, convents, and orphanages. Many saw him as a sweet-tempered, humble man and others as pompous and autocratic. See Julián de Nieves, pp. 95–99.

25. Julián de Nieves states that through their activities the Knights fomented "love of country, meaning the United States, loyalty to the regime and cultural assimilation." And that "at their annual convention in 1924, they resolved to seek the incorporation of the insular diocese to the Catholic hierarchy of the United States" (p. 130).

26. This is still the case today. In the 1970s, after much heated debate and conflict in the Catholic Church in Puerto Rico, the Catholic seminary in Ponce was closed. Henceforth any candidate to the priesthood has had to leave the island, many being sent to the U.S. (Florida) for their training. See Díaz-Stevens, "La Misa Jíbara," in *Revista de Ciencias Sociales* 30, nos. 1–2 (Jan.–June 1993): 139–61.

27. Madre Elena was a lay woman who at the turn of the century took upon herself the role of preacher and teacher to counteract the efforts of the Protestant missionaries in Puerto Rico in the areas of Caguas, Cayey, Yabucoa, San Lorenzo, Patillas, and Guayama. Among other things she would gather the young women of the area to teach them reading, writing, and arithmetic, and to instruct them in the teachings of the Catholic faith. Today she is referred to as *Vuestra Madre* or Madre Elena and some believe she was the personification of Our Lady of Mount Carmel, to whom many Puerto Ricans are devoted. A sanctuary has been built in the mountain where she settled (La Santa Montaña de San Lorenzo), and dedicated to Our Lady of Mount Carmel in 1985. It has been placed under the directorship of a Puerto Rican Benedictine Priest, Jaime Reyes, who has written a book on Madre Elena. He is assisted

by members of a new congregation of religious women known as Las Hermanas de Nuestra Señora de la Aurora. The santuary is open to visits and pilgrimages.

28. In practice, the territorial parishes in the northeast were often dominated by the Irish, who had arrived in this country with experience of the Anglo-Saxon world and knowledge of the English language. It is probable that they saw themselves as closer to assimilation as "Americans" than most other groups. Irish clergy, who staffed many of the territorial parishes, outnumbered other ethnic groups both in terms of ordinary clergy and bishops, and thus held much control and political influence in their hands (see Ana María Díaz-Stevens, *Oxcart Catholicism on Fifth Avenue* [Notre Dame: University of Notre Dame Press, 1993], pp. 66–90). Many national parishes were left in the care of religious orders (or religious congregations) with no direct participation in diocesan governance. The national parishes in effect exercised far less influence in the institutional church and general society. In 1902, the Archdiocese of New York (which does not include Brooklyn and Queens) had thirteen German churches, two French, one Bohemian, four Polish, one Maronite, two Slovak, one Hungarian, eleven Italian and one Spanish.

29. Cubans, while not resorting to the national parish, received after 1959 a number of native Cuban priests and ministers who came of their own accord. In 1961 an additional 135 Cuban-based clergy were deported, including among them Bishop Eduardo Boza Masvidal and forty-five native Cuban priests.

30. Ivan Illich, a priest of Yugoslavian and Jewish ancestry, had been trained in Europe and held various doctorates before asking to be incardinated in the Archdiocese of New York. He was assigned to Incarnation parish in Upper Manhattan, where his mother was living. There he came in contact with the Puerto Rican community and was challenged by their presence to learn their language and culture. After his tenure with the Institute of Intercultural Communications, he went for a short time to Fordham University. Ultimately, he left for Cuernavaca, Mexico, where he established a center for investigation and documentation known as CIDOC, thus continuing for missionaries assigned to Latin America and other religious personnel in the United States who wanted to

work among Hispanics, what he had already instituted on behalf of the Puerto Rican apostolate in the Archdiocese of New York.

31. The terms "men religious" and "women religious" are common in Catholic circles. They are used to name men and women who through the vows of poverty, chastity, and obedience have dedicated their entire lives to serving the Church through "the religious life" in a monastic religious order or other official institutional religious congregations, societies, or institutes established for that purpose.

32. Fox, a social worker by training, was the third priest assigned to direct the apostolate at the archdiocesan level. He had also been trained in Social Catholic Action in Uruguay. Coming to this responsibility, as he did, during the years of the Johnson administration and the War on Poverty, Fox was able to secure federal funding for community work. However, under the title Summer In The City, the program that was established with the backing of these funds had to be of a nonsectarian nature. It was then that the emphasis on the Puerto Rican apostolate was lost, because the effort was refocused to be inclusive of the urban poor, including other Hispanics and African Americans.

33. For an interpretation of the Hispanic presence vis-à-vis cultural diversity in the Church, see Joseph P. Fitzpatrick, S.J. *One Church, Many Cultures: The Challenge of Diversity* (Kansas City, Mo.: Sheed and Ward, 1987), pp. 125–26.

34. The New York study goes under the title *Hispanics in New York: Religious, Cultural and Social Experiences* (1982), and the Newark study is *Presencia Nueva: Knowledge for Service and Hope, A Study of Hispanics in the Archdiocese of Newark*, (1988).

35. Interestingly, when Boston and Washington, D.C., looked for possible candidates, they found and consecrated two Puerto Ricans, Roberto González, a Capuchin, and Alvaro Corrada del Río, a Jesuit.

36. For such a declaration, see Robert Sam Anson, "The Irish Connection." *New Times*, May 17, 1974, pp. 29–33.

37. The impact of the changes of the Second Vatican Council on the Church of Puerto Rico merits a different chapter. For an analysis of how experimental parish and liturgical innovations impacted and were impacted by political issues, see Díaz-Stevens,

"La Misa Jíbara como campo de batalla sociopolítica," in *Revista de Ciencias Sociales* 30, no. 1–2 (Jan.–June, 1993): 139–61.

38. The history of the deaconate program in New York has not been exempt from conflicts. At one point the Hispanic component of the deaconate program was very successful. According to Dr. Jaime Vidal of the Notre Dame Cushwa Center for the Study of Catholicism, who was actively involved in preparing candidates for the deaconate in New York, there was at least one year where the number of candidates ordained surpassed twenty. At the insistence of the chancery, the Spanish-speaking component was fused with the English-speaking. Within a few years Hispanic candidates had decreased to negligible numbers, necessitating a reversal in the decision to combine the two components. When the Hispanic component was reinstituted as a separate program, it began again to attract larger numbers of candidates. However, the initial leaders, who had professional training (most of them at the doctoral level) in liturgy, philosophy, culture, and biblical and theological studies, were not invited back. Interview with Dr. Jaime Vidal, Assistant Director of the Notre Dame Cushwa Center for the Study of American Catholicism, Notre Dame, October 21, 1993.

39. Beyond the scope of this essay but of great importance is the role that the Catholic school system has assumed and can assume in the academic and moral education of the Puerto Rican and Hispanic communities, especially in the inner cities. Given the decrease in resources, especially in terms of ordained clergy, that the Catholic Church is facing, another question deserving further analysis is this: What role will religion and Church agencies assume amidst political and social turmoil, especially as Puerto Ricans move to smaller cities and as government cutbacks in services continually drain the vitality of their communities?

BIBLIOGRAPHY

Albizu Miranda, Carlos, and Héctor Marty Torres. 1958. "Atisbos de la personalidad puertorriqueña." *Revista de Ciencias Sociales* 2, no. 3.

Alegría, Ricardo E. 1983. *La vida de Jesucristo según el santero puertorriqueño Florencio Cabán*. San Juan de Puerto Rico: Centro de Estudios Avanzados de Puerto Rico y el Caribe.

Anson, Robert Sam. 1974. "The Irish Connection." *New Times*, May 17, pp. 29–33.

Berbusse, Edward J. 1966. *The United States in Puerto Rico*. Chapel Hill: University of North Carolina Press.

Cole, Mary. 1968. *Summer In The City*. New York: Kenedy.

Díaz Alfaro, Abelardo. 1971. "Peyo Mercé enseña inglés." In Kal Wagenheim, ed., *Short Stories from Puerto Rico*. San Juan de Puerto Rico: Instituto de Cultura Puertorriqueña.

Díaz-Stevens, Ana María. 1990. "From Puerto Rican to Hispanic: the Politics of the Fiestas Patronales in New York." *Latino Studies Journal* 1, no. 1 (January): 28–47.

———. 1993a. *Oxcart Catholicism on Fifth Avenue: The Impact of the Puerto Rican Migration upon the Archdiocese of New York*. Notre Dame: University of Notre Dame Press.

———. 1993b. "La misa jíbara como campo de batalla sociopolítica en Puerto Rico." *Revista de Ciencias Sociales* 30 (Jaunary–June): 139–61.

———. 1993c. "The Saving Grace: The Matriarchal Core of Latino Catholicism." *Latino Studies Journal* 4, no. 4 (September): 60–78.

Fernández Méndez, Eugenio. 1967. *Encomiendas y Esclavitud de los Indios de Puerto Rico 1508–1550*. Seville: Escuela de Estudios Hispanoamericanos.

———. 1970. *Historia Cultural de Puerto Rico 1493–1968*. San Juan de Puerto Rico: Ediciones "El Cemí."

Figueroa, Loida. 1972. *History of Puerto Rico*. New York: Anaya Book Co.

———. 1977. *Breve Historia de Puerto Rico*. Second Part. Rio Piedras: Editorial Edil.

Fitzpatrick. S.J., Joseph P. 1987. *One Church, Many Cultures: The Challenge of Diversity*. Kansas City, Mo.: Sheed and Ward.

James, Arthur. 1927. *Thirty Years in Puerto Rico*. N.p.

Julián de Nieves, Elisa. 1982. *The Catholic Church in Colonial Puerto Rico: 1898–1964*. Rio Piedras: Editorial Edil.

La Democracia. San Juan de Puerto Rico: January 18, 1919.

Mixer, Knowlton. 1926. *Porto Rico: History and Conditions, Social, Economic and Political*. New York: Macmillan.

Moore, Donald T. 1969. "Puerto Rico para Cristo." Ph.D. diss., Southwest Baptist Seminary, Forth Worth, Texas.

National Council of Catholic Bishops. 1983. *The Hispanic Presence: Challenge and Commitment: Pastoral Letter*. Washington, D.C.: NCCB.

Negrón de Montilla, Aida. 1975. *Americanization, Puerto Rico and the Public School System, 1900–1930*. Río Piedras: Editorial Universitaria.

Office of Pastoral Research. 1982. *Hispanics in New York: Religious, Cultural and Social Experiences*. New York: Roman Catholic Archdiocese of New York.

Office of Research and Planning. 1988. *Presencia Nueva: Knowledge for Service and Hope. A Study of Hispanics in the Archdiocese of Newark*. Newark: Archdiocese of Newark.

Pantojas García, Emilio. *La iglesia protestante y la americanización de Puerto Rico*. San Juan de Puerto Rico: PRISA, n.d.

Pérez y Mena, Andrés Isidoro. 1991. *Speaking with the Dead: Development of Afro-Latin Religion among Puerto Ricans in the United States*. New York: AMS Press.

Puerto Rico, Commissioner of Education Office. 1900. *Annual Report of the Commissioner*.

Seabury, Joseph B. 1903. *Porto Rico: The Land of the Rich Port*. New York, Boston and Chicago: Silver, Burdett and Co.

Silvestrini, Blanca, and María Dolores Luque de Sánchez. 1987. *Historia de Puerto Rico: Trayectoria de un pueblo*. San Juan de Puerto Rico: Cultural Puertorriqueña, Inc.

Stevens-Arroyo, Anthony M. 1980a. "The Indigenous Elements in the Popular Religion of Puerto Ricans." Doctoral diss., Department of Theology of Fordham University.

———, ed. 1980b. *Prophets Denied Honor: An Anthology of the Hispanic Church in the United States*. Maryknoll, N.Y.: Orbis Books.

Stevens-Arroyo, Anthony M., and Ana María Díaz-Stevens. 1994a. "Religion and Faith among Latinos." In Félix Padilla, ed., *Handbook of Hispanic Cultures in the U.S.* Houston: Arte Público Press.

———, eds. 1994b. *An Enduring Flame: Studies on Latino Popular Religiosity*. New York: Bildner Books.

Thieme, Fred P. 1959. *The Puerto Rican Population: A Study in Human Biology*. Ann Arbor: University of Michigan Press.

Vidal, Jaime. 1994. "Towards an Understanding of Synthesis in Iberian and Hispanic American Popular Religiosity." In Stevens-Arroyo and Díaz-Stevens, eds. *An Enduring Flame*. New York: Bildner Books.

U.S. Commission to the Secretary of War. 1898. *Insular Affairs. Report of the U.S. Commission to the Secretary of War: Upon Investigation Made into the Civil Affairs of the Island of Porto Rico, with Recommendations*. Washington, D.C.: Government Printing Office.

Part Two ───────────────────────────────

POLICY ISSUES

───

7

Hispanics and Wage Inequality in New York City

EDWIN MELÉNDEZ

What factors determine wage differences among workers is the question that has attracted perhaps the most attention from labor economists and sociologists in the last decades, and for good reasons. Income is the most widely used variable for measuring relative socioeconomic status and economic change through time. If other sources of income are not included, annual income is the product of the wage rate times the amount of time worked. Like any other price in markets, wages serve as an allocation mechanism for labor across firms and industries as well as a distributional mechanism for the rewards of labor services. Although the determinants of wage differences for blacks and women have received extensive attention in the literature, not until recently has substantial attention been paid to the question of what determines wage differences for Hispanics.[1] This chapter is concerned with how differences in education, immigrant characteristics, labor market segmentation, and racial or ethnic discrimination explain wage differences among white, black, and Hispanic workers in New York City.[2]

Understanding the factors contributing to Hispanics' wage inequality is important for many reasons. Hispanics are one of the fastest-growing groups in United States labor markets. According to the Bureau of the Census, the Hispanic population of the United States grew from 14.6 million in 1980 to 22.7 million in 1993, or

The author wishes to acknowledge the financial support of the Committee of Public Policy Research on Contemporary Hispanic Issues and the Ford Foundation. The Center for Puerto Rican Studies-Hunter College provided the data for some of the tables in this chapter.

from 6.45 percent of the total population to 8.9 percent. During the same period the percentage of Hispanics among all employed persons increased from 5.59 to 8.1. These figures represent a population rate of growth five times as high, and an employment rate of growth three times as high, as the average for the rest of the population. Hispanics are also highly concentrated in a few regional labor markets. In 1993 the four states with the largest Hispanic population were: California (34%), Texas (20%), New York (9%), and Florida (7%); these states accounted for approximately 70 percent of all Hispanics in the U.S.[3]

In contrast to earlier immigrants whose populations grew at a similar rate and whose primary language was not English, a large proportion of Hispanics are natives. In addition Hispanics do not conform to existing notions of racial categories. In many ways the incorporation of Hispanics into labor markets represents a new situation that remains to be fully understood. Persistent wage inequality may be signaling that the experience of Hispanic workers in labor markets is not similar or comparable to that of previous immigrants.

The assimilation of Hispanic workers into labor markets is a topic that has attracted much attention during the last decade. A common index of immigrants' socioeconomic progress and successful incorporation in their new work environment is these workers' wage gains over time. In reference to all immigrants Chiswick (1978) proposes that, over time, they adapt their occupational skills, learn the new language, and become accustomed to a new labor market. Immigrants' productivity increases as they improve their human capital, i.e., education and country-specific experience. In turn, gains in productivity lead to wage gains over time. Indeed, typically immigrants initially earn less than the native-born, but "their earnings rise rapidly, particularly during their first few years in the country. After 10–15 years, their earnings equal and then exceed that of the native born" (Chiswick 1978:920). However, Borjas (1982) found that there is a great disparity in wage gains over time among Hispanic males. While the pattern for Cubans and Central Americans conforms to that of previous immigrants, it takes fifteen years for Mexicans and twenty-five years for Puerto Ricans to have statistically significant wage gains.[4]

This persistent divergence in labor market outcomes is not

confined to Hispanics of immigrant background. Recent studies (Bean and Tienda, 1987; Sandefur and Tienda, 1988) have found that socioeconomic inequality for all Hispanics has increased during the 1970s and 1980s, in patterns very similar to that of blacks. Carnoy, Daley, and Hinojosa (1989) suggest that labor market dynamics are perhaps more important then demographics, policy, or other factors influencing trends in socioeconomic divergence. In a study of the causes of family income inequality, using cross-sectional data from the 1976 Survey of Income and Education, Reimers (1984) concluded:

> The most important single reason for lower family incomes of Hispanics and blacks than of white non-Hispanics is lower wage rates—especially for men, but also for Mexican and Cuban women—even after differences in age, education, and regional distribution are controlled.

It is apparent from the previous discussion that understanding the relative importance of the different factors contributing to Hispanic wage inequality has both policy and political implications. To the extent that differences in human capital explain most variations in earnings, corrective policies should emphasize workers' education and training. In this light, it should be noted that a disproportionately large number of young workers among Hispanics give the impression that Hispanic workers are paid relatively lower wages than equally well trained white workers, whereas in reality a significant proportion of the wage gap could be attributed simply to differences in the proportion of the Hispanic and white population that occupies each age cohort. Nevertheless, although the passage of time alone is likely to reduce wage inequality, labor market policies could help youth to gain access to jobs and experience. A significant proportion of wage differences could also be attributed to factors pertaining to Hispanics' immigrant background. In this case, English as a Second Language and other programs focusing on the adaptation of worker's skills to U.S. labor markets are likely to be very effective.

However, the institutional context in which Hispanic workers are situated in labor markets may play a very important role in inducing divergence in labor market outcomes. The industrial and occupational distribution of Hispanics, together with employer's

ethnic discrimination, could induce a tendency to undervalue Hispanic's productivity in labor markets. Labor market segmentation
exists when a different set of rules and institutional arrangements
determines labor market outcomes for distinct groups of workers,
such as racial and ethnic minorities. Hispanic workers may be
adversely affected by hiring and promotion practices that are characteristic of secondary labor markets. As race is a basis for discrimination against blacks, various ethnic traits could be the basis of
employers' discrimination against Hispanic workers. Thus, wage
inequality could be attributed to barriers that prevent Hispanics
access to good jobs. Removing barriers on the demand side of the
market requires a different set of policies, such as affirmative action
and pay equity, from those that focus on workers' human capital
or immigrant background. Such policies in turn require political
action to make them viable at state and city levels.

The rest of this chapter is an examination of the determinants
of Hispanic wage differences in New York City. The first section
deals with income inequality in New York City. There follows a
brief summary of the main arguments regarding the determinants
of Hispanics' wage differences. Then, I will turn to a detailed analysis of the factors contributing to wage inequality and an assessment
of their relative importance. The chapter ends with a discussion of
some policy implications.

Income Inequality in New York City

Understanding wage inequality has become increasingly important
in New York City. A traditional entry port for immigrants, the city
has experienced a rapidly changing demographic composition and
a rising demand for specialized white-collar and unskilled service
workers. Both factors are inducing a rapid polarization of income
and a concentration of disadvantaged workers in the city, a significant proportion of whom are of Hispanic origin. (Sassen-Koob 1986).
A study by the Community Service Society (Stafford 1985) attributes
growing underrepresentation of blacks, Hispanics, and women in
New York City's core industries and jobs to the combined effects of
industrial restructuring and labor segmentation. If indeed exclusion
from good jobs disproportionately affects minority workers, ongo-

Table 1
Distribution of Persons by Household Income
New York City, 1979

	White	Black	All Hispanic	Mexican	Puerto Rican	Cuban	Other Hispanic
Total Persons (000)	3,687	1,702	1,410	24	864	68	473
Income							
Less than $9,999	23.6	40.7	46.4	39.9	52.4	27.0	36.7
$10,000 to $19,999	25.8	29.6	30.5	33.4	29.3	30.2	35.2
$20,000 to $29,999	23.1	17.2	14.6	12.6	12.5	22.8	17.3
$30,000 and over	27.6	12.5	8.4	12.6	5.9	20.0	10.8
Index of dissimilarity[a]	....	20.95	27.85	24.70	32.30	7.85	22.55

[a]Indicates the percentage of persons that would have to move from income categories to achieve income distribution parity with whites.

SOURCE: 1980 Census, 5 percent Public Use Microdata Sample. Tables compiled by the Center for Puerto Rican Studies, Hunter College, City University of New York.

ing changes in the demand for labor could lead to increasing income inequality.[5]

Table 1 summarizes the distribution of persons by household income and by race and ethnicity for New York City in 1979. Blacks and Hispanics are concentrated at the lower end of the income distribution. In 1979, 41 percent of blacks and 46 percent of Hispanics lived in households with less than $9,999 yearly income, while only 24 percent of whites were below that level.[6] Whites were evenly distributed across the four specified income categories, and the $20,000 cutoff divided the white population by half. In contrast, only 30 percent of blacks and 23.2 percent of Hispanics lived in households with annual income of $20,000 or more. Income distribution was also very inequal within the total Hispanic population. While only 18 percent of Puerto Ricans lived in households with $20,000 income or more, 43 percent of Cubans were in the upper income categories.

The index of income dissimilarity indicates the percentage of individuals in each minority group who would have to change income categories in order for the group to achieve a similar income distribution to that of whites. The index of income dissimilarity is a measure of black and Hispanic relative income inequality with respect to whites. In 1979, 21 percent of blacks and 28 percent of Hispanics would have had to change income categories to achieve income distribution parity with whites. The Hispanic average reflects the high concentration of the largest Hispanic groups, Puerto Ricans and Other Hispanics, at the lower end of the distribution.[7] Cubans have a very similar distribution of income to that of whites; Puerto Ricans have the most dissimilar. Mexicans and Other Hispanics are slightly worse off than blacks but their distribution of income is closer to blacks' than to Puerto Ricans or Cubans.

An alternative way to look at racial and ethnic income inequality is at the family level. Table 2 presents family income and poverty data by race and ethnicity for New York City in 1979. In this table, median family income was higher for whites ($21,515) and Cubans ($17,155) than for all the other groups. Blacks, Mexicans, and Other Hispanics had median family income of around $12,000 a year, and Puerto Ricans were at the bottom with $8,705. Income stratification is also reflected in the percentage of families in poverty: Puerto Ricans have the highest family-poverty rate, whites and Cubans the lowest. Families headed by women are disproportionately represented among the poor. Average family-poverty rates range from 7 percent for white families to 41 percent for Puerto Ricans, while poverty rates for female-headed families range from 35 percent for whites to 74 percent for blacks.

These patterns of Hispanics' income distribution and poverty are directly related to their relative low earnings. Other factors such as comparative percentages of labor force participation, full-time employment, and unemployment are also very important in determining annual earnings. To control for the influence of these employment-related factors, I have estimated average hourly wages only for workers with positive earnings.

Hourly wages in New York City are stratified along race, sex, and ethnic lines. For each dollar earned by white men (table 3), black men earned 75 cents. For most Hispanic men the ratio was even smaller: Mexicans, 70 cents; Puerto Ricans, 70 cents; and Other Hispanics, 67 cents. Among all Hispanic men, Cubans had the highest ratio of earnings, earning 85 cents for each dollar earned by white men. Black women earned almost as much as white women, 91 cents per dollar. Hispanic women earned relatively more

Table 2
Family Income and Poverty
New York City, 1979

	White	Black	Mexican	Puerto Rican	Cuban	Other Hispanic
Total Familes	955,040	402,740	4,520	213,880	18,760	111,380
Median family income ($)	21,515	12,210	12,575	8,705	17,155	12,435
Mean family income ($)	24,747	15,103	15,614	11,266	19,198	14,682
% Family in poverty	7.0	23.7	22.6	41.4	13.6	26.0
% Female-headed familes in poverty (as percentage of familes in poverty)	35.3	73.7	51.0	71.0	43.8	60.9

SOURCE: 1980 Census, 5 percent Public Use Microdata Sample. Tables compiled by the Center for Puerto Rican Studies, Hunter College, City University of New York.

compared to white women than Hispanic men earned relative to white men, but a wide wage gap between Hispanic and white women persisted. Mexican, Puerto Rican, and Other Hispanic women earned 80 cents or less, Cuban women 90 cents for each dollar earned by white women. The hourly wage data also show that, for any given ethnic or racial background, women earned less than men. White, black, and Hispanic women earned substantially less than white, black, and Hispanic men respectively.

Factors Contributing to Hispanics' Wage Differences

The factors determining differences in hourly wages can be broadly categorized as supply- or demand-side. Supply-side factors pertain to the quality and quantity of labor offered, as determined for example by education, experience, English proficiency, and the presence of preschool children. Demand-side factors include employers' hiring, promotion, and employment practices as well as employers' size and product market power, the presence of unions and other

Table 3
Observed Hourly Wages[a]
New York City, 1979

	White	Black	Mexican	Puerto Rican	Cuban	Other Hispanic
Men	8.83	6.60	6.20	6.17	7.47	5.96
Women	6.90	6.27	4.71	5.57	6.20	4.90
Ethnic to White Ratio[b]						
Men	. . .	0.75	0.70	0.70	0.85	0.67
Women	. . .	0.91	0.68	0.81	0.90	0.71

[a]Workers with postitive earnings, ages 16 to 65, are included in the sample. Data for whites and blacks is based on a subsample of cases, see text for explanation.

[b]Observed hourly wages ratio = Wl / wh, where l refers to the low income group (blacks and Hispanics) and h refers to the high income group (whites).

SOURCES: 1980 Census, 5 percent Public Use Microdata Sample.

institutions affecting these practices. The interaction of demand- and supply-side factors, sometimes influenced by government policies, determines wages and other labor market outcomes such as employment stability, career paths and industrial and occupational distribution. Within this context, human capital and immigrant background are the variables that affect the supply side of labor markets; segmentation and discrimination affect the demand side. Other things being equal, the more productive workers are, the higher their hourly wages; the more highly concentrated a group is in secondary labor markets and the higher the racial or ethnic discrimination in those markets, the lower that groups' hourly wages.

Research on Hispanics' earnings has focused on two main and related questions. First, to what extent can earnings differences be attributed to Hispanics' endowment of human capital or their immigrant background? Second, to what extent is discrimination against Hispanics a critical determinant of earnings? Most researchers base their analysis on a human capital model in which years of schooling and postschool experience are the most important variables affecting productivity (a variable that itself is very difficult to measure directly). Since a significant proportion of Hispanics are foreign-born, the problem of immigrant background has attracted considerable attention as well. Variables such as foreign birth,

English proficiency, length of time in the host country, and nationality are often included in the analysis. Such factors affect workers'
productivity to the extent that some skills and knowledge are not
transferable across national, cultural, and language boundaries. Discrimination on the basis of race or ethnicity is indicated, then, simply
by unexplained difference in wages between groups of workers
after controlling for the relative influence of all other factors.

Although empirical findings based on either the immigrant or
the extended human capital model vary significantly, there are some
clear areas of consensus and disagreement among researchers. The
most important finding is that, in contrast to the discrimination that
affects the earnings of black men, differences in education and other
measurable characteristics are the most important factors explaining
Hispanics' wage differences (Stolzenberg 1982; Cotton 1985; Hirshman and Wong 1984). This general statement, however, has been
qualified in some important ways. First, returns on education are
generally lower for Hispanics than for whites and there are
important variations among Hispanic groups (Reimers 1983, 1985;
Gwartney and Long 1978; Kalacheck and Raines 1976; Long 1977).
According to Reimers, for example,

> All Hispanic groups have lower returns to education than Anglo
> men. Their returns range from 3.4% higher wages per grade for
> Other-Hispanics to 4.5% for Mexican, whereas Anglo men earn
> 6.1% more for each additional grade of school completed.
> (1985:41)

A second qualification, although more important in explaining
blacks' lower wages, is that discrimination significantly affects some
Hispanic groups, particularly Mexicans and Puerto Ricans (Verdugo
and Verdugo 1984; Tienda 1983; Carliner 1976; Poston, Alvirez and
Tienda 1976; Reimers 1983). Quoting again from Reimers,

> Discrimination in the labor market may be responsible for a wage
> differential, compared to Non-Hispanic white men, of 18% for
> Puerto Rican men, 14% for black men, and 12% for Other-Hispanic
> men, but only 6% for Mexican men. (Reimers 1985:55)

Thus, these variations in the effects of discrimination and other
factors have induced researchers to avoid lumping Hispanics into
a single category but to conduct their analyses taking into account
the national origin of different Hispanic groups.

Empirical findings regarding the effects of immigrant background on Hispanic earnings are less conclusive. For example, some researchers have attributed one-third to one-half of the wage gap to lack of English-language proficiency (McManus, Gould, and Welch 1983; McManus 1985; Grenier 1984). Others have found the effects of language proficiency to be relatively small, accounting for less than ten percent of the wage difference (García 1984; Reimers 1982, 1983, 1984). The effects of English fluency also show wide variation among Hispanic groups.

Hispanics and Segmentation

While it is true that the question of how earnings are affected by labor market structures or segmentation has received extensive attention, relatively little research directly addresses Hispanics. Segmentation theorists reject the implicit assumption that labor markets are essentially competitive in nature and that labor market forces tend to eliminate wage and employment differences in the long run. Choosing among several different segmentation theories, I will base the organization of the data and the following explanation on the Gordon-Edwards-Reich model. (Edwards 1979; Gordon 1971; Gordon, Edwards, and Reich 1982; Reich 1984; Reich, Gordon, and Edwards 1973).

For segmentation theorists, labor markets are organized along occupational segments, although industrial sectors (core, periphery) are important to differentiate orders in the lower strata of occupations. Jobs in the primary labor market are divided between subordinated and independent segments, the difference being defined to a considerable extent by educational credentials and/or state regulation of the occupation. Jobs in the primary independent segment offer clear paths for advancement and have a well-defined hierarchial structure. Administrators and managers, together with professional and technical workers who enjoy great autonomy in their work (such as engineers, scientists), college professors and teachers are included in this category. Jobs in the primary subordinated segment tend to be unionized and to have machine-paced systems of labor control. In this segment educational requirements are lower, but the institutional organization of labor markets insures relative job security and higher wages. Examples of occupations included in the primary subordinated segment include registered nurses, air traffic controllers, bank tellers, police and detectives, and operators in monopolistic industries.

By contrast, jobs in secondary segments require very little formal training, and they depend on direct supervision. To the extent that there are barriers to workers' mobility and to the extent that ascribed characteristics such as race, ethnicity, and gender are stratifying factors, there is a premium attached to labor market location. The crowding of given groups of workers along industrial and occupational categories and the ethnic, racial, and gender divisions of labor, which are conducive to divisions and conflict among workers, tend to lower wages and increase employment instability. Examples of secondary labor market jobs include messengers, child-care workers, guards, and operators and laborers in competitive industries and small firms.

In sum, wages and other labor market outcomes result from the interaction of demand- and supply-side factors. From an analytical or practical point of view, observed wage differences say very little beyond signaling the existence of a problem. The real task is to assess the underlying causes of wage differentiation. An accurate estimation of the relative importance of supply-side (education, immigrant background) or demand-side (segmentation, discrimination) forces inducing wage inequality is the best guide for designing corrective policies and for assessing community strategies aimed at exerting pressure on the private and public sectors.

A Closer Look at Wage Inequality in New York City

Table 4 shows the distribution of highest educational level for individuals twenty-five years old and older. The percentage for blacks and Hispanics, with larger concentrations below the level of high school graduates and a small proportion at college educational levels or higher, have an asymmetrical structure when compared to those of whites. Proportionally almost three times as many white men have college or higher education than do blacks and Hispanics, with the exception of Cubans, who have the highest proportion among Hispanic groups. Among white and black men the lowest

Table 4

Percentage Distribution of Population by Highest Educational Level
New York City, 1979[a]

	White	Black	Mexican	Puerto Rican	Cuban	Other Hispanic
Men						
Total Persons	1,202,140	379,220	5,600	171,900	22,000	108,740
8 years or less	7.35	7.15	14.24	13.99	14.57	13.22
Some high school	6.47	9.13	8.51	11.61	5.97	8.19
High school grad	11.22	13.10	11.28	9.25	11.04	9.79
Some college	6.13	5.44	4.69	3.42	5.79	5.23
College or more	11.55	3.34	3.82	1.57	6.82	3.59
No school at all	0.52	0.41	1.74	0.82	0.47	0.83
Attending now	1.80	2.63	4.34	1.82	2.22	2.79
Women						
Total Persons	1,466,540	541,460	5,920	232,900	24,940	140,400
8 years or less	10.55	9.76	15.63	21.03	19.13	21.78
Some high school	7.86	13.59	9.38	14.26	6.39	8.94
High school grad	18.40	19.76	12.67	12.66	13.08	13.17
Some college	6.01	6.85	4.17	3.65	5.24	4.31
College or more	8.99	3.93	3.65	1.29	5.75	3.22
No school at all	0.96	0.54	1.56	2.04	0.94	1.66
Attending now	2.18	4.39	4.34	2.61	2.60	3.31

[a]Individuals 25 years and older.

SOURCE: 1980 Census, 5 percent Public Use Microdata Sample, Tables compiled by Center for Puerto Rican Studies, Hunter College, City University of New York.

proportion are without a high school education; among Hispanics, the highest. Educational attainment among Puerto Rican men is particularly low; this group has the highest proportion without a high school diploma and the lowest proportion with education at college level or above.

Hispanic women are in a similar situation to Hispanic men: a very high proportion without a high school diploma, very few with college degrees. However, among white women a lower proportion have college degrees than do white men, and a much higher proportion lack a high school diploma than do men. In contrast, Hispanic women are not at a great disadvantage when compared to Hispanic men. Again, the statistics for Puerto Rican women are noticeable for an extremely low percentage of college graduates

Table 5
Ethnic and Racial Groups' Nativity
New York City, 1980

	White	Black	Mexican	Puerto Rican	Cuban	Other Hispanic
Number of Persons	3,686,600	1,701,880	24,040	863,900	67,900	473,320
% U.S.–born	74.72	80.94	60.89	49.37	23.83	31.73
Outside NYS	11.07	30.34	15.97	1.32	2.18	1.48
New York State	67.65	50.60	44.84	48.05	21.65	30.25
Foreign-born from selected countries	21.28	19.06	39.19	50.63	76.17	68.27
Mexico			28.04			
Puerto Rico				47.07		
Cuba					69.72	
Dominican Rep.						24.77
Central America						8.80
Columbia						8.41
Ecuador						8.04
Panama						2.75
Peru						2.15

SOURCE: 1980 Census, 5 percent Public Use Microdata sample. Tables compiled by the Center for Puerto Rican Studies, Hunter College, City University of New York.

and an extremely high percentage without a high school diploma.

The disproportionate number of immigrants among Hispanic groups could be an important factor explaining income differences. The majority of Puerto Ricans (50.6%), Cubans (76.2%), and Other Hispanics (68.3%) are immigrants (table 5). Almost all native Puerto Rican, Cuban, and Other Hispanics were born in New York State. Of the foreign-born, Other Hispanics, Dominicans, and Central Americans constitute the largest group. This high proportion of foreign-born among Hispanic groups is reflected in a high number of Hispanics who are not fluent in English. Table 6 shows that between one-fifth and one-third of Hispanics speak English poorly or not at all. Puerto Ricans and Mexicans have the lowest proportion of those who are not fluent (21.1 and 21.8 respectively), while Other Hispanics and Cubans have the highest proportions (34.4 and 29.4 respectively).

Table 7 shows the distribution of ethnic groups by segments. The immense majority of blacks, Hispanics, and white women are concentrated in low-wage occupational segments. A majority of

Table 6
English Fluency Percentages by Ethnic and Racial Groups
New York City, 1980[a]

English Fluency	Non-Hispanic White	Non-Hispanic Black	Mexican	Puerto Rican	Cuban	Other Hispanic
Only English	74.86	92.88	35.73	8.96	10.47	10.38
Very well	14.37	4.13	27.07	43.13	36.55	30.71
Well	7.00	2.11	15.38	26.82	23.62	24.49
Not well	3.01	0.74	12.71	15.25	19.52	21.33
No English	0.75	0.15	9.12	5.84	9.84	13.09

[a]All persons 3 years and over.
SOURCE: 1980 Census, 5 percent Public Use Microdata Sample. Tables compiled by the Center for Puerto Rican Studies, Hunter College, New York City.

Hispanic men occupy the secondary segment, while a majority of Hispanic women occupy the primary subordinated segment. The proportion of black and Hispanic men in primary subordinated and secondary segments ranges between 60.6 percent for Cubans to 70.9 percent for Puerto Ricans. Women are even more concentrated in these low-wage occupations; the proportion of women ranges from 66.8 percent of whites to 86.0 percent for Other Hispanics. The majority of white men are concentrated in the categories of managers and supervisors and professional and technical categories; white women are concentrated in the primary subordinated segment. Thus, the segment location data reveal that whites are overrepresented in the upper tier of labor markets in New York City, while blacks and Hispanics are concentrated in low-wage jobs.

Decomposition in the Wage Gap

The above analysis suggests that all of the key factors reviewed are likely to be determinants of wage differences between Hispanics and non-Hispanic white and black workers. The question is to what degree does each factor contribute to the observed wage differences.

Labor market analysts use regression analysis to determine the relative effect of a given variable on wages, assuming that the remaining explanatory variables are held constant. For example,

Table 7
Percentage Distribution of Racial and Ethnic Groups by Segment Location
New York City, 1980[a]

	White	Black	Mexican	Puerto Rican	Cuban	Other Hispanic
Segment						
			Men			
Primary Independent						
Managers &						
Supervisors	21.8	10.9	14.9	10.7	19.6	11.0
Professional &						
Technical	16.7	7.3	5.2	5.6	9.8	6.6
Craft	12.9	11.8	14.1	12.8	10.0	14.7
Primary	25.9	28.7	17.7	23.9	26.8	22.1
Subordinated						
Secondary	22.7	41.3	48.1	47.0	33.8	45.6
			Women			
Primary Independent						
Managers &						
Supervisors	14.8	10.1	6.2	7.5	8.9	7.0
Professional &						
Technical	16.4	8.5	8.5	8.9	10.3	5.2
Craft	2.0	1.5	1.5	1.7	1.6	1.8
Primary	51.7	52.8	43.1	47.5	44.3	36.9
Subordinated						
Secondary	15.1	27.1	40.7	34.9	34.9	49.1

[a]Workers with positive earnings, ages 16 to 65, are included in the sample. Data for whites and blacks is based on a subsample of cases, see text for explanation.
SOURCE: 1980 Census, 5 percent Public Use Microdata Sample.

the regression coefficient for education could be interpreted as the estimated gains for one additional year of schooling, assuming that labor market experience, immigrant and socioeconomic background, and other factors remain constant. I used microdata from the 1980 census (5% sample) to estimate wage equations for white, black, and Hispanic salaried workers sixteen to sixty-five years old with positive earnings in New York City.[8] I used these equations to decompose wage differences into portions attributable to education, immigrant background, and primary segment location, and the residual or unexplained wage difference is then attributed to discrimination.[9]

Table 8 depicts the results of the experiment. For analytical

Table 8
Estimated Effects of Education, Discrimination and Segmentation*

	Black	Mexican	Puerto Rican	Cuban	Other Hispanic
			Men		
Observed Wage					
Difference ($)	2.23	2.63	2.66	1.36	2.87
Education (%)	25.7	42.6	41.9	51.1	33.5
Discrimination (%)	54.9	34.0	31.6	33.4	49.0
Segmentation (%)	21.9	15.9	18.9	16.4	15.9
			Women		
Observed Wage					
Difference ($)	0.63	2.19	1.33	0.70	2.00
Education (%)	68.4	38.8	42.1	45.6	39.9
Discrimination (%)	−6.2	23.1	25.1	24.5	18.4
Segmentation (%)	81.7	37.8	36.1	57.7	41.9

*Total effect may not add to 100% because the effect of other variables affecting wage differences are not included in the table.
SOURCE: Author's estimates based on 1980 Census data, see text for explanation.

convenience, the explained effect is divided into partial sums corresponding to education, immigrant background, and segmentation and expressed as a percentage of the observed wage difference.[10] The most important points are summarized as follows:

1. *Labor market segmentation explains a substantial proportion of Hispanics' wage differences.* The overall proportion of the observed wage difference explained by primary segment location is between 16 and 19 percent for Hispanic men and between 36 and 58 percent for Hispanic women. Most of the effects of segmentation are attributable to underrepresentation in control or professional and technical subsegments.

2. *Differences in measurable characteristics explain most of the wage gap for Hispanic men and women, but the effect of discrimination is very significant for Hispanics, and it explains most of black men's wage gap.* Discrimination accounts for two-thirds of the wage gap for black, one-half for Other Hispanic, and one-third of Mexican, Puerto Rican, and Cuban men. Considering that black women have the smallest observed wage

difference ($0.40), black women's earnings are not substantially affected by discrimination; however, discrimination represents between one-fifth and one-half of Hispanic women's wage gap.

3. *Education is the single most important factor explaining earning differentials for all groups of men and women except for black and Other Hispanic men.* The portion of the wage gap explained by differences in education, however, varies greatly among ethnic groups. In consideration of differences in both education and experience, human capital variables explain between one-fourth and one-half of ethnic men's wage differences and eliminate or reduce by more than half ethnic women's wage differences.

The combined effect of demand-side factors—segmentation and discrimination—accounts for half of Hispanic men's wage differences, between 55 and 82 percent of Hispanic women's, 77 percent of black men's, and 75 percent of black women's. Thus, demand-side factors account for a substantial portion of black and Hispanic wage differences relative to non-Hispanic white workers. These effects are significant even after controlling for differences in education and immigrant background between whites (the high wage reference group) and Hispanics. The relative importance of demand-side factors, however, varies among Hispanic groups and between men and women of similar ethnicity and race.

These findings indicate the need to implement policies aimed at correcting the problematic concentration of Hispanics in low-wage segments and at attacking discrimination. They also suggest the need for flexible policies that take into account gender differences and the particular barriers that affect Hispanics of different national origins.

Policy Implications

The analysis of wage differences is consistent with emphasizing the need for more active public and civic intervention in the demand side of labor markets in New York City. Previous research on Hispanic earnings has focused on supply-side factors (human capital, immigrant background) and therefore has emphasized policies pertaining to the adaptation of Hispanic immigrants to labor markets. This immigrant approach assumes a significantly competitive labor market in which wage inequality based on differences in workers' attributes will disappear with time. To the extent that public policy accelerates their adaptation to labor markets, Hispanics, like European immigrants in previous decades, will achieve income parity.

The optimistic outlook related in the immigrant approach to Hispanics' situation in labor markets is tempered by the evidence. The analysis presented in this chapter indicates that demand-side factors play an important role in explaining wage inequality in New York City. Thus follows the need to pursue both supply- and demand-side policies as complementary strategies to increase blacks', Hispanics', and white women's earnings. As is made clear in policy recommendations from previous studies, promoting education and training opportunities to increase Hispanics' skills, language fluency, and country-specific experience are important. These conventional policy recommendations, however, are bound to stop short of correcting employers' discriminatory hiring, compensation, and promotion practices.

Employers' discriminatory valuation of workers' productivity in labor markets can be remedied by affirmative action and pay equity policies. Affirmative action promotes equal treatment of minority workers in hiring, promotion, and employment security. Hispanics and blacks are extremely underrepresented in the upper tier of primary segments. Affirmative action promotes the mobility of workers from secondary jobs to good jobs with higher earnings, employment stability, and more advancement opportunities. Pay equity promotes the equal valuation of jobs in which minority workers are concentrated. Rather than offering "access" to "good" jobs—as affirmative action proposes—pay equity aims at transforming a poor job into a good job. Pay equity is a necessary policy when the concentration of minorities or women in a particular job is the main factor inducing the undervaluation of workers' productivity.

Conventional wisdom is that supply-side policies are more politically viable than demand-side policies, to the extent that the latter are perceived as promoting preferential treatment for minorities. The truth is that demand-side policies will benefit the majority of workers in New York City. To the extent that monetary gains represent workers' invested interest in alternative policy scenarios, there are reasonable conditions for a multiracial and multiethnic alliance behind affirmative action and pay equity. Hispanic men and women are among those who will benefit the most from these policies.

NOTES

1. I have decided to use "Hispanic" and not "Latino" for two reasons. First, Hispanic is the term most used in the labor market literature. Second, Hispanic is gender neutral and Latino is not; trying to correct for the gender bias for "Latino" makes a more difficult reading of the essay.

2. These are mutually exclusive categories. "Hispanics" refers to persons of Mexican, Puerto Rican, Cuban, or other Spanish-speaking origin; "white" refers to non-Hispanic white and "black" to non-Hispanic black persons.

3. U.S. Bureau of the Census, *The Hispanic Population in the United States: March 1993* (CPR, Series P–20–475).

4. Borjas's findings are based on the *Survey of Income and Education*, U.S. Bureau of the Census, 1970. In a more recent study using 1980 census data, Frank Bean and Marta Tienda (1987) found similar discrepancies in the earnings of Central Americans and Mexicans.

5. My argument in this chapter is based on cross-sectional data from the 1980 census. It is not intended to measure trends, but it provides a detailed account of the relative effect of labor market location on different groups of workers at one point in time.

6. The argument that follows is based on an analysis of 1980 census data, by now more than a decade old. Unfortunately, census data are the only reliable available source for examining small population subgroups such as Puerto Ricans and Cubans. [Editors' note: We believe the 1990 census data support the argument put forth in this chapter.]

7. The Other Hispanics category includes all persons of Hispanic origin not previously classified as Mexican, Puerto Rican, or Cuban. Persons born in the Dominican Republic constitute the largest group, representing 25 percent of other Hispanics.

8. To save on computational cost, a subsample corresponding to 1% of the population has been included for whites and blacks. Variable definitions, regression coefficients and means are available from the author upon request.

9. A detailed explanation of the statistical technique employed in the analysis of wage differences as well as tables reporting all the results are available from the author upon request.

10. Additional variables were included to control for postschooling experiences, socioeconomic background (marital status, presence of school-aged children in the family, veteran or not veteran status, and mobility to work because of health problems), and government employment (federal, state, and local).

REFERENCES

Bean, Frank D., and Marta Tienda. 1987. *The Hispanic Population in the United States*. New York: Russell Sage.

Borjas, George J. 1982. "The Earnings of Male Hispanic Immigrants in the United States." *Industrial and Labor Relations Review*, April.

Carliner, Goffrey. 1976. "Returns to Education for Blacks, Anglos, and Five Spanish Groups." *Journal of Human Resources* 11 (Spring): 172–84.

Carnoy, M.; H. Daley, and R. Hinojosa. 1989. "The Changing Economic Position of Hispanic and Black Americans in the U.S. Labor Market since 1959." Unpublished paper, Inter-University Program for Latino Research.

Chiswick, Barry R. 1978. "The Effects of Americanization on the Earnings of Foreign Born Men." *Journal of Political Economy*, October: 897–922.

Cotton, Jeremiah. 1985. "A Comparative Analysis of Black-White and Mexican-American-White Male Wage Differentials." *Review of Black Political Economy*. Spring: 51–69.

Edwards, Richard. 1979. *Contested Terrain*. New York: Basic Books.

García, Philip. 1984. "Dual-Language Characteristic and Earnings: Male Mexican Workers in the United States." *Social Science Research* 13:221–35.

Gordon, D. 1971. "Class, Productivity, and the Ghetto: A Study of Labor Market Stratification." Unpublished Ph.D. diss., Harvard University.

———, Richard Edwards, and Michael Reich. 1982. *Segmented Work, Divided Workers*. Cambridge: Cambridge University Press.

Grenier, Gilles, 1984. "The Effects for Language Characteristics on the Wages of Hispanic-American Males." *The Journal of Human Resources* 19 (1): 35–52.

Gwartney, James P., and James E. Long. 1978. "The Relative Earnings of Blacks and Other Minorities." *Industrial and Labor Review* 31 (3) (April): 336–46.

Hirshman, C., and Morrison G. Wong. 1984. "Socio-economic Gains of Asian Americans, Blacks, and Hispanics: 1960–1976." *American Journal of Sociology* 90 (3): 584–607.

Kalacheck, Edward, and Frederic Raines. 1976. "The Structure of Wage Differences among Mature Male Workers." *Journal of Human Resources* 11 (4): 484–506.

Long, James E. 1977. "Productivity, Employment, Discrimination and the Relative Economic Status of Spanish Origin Males," *Social Science Quarterly* 58 (December): 357–73.

McManus, Walter. 1985. "Labor Market Cost of Language Disparity: An Interpretation of Hispanic Earning Differences." *American Economic Review* 75 (4) (September): 818–27.

————, W. W. Gould and F. Welch. 1983. "Earnings of Hispanic Men: The Role of Proficiency in the English Language." *Journal of Labor Economics* 1 (April): 110–30.

Poston, Dudley L., David Alvirez, and Marta Tienda. 1976. "Earning Differences between Anglo and Mexican American Male Workers in 1960 and 1970: Changes in the 'Cost' of Being Mexican American." *Social Science Quarterly* 57 (December): 618–31.

Reich, Michael. 1984. "Segmented Labour: Time Series Hypothesis and Evidence." *Cambridge Journal of Economics* 8: 63–81.

————, David M. Gordon, and Richard Edwards. 1973. "A Theory of Labor Market Segmentation." *American Economic Review* 63 (May): 359–65.

Reimers, Cordelia W. 1983. "Labor Market Discrimination against Hispanic and Black Men." *Review of Economics and Statistics* 65 (4): 570–79.

————. 1984. "Sources of Family Income Differentials among Hispanics, Blacks, and White-Non-Hispanics." *American Journal of Sociology*, 89 (4): 889–903.

————. 1985. "A Comparative Analysis of the Wages of Hispanics, Blacks, and Non-Hispanic Whites." In G. Borjas and M. Tienda, eds., *Hispanics in the U.S. Economy*. Orlando: Academic Press.

Sandefer, Gary D., and Marta Tienda. 1988. *Divided Opportunities*. New York: Plenum Press.

Sassen-Koob, Saskia. 1986. "New York City: Economic Restructuring and Immigration." *Development and Change* 17: 85–119.

Stafford, W. 1985. "Closed Labor Markets: Under-representation of Blacks, Hispanics, and Women in New York City's Core Industries and Jobs." New York: Community Service Society.

Stolzenberg, Ross M. 1982. *Occupational Differences between Hispanics and Non-Hispanics*. Santa Monica: Rand Corporation.

Tienda, Marta. 1983. "Nationality and Income Attainment among Native and Immigrant Hispanic Men in the United States." *The Sociological Quarterly* 24 (Spring): 253–72.

U.S. Bureau of the Census. 1989. *The Hispanic Population in the United States: March 1988* (Advanced Report).

————. 1994. *The Hispanic Population in the United States: March 1993*. (CPR, Series P–20–475).

U.S. Department of Commerce. 1980 Census of Population—Public Use Microdata Sample (A).

Verdugo, Naomi T., and Richard R. Verdugo. 1984. "Earnings Differentials among Mexican American, Black, and White Male Workers." *Social Science Quarterly* 65 (June): 417–25.

8

Education and Community: Puerto Ricans and Other Latinos in the Schools and Universities

JESSE M. VÁZQUEZ

Educational institutions do not stand alone, nor do they stand apart from the larger social structure; they are social, economic, and cultural products. The same societal factors which come together to create ghettos in some communities and tree-lined streets in others will also, in large measure, shape the nature and quality of our neighborhood schools and our private and public universities. In order to better understand the current situation of Puerto Ricans and other Latinos in the schools and colleges in New York, this chapter encourages the reader to go beyond the neighborhood school building or the local college campus and consider the myriad social, political, economic, and cultural processes which, when combined, create a network of interacting forces which shape the substance and quality of our educational institutions. Given the complexity of this interconnecting network, this chapter will place the Latino educational experience into a broader societal framework.

The events and debates that are taking place in and beyond the schools and colleges are presented in a way that enables the reader to fully appreciate the multidimensional nature and urgency that surrounds the "educational crisis" as that crisis is currently unfolding in our public schools and universities across this nation. Our analysis and discussion will also turn the reader's attention to more distant events and policies which continue to affect the long-term agenda for our nation's educational system.

In an effort to familiarize the reader with how current educational debates are affecting the Latino community, we have selected a number of key issues that are presently unfolding in our schools and colleges. The educational issues presented will enable us to shed some light on the broader societal implications of education and its importance for the development of the Latino community. The reader should note that the issues that have been selected for discussion in this chapter represent only a small fraction of a greater number of problems and debates which continue to have a direct impact on the quality of education for all children and young adults in New York schools and colleges. A good many of these issues have existed for as long as Puerto Ricans and other Latinos have been a significant segment of the school population, but many others are part and parcel of the growing number of seemingly intractable social and economic problems now facing all inner-city schools in the United States. As pointed out in a report by the National Council of La Raza, "the United States is undergoing a serious educational crisis, with Hispanics among those suffering its worst impact" (Miranda and Quiroz 1990:13).

Selecting Issues to Study in Education

Even identifying the basic problems, issues, and questions in education, and how they might affect the Latino community can be problematic. By no means is it an easy task to point to specific educational problems and select those as *the overriding educational problems facing the Latino community*. By setting forth even a partial list of what one considers to be the fundamental problems (e.g., my own favorite list of basic educational problems) in our schools, we automatically establish our own biased agenda and priorities for (a) identifying a problem, and (b) proposing solutions for those select problems. If I say, for example, that the most critical problem facing our children and our schools today is the question of *language and culture*, then I have already predetermined that we need to look for resolutions for this particular problem through the implementation of various curricular reforms (e.g., the imposition of bilingual-multi-cultural education programs, English as a second language programs, etc.). If on the other hand I decide that drug treatment and education—a problem which cuts across all communities—is the number one need facing our children, then all efforts will be expended toward mounting a powerful and effective antidrug program and campaign in our schools. If we don't, I warn the parents, we risk having our children swallowed up by a plague that seems to be affecting all communities. Similarly, if I promote the idea that school safety is the key to assuring that our children learn in a secure and nonthreatening environment, then obviously my list of program priorities will include that a large portion of our annual district budget will be given over to hiring more security guards, the purchasing of metal detectors, and organizing street patrols to assure the safety of children, teachers, and so on.

Sometimes, simply having the power to name the problem or problems in our schools is the thing that determines the future direction of those institutions. Those who manage and control our educational institutions rarely agree upon what the most critical problems are, much less on what the proposed solutions to these problems might be. But problems and obstacles there are.

Except in the most abstract scholarly reports, usually written for a small audience of researchers and academicians, Latinos have had little opportunity to develop their own corrective agenda for what ails this nation's educational establishment. Historically, it is safe to say that those who have had the power to define and to act upon the educational inequities facing the Latino community have been those who are non-Hispanic and those who sit at the top of the educational pyramids. Not until very recently in education history have Latinos and other ethnic or racial minorities sought to shape educational policy from the bottom up.

The hope for racial equality and social justice was made palpable in America by the 1954 landmark Supreme Court decision of *Brown vs. The Board of Education*. That Court decision, which held "that segregated public schools are unconstitutional," offered the promise of setting this nation on the right course toward freedom and equality for all (Bell 1987:3). One can't help but wonder why it is that our nation's racial/ethnic minorities, more than forty years after the *Brown* decision, are still busy fighting front-line skirmishes in education in an even larger war to secure social justice in American society. Kozol's revisiting of the schools in the late 1980s reminds Americans that our schools are far more segregated in the North than in the South, that our property-based school/land taxes are perpetuating scandalous inequities in our nation's schools, and that "nowhere is the pattern more explicit or more absolute than in the public schools of New York City" (Kozol 1991:83).

By and large, the voices protesting the educational injustices perpetrated against the Latino community have come from grass-roots organizations. These would include, among many others, Aspira, the Puerto Rican Legal Defense Fund, the Puerto Rican Educators Association, Puerto Rican Association for Community Affairs, New York State Association for Bilingual Education, the National Congress for Puerto Rican Rights, the Puerto Rican–Latino Education Roundtable, and the Puerto Rican Council on Higher Education. In the greater New York metropolitan area, Dominicans and other newly arrived Central, South American, and Caribbean immigrants have not only formed their own organizations, but have also joined forces with the Puerto Rican organizations in an effort to create a united broad-based education coalition.

Over the years these organizations have tended to be reactive to single-issue crises as they present themselves on the educational horizon. They focus a good deal of their energy and resources on campaigns attempting to secure positions and representation on the boards of education, the trustees of CUNY's Board of Higher Education, in looking for candidates for the presidency of select CUNY campuses, holding voter registration campaigns for the local community boards, and so on. When a policy or practice is revealed to be potentially harmful, or not in the interest of the greater Latino community, these organizations spring into action. As a result of their aggressive political action, bilingual educational consent decrees have been passed; school chancellors have been supported or toppled; college presidents and board members have been selected, recommended, and installed; testing policies have been revised; placement practices challenged; ethnic studies programs have been established in the colleges; and, most recently, the New York State's schools curriculum has been deemed inappropriate and potentially damaging to ethnic or racial minorities in the state and will soon be revised. There is little doubt that much has been accomplished by this kind of educational activism which seeks to gain control of policy-making positions. And it is also the kind of advocacy which in its various forms is attempting to dismantle the kinds of practices in our schools and colleges that have contributed to mass educational failure for children and young adults and which inevitably result in major losses in the economic sector as well.[1]

Given the broad variety of issues to which the Hispanic community has responded in its struggle to correct the inequities and problems in our educational institutions, it would be presumptuous of me to simply list the issues and propose the resolutions. This is especially true if the reader accepts the main thesis of this chapter: that problems usually presented as school-related are rarely limited to the school environment but also have their origins and partial resolutions in the society that surrounds, shapes, and sustains the schools that we have come to know as either effective or failed institutions. Therefore, the sample problems, issues, and areas of concern that I will identify and discuss in the following sections of this chapter *should by no means be viewed as the only critical educational problems and issues facing the Latino community.* Instead, they are presented as an opportunity for the reader to look more closely at the complexity of educational policies and practices in a complex society. Perhaps viewing the issues from this perspective may help us understand why it is that, while winning some battles, we may be ultimately losing the war in education.

The school organization as we have come to know it in the latter part of the twentieth century constitutes the prevailing structure of choice for the education of our children. In no way, therefore, should the rest of this discussion be considered a blueprint for educating the Latino in the 1990s. Rather, this exercise should simply suggest ways for us to look at and study the complex and dynamic nature of the educational issues currently facing the Latino community. Being able to identify the participants who are engaged in the debate, examining some of the fundamental underlying arguments, understanding the social, historical, and political contexts which shape our educational institutions are among the many considerations in our analysis.

Latinos, the Schools, and the Social Structure

Whatever is taking place in our schools today is the result of a long series of complex historical events and interactions which continue to unfold as new conditions and factors emerge in the social and economic landscape. When one sets out to examine the current problems of our schools, whether the schools we study are in or out of the Latino community, the problems we look at must be placed in their larger historical, social, and economic context. For example, the fact that the dropout rate for Puerto Ricans and other Latinos in New York was estimated at approximately 62 percent (Task Force on the New York State Dropout Problem 1986:6) and is higher than it is for other ethnic groups, specifically African Americans and Native Americans in the state, is no doubt a singularly alarming statistic for any observer.[2] However, this piece of information will take on a more expansive meaning only when we begin to understand the numerous events, forces, and conditions— both in and out of the school system—that directly and indirectly contribute to this particular social, economic, and individual tragedy. The escalating dropout rate for Latinos and other ethnic and racial minorities in New York is not simply a measure of the failures of schools, but a societal failure as well (Nelson Rockefeller Institute of Government 1986: 78; Aspira of New York 1983: 1).

Education is only one of several social institutions in our society which are linked to one another by virtue of economic structures, societal organizational patterns, cultural values and traditions, and historical and political processes. For example, it can be said that the racism that exists in the society at large is replicated in countless numbers of ways in our educational institutions from kindergarten to graduate schools. Those confirming significant obstacles in their education simply because they are poor, Latino, African American, Asian, or Native American are forced to face the negative consequences of racism and the profound limitations of family and community resources. However, because we have a public education system that is open and accessible to all, and *theoretically* founded on a principle of equal opportunity for all, Latinos and other ethnic or racial minorities are expected to overcome these barriers, regardless of social and economic background. For many, the disadvantage of being a member of a racial or ethnic minority group or coming from poor or working-class families is compensated for in very limited and circumscribed ways in the schools as we know them today. Yes, there have been countless numbers of federal and state funded programs (e.g., Project Headstart, SEEK, Bilingual Education, Title VII Programs) designed to compensate for disadvantages in income, education, and differences in language and culture, but these programs continue to be the targets of government cutbacks and the public's growing disenchantment with past efforts at educational reform. The twelve years of the Reagan and Bush administrations served to set back social and educational programs for almost two decades. Kozol, however, would argue that "in public schooling social policy has been turned back almost one hundred years" (Kozol 1991:4).

As such, our schools, like so many other social institutions, are creations of the interests and beliefs of the people who manage them and are designed to reflect the images, values, and beliefs of the dominant society. Those who manage and guide our schools on a day-to-day basis (teachers, counselors, principals, district superintendents, local community boards, etc.), as well as those who establish the policies which govern the schools and universities (chancellors, boards of education, trustees, state education department personnel, and members of the board of regents, etc.) are not isolated, or protected individuals of social groupings; nor are they immune from the influences and the pressures that emanate from numerous interconnecting social institutions, political pressures and processes, and class interests. Whether these individuals make school policy or design a social studies curriculum, they are doing so as representatives of different classes, ethnic groups, and interest groups expressing the divergent views of these various political and social constituencies. To create school or university policy, therefore, is ultimately an act of creating social policy. It is a process which, by and large, has systematically excluded the poor and the undereducated, especially Latinos, African Americans, and Native Americans.

A number of critical issues and debates now occupy a central place on the nation's educational agenda. These are not only at the forefront of the national debate on educational reform but are also of primary significance to Latino communities in the city and state of New York. How Puerto Ricans and other Latinos in New York understand and, as active participants in the process, attempt to resolve these educational challenges will also bear some resemblance to how other Latino groups throughout the nation confront these same issues and problems. The educational experiences, employment patterns, types of housing, health problems, and other social factors affecting Puerto Ricans and other Latinos in New York make up a socioeconomic profile which is very much like that of the Chicanos and Puerto Ricans in Chicago or, for that matter, the Chicanos in California and in the Southwest. While the focus of this book may be on the Latino experience in New York, the reader must be mindful of the broader implications for other similarly disenfranchised groups in American society. The educational crises and social inequities faced by the Hispanic community in New York are indeed very much like those of other Latinos and other racial/ethnic minorities in communities all over the United States.

Changing Demographics and Unchanging Schools

With some notable exceptions, Puerto Ricans and most Latinos in the United States share the experience of migration and immigration. The earliest Spanish settlers in the Southwest and parts of the West predate the territorial and certainly the statehood annexations of these regions by the United States. There were Spanish settlements in some of these areas well before the New England colonies were getting started in the northeastern United States. "Hispanos" in New Mexico, who may be seen as the Hispanic's equivalent of the founding fathers of the Southwest, continue to live in areas settled by their ancestors well over four hundred years ago; and some would rather identify themselves as "descendents of Spanish conquerors than as 'Mexican' or 'Chicano'" (Langley 1988: 81).[3] However, when those in the Northeast, particularly in New York, think of the Hispanic settlements, they generally think very narrowly about the most recent waves of South and Central American, Cuban, and Dominican immigrants, and slightly before them, the great Puerto Rican migrations of the 1940s to 1960s. They do not think of the over four-hundred-year-old settlements in New Mexico, other parts of the Southwest, and Florida (in particular St. Augustine, which is the oldest Spanish settlement in North America). Most casual observers fail to see the complexity of the ethnic diversity which makes up the Latino reality and experience in the United States.

While emigration from Latin America to New York had been occurring since the early 1900s and before, the early and middle 1950s marked the first dramatic high point of the Puerto Rican migration to the United States. During that period, approximately 80 percent of the Puerto Rican migrants settled in New York City (Fitzpatrick 1987: 15). Since that time, and for well over forty years, Puerto Ricans and other Latinos have continued to migrate not only to New York but to other major urban centers in the northeastern and midwestern parts of United States (e.g., Philadelphia, Boston, Chicago, Newark, Hartford, Trenton). New York City, however, continues to be home to the greatest number of Puerto Ricans, Dominicans, and other selected Latino groups in the continental United States. According to recent estimates one out of every eight New Yorkers is Puerto Rican and one out of every sixteen is a Dominican (Puerto Ricans make up 12.6 percent of New York City"s population and Dominicans make up 6.3 percent) (Rodríguez 1989: 28).

The New York public school system has been the primary educational institution that first-, second- and now third-generation Puerto Rican New Yorkers and other Latinos have turned to for the elementary, secondary, and college education of their children. One would think that after almost four decades of Latinos being a significant part of the New York scene that time alone would have made a significant difference in how Hispanic children have fared in the nation's largest educational school system. But this is not the case; in fact, the educational future of Hispanic children does not seem very bright at all. Hispanic pupils continue to be the victims of a system which has thus far failed to provide their fundamental educational needs. And as we move rapidly toward an information-based society, the high school dropout or even the high school graduate without technological skills will find himself or herself far less employable than his or her counterpart did twenty-five years ago. It is ironic that as far back as 1953 the New York City Board of Education mounted one of the most extensive studies of the Puerto Rican community, which sought to address a broad range of issues and problems facing that first large wave of migrant Puerto Rican children in New York City's public schools. The Puerto Rican Study was "a four-year inquiry into the education and adjust-ment of Puerto Rican pupils in the public schools of New York City ... a major effort ... to establish on a sound basis a city-wide program for the continuing improvement of the educational oppor-tunities of all non-English speaking pupils in the public schools" (Cordasco 1972: 341). It must be noted that this study predated the bilingual education movement of the 1960s, and yet it addressed, in a most comprehensive fashion, the fundamental elements of the multifaceted needs of the recent migrant children, their parents, and of educators who, by virtue of the gaps in their earlier training, were unable to attend to the educational and social complexities of this non-English-speaking population. The 1953 Puerto Rican study followed a less comprehensive study carried out by the Mayor's Advisory Committee on Puerto Rican Affairs in 1951. This report, entitled *Puerto Rican Pupils in the New York City School, 1951* was a survey of "75 elementary and junior high schools as well as a report on day classes for adults, evening schools, community centers and vacation playgrounds" (Cordasco 1972: 347). While the report ostensibly demonstrated a genuine concern for the earlier waves of Puerto Rican and other Latino migrants, the New York schools seemed to have continued on a downward spiral, in spite of well-intentioned efforts at devising programs for Latino youth. So what happened, what went wrong? According to a report on Puerto Rican New Yorkers, "despite generational improvement . . . both Puerto Rican males and females ages 18 to 24 in 1980 remained substantially below the high school graduation achievement level of all 18 to 24 year olds, more than 25 percentage points lower" (Salvo and Mann 1985: 10).

When Puerto Ricans—who continue to be the most populous Latino ethnic group in New York City—are statistically merged with other Hispanics from the Caribbean, Central and South America, it is estimated that as an aggregate group Latinos make up 33.6 percent of the total kindergarten through twelfth-grade population in New York City's public schools (Reyes 1987: 3). This increase in the Hispanic school population has not been restricted to New York State. The nation's Latino population has increased at a much greater rate than non-Hispanics. From 1980 to 1988 alone the total number of Hispanics in the United States increased by 34 percent (U.S. Census Bureau 1989: 1). Hispanics now constitute approximately 8.8 percent of the total U.S. population (about 21.1 million) (U.S. Census Bureau 1993), an increase of approximately 7.8 million persons since 1980. Because the Latino community, in mean age, tends to be much younger than the non-Hispanic, the dramatic shifts in population will have their greatest impact on our urban schools. In other words, schools will continue to be the single most important resource for this rapidly expanding group. Does this mean that our schools will simply continue to perpetuate the miseducation of Latinos at an even greater rate or will schools, educators, parents, and community begin to address the economic and social disaster that threatens these communities and, by extension, the nation as a whole?

The Task Force on the Education of Children and Youth at Risk described the state's public school system as "a two tier system that has essentially given up on the neediest students" (see Kolbert 1988: 1 and 31). In other words, while culture and language differences are crucial considerations in the education of the Latino child, racism, poverty, and political powerlessness continue to play a central role in shaping the poor educational outcome of the schools in these communities. To educators responsible for teaching the ever-increasing number of Hispanics and other ethnic minorities, the challenge has been profound and the failures have been equally astounding. The problems resulting from inadequate and bankrupt educational systems are not new to minorities and the poor in this country, but these conditions do seem to be worsening. In fact, the crisis in education in New York is so profound that former Education Commissioner Thomas Sobol, in an address to top school administrators in Westchester County, said "if we don't come up with genuine fundamental reform soon, we are going to lose the whole game" (see Keagan 1989: 4). These are remarkable words, especially when one considers that they come from the highest ranking education official in New York State. If he shares these demoralizing thoughts publicly, it makes one wonder whether or not these conditions are far worse than one could imagine. And, if this is his assessment of education in general, what then is the educational future for the Latino community?

Parental Involvement in the School System

We have been taught to believe, rather erroneously, that a child's journey through the educational system is a social interaction that simply involves the child and his/her succession of teachers from kindergarten through high school and into college. Many are also under the misapprehension that this particular social interaction— the teacher and the pupil in the classroom—is all that really counts in the child's struggle to survive in the educational system. In point of fact, most Americans have quite a limited understanding of what specific elements are needed to produce an effective and successful educational system.

We do know generally that poor educational outcomes (high dropout rates, low reading and math scores) go hand in hand with poverty, racism, poor housing conditions, high unemployment, poor health care, inadequate prenatal and neonatal care, and teenage pregnancies. As suggested by a New York Board of Education report, *"overall educational performance at the district and high school level is alarmingly associated with the demography of the districts' and high schools' enrollment and with characteristics of the communities that comprise the districts"* (Task Force on Human Relations 1989: 23, my emphasis).

For the most part, as has become increasingly evident in scandals in which local community school boards have been charged with "corruption and improprieties" parents continue to be locked out of the educational decision-making process which is directly affecting the future of their children (Purdum 1988). However, parents who tend to have a higher level of education, income, and political awareness are also more likely to be involved in the inner workings of the community school. Suburban parents, for example, who often select places of residence after they have made a careful assessment of the quality of local schools and who pay direct school taxes based on property values, make certain that they *know* what the school budget will be for the next academic year. They know full well that maintaining an active connection with the teachers, the schools, and its policymakers is critical for the success of their children, especially if their child's educational experience is expected to result in a "good college" placement. These same parents have the power to reject or accept these school budgets, whereas, poor inner-city parents do not.

This kind of involvement and empowerment comes as a result of privilege, class, political awareness, and education. On the other hand, the poor or working-class parents, who tend to be predominantly Hispanic and African American and who generally live in the inner city, are on the whole kept uninformed and for the most part feel no sense of connection to the mysterious inner workings of the school. Many feel threatened and awed by the complexities of the system. These parents are far more likely than their suburban counterparts *not* to participate in school governance activities such as school board elections or activities of the parents' association. They are, by and large, kept out of the inner circle of policy-making bodies.

In their recent report to the Commissioner of Education of the State of New York, the Task Force on the Teaching Profession, while setting forth far-reaching recommendations for the "fundamental restructuring of our schools," also "recognizes the crucial need for parents to be involved in the schools, both as interested supporters of their own children's educational progress and as collaborators in developing strong educational programs" (Commissioner's Task Force 1988: 5, 22). But this report doesn't seem to go far enough. While the Task Force acknowledges the need for parental involvement along with other sectors of the community, it nevertheless fails to address the fundamental inequities that exist between the undereducated poor parent and the one who is solidly middle class and sufficiently educated to enable him or her to effectively challenge the system and its personnel. If we are going to move ahead in the area of parental involvement, it is an issue that must be addressed in a far more effective way than it has been in the past. Parental involvement takes on a special urgency in the Latino community, because language and cultural and economic factors continue to pose significant obstacles to effective communication and engagement in the process of school reform. Despite the recent scandals involving members on local community boards in New York City, and the subsequent investigations into wrongdoing, the idea of community control and direct parental involvement in local school boards still remains as sound an idea as it was when these boards were first established in 1970. Parents need to be trained, informed, and brought directly into the educational process. The long and tumultuous struggle to secure community control in New York City, as suggested by Marilyn Gittel, was "an attempt to achieve a new balance of power by reintroducing competition into the system. Local community groups are competing with the professionals for power, resources and a larger share in the decision-making process" (Gittel 1970: 115).

While the struggles for power continue on many levels throughout the system, especially between the central board and the local community school boards, this system of direct community participation remains the best method to date to assure parental involvement in the education of their children. Power struggles notwithstanding, the need for cooperation between all of the segments of the community must take precedence. The school-based or on-site management models, now gaining in popularity throughout the United States, seem to offer an excellent opportunity for direct parental involvement on the grassroots level where parents can work closely with teachers, counselors, paraprofessionals, and school administrators.[4] Former New York City schools Chancellor Joseph Fernández initiated an "innovative project: the School Based Management/Shared Decision-Making initiative (SBM/SDM).[5] A strong proponent of school-based management, Chancellor Fernández reached out to all segments of the New York City education community, including university faculty, in order to provide community schools with direct technical assistance as school-based teams began to develop new strategies to improve their programs. While most see this as an opportunity for improved change, others wonder whether or not this practice will take hold in the nation's largest school system where a new chancellor continues to work under even greater fiscal pressure than his predecessor.

The Politics and Pedagogy of Bilingual-Multicultural Education

Another educational battle which has claimed many casualties in the Latino community and which is probably one of the most highly contested public debates in education today is the issue of *bilingual education*. Ironically, Hispanic parents (and now other language minority parents as well) turn out to be unwitting victims of this struggle as it is currently being played out in our schools. Some parents, who are naturally concerned about securing the best for their children and who unfortunately in many instances have not been fully informed about the benefits and expectations of these programs, form a frontline offensive attack against the school-based bilingual program. A variety of factors contribute to their fear of having their children placed in a bilingual classroom. One of their overriding concerns is that their children will be irrevocably labeled as limited English proficient (LEP) and stigmatized as slow learners for the rest of the child's educational life. Sometimes, the scattered negative experiences that their friends and relatives have passed on to them about bilingual education do not put these programs in a good light; they only serve to promote distrust and fear.

What many parents don't know is that bilingual education is a highly complex pedagogical method of instruction which unfortunately has been misrepresented because of political, social, and cultural misinformation. The controversy surrounding bilingual education has its roots in the social structure of the society. Unlike introducing a new way of teaching math or science, the failure or success of bilingual education—because of the power of language and culture—is tied to beliefs, values, attitudes, and mythologies that seem to go well beyond the experience of children in the classroom and serve to keep supporters of this innovative teaching experiment on the defensive.

Language and *culture* in American education continue to be debatable and negotiable issues. This ambivalence toward culture and language seems to be an expression of a fundamental contradiction in American ideals and actual practice in our schools and in the larger society. While we encourage second-language learning in secondary and postsecondary education, many continue to discourage the use of a child's native language in the primary and most critical years of learning. Lamentably, many teachers, parents, and school administrators are too easily persuaded to squander this vital learning resource that the child brings to his or her first encounter with the educational process.

To teach children in any language other than English seems to many to be a violation of a fundamental American belief and practice. For example, the movement to make English the official language of the United States seems to be a direct response to an imagined threat that is perceived to come not only from the Hispanic community but also from other language minority groups. The ever-increasing flow of both documented and undocumented workers from Latin America into the United States has served to fuel these old xenophobic fantasies.

The proponents of the U.S. English movement hope that making English the official language would effectively put an end to bilingual education in America. The U.S. English movement is a political manifestation of the more deeply rooted fears of language and cultural assimilationists who believe that one needs to give up one's native language in order to become a "true" American. This pro-English antiforeign-language sentiment was widespread during and after World War I and up through about 1950. So what seems to be the issue for many in this debate is how one would define what it means to be an American. The fear of balkanization leads many to reject the potential consequences of encouraging the maintenance of native languages in the schools. The old fear of split national loyalties also prompts detractors to reject the notion of language continuity. This fear seems to be a variation of the war hysteria that provoked what many feel was a racist policy during World War II that resulted in the internment of thousands of Japanese Americans in concentration camps.

In the wake of the Japanese attack on the United States naval base in Pearl Harbor in 1941, the American government quickly enacted a series of policies which effectively removed all Japanese Americans from their homes, businesses, and schools in an effort to stave off possible collaboration with Japan. These racist actions were prompted by the fundamental belief that the uncontrolled presence of Japanese Americans in their homes constituted a real threat to United States' national security. It must be noted that these were naturalized first-, second-, and third-generation Americans who were imprisoned, and whose businesses, property, and homes were confiscated.

While the same kind of threat was never attributed to German Americans during World War II, the strong anti-German sentiment that swept the nation during and after World War I resulted in strong state and local efforts to eliminate the use of German in a variety of areas. Kenji Hakuta points out that "German was barred not just from many private and public schools but also from public meetings, telephone communications, and the streets." (1986:168). Hakuta goes on to state that the laws prohibiting German and other foreign languages were eventually "declared unconstitutional by the Supreme Court in 1923." However, so much stigma had been attached to the study of German that by the time this ruling was issued, the number of students enrolled in German classes had dropped from 24 percent in 1915 to one-sixth of one percent in 1992. This strong sentiment against foreign-language use in our public schools can be seen today in the antibilingual-education pronouncements of the group that calls itself the U.S. English movement.

The racism and ethnocentrism inherent in the policies and actions carried out against the Japanese Americans, and the projected fears of speakers of other languages, while not on the same order or magnitude, do grow out of the same xenophobic tradition that is deeply rooted in the American cultural psyche. Placed in this larger social-cultural context, the U.S. English movement and its broad-based assault against bilingual education and other forms of bilingualism in the public arena (e.g., bilingual ballots, bilingual signs, instructions in public places, etc.) can be understood in a framework that goes well beyond the classroom. It was reported by the Language Rights Committee of the National Congress for Puerto Rican Rights that the group U.S. English—in a "blatant attack on our language and culture—hit Puerto Rico in an attempt to organize a chapter there. The people of Puerto Rico responded with a firm and uncompromising statement: 'Spanish is not negotiable under any political circumstances.'"[6]

This represents a rather bold incursion into a Latin American society, controlled by the United States, but proud of its traditions. So the issue of how, when, and at what pace children are to be introduced to a second language (English), takes on a dimension which seems to have very little to do with the actual pedagogical merit of one method of instruction versus another. It has more to do with what one group's idea of how being American is to be defined, and the role that English-language competence plays in that definition. Of course, this notion seems to be in direct conflict with those who believe that language is a psychological, social, and cultural resource, a birthright that must be used and preserved in our culturally diverse society. It also conflicts with the idea which is promoted in high schools, colleges, and universities that an educated person should be proficient in at least one foreign language.

The controversies over bilingual education in America and the tenacious resistance expressed by many mainstream educators have combined to keep the proponents of bilingual education on the defensive. The all-out assaults on bilingual education from its inception in the 1960s exploited some of the early-phase difficulties and inconsistencies of this new educational experiment. It must be noted, however, that bilingual education or the conflicts over it are not new to the American educational scene. Keller and Van Hooft document the history of bilingual education and bilingualism from colonial times to the present. According to these writers, the languages used most frequently in the 1700s in Pennsylvania, Maryland, Virginia, and the Carolinas were German, one or another Scandinavian language, Dutch, Polish, and French. English was taught as a separate subject in some instances and the native languages were used as a medium of instruction (1982: 3, 4). The variation in focus and use of English and other languages varied greatly. In the Southwest, where the Spanish had established colonial territories, bilingual schooling continued to exist until the war with Mexico in 1848, and in some places it continued until statehood was granted to these southwestern territories. In fact, as early as 1753, according to Stalker, Benjamin Franklin, "in a letter to a friend, expressed the fear that German would be so prevalent in Pennsylvania that the legislature would need interpreters. He noted that a good many of the street signs in Philadelphia were in German, without English translation" (1988: 19). What is most fascinating about this historical footnote is that the same arguments were recently repeated in Florida's debate over the imposition of an official state language, except that Spanish was at issue, not German.

The history of bilingualism in the United States makes for interesting reading and gives one an entirely different perspective on the language and ethnic development of this nation. It should be clear to even the most casual reader of this documentation that American history is indeed ethnic history in the truest sense and that these debates have been a significant part of the ever-evolving question of what it means to be an American—a debate which was initiated by ethnic studies programs more than twenty years ago and recently reignited by the multicultural debate in our schools and universities.

Today the research literature on bilingualism and bilingual education has become increasingly specialized; a new generation of bilingual teacher has now entered the classroom with well-honed skills in linguistics, and cultural knowledge of the pupils in their classes. This is not to say that the problems have all disappeared, but I do suggest that the proliferation in research literature and its increased level of sophistication have served to generate new and more refined information about methods, materials, first- and second-language acquisition, psycholinguistic and sociolinguistic aspects of bilingualism, language development and cognitive development, transfer of learning skills from one language to the second, and so on. While this increased interest in both theoretical and applied research is significant, we still need to learn a good deal more about the social as well as psychological aspects of bilingualism in the community and in the educational setting. There is much to be accomplished in this area, but because the question of bilingual education is so emotionally and politically charged and its method of instruction is relatively new, it will continue to be challenged and questioned, despite widespread awareness of the profound failings of our regular school system.

Meanwhile millions of students with limited English proficiency (LEP) in public schools throughout the United States are continuing to struggle and fail because of language barriers. The official numbers published by the New York State Department of Education have been challenged because, as a recent study by Reynaldo Macías points out, "the LEP student count was closer to 350,000 rather than the 100,000 identified by district reporting" (1989: 46). This undercount was compounded until quite recently by pushing students into mainstream classrooms before they were sufficiently proficient in English. Acknowledging this problem, the New York State Department of Education reported that it has now raised the eligibility standard to the fortieth percentile instead of the twenty-third, which effectively "broadens the range of students eligible for bilingual or English as a second language (ESL) funding."[7] In this same report, Education Commissioner Thomas Sobel suggests that the higher cutoff score would give students "a much more reasonable chance of succeeding in a mainstream classroom" (New York State Education Department 1989: 1).

This shift in language assessment and placement is just one more example of the complexity of this issue. Even when it has been agreed and legally mandated that students with limited English proficiency must receive special language instruction, how one defines and measures the level of proficiency will determine who does or does not receive bilingual or ESL services. Bilingual education is not a panacea for the deeply rooted failures of our current educational system, and it is also not a method that lends itself to simplistic pro and con arguments. It is, however, an instructional approach that should be given an opportunity to grow in a variety of places and through a variety of models. When the term "bilingual education" is used it is erroneously assumed that the methods of one are necessarily the methods of all such programs. It is rarely acknowledged that these programs are as diverse as the so-called "standard" monolingual school programs. In his appeal to allow bilingual education programs the room to grow and develop, Joshua Fishman suggests:

> Let us not permit bilingual education to "self-destruct" in a decade like the countless educational fads of former years. Bilingual education is not a fad or gimmick. We need information and perspective and conviction to make it work, and we need them every bit as much as we need the time, the money, and the manpower that are so much more frequently mentioned. (1976: xii)

The Multicultural Debate: Implications for Latinos

There are a number of places along the educational pipeline (from the pre-service teacher training process to in-service practice) where the standard curriculum can be expanded and enriched to account for the society's multiplicity of cultures, races, and languages. Currently, curricular changes are taking place most rapidly in those community schools where demographic shifts seem to be a step ahead of yesterday's ethnocentric (Anglo-centric) and monocultural curriculum. Responsive community educators and officials in many state education departments have acknowledged the need to have the curriculum reflect the lives and realities of those who populate the schools.

Are our teacher-training institutions doing everything they can to address these new realities? How effectively our universities prepare to meet this challenge in the restructuring of their own multicultural curriculum and antiracist strategies will have a profound impact on the educational outcome of Latino and other racial/ethnic minority children for the next decade and well into the twenty-first century.

In New York State several reports on diversity in the curriculum have been released. A 1989 report entitled *A Curriculum of Inclusion*, represented the state's most ambitious effort and perhaps its most controversial one. It pushed educators in the direction of shaping a more inclusive multicultural curriculum. The earlier Task Report noted:

> to the extent that the curriculum treats any culture inappropriately, it treats all cultures inappropriately. To the extent that contributions from non-Europeans are omitted from the curriculum, European American children grow up erroneously believing that the only people who contributed to the society were from their culture. Thus, if the Regent's goals of an education recognizing our pluralistic society are to be met, an accurate, inclusive curriculum is essential for all children in every school district in the state. (Commissioner's Task Force 1988: 3)

This report generated a good deal of discussion and controversy. However, two years later, a second report—*One Nation, Many Peoples: A Declaration of Cultural Interdependence*—prepared by the New York State Social Studies Review and Development Committee (1991) superseded the earlier report. Although there was controversy and some dissent on the part of the committee's membership, the *One Nation* report was perceived as a far more acceptable document because for many it represented a more temperate approach to diversity and seemed less politically strident than the earlier *Curriculum of Inclusion* report. Nonetheless, these two reports and other similar reports throughout the nation have drawn sharp criticism and set off a heated round of debates that are still reverberating in all quarters of our educational establishment.

Similarly, the New York City Public Schools, although an early proponent of multicultural curricula, joined in the culture wars controversy when it issued its *Children of the Rainbow* curriculum guidelines (New York City Public Schools 1991). The controversy seemed to center around the suggested guidelines for how to sensitize children to the fact that there are indeed homosexual parents in the community who should be viewed with the same level of acceptance accorded to all parents and families. Joseph Fernández, the former schools chancellor, said that "we took more heat in 1992 with our 'Children of the Rainbow' multicultural curriculum, which included a small segment (two pages out of 443) dealing with tolerance of 'non-traditional' (including homosexual) family structures"

(Fernández 1993: 239). This curricular suggestion created one of the most impassioned, emotionally laden public debates heard to date. The *Rainbow* curriculum had apparently touched a core psychological and cultural value in certain segments of the community. In many of the Latino school districts the objections were as forceful as those of the European ethnic communities in other sections of the city. That curriculum package has been redrafted and is tentatively being called the "Comprehensive Instructional Program" (Diana Caballero, personal communication, April 1994).

These kinds of curricular reform mandates are by no means new. They follow earlier calls for broadening the cultural curriculum base. What is at issue is if and how these changes will be effectively implemented and, secondly, whether or not these educational reforms will ultimately have an impact on a society that has for so long struggled to eliminate the consequences of cultural and institutional racism. I am not sure, however, that curricular change will reduce ethnic friction in our society at large, as suggested in the *Curriculum of Inclusion* report (Commissioner's Task Force 1989: 7). Before this can happen, it would seem that other, more fundamental socioeconomic structural changes have to occur in the society at large. It does seem plausible that a more inclusive curricular approach potentially can help reduce the high dropout rates for Latinos and other racial/ethnic minorities. And it also seems likely that poor academic performance and ethnic friction in the schools may be reduced by some measure, especially as educators start to look more carefully at the hidden messages that are conveyed through a biased curriculum. Beyond these kinds of benefits, our citizenry might also be encouraged to develop a more culturally expansive understanding of this nation's history.

Many of the critics of the earlier *Curriculum of Inclusion* report seemed to be offended by the choice of language, underlying assumptions, and potential damage to the education of the children who might be touched by these kinds of proposed curricular changes. Diane Ravitch, educational historian, emerged as one of the chief critics of this report and other similar calls for a vigorous multicultural curriculum. In her seeming determination to undermine and challenge the findings, interpretations, and recommendations of that earlier report, she introduces her own set of assumptions, interpretations, interesting jargon and phrasing, and a rather puzzling series of textual contradictions (Ravitch 1990). For example, Ravitch at one point in her critique says, "That influence (the European influence) is a historical *fact* [italics are mine], reflected in our Constitution as well as our cultural and economic institutions" (Ravitch 1990: 47). And shortly thereafter, she suggests that

> it is important to teach students about conflicting interpretations and about debates among experts. Every subject field has dis-agreements among the experts, and the study itself becomes more interesting if students are let in on these disagreements. History is not just a bunch of facts and dates and names that must be regurgitated for tests; it's a field that is alive with controversy. (1990: 48)

These mixed messages can become somewhat confusing. Is it or is it not a *historical fact* that a European influence is reflected in the Constitution, and in our cultural and economic institutions? Or is it something that can be interpreted in a slightly different way? And if it is a historical fact, then would it not also follow that it is the European value of property and property rights that propelled the founding fathers to build the institution of slavery into the Constitution (Bell 1987)? This would lead one to consider several alternative hypotheses for this particular moment in American history, would it not?

Ravitch was joined by others in her critique of the *Curriculum of Inclusion*. Many well-known scholars have joined the public assaults on the multicultural education reform. Historian Arthur Schlesinger, Jr., added his voice to the debate in the *Wall Street Journal* commentary entitled "When Ethnic Studies Are Un-American" (Schlesinger 1990: 14). Their arguments have a ring of similarity in that there is a call to arms to protect the democratic principles upon which this nation is built. We are asked to revel in and take pride in our European inheritance and warned that "if we repudiate the quite marvelous inheritance that history has bestowed on us—and this is truly the ironic part—we "would invite fragmentation of our own culture into a quarrelsome spatter of enclaves" (Schlesinger 1990: 14).

Ironically, Ravitch, in her presentation of California's model for multicultural education, invokes a similar warning, which she articulates as follows:

> The California history framework explicitly recognizes the positive value of pluralism in American society. Pluralism is presented as a key to understanding and defining the American community—a society and a culture to which we all belong. If there is no overall community, if all we have is a *motley* [my italics] collection of racial and ethnic cultures, there will be no sense of the common good. Each group will fight for its own particular interests, and we could easily disintegrate as a nation, becoming instead embroiled in the kinds of ethnic conflicts that often dominate the foreign news each night. (1990: 19)

And to this rather grim futuristic scenario, she adds that we might yet arrive at a time when these kinds of ethnic-specific interests may possibly lead to an end to the support of public education as we've known it. One may ask each of these scholars, and others who are similarly inclined, what was it in our societal structure before the introduction of ethnic studies or multicultural education proposals that contributed to the creation of ghettos, barrios, and Native American reservations? And do they really believe that the effort to introduce other complementary and perhaps competing interpretations of history into the standard school curriculum would necessarily lead to the kind of social chaos they predict?

These attempts to ward off the inevitable changes that must take place in our schools and in our communities only serve to illustrate how deeply rooted the need is in this society to prevent our nation from recovering a history that accurately reflects the experiences of racial/ethnic minorities in American society. The culmination of Schlesinger's assaults on multiculturalism came with the publication of *The Disuniting of America: Reflections on a Multicultural Society* (1992). In this work, Schlesinger carries his argument to the point where he suggests that multiculturalism may indeed be a threat to the very foundation of the republic (Vázquez 1993a). The hyperbolic language and ideology proposed by critics like Schlesinger, Ravitch, and others only serves to escalate the discourse and further distort what this debate is all about (Vázquez 1991).

Because New York State has always been a place of great ethnic diversity, there continues to be a pressing need for a truly multicultural curricular approach in our schools. In response, a great many school districts are beginning to make significant changes in their curriculum. However, professional training does not begin in the community school or in state educational agencies, but in our schools of education. This is the arena where a multicultural education approach can have a significant impact. For it is in the preprofessional training sequence that the future educator either is or is not sensitized to the complexities, subtleties, and the importance of understanding the impact and role of race, culture, and language in the educational process. The challenge facing our teacher-training faculties, through a broad range of specializations which are to be found within our schools of education, is how to best lay down a solid foundation in this very critical area of pedagogy. It is suggested by Watson (as cited in Modgil et al. 1986) that without "reform taking place in teacher education institutions there is unlikely to be any real change in classrooms and the curriculum."

With new mandates being issued by the state for a restructured teacher education curriculum in our universities, and with the recent reports calling for curricular change in our schools, our teacher-training institutions are now beginning to take initial steps to broaden and enrich the cultural content of the existing teacher education curriculum.

Researchers in the field have delineated a number of distinct types or approaches to multicultural education which are based on select assumptions about race and culture and how these should be used in the school curriculum (Banks and McGee Banks 1995). And, of course, these diverse perspectives add to the confusion in our community schools were practitioners are required to apply these varied theoretical approaches. As suggested by Modgil et al., "the very term [multicultural education] is without agreed definition, and the implementation of the concept appears to depend largely upon the standpoints of individuals, whether they take an assimilationist, cultural pluralist, or anti-racist approach (1986: 5). This was borne out in a preliminary survey of faculty in the School of Education at Queens College (CUNY) (Vázquez, Proefreidt and Truesdell 1988).

Some critics of multicultural education propose that it is a pedagogy which, in its most benign form, tends to hide behind the more liberal notions of "cultural pluralism" and, in doing so, denies the centrality of racism and class struggle in American society (Berlowitz 1984: 134). So the fundamental and persistent problems of racism and economic neglect continue to go unchallenged in the very institutions that offer us the greatest hope of addressing these issues head-on. Kozol found that racial segregation in the inner-city schools of the late 1980s had simply intensified, and what mystifies him "is that the nation, for all practice and intent, has turned its back upon the moral implications, if not yet the legal ramifications, of the *Brown* decision. . . . The dual society, at least in public education, seems to be unquestioned" (1991: 4).

Conceptual language in multicultural education is something we must carefully define, examine, and re-examine before establishing firm curricular guidelines and objectives. Who trains the trainers, and what are our curricular, personal, and ideological agendas?

As James Lynch suggests, "Most staff and students in teacher education derive their cultural biography from an Anglo-centric socialization of many years' duration and manifest efficiency, so that the question inevitably arises of where the expertise is to come from to implement such revolutionary and innovatory programmes, even given the dubious hypotheses that the consensual will exist" (Lynch 1986: 154).

This simply means that the professors who teach the teachers and the teachers who teach the children must come to terms with themselves, acknowledge their own racial and cultural biases, and perhaps their own negative internalized values and assumptions regarding race, culture, and language in American society. On the whole, our training programs, in curricular content and approach, have failed to keep pace with the rapidly changing demographics of our schools and communities. As a consequence, generations of teachers trained for service in the urban school have not been given the kinds of skills that would allow them to successfully serve one of the most culturally and racially diverse school populations in the nation.

Most of us, as indicated above, approach the issue of multicultural education from a perspective that is essentially a fusion of personal experiences and beliefs, and informed in part by our professional understanding of what the role of culture and race should be in the educational process. We are all products of an educational system and a society which has promulgated countless ethnic myths, fallacies, racist distortions, and stereotypes which in turn have been internalized and have become part of our own personal belief system. Few teachers or trainers of teachers (e.g., university professors) have undertaken a formal in-depth study of the dynamics of culture and race. So, when called upon to introduce these factors into a mainstream teacher education curriculum, we do so in light of what our own personal/professional understanding is of each of these issues and concepts (Vázquez et al. 1988).

Those who believe that multicultural education, in its many varied forms and models, should be made a permanent part of the educational process will have to answer a number of fundamental questions which take us beyond the boundaries of the classroom. For example, are our pedagogical objectives aimed at correcting the built-in structural inequities in our socioeconomic system? What are the links between these two societal domains? Teachers must be aware of these connections. Or, on the other hand, are our pedagogical concerns with culture and race merely an attempt to reduce potential conflict between people? Both laudable objectives, but certainly different politically and perhaps philosophically. Are we engaged in an aggressive radical "anti-racist education" or a more moderate "multicultural education," which to some may seem more of a palliative strategy than the former? Similarly, if educators believe that culturally different students simply have to be helped to move into the American mainstream, they too would be reluctant to use a *social reconstructionist* approach to multicultural education.[8]

The "Multicultural and Social Reconstructionist" approach, as discussed by Sleeter and Grant (1987), is the multicultural approach that prepares students to challenge social structural inequality and to promote cultural diversity. It is the one approach that clearly answers the question: What is the ultimate purpose in a curriculum that encourages our understanding and appreciation of differences in race, culture, class and language? Furthermore, it openly promotes the idea of social change through the educational establishment. It also encourages a democratization of the educational environment as a model for collective action as empowerment, as opposed to unquestioned obedience. This model actively pursues the goal of social structural change. It uses ethnic studies as a way of teaching the student to go beyond the one-dimensional cultural focus of the traditional multicultural agenda. It is an approach that is rooted in the radical beginnings of the multicultural movement.

Is College Admission for Latino Students the Ticket In—or the Ticket Out?

For those Latinos who survive twelve years of inadequate primary and secondary schooling, college seems to be the most logical place for them to go, despite the high probability of dropping out. It may indeed be the answer for a select few, but for far too many students, attending college may prove their educational undoing. Traditionally, when one enters college in American society it is assumed that certain basic academic skills have been mastered and that a sufficient level of general knowledge has been absorbed so that the student can begin to tackle a more complex set of intellectual problems (college-level courses). Without this fundamental preparation, the student will likely flounder. Far too many students entering college today are simply underprepared for the rigors of a standard university curriculum. For example, in 1986 more than 75 percent of City University of New York's incoming first-year students needed remedial help (Mayor's Commission 1986: 21). While this percentage of students includes whites as well as racial/ethnic minorities, the greatest need for compensatory and remedial courses comes from the Hispanic, African-American, and in many instances the Asian-American students. The CUNY budget investment in the area of remedial programs, intended to offset the ill effects of twelve years of a New York public school education, is laudable and necessary, but frequently much too little comes much too late in the student's academic life before he or she is pushed out of the university.

These college-level remedial and compensatory programs are simply another measure of the public school system's inability to come to terms with the complexities of educating the poor and ethnic/racial minorities. When the public schools fail our minority communities, and when our society makes it possible for underprepared students to enter two- and four-year schools with minimum basic academic skills, we are all participating in a grand educational illusion. And by extension, as is so frequently noted, the educational marginality of Puerto Rican and Latino students ultimately contributes to the economic marginality of an increasing Puerto Rican and Latino population in the Northeast.

The National Council of La Raza report, *Moving from the Margins: Puerto Rican Young Men and Family Poverty* (Pérez 1993) and the Latino Commission on Educational Reform (1992) study are only two reports which amply demonstrate the linkages that exist between reduced educational opportunities, persistent poverty, and bankrupt educational policies that fail to address the basic learning needs of Latino children, young adults, and adults in this region.

There is no doubt that a select number of students who need some brush-up on basic skills are indeed helped by some of these remedial and compensatory programs, but a significant portion of those requiring remediation face serious setbacks in their academic advancement. Two major studies which focused on the Latino student experience in the City University of New York, raise significant policy and practice questions about how the university utilizes its screening and placement tests, how it manages its English as a second language (ESL) programs, and how the imposition of basic skills (non-credit) prerequisite courses ultimately contribute to the unusually high dropout rate of Puerto Rican and other Latino students (Pereira et al. 1993; Otheguy 1990).

The concerns of these two reports were first articulated by the Puerto Rican Council on Higher Education (PRCHE) in the middle to late eighties. PRCHE, an educational advocacy group of concerned Puerto Rican and Latino educators, set forth a number of research initiatives within the City University of New York. Two of those initiatives called for focused research in the area of language and language policy in CUNY, as well as research into the question of retention of Puerto Rican and other Latino students. The CUNY administration and PRCHE endorsed these two major research projects. A third important area of concern, which has yet to be explored, is that of Puerto Rican and Latino faculty and staff recruitment and retention and promotion.

Once in the college setting, the question of retention becomes critical. The student with poor or marginal academic skills requires constant monitoring to assure that he/she doesn't fall between the cracks. Often the courses in remediation taken by many students simply are not enough to offset their poor skills and years of academic neglect. Ricardo Otheguy asserts that "as matters stand now, large numbers of Latino students enter the University only in name, since instruction in remedial programs is mostly at the secondary school level, and since instruction in ESL programs, despite being at tertiary levels, is usually not granted credit" (1990: 60). Both four-year and community colleges must make a greater commitment to the issue of retention. If underprepared students continue to enter these institutions in ever-increasing numbers, then higher education must of necessity re-examine its long-standing mission and commitment to the liberal arts and preprofessional preparation.

Some higher education researchers suggest that we ought to look at a statistical notion called a "persistence rate": the rate of completion or the actual time it takes to get a degree after the formal year of admission. They assert that the students now entering school are not only facing academic obstacles but must contend with multiple factors which increase the time it takes to graduate. The former chancellor of New York City schools, Anthony Alvarado, in an earlier report on the CUNY Community Colleges says: "most students need significantly more time, given the need for remediation and the financial concerns, employment pressures, and family responsibilities of adult urban life. Therefore, I believe that analyzing retention data over a broader time span provides a clearer picture of the dropout problem" (Alvarado 1985: 7).

It is interesting to note that after seven years, the community college class of 1978 had a "staggering" dropout rate of 74 percent (Alvarado 1985: 8). That means that in 1985 only 26 percent of the students had graduated. Alvarado points out, however, that the community college dropout rate is a problem that is national in scope. Using California as a case in point, he cites that their graduation rate after three years is only 16 percent. By anyone's measure, these are still quite dismal statistics about the so-called "persistence rate" for Latino undergraduates.

Lavin et al. (1986), in their report on the impact of the short-lived CUNY open admissions policy, suggest that there were indeed dramatic gains by minorities during that period. Yet, the fact that it took some students up to eight or nine years to graduate (the "persistence rate"), is presented in a most positive manner, as a kind of optimistic alternative way of looking at what might otherwise be seen as a dismal retention record for Latinos and African Americans in higher education. The positive jargon or labeling used to report what for many minority students turns out to be a nine- to ten-year sojourn through college is presented in such a way that we are asked to be delighted with these kinds of educational achievements. These persistence statistics are more a measure of the tenacity of a minority individual than they are a reflection of the success or failure of compensatory college education programs. A Latino student who takes this long to complete a college degree, while exhibiting great tenacity and determination, also enters the labor market as a much older individual with a significant loss of earning power over a lifetime.

Encouraged by some guidance counselors, teachers, friends, and relatives, discouraged by others, far too many Latino students who enter a two- or four-year college with the greatest hopes are likely not to graduate (Governor's Advisory Committee 1985). While both financial and academic support programs can do much to slow down the revolving-door syndrome in higher education, the lack of adequate preparation in the public schools continues to produce students who are eventually forced out of the system. The irreparable loss to individuals, to families, and to communities is ultimately translated into a loss in human resources to the city, the state, and to the nation. As a report of a Ford Foundation education task force assesses the problem:

> If our nation is truly "at risk" due to declining quality of educa-
> tion, as recent commissions have concluded, then majority
> America is confronting a situation minority parents have histori-
> cally encountered in schooling for their children. Disenfranchise-
> ment and marginalization incontestably characterize Hispanic
> education in the U.S., and evidence is mounting which suggests
> an overall deterioration of this condition. (Institute for Puerto
> Rican Policy 1984: 23)

And a decade later, The National Council of La Raza report "Moving from the Margin" echoes this dismal outlook for Latino youth.

> Hispanic youth, overall, remain the most undereducated major
> segment of the U.S. population at a time when they represent
> one in ten elementary and secondary school students. Among
> Hispanic youth aged 18–24, 55% have completed high school,
> compared to 75% of Blacks and 82% of Whites. Recent national
> data show that more than one in three Latino youth aged 16–24
> do not have a high school diploma. Additional studies have
> shown that the quality of education received by a substantial
> proportion of Puerto Rican and Latino youth is poor, that they

are especially likely to learn in segregated schools from teachers
with fewer credentials than those in other school districts, that
often they are held back and enrolled below the grade level
expected for their age, and that they have low rates of college
enrollment and completion. (Pérez 1993: 18)

We cannot expect to wash away the profound failure of our
primary and secondary school systems by simply redefining what
educational success and failure mean in postsecondary education.
If we simply accept the fact that it takes Latino students a longer
time to complete college than it does other nonethnic or racial
minority students, then we have the beginnings of a separate and
unequal system of higher education.

In an effort to understand why it is that almost 50 percent
of Latino and African-American students drop out within their
first two years at college, Pereira, Cobb, and Makoulis (1993) conducted one of the most comprehensive studies of Puerto Ricans
and other Latinos in the City University of New York. The Pereira
et al. report carefully examined the academic profiles of Latino and
non-Latino subgroups entering CUNY in 1980 and 1988. Among
dozens of factors contributing to success or failure of these cohorts,
they looked at areas such as admissions of specific racial/ethnic
groups; high school academic measures; skills assessment test outcomes; performance on CUNY entrance and skills exams; degree of
attainment; persistence and dropout attribution; total course loads;
non-credit hours; and credit hours attempted, completed, and
earned.

On the whole, the data gathered by these researchers will give
us more than enough to look at as we try to make sense of the
complexity of factors which contribute to the persistence of some
Latino students and failure of others in the CUNY system and
perhaps, by extension, in other institutions of higher education.
However, if as recommended by Pereira et al. (in what seems a
most thorough report on the state of Puerto Ricans and other Latinos
in CUNY) we simply redefine what it means to earn college credit,
then we are in danger of creating a two-tiered system in the university in the same way that we have created a dual-tracking system
in our public schools. The solution proposed by Pereira et al. to
solve the problem of low credit accumulation is that a credit add-
on of twenty credits or 16 percent of the total requirement for a

bachelor's degree be awarded for "acceptable work done, even if it is work on learning the curriculum of non-regular courses" (Pereira et al. 1993: 163). Toward the end of their report, however, they reduce this add-on to only 5 percent and their recommendation is that CUNY allow "full credit for no more than four basic skills courses in the first year of college (Pereira et al. 1993: 185). No mention is made of the second year.

There is little question that poor screening tests, placement policies and practices, and the persistence of non-credit courses contribute to years of low percentages of credits earned and eventual disillusion with the college experience, as pointed out by the Otheguy and the Pereira studies. And this lengthening of the college experience, coupled with other social and economic burdens, ultimately discourages many and leads to the dropping out of the college system. However, by simply giving credit for precollegiate skills, these researchers are avoiding and once again deflecting the real problem faced by many of our students in high school. And saying that the emperor has clothes when he does not, will not make it so. By rewarding effort in precollegiate (high-school-level) remedial courses, we will be telling some students that admission into the university with reading, writing, and math deficiencies is acceptable. By reconfiguring the college credit system, Pereira et al. are sending the message that we will make things right after one or two years of credit-bearing remedial courses. But will this really help Latino students? Will we not be guilty of creating yet another educational delusion? And, will we not be constructing a second tier, as suggested above, that will mean one thing for one set of students and something else for yet another?

With regard to the question of "standards" and college admission, a complex and politically charged issue, I believe that Pereira et al. oversimplify with their assessment that "there is still an ideological split at the University. On the one hand, there are those who oppose 'open enrollment' and the idea of admitting academically underprepared students into the university . . . because they believe that by allowing that to happen academic standards will be corroded. On the other hand, there are those who see arguments about the 'corrosion of standards' as a way of denying equal access to those groups who have traditionally been denied access to college" (Pereira et al. 1993: 160).

I would submit that there is yet another group which has been an enthusiastic supporter of open enrollment all along, and which would also *not* deny equal access to an increasing number of Puerto Rican and other Latino students. This group, however, is profoundly concerned that we might simply be perpetuating a great disservice to young Latino college students by continuing to pretend that success in this society is simply a matter of accumulating college credits. It is true that an individual graduates when the required amount of credits have been completed, but it is also expected that the individual will have mastered skills in a variety of academic domains. If the mastery of those skills is not apparent or is artificially inflated by adding twelve to twenty credits for non-college-level work, which do not reflect the mastery of those advanced college-level skills but are simply a compensation for high school work never learned, then the degree granted becomes a sham. And, what is worse, the students, the communities, their families, and the society at large in the final analysis are the losers. What we will have accomplished is not equal access to the university but unequal educational attainment.

What seems to make a good deal of sense in the Pereira et al. report is their support of the many "instructional options" outlined in the Chancellor's Advisory Committee on the Freshman Year (1992). Looking for new ways to bolster, enhance, and reconstruct the existing support services by expanding some of the best and most effective methods currently being used to improve college skills and promote potential success in content courses seems to go to the heart of the matter when it comes to helping students who are academically underprepared. If basic skills courses are paired or bridged with academic content courses and credit is awarded for these as corequisites for courses offered by academic departments, then we might more effectively combat the problem of low percentage of courses completed for credit (Pereira et al. 1993: 184).

So, problems with testing, the complexity of placing students who are academically underprepared in classes that may carry only partial or no credit, and of course the profound challenges of overcoming significant family and financial obligations all seem to present almost insurmountable obstacles for many Latino students in institutions of higher education. But despite the continued struggle of many college-level students, there is some evidence that "Puerto

Ricans made significant gains in educational attainment between 1980 and 1990" (Pérez 1993: 8). This same report, however, points out that the "proportion of Puerto Ricans who are college graduates remains low compared to the non-Hispanic population. While the college completion rate steadily increased during the early part of the 1980s, the rate grew stagnant in the latter half of the decade (Pérez 1993: 8).

Puerto Rican and Latino Ethnic Studies in the University

While the preceding section focused on some of the problems of academic survival in the university, this final section will focus on how the Puerto Rican community (students, scholars, and community-based organizations) created a space in the university where Puerto Ricans and other Latinos could analyze and research their own reality. The emergence of Puerto Rican and Latino studies, as well as other ethnic studies in higher education, illustrates how a community can shape the course of education in American society.

As indicated above, we know that our educational institutions are reflections of the societal structures that shape them and their policies. What motivated many in the 1960s, especially the earliest proponents of Puerto Rican and other ethnic studies was the untested belief, and perhaps the hope, that the institution of higher education could be one of several institutions that would ultimately contribute to a societal transformation beyond the gates of our campuses. The following will give the reader a sense of some of the central pedagogical and societal concerns that were an essential part of the early development of Puerto Rican, Latino, and other ethnic studies programs:

> Puerto Rican Studies (therefore) was an organizational form through which we challenged the university and created a separate space in which to test and develop our own educational agenda. The commitment of Puerto Rican faculty and students to examine facts or principles in order to act on our condition as a people formed the essence of our intellectual work in the university. Like Black Studies and Chicano Studies, and Women's Studies, Puerto Rican Studies began with a purpose and content which went beyond intellectualism. The era of social upheaval,

community conflict, and demands for institutional change, gave these ethnic programs a stamp and character of social practice and theory building different from most other university programs. . . . Our efforts involved, in particular, a critique of the way in which social science theory and methods had served to legitimize our colonial history. Hence a basic set of principles was almost uniformly established in all colleges. (Nieves et al. 1987: 5).

Given the range of these concerns, one could easily see that Puerto Rican and other ethnic studies programs laid the foundations for what is now being called the "multicultural education movement" (Vázquez 1993b). A significant part of the university's current move to transform the general curriculum to one which is more inclusive with regard to culture, race, and gender can be seen as a direct outgrowth of the ethnic studies movement of the 1960s and early 1970s. The foundations of what to many appears to be a new educational reform movement are directly rooted in the earliest articulated expressions of Puerto Rican studies, Chicano studies, African-American studies, Native-American studies, and Asian-American studies. Furthermore, the more than twenty-year struggle to maintain these programs in the university contributed to an on-going ethnic studies presence, which in turn produced new scholarship and a new curriculum. When university faculty talk about diversity in the curriculum, they must acknowledge the fact that departments and programs in Puerto Rican and Latino and the other ethnic studies (Asian-American, Native-American and African studies) were the ones that brought academic diversity to the American university.

Few, however, will acknowledge the contributions by ethnic studies scholars, for a complex set of political, ideological, and pedagogical reasons. Some of the detractors of ethnic studies still recall that ethnic studies programs did not come into existence in the same way that new academic disciplines usually come into their own in the university. Ethnic studies were born out of campus and community struggle and turmoil. Except for a very limited number of courses in sociology and anthropology departments, most universities simply did not deal with America's racial and ethnic reality in any systematic and direct way. The Latino, African-American, Native-American, and Asian-American reality in the curriculum of the American university was simply not there—it was missing. So students, along with a handful of committed faculty, some ethnic/racial minority and some Anglo, took to the campuses to demand that colleges create a space and provide the resources for what many detractors saw as a politically and racially motivated curricular transformation. Hu-DeHart in an essay on the origins of ethnic studies in American higher education writes "In the late sixties, inspired by the Civil Rights movement and further buoyed by the energies of the anti-war movement, a generation of college students across this nation took to their own campuses, invaded and occupied administration offices, startled and no doubt terrified a few presidents, deans and professors" (Hu-DeHart 1994: 696).

Others' writings about this period in American education usually recount the same kinds of campus confrontations against a backdrop of great political and cultural volatility (Bataille 1988). Inside and outside of these institutions there was great resistance to the idea of providing for the formal study of what many considered a frivolous and unworthy academic enterprise. Many suggested that there was no literature to study, while other critics thought that university administrators were capitulating to campus radicals. How could we dare to suggest that there was something in our collective American history and in our contemporary reality in the United States that would justify the bringing together of a multiplicity of disciplines to better comprehend and examine this unique American experience? How dare we be so presumptuous? Ethnic studies practitioners shared a principled belief that all scholars had to begin to look more critically at racial, cultural, ethnic, and class history in a very new way. In part our insistence upon a new scholarship grew out of a widespread rejection and our disappointment with so many earlier community studies that often simply distorted, romanticized, or trivialized the reality of ethnic groups in American society.

Up to that point, traditional American scholars had, with few exceptions, studied ethnic groups as "others" within the larger society. Many of these studies presented ethnic and racial issues as contained within ghetto borders, barrios and reservations, isolated from the mainstream and with very limited class or cultural analysis that went beyond dismal demographic reporting. On the other hand, ethnic studies scholars sought to position the reality of racial/

ethnic minorities within the much larger social-economic, political, and cultural framework of American society. In the case of Puerto Rican studies, scholars had ample opportunity to look more closely at the connections between U.S. government policies and the socio-economic shifts on the island which determined places of settlement in the mainland, U.S. school experiences, religious practices, cultural change and cultural resistance, housing and jobs, health and mental health problems, and a host of other issues (Vázquez 1992). With the advent of the new ethnic studies programs, the study of the exotic "cultures of poverty" was quickly going to become a thing of the past.[9]

For many Puerto Rican studies practitioners, the university represented a place where we had the opportunity to examine more closely the role of race, ethnicity, class, and gender in American society. And since our work in the university was scholarship and teaching, our obligation included bringing the concerns of our communities into our programs of research and into our classrooms. Those community concerns—both historical and contemporary— were transformed into research questions as well as into an interdisciplinary curriculum of study. In order to accomplish this, we had to have an autonomous space in the university. Program autonomy would allow us the same departmental rights and privileges that other more traditional departments had—to hire faculty, develop curriculum, and set a research agenda.

What is interesting about the structural evolution of Puerto Rican and other Latino studies programs and departments is that they have been able to survive and grow in a variety of settings, under a wide range of administrative structures and entities. For example, in a place like the City University of New York, the fact that we have such a great variety of models of Puerto Rican and Latino studies programs and departments is really a reflection of how one goes about the task of establishing a program and how one keeps it alive and flourishing even in the most hostile of environments—and we have had some very hostile environments.

Yet with all of the resistance, we have managed to create a space and keep it, despite the constant struggles. The variety of organizational structures is reflected in some of the following titles of programs and departments throughout the CUNY system and elsewhere in the Northeast. The City College of New York has a department of Latin American and Hispanic Caribbean Studies, formerly the Department of Puerto Rican Studies. Its curriculum continues to offer a Puerto Rican Studies course sequence, but it has gone beyond that to include Dominican Studies, and other Hispanic Caribbean and Latin American Studies courses as well. City College also has an Institute for Dominican Studies and at Baruch College, the Black and Puerto Rican Studies Department recently submitted a curriculum proposal which redesigned its course sequences and renamed itself the Department of Africana and Latino Studies. It continues to have a Puerto Rican Studies course sequence. The Borough of Manhattan Community College has a Center for Ethnic Studies, which includes courses in Puerto Rican and other Latino studies. And Brooklyn College, one of the oldest and largest departments, continues to support a Puerto Rican Studies major as well as a Latino Studies Institute. Hunter College, since the inception of its ethnic studies program, continues to have a Department of Black and Puerto Rican Studies. John Jay College has a Puerto Rican Studies Department. Queens College offers a minor concentration through its Puerto Rican Studies Program. Some of the courses in that concentration have over the years broadened its focus by addressing the issues of other Latinos in the New York area. Lehman College has a Latin American and Puerto Rican Studies Department that has been historically linked to that institution's bilingual studies program.

Northeastern University in Massachusetts now has a Latino, Latin American, and Caribbean Studies Program, while in New Jersey, Rutgers University has Puerto Rican and Hispanic Caribbean Studies. An American Studies Program houses Puerto Rican Studies at the State University of New York (SUNY) at Buffalo, and at another SUNY campus at Albany, Puerto Rican studies course sequences are linked to Latin American studies under the department title of Latin American and Caribbean Studies. Fordham University in New York City has a program which also links two related areas under the rubric of Puerto Rican and Latin American Studies.

These are just a few examples of how Puerto Rican and other Latino studies models survived and were shaped and reshaped over the last several decades. And as noted, in some instances, Latin American area studies programs have come together with Puerto

Rican and Latino studies in a broad range of diverse programs and departments, centers, and instituted.

During the last few decades, Puerto Rican studies practitioners have maintained an active network of scholars scattered throughout the United States (including Hawaii) and Puerto Rico. And in that time we have witnessed the emergence of a significant body of literature and scholarship in Puerto Rican and other Latino studies. These scholars are "engaged in socio-linguistic studies, migration and immigration studies, second language acquisition research, the exploration of ethnic voting patterns, the epidemiological studies that might bring to light health problems limited to certain ethnic communities, labor market studies that look carefully at employment and underemployment patterns among distinct ethnic communities, the psychological research the examines the stress related to relocation and immigration, the studies that examine the oral and written traditions of particular ethnic communities, and so on" (Vázquez 1992: 1044). Included in this great array of academic interests is the study of the rich creative literature of the island and the writings of those who find themselves in the United States as migrants, as well as the sons and daughters of migrants who express themselves in a wide range of art forms. While Puerto Rican studies scholars have forged an informal network throughout the years and many have taken part in education advocacy groups such as the Puerto Rican Council on Higher Education mentioned above, as well as other community and campus efforts, it was not until 1992 that the Puerto Rican Studies Association was formed as an international association of scholars.[10]

This very brief overview of Puerto Rican and Latino studies may provide a sense of how this particular educational reform in the university has both direct and indirect connections with the other educational issues discussed in this chapter's earlier sections.

Conclusion

The issues selected have been used to illustrate some of the fundamental societal interactions which enable us to begin to unravel the complexities of an educational system that has consistently failed an overwhelming majority of Latino children who start their school experiences with hope and smiles, and much too frequently end with boredom, disillusionment, rejection, frustration, and even despair.

We know that there are many structural factors in the society and within our educational institutions that allow for the continued miseducation of our Latino children and other minorities in American society. In many instances this miseducation replicates and seems to be an extension of the relationships that exist in the larger society between the poor, the racial/ethnic minorities, and those who are not poor and who are members of the dominant social structure. Our schools and universities often seem to be playing their part in sustaining these unequal relationships. Socialists' criticism of American education, as William Proefriedt suggests, "stresses education's function as a ruling-class ideology that provides false hope, diverts energies from economic reform, and legitimizes the existing social order" (Proefriedt 1980: 470). He continues,

> much of what goes on in the schools can be understood as a reflection of existing economic relations in the society and ... both accepted practices and efforts at reform will reflect those relations. The genius of the socialist criticism is to have worked through the Marxist understanding of the influence of production relations on other aspects of society and to have spelled out specifically how school policies and practices mirror those productive relations (Proefriedt 1980: 472).

It is unrealistic, therefore, to point to any one single issue or suspected cause and simply suggest that a correction of that particular problem will result in an improved educational experience for the Latino child or adult. Neither would it serve us well to point to a single group as the primary culprit in our educational failures. And it would be equally naive for us to believe that educational reform will necessarily result in direct societal change. That many children are able to transcend their poverty-stricken beginnings and rise above the conditions that keep countless others prisoners of their surroundings is a testament to their tenacity and will. *Sometimes* it can be directly attributable to the helping hand of caring and dedicated teachers, counselors, and other education professionals. That these exceptions have emerged from some of our worst schools is noteworthy, but that so many thousands of others have been and may continue to be lost in the societal and educational chasms is a continuing tragedy. It is critical, therefore, that we address the complex and multifaceted interactions between issues and that we maintain a dialogue with those who promote different analyses and propose competing resolutions for these issues. None of our problems lend themselves easily to the quick fix or the superficial answer.

NOTES

1. There are indeed economic consequences for Hispanics with poor educational credentials, as pointed out by Miranda and Quiroz in the La Raza report. "For all groups, including Hispanics, low education attainment is closely associated with low incomes and high poverty. In 1988, Hispanic householders with less than four years of high school had a median household income of $14,496—43% less than the $25,282 median household income of Hispanic householders with four years of high school or some college. Hispanic householders completing four years of college had a median income of $38,140—51% higher than that of Hispanics completing only high school" (Miranda and Quiroz 1990: 14).

2. It should be noted that the figures cited in various dropout reports vary significantly depending on the source. For example, the Task Force on the New York State Dropout Problem (1986) reported that an earlier Aspira of New York study (1983) had estimated a dropout rate of 80 percent for Latinos—18 percentage points more than the Task Force estimate. These figures continue to vary, depending on sources and methods of estimating dropouts (Report of the Task Force 1986 and Aspira of New York 1983).

3. The question of how "Hispanic" or "Latino" is defined in the United States is something which is explored in other chapters of this book, and an issue which is as complex politically, culturally, historically, and psychologically as the questions and controversies which surround African-American and Native-American communities with regard to the boundaries of identity.

4. The following articles provide examples of the kinds of issues, problems, and concerns being addressed as our schools attempt to restructure and improve the learning environments: L. W. Aronstein, M. Marlow, and B. Desilets, "Detours on the Road to Site-Based Managements," *Educational Leadership*, 47 (7) (1990): 61–63, and S.K. Strauber, S. Stanley, and C. Wagenknecht, "Site-Based Management at Central-Hower," *Educational Leadership* 47 (7) (1990): 64–67.

5. The New York Alliance for the Public Schools, Memorandum from Barbara Probst, Executive Director, May 10, 1990, announcing the *University Consultant Service Invitation to Participate in the Chancellor's School Based Management/Shared Decision Making Initiative* (SBM/SDM), pp. 1–2.

6. This information appeared in a memorandum from the Language Rights Committee of the National Congress for Puerto Rican Rights which was sent to its membership on May 24, 1990.

7. See New York Department of Education 1989: 1. This shift in test placement policy is the kind of issue that New York state-based Puerto Rican and Latino grassroots organizations have been involved with for quite some time. This change in policy also serves to underscore the need to monitor, field-test, and challenge, when necessary, policies and practices which seem to be contributing to the mis-education of Latino children. This policy in its original form was sending thousands of youngsters to certain failure in their early years of schooling.

8. The "social reconstructionists" approach is one of the five basic multicultural approaches identified by Sleeter and Grant (1987) in their typology.

9. The reference here is to the 1966 work of Oscar Lewis, *La Vida: A Puerto Rican family in the culture of poverty—San Juan and New York.* His description of the "culture of poverty" and how it shaped the lives of poor Puerto Ricans (what we might now call the underclass) drew widespread heated reactions from both scholars and the lay public. For a thorough examination of the place of Lewis's work within the larger framework of the social science literature, see Clara Rodríguez (1995).

10. The bylaws of the Puerto Rican Studies Association were adopted on September 20, 1992, in White Plains, New York. The current president is Emilio Pantojas-García, Centro de Investigaciones Sociales, University of Puerto Rico, Río Piedras, Puerto Rico.

REFERENCES

Alvarado, Anthony. 1985. *Toward reshaping the mission and vision of New York City's community colleges.* New York: Center for Public Advocacy Research, Inc.

Aspira of New York, Inc., 1983. *Racial and ethnic high school dropout rates in New York City: A summary report*, New York: Aspira of New York, Inc.

Banks, James A. 1988. *Multiethnic education; theory and practice.* 2nd ed. Boston: Allyn and Bacon.

———, and Cherry A. McGee Banks. 1995. *Handbook of research on multicultural education.* New York: Macmillan.

Bataille, Gretchen, M., ed. 1988. [Special issue] *Explorations in Ethnic Studies: The Journal of the National Association for Ethnic Studies* 11 (1).

Bell, Derrick. 1987. *And we are not saved: The elusive quest for racial justice.* New York: Basic Books.

Berlowitz, Marvin, J. 1984. "Multicultural education: Fallacies and alternatives." In M. J. Berlowitz, and R. S. Edari, eds., *Racism and the denial of human rights: Beyond ethnicity.* Minneapolis: MEP Publications.

Chancellor's Advisory Committee on the Freshman Year (CACFY). 1992. The Committee's unpublished report is available from the Board of Higher Education, City University of New York.

Commissioner's Task Force on the Teaching Profession. 1988. *The New York report: A blueprint for learning and teaching.* New York: reprinted by the New York State United Teachers, AFT.

Cordasco, Francesco. 1972. "The Puerto Rican child in the American school." In Francesco Cordasco and Eugene Bucchioni, *The Puerto Rican community and its children on the mainland: A sourcebook for teachers, social workers and other professionals.* Metuchen, N.J.: Scarecrow Press. The article first appeared in *Journal of Negro Education* 36 (1967): 181–86.

Fernández, Joseph A., with John Underwood. 1993. *Tales out of school: Joseph Fernández's crusade to rescue American education.* Boston: Little, Brown and Company.

Fitzpatrick, Joseph P. 1987. *Puerto Ricans: The meaning of migration to the mainland.* Englewood Cliffs, N.J.: Prentice-Hall.

Fishman, Joshua A. 1976. *Bilingual education: An international sociological perspective.* Rowly, Mass.: Newbury House.

Gittell, Marilyn. 1970. "The balance of power and the community school." In Henry M. Levin, *Community control of schools.* New York: A Clarion Book.

Governor's Advisory Committee for Hispanic Affairs. 1985. *New York State Hispanics: A challenging minority.*

Hakuta, Kenji. 1986. *Mirror of language: The debate on bilingualism.* New York: Basic Books.

Hu-DeHart, Evelyn. 1995. Ethnic studies and higher education. In J. A. Banks and C. A. M. Banks, eds., *Handbook of research on multicultural education,* pp. 696–707. New York: Macmillan.

Institute for Puerto Rican Policy. 1984. *Public policy research and the Hispanic community: Recommendations from five task forces.* A report to the Ford Foundation, October, disseminated by the Institute for Puerto Rican Policy, New York, N.Y.

Keegan, Patricia 1989. "Challenge issued to local educators." *New York Times*, June 4, p. 4.

Keller, Gary D., and Karen S. Van Hooft. 1982. "A chronology of bilingualism and bilingual education in the United States." In J. A. Fishman and G. D. Keller, eds., *Bilingual education for Hispanic students in the United States*, pp. 3–22. New York: Teachers College, Columbia University.

Kolbert, Elizabeth. 1988. "A New York report says racism creates two school systems." *New York Times*, October 22, pp. 1, 31.

Kozol, Jonathan. 1991. *Savage inequalities: Children in America's schools.* New York: Harper Perennial.

Langly, Lester D. 1988. *MexAmerica: Two countries, one future.* New York: Crown Publishers.

Latino Commission on Educational Reform. 1992. *Toward a vision for the education of Latino students: Community voices, student voices.* [Interim Report] May 20, New York, N.Y.

Lavin, D., J. Murths, B. Kaufman and D. Hyllegard. 1986. "Long-term educational attainment in an open-access university system: Effects of ethnicity, economic status, and college type." City University of New York. Paper presented to annual meeting of the American Educational Research Association, April, San Francisco.

Lynch, James. 1986. *An initial typology of perspectives on staff development of multicultural teacher education.* In S. Modgil, G. K. Verma, K. Mallick, and C. Modgil, eds., *Multicultural education: The interminable debate.* London and Philadelphia: Falmer Press.

Macías, Reynaldo F. 1989. *Bilingual teacher supply and demand in the United States.* University of Southern California Center for Multilingual, Multicultural Research, and The Tomás Rivera Center.

Mayor's Commission on Hispanic Concerns. 1986. Report of the Mayor's Commission on Hispanic Concerns, December, City of New York.

Miranda, L. and J. T. Quiroz. 1990. *The decade of the Hispanic: An economic retrospective.* Washington, D.C.: National Council of La Raza, Policy Analysis Center, Office of Research, Advocacy and Legislation.

Modgil, S., G. K. Verma, K. Mallick and C. Modgil. eds. 1986. *Multicultural education: The Interminable debate.* London and Philadelphia: Falmer Press.

Nelson A. Rockefeller Institute of Government, Center for Social and

Demographic Analysis. 1986. *New York State Project 2000. The people of New York: Population dynamics of a changing state.* Albany, New York.

New York City Public Schools, Board of Education. 1991. *Children of the rainbow, first grade.* Produced under the auspices of the Chief Executive of Instruction, Nilda Soto Ruiz.

New York State Education Department (1989, January 13). "Helping more students succeed in the goal of new Regents bilingual education policy." [News release.] The University of the State of New York, New York State Education Department, p. 1.

New York State Social Studies Review and Development Committee. 1991. *One nation, many peoples: A declaration of cultural interdependence.* New York State Education Department, July.

Nieves, J., M. Canino, S. Gorelick, H Ortíz, C. Rodríguez, and J. M. Vázquez. 1987. "Puerto Rican studies: Roots and challenges." In M. Sánchez and A. Stevens-Arroyo, eds. *Towards a renaissance of Puerto Rican studies: Ethnic and area studies in the university,* pp. 3–14. Highlands Lakes, N.J.: Social Science Monographs; Boulder, Colo.: Atlantic Research Publications, Inc.; Columbia University Series on Societies and Change. Distributed by Columbia University Press.

Otheguy, Ricardo. 1990. *The condition of Latinos in the City University of New York.* A report to the Vice Chancellor for Academic Affairs and to the Puerto Rican Council on Higher Education, June, New York, N.Y.

Pereira, J. A., E. S. Cobb, and H. Makoulis. 1993. *The nature and extent of the undergraduate educational experience at the colleges of the City University of New York: A comparison of Latino and non-Latino subgroups.* Bronx, N.Y.: Latino Urban Policy Initiative, Lehman College-CUNY.

Pérez, Sonia, M. 1993. *Moving from the margins: Puerto Rican young men and family poverty.* Poverty Project. Washington, D.C.: National Council of La Raza.

Proefriedt, William A. 1980. "Socialist criticism of education in the United States: Problems and possibilities." *Harvard Educational Review* 50 (4): 467–80.

Purdum, Todd S. 1988. "Koch panel with broad powers to investigate 32 school boards." *New York Times,* December 23, pp. 1, B3.

Ravitch, Diane. 1990. "Diversity and democracy: Multicultural education in America." *American Educator* 14 (1): 16–20, 46–48.

Report of the Commissioner's Task Force on Minorities: Equity and

Excellence. 1989. *A curriculum of inclusion*. The State Education Department/The University of the State of New York.

Report of the Task Force on the New York State Dropout Problem. 1986. *Dropping out of school in New York State: The invisible people of color*. Commissioned by the New York State African American Institute of the State University of New York.

Reyes, Luis, O. 1987. *Demographics of Puerto Rican/Latino students in New York and the United States*. Office of Research and Advocacy, Aspira of New York, Inc.

Rodríguez, Clara E. 1989. *Puerto Ricans born in the U.S.A.* Boston: Unwin Hyman.

———. 1995. "Puerto Ricans in historical and social science literature." In J. A. Banks, and C. A. McGee Banks, eds. *Handbook of research on multicultural education*, pp. 223–44. New York: Macmillian.

Salvo, Joseph J., and Evelyn S. Mann. 1985. *The Puerto Rican New Yorkers: Part I, Socioeconomic characteristics and trends 1970–1980*. Department of City Planning, City of New York.

Schlesinger, Arthur. 1990. "When ethnic studies are un-American." *Wall Street Journal*, April 23, p. A14.

———. 1992. *The Disunitng of America: Reflections on a multicultural society*. New York: W.W. Norton.

Sleeter, C. E. and C. A. Grant. 1987. "An analysis of multicultural education in the United States." *Harvard Educational Review* 57 (4): 421–44.

Stalker, James C. 1988. "Official English or English only." *English Journal* 77 (3): 18–23.

Task Force on Human Relations. 1989. *New York City Board of Education Human Relations Task Force Final Report*. New York: New York City Board of Education.

U.S. Census Bureau. 1989. *The Hispanic population in the United States; March 1988*. Current Populations Reports, Series P–20, No. 438, Washington, D.C.: U.S. Government Printing Office.

———. 1993. *The Hispanic population in the United States: March 1992*. Revised. Current Population Reports, Population Characteristics, P20–465V.

Vázquez, Jesse M. 1988. "The co-opting of ethnic studies in the American university: A critical view." *Explorations in Ethnic Studies: The Journal of the National Association for Ethnic Studies* 11 (1): 23–36.

———. 1989. Puerto Rican studies in the 1990s: Taking the next turn in the road." *Bulletin: Journal of the Center for Puerto Rican Studies* 2 (6): 8–19.

———. 1991. "The public debate over multiculturalism: Language and ideology." *California Sociologist: A Journal of Sociology and Social Work* 14 (1–2): 11–32.

————. 1992. "Embattled scholars in the academy: A shared odyssey." *Callaloo* 14 (4): 1039–51.

————. 1993a. "Arthur M. Schlesinger's vision of America and the multicultural debate." [Review of the book: *The disuniting of America: Reflections on a multicultural society*]. *Exploration in Sights and Sounds: A Journal of Reviews of the National Association for Ethnic Studies* 13: 1–13.

————. 1993b. "A Re-examination of the founding principles of Puerto Rican studies: Ethnic studies and the new multiculturalism." *IMPART: Journal of Open Mind* 1: 77–90.

————, W. Proefreidt, and L. Truesdell. 1988. *New perspectives in multicultural education: Three reports on multicultural education.* School of Education, Queens College, CUNY. These reports were sponsored by the Queens College Teacher Opportunity Corp. Grant, funded by New York State Education Department.

Watson, K. 1984. "Training teachers in the United Kingdom for a multicultural Society: The rhetoric and the reality." *Journal of Multilingual and Multicultural Development* 5 (5): 385. Reprinted in S. Modgil, G. K. Verma, K. Mallick, and C. Modgil, eds., *Multicultural education: The interminable debate.* London and Philadelphia: Falmer Press, 1986.

9

Puerto Rican Politics in New York: Beyond "Secondhand" Theory

JOSÉ R. SÁNCHEZ

> The first rule for understanding the human condition is that men live in second-hand worlds. They are aware of much more than they have personally experienced; and their own experience is always indirect.
>
> C. Wright Mills (1967: 405)

This reminder that concepts, theories, and beliefs mediate social life suggests that theory, and not just social life, must come under scrutiny. Much of the literature on the political experience of Puerto Ricans in the United States does not yet do that. Most seem to rely blindly on second-hand theory. These researchers have unselfconsciously incorporated, as their own, the meanings and images of the world found in the theories that dominate political science as a discipline. With few exceptions, these studies lack the critical perspective necessary to make useful sense of the particular political experience of Puerto Ricans in the United States. What these researchers do not understand is that second-hand theories, like clothes, do not always fit the social reality they attempt to cover.

Three approaches to the distribution of power in American society dominate the field of political science and the study of Puerto Rican politics. These are the pluralist, the elitist, and the political-economic. Each stakes out a certain range of political behavior for study and asks very different questions about the nature of politics. The pluralist finds political power "out there" with different groups

---

Angelo Falcón made a significant contribution to the early development of this paper. He, of course, has no responsibility for any errors in perception or understanding this paper may contain. Those errors are, of course, all mine.

competing to grab it. For the elite theorist, political power resides in the hands of a few people who manipulate social conditions to keep it. And, finally, the political-economist often sees political power as an attribute of economic wealth or class standing, structurally distributed in very uneven ways within society.

This article critiques the "secondhand" nature of these various attempts to explain the politics of Puerto Ricans in the United States. We will argue that such an uncritical adoption of theory jeopardizes the attempt to improve understanding. From that critique will emerge the tentative outlines of a different approach, a "social power" approach. We think it overcomes some problems of the other three and takes into account the specific political and social experiences of Puerto Ricans in the United States. The application of this social power approach to the study of Puerto Rican politics also provides, we think, lessons about the possible future political trajectories of other Latinos and racial-ethnic groups in the U.S..

The Pluralist Approach

The consensus in the literature on Puerto Ricans in the United States is that it is a somewhat powerless community compared to other groups. The pluralist suggests that Puerto Ricans can have power. If they don't, it must be due to a lack of political intelligence, legitimacy, aggressiveness, or group organization. As a founder of this approach, David B. Truman once stated the pluralist belief is that groups gain power because there is "cohesion among members sufficient to give force to their claims" (1971:269). A lobbying group, community-based organization, or professional association is thus effective in the political arena to the extent that it has internal consensus, commitment, and leadership. The assumption is that political power originates in the activities of middle-level social organizations; that is, in the organizational "cohesiveness" of interest groups, such as labor unions, rather than in political parties or larger social processes.

The American political system is essentially open, according to pluralists. It provides opportunities to influence decision makers both through the electoral process and through the lobbying and the competition that occurs between various interest groups. The pluralist assumption that political power rests in the capacity of groups to press for their interests can be found most readily expressed in an article by Cohen and Kapsis, "Participation of Blacks, Puerto Ricans, and Whites in Voluntary Associations: A Test of Current Theories" (1978). They assess whether socioeconomic deprivation or group cultural norms account for the different rates of political participation by Puerto Ricans, blacks, and whites.

Cohen and Kapsis find that "blacks, especially black women, are more likely to join voluntary organizations than are whites or Puerto Ricans with like social and demographic characteristics" (1978:1066). They conclude from this that it is the presence of "activist norms" within particular ethnic cultures, rather than deprivation, that accounts for participation differences. In this sense, they explain the political powerlessness of the Puerto Rican community as a product of Puerto Rican cultural attributes that limit their participation in voluntary organizations or "interest groups," as Truman called them. Cornacchia (1985) comes to essentially the same conclusion in his study on participation. Compared to blacks and whites, he argues, Puerto Ricans are least active in electoral politics because their ethnic culture does not produce political attitudes "conducive to participation."

Several factors, however, suggest that the emphasis in these studies on group cultural norms as a determinant of participation levels and styles in misleading. If Puerto Rican culture is responsible for the low rates of political participation among Puerto Ricans in the United States, one would expect to see equally low rates in Puerto Rico itself. That is not so. As Falcón has shown, it is not culture but "structural differences between political systems that gain in prominence in explaining differences in levels of participation" (1980:3). Whereas in 1980 the turnout to vote by Puerto Ricans in some electoral districts in New York City was as low as 5 percent of eligible voters, the results in Puerto Rico have been dramatically different (ibid.:1). Since 1948 between 73 and 87 percent of eligible voters have participated in the gubernatorial elections in Puerto Rico.

These New York/Puerto Rico differences are the result of various factors. For instance, Puerto Rico has a stronger political party structure, fewer general elections, extensive voter registration campaigns underwritten by the state, and a strong patronage system

(Falcón 1980: 20). These structures encourage participation among all sectors of the Puerto Rican population by providing immediate political and practical rewards. The assertion that culture accounts for the low rates of participation among Puerto Ricans in the United States is, thus, highly questionable.

One cannot redefine the cultural explanation as a simple problem of "assimilation" of Puerto Ricans to the political styles found in cities like New York, as Estades has suggested (1978: 87). Puerto Ricans have lived in New York City for decades without seeing any significant increase in participation. Nelson finds that "assimilated Puerto Ricans are less rather than more likely to exhibit political attitudes supportive of political participation" (1980: 101). It appears that assimilation does not produce increased participation. This is true even when measured against the traditionally low participation rates found among contemporary U.S. citizens. Even in presidential election years, the average voter turnout in the U.S. is 50 percent, far below the rate in Puerto Rico. The explanation for the low participation levels of Puerto Ricans in the U.S. therefore lies in factors other than culture. Do Puerto Ricans lack political will?

In his influential study of New Haven politics, Dahl concluded that "all active and legitimate groups in the population can make themselves heard at some crucial stage in the process of decision" (1956: 84). He assumes not only that all groups can make themselves heard, but that they want to. Political participation, after all, often produces economic and social benefits in return. Hester (1976) confirms this commonplace observation in a study of the Puerto Rican community in Connecticut. He found that the more active a group or community was, the more likely they were to receive benefits from their involvement; the two were "positively associated" (1976: 189). But one has to be careful not to make too much out of this "correlation," as Dahl and other pluralists so often do.

Puerto Ricans in other parts of the United States are aware that participation often produces benefits. History also shows that high levels of political organization and mobilization have not always improved the Puerto Rican ability to get what they need. The more interesting historical cases are, in fact, those where Puerto Ricans were highly politically organized and active and yet were essentially powerless. Estades, for example, found that in New York

City "the campaign and elections of 1972 marked a turning point in the participation of Puerto Ricans in partisan politics" (1978: 85). A massive voter registration drive was underway in that year that was supported by many Puerto Rican community organizations in New York as well as the government of Puerto Rico. Puerto Rican congressman Hermán Badillo led the campaign. Writing in the immediate aftermath of this mobilization, Estades wondered "whether the unification gained in the 1973 campaign will continue" (1978: 86). She should have asked whether adding an additional 200,000 Puerto Ricans to the pool of eligible voters made any discernible difference to the status of power for this community.

Case Study 1: The Struggles for Public Housing

Falcón once cautioned that one should not assume a "correspondence between voting and elite responsiveness" (1980: 21). It is facile to assume that political power hinges on voting rates or even on other political actions like demonstrations and sit-ins. What dramatic and routine acts of political will, such as rallies and voting, do is to provide information about what a group or community can do in some sustained, independent fashion against its opponents. But amassing political "firepower" by itself doesn't always do much damage or result in a noticeable change in power. One example of this was the struggle by Puerto Ricans during the 1972–73 period to expand the admission of Puerto Rican families to public housing in New York City.

As their housing conditions worsened during the early 1970s, Puerto Ricans turned their attention to public housing. Many community leaders became aware of the persistently low level of Puerto Rican participation in public housing. Actually, much of the alarm, especially by Puerto Rican public officials, centered on evidence of the dispersal of Puerto Ricans within the public housing system. The concern was that this would result in lower geographic concentrations of Puerto Ricans, thus diluting the impact of the Puerto Rican vote. Though this was a legitimate worry for Puerto Rican politicians, Puerto Ricans themselves were more worried about getting into public housing in the first place. The Spanish daily *El Diario-La Prensa* (February 14, 1972) articulated some of these fears in an article that stated,

[W]e are still the poorest among the low-income groups. We are therefore living in slums and are still at the tail end of being considered regarding our housing needs. Some people attribute this to an unwritten policy in the Housing Authority favoring one group against another. There are those who say this is the attitude of that agency toward the needs of the Puerto Rican families. What is true is that, though they have the smallest share of public housing, the tendency continues to reduce their share in that program even more. (Author's translation of Spanish original)

Puerto Ricans became alerted to these inequities when they compared the proportional increase and decrease of blacks in public housing to that of Puerto Ricans. Blacks had increased as a proportion of the tenant population in 119 projects and decreased in only ten. Puerto Ricans, on the other hand, increased their proportion in 85 but went down in 44 (*El Diario-La Presna* 1972). Puerto Ricans protested these patterns and prodded the U.S. Commission on Civil Rights to investigate their charges. The Commission held a public hearing in February 1972 to assess the civil rights of Puerto Ricans, particularly "the problem of access to public housing" (Buggs 1972).

The Puerto Rican organizations that took a leadership role in protesting Housing Authority policies toward Puerto Ricans were primarily War on Poverty funded groups with a smattering of private social and civic associations. At least nine Puerto Rican and South Bronx organizations, for instance, met with Housing Authority Commissioner Aramis Gómez (the Puerto Rican leader of an earlier 1960s protest by Puerto Ricans against the West Side Renewal plans) and Amalia Betanzos, the Commissioner of Relocation, during 1971 and early 1972 to discuss Puerto Rican community concerns. Because of countless letters, petitions, and mass sit-ins, Puerto Ricans could press their case onto the local policy agenda.

Puerto Rican attacks on the Housing Authority, however, went beyond petitions and letters. New legislation and the use of public elected officials to influence the Housing Authority accompanied the sit-ins and demonstrations. Puerto Rican tenants from the South Bronx, for instance, demonstrated at Housing Authority central offices in March of 1972 "to protest the nature of tenant selection at Betances Houses" (NYC Housing Authority 1972). Another demonstration, which the Authority dubbed a "community upheaval," in Seward Park also forced the Housing Authority to close an extension office of the Housing Authority Tenant Selection Division (Weiss and Tenner 1973: 12). The response of the Housing Authority suggests that it was more bewildered than offended by the charges that it discriminated against Puerto Ricans. After one heated demonstration at Housing Authority headquarters by a Puerto Rican group from the Lower East Side, a Housing Authority official casually dismissed the charges leveled against the Authority, sure they were inspired by nothing more than opportunism. The Lower East Side group, he said, had "apparently evaluated the Housing Authority as a most vulnerable public agency with which it has contact and intends to attack other elements of the official establishment through the Housing Authority" (Roye 1969).

In an effort probably intended to make sense of, as well as respond to, Puerto Rican protests, dazed officials at the Housing Authority began to issue weekly "Tension Reports" on the recurrent demonstrations. The Tenant Selection Division of the Housing Authority was also required to warn its staff about the constant pressure they would face on the job since individual and mass sit-ins had become "the order of the day." The Division's staff handbook further declared that "our atmosphere is so frequently charged with tension that although all Chiefs have had experience in the Division, none are anxious for an assignment here" (Weiss and Tenner 1973: 2). Elected officials who represented Puerto Rican areas also pressured the Authority.

Various local and state elected officials wrote to Housing Commissioner Simeon Golar to ask about the status of Puerto Ricans in public housing. In one case, State Senators Luis Nine and Robert García managed to get the State Legislature to pass a bill during May 1972 that prohibited discrimination by public housing "against women who have had children out of wedlock" (El Diario-La Prensa 1972b). The Housing Authority's response at first was to insist that its tenant selection process gave "fair and equal treatment for all applicants" (Weiss and Tenner 1973: 2). But the demonstrations and the mobilization of support from elected officials served as a lucid expression of what Janeway once called the "ordered use of the power to disbelieve." This is the ultimate power of the weak to refuse "to accept the definition . . . that is put forward by the powerful" (1980: 167). Despite the Authority's claim of innocence, Puerto

Ricans didn't believe it and continued to protest. The result was that subtle and slow changes occurred in Housing Authority admissions policies, changes that had a mixed impact on the admissions of Puerto Ricans to public housing.

Their distrust empowered the Puerto Ricans. They forced the Housing Authority to undertake a special study of its admissions procedures. This report concluded that "Puerto Rican families who file applications with the Authority . . . appear to be getting their fair share of available apartments." This denial of bias included a hidden caveat in the form of a handwritten note by Gómez attached to the original draft of this study. The note read that there remains the question, however, as to whether Authority "procedures are such as to discourage Puerto Rican families in need of housing from filing applications" (1972). This carefully worded admission that something could be wrong led to some limited remedies from the Authority. Though most of the recommendations in this report aimed at no more than further study of the problem, one recommendation appeared to have been taken more seriously.

The Gómez report to Housing Authority Chairman Golar advised the Authority to "mount a special program to direct additional Puerto Rican families to apartments that become available in the following projects that have had marked changes in occupancy, particularly in the last two years: Douglas, Carver, Wagner, Mott Haven, Mitchell" (Gómez 1972: 3). Data on all of these projects are not available, but what they show is that the Carver, Mott Haven, Mitchell as well as several other projects that had experienced drops in their Puerto Rican population prior to 1972 recorded very significant gains after that in the percentage of Puerto Rican tenants. From 1972 to 1980 the Puerto Rican percentage in Carver Houses, for instance, increased by almost three percentage points. East River Houses recorded a gain of almost eleven points in the percentage of Puerto Ricans in that same period. These gains in the percentage of Puerto Ricans in these specific projects, furthermore, continued into the 1980s. Clearly, whether or not the Authority formally implemented the Gómez recommendation, the changes in tenant population intended by it were in fact achieved. The Housing Authority's response to Puerto Rican dissent resulted in a redistribution of Puerto Rican families admitted into public housing as a whole rather than in substantially increasing the share of Puerto Ricans who gained admittance. The percentage of Puerto Ricans in public housing has remained fairly constant since 1972.

There are more Puerto Ricans in public housing today than ever before, but less than one would expect. There has been some increase in the Puerto Rican proportion of tenants in public housing, but that growth has leveled off. Thus, whereas in 1975 Puerto Ricans comprised 24 percent of all families in public housing, in 1983 they were only 26 percent. This is a very minor increase. The effect of Puerto Ricans protests was thus to produce small increases in the Puerto Rican share of public housing tenants. It also forced the Housing Authority to maintain or increase the concentrations of Puerto Ricans in particular projects.

One can argue that it was the Puerto Rican protests rather than independent changes in Authority policies that produced these new admissions patterns, since records show that the Authority had not abandoned its bias for submerged middle-class (generally white) tenants. An internal management memo, for instance, reaffirmed that the Authority's "immediate concern should be the continuation of a tenant selection process that will result in attracting higher income stable families" (Mattuck 1972). The Housing Authority did not give up its desire to play public landlord, though public and Puerto Rican pressure forced it to admit more "unstable," low-income families. It budged ever so slightly on its admissions policies and hoped that with time and patience the pressure would lessen.

By 1975, when the Office of the New York State Comptroller performed an audit of the New York City Housing Authority's tenant selection processes, it found evidence of severe irregularities. After reviewing the Authority's decisions on a small sample of applicants, the Comptroller's report concluded that the Housing Authority had classified about 28 percent of the applicants incorrectly. This resulted in a lack of adherence to the Authority's priority system. Consequently, applicants were being housed too early, too late, or not at all (NYS Comptroller 1976: 4).

The audit found that the Authority was not consistently following its own official admissions policies. It also documented that the Authority practiced specific exclusion of welfare and Puerto Rican applicants by labeling them as "problem cases." Much of this discrimination had gone unnoticed by outside observers and by the applicants themselves because of how it occurred. Applicants typically went through a series of indirect, passive obstacles that delay, reevaluate, bypass, and generally shunt unwelcomed applicants through the bureaucratic maze of the Authority. The comptroller further elaborated that: "[S]ince no records are kept of instances of bypassing of priorities, we could not determine the frequency of such occurrences. The Housing Authority has formulated a guide for the eligibility interviews, which states that particular racial groups may or may not be placed in an individual project. While all groups may be able to obtain an apartment in some projects, other projects will be restricted to only whites. . ." (NYS Comptroller 1976: 10).

Similarly, the auditors found that "applicants receiving public assistance may encounter difficulties in some projects because the Interviewers Guide directs the interviewers to offer only certain projects to them" (ibid.). Ironically, around this time, reports filled the newspapers that an increasing incidence of "problem" and destructive tenants were plaguing the housing projects (New York Times, June 29, 1975). These alarmist but, as history has shown, false reports made it possible for the Housing Authority to get state approval to raise the maximum eligible income for applicants in an attempt to decrease the number of welfare and "problem" tenants it would be forced to accept (New York Times, January 22, 1975).

The policy of rejecting housing-needy Puerto Rican and welfare applicants to public housing continued apace. Puerto Rican protests, mobilization, and organization did very little to change Housing Authority policies. Political efficacy is, thus, not achieved by acts of political will alone. The strength of the opponent, of course, also plays a role. For Puerto Ricans, opponents are not only other groups but much of the entire social edifice of political and economic institutions and structures in the United States. Power is not something Puerto Ricans can get easily by simply striving for it. Power is located in existing social structures, and what these existing structures mediate and make possible has, over the years, hurt and excluded Puerto Ricans.

Some studies within the pluralist school recognize that social structures are strong mediators of political participation and power for Puerto Ricans. Gutiérrez, for instance, explains that most of the

Puerto Rican, Chicano, and Cuban groups that have been created around the issue of bilingual education owe their existence not to community pressure or individual leadership but to the federal government agencies and private foundations that fund them. This is, of course, not limited to Latinos. Afro-Americans don't escape this dependence on external institutions but they enjoy more autonomy because of a different institutional history and configuration, as is true with the independent black church. The black church has been an organizer of Afro-American values and opinion as well as an incubator of Afro-American leadership and movements for change. The profound contribution of the autonomous black church not only explains some of the differences between politics in the Latino and in the Afro-American communities but within the Afro-American community itself.

In the study already mentioned, Cohen and Kapsis found that black women were not only more active in voluntary associations compared to whites and Puerto Ricans of both sexes, but that they were more active compared to black males. Ethnic culture would thus presumably have little to do with these patterns. A closer look at the Cohen and Kapsis data suggests a simpler explanation. These data reveal that black women were active in church-related groups at a rate that was twice that of black men, as well as of white men and women, and eight times the rate of Puerto Rican men and women. The church membership and activism of black women, then, played an important role in participation. What black women have that black men have less of and Puerto Ricans don't possess at all is participation in an independent institution that provides routine opportunities for congregating, sharing joys and hopes, and assisting often in the mobilization of values, resources, and people on behalf of the autonomous needs and demands of the black community. Black men take part in this religious culture. Men are usually the ministers of black churches and men as a whole certainly benefit from what the church contributes to the life and welfare of the black community. Thus, it is not apparent that male-female differences in religious participation results from anything intrinsic or unique to black cultural traditions. What Puerto Ricans lack is not a participatory culture but supportive and autonomous institutions such as the black church. It is an institutional rather than a cultural deficiency that limits political participation among Puerto Rican males and females.

Gutiérrez argues, however, that what Puerto Ricans lack is not an independent system of churches but organizations to represent their interests "at the federal level." (1987: 2) He explains the lack of national-level organizations capable of representing the interests of Puerto Ricans (or Chicanos or Cubanos) as a function of government and foundation policies. Truman had assumed that interest groups formed in response to "disturbances" in society. Gutiérrez argues that "disturbances" (i.e., unemployment, AIDs, etc.) may spur action but that the organization of groups around specific issues reflect "the issues, policies, and programs that concern the federal government and private foundations" (1987: 71).

The evidence that external organizations control Puerto Rican politics is suggestive and supported by the personal experiences of some prominent actors in the development of Puerto Rican social and political organizations. Longtime Puerto Rican activist Antonia Pantoja, for instance, is very critical about the institutional autonomy of many Puerto Rican organizations because she says "some of the current and recently emerged professional leadership perceive themselves beyond the accountability of the Puerto Rican community" (1989: 28). To block control by outside forces, Pantoja has proposed the creation of a "Puerto Rican community-owned corporation" that would "perform the functions of production, distribution, and consumption of the basic resources needed by Puerto Ricans in New York City" (ibid.).

Baver also asserts the importance of external influences on participation in her claim that "the minimal presence of Puerto Ricans in New York politics in the 1950s" was the result of unbenign neglect by the Democratic Party in the city (1984: 65). Thus, for Baver, Puerto Ricans did not participate in pluralist politics because the Democratic Party left them out. There are reasons to doubt, however, that simple exclusion from the Democratic Party adequately accounts for the powerlessness of the Puerto Rican community. The reasons she gives for the Democratic Party's decision to exclude Puerto Ricans are themselves too one-dimensional. For instance, Baver cites Puerto Ricans being "non-white" as a cause of the racist, exclusionary actions by the Democrats. She doesn't explain why such racial fears did not prevent the party from courting and wooing black New Yorkers during that same period. A more basic problem in the Baver argument, however, comes from her uncritical acceptance of pluralist dogma that the existing array of political institutions configure politics and political power. Thus, she assumes that the absence of politics and power where interest groups and political parties are not evident. This is not only wrong as a general principle of inquiry but wrong as an explanation of Puerto Rican political experience.

Case Study 2: Politics in the 1950s

The 1950s period, for example, was far from being, as Baver calls it, a "tiempo muerto" of little political activity for Puerto Ricans. It was actually a time of intense political conflict. Baver was right about Puerto Ricans being excluded from politics during the 1950s. But she was wrong about the kind of exclusion that took place as well as the reasons why it happened. The key processes of political exclusion for Puerto Ricans during the 1950s were not from the Democratic Party but from local government and the Liberal Party.

Puerto Ricans were both "excluded" and "incorporated" into New York City's mainstream political system. They were ignored by the Democratic Party but City hall paid unusual attention to the rapidly-growing Puerto Rican community. On September 12, 1949, New York City Mayor William O'Dwyer established the Mayor's Commission on Puerto Rican Affairs (MCPRA) with a mandate to ease "the integration of U.S. citizens from Puerto Rico into the life of the city" (MCPRA 195:4). This initiative was unusual in that it originated in government with little demand from Puerto Ricans living in the city and because of its broad composition. Practically all the heads of the City's government departments, as well as a large representative sample of the Puerto Rican leaders served as members of the MCPRA. The MCPRA proved effective in adapting the delivery of NYC social services to the special needs of Puerto Ricans. The Department of Welfare, for example, hired over 480 Spanish-speaking caseworkers and personnel in 1953 (Sánchez 1990: 59). The MCPRA undertook similar reforms in education and housing services.

The MCPRA gave Puerto Ricans unprecedented access to local government by incorporating them and their needs in the policy process. Puerto Ricans did not enjoy this level of access prior to 1949, nor have they since the dissolution of the MCPRA in 1955. What accounts for the creation of the MCPRA? The reasons are complex and generally have little to do with interest-group organizing by Puerto Ricans. An important catalyst for local government was the fact that Puerto Ricans in the late 1940s and early 1950s played a major role in salvaging the city's manufacturing sector with their cheap labor. City Hall wanted to encourage and maintain this influx of cheap labor into the city. Mayor O'Dwyer was also motivated by his close relationship with Luis Muñoz Marín, the new governor of Puerto Rico. Puerto Rico initiated political and economic policies during the 1940s that demanded siphoning off "excess" Puerto Ricans from the island. The MCPRA provided information, recruitment, and socialization programs that encouraged Puerto Rican migration to New York.

The third reason is more political. Vito Marcantonio was a radical U.S. congressman who represented East Harlem. Throughout his long tenure in the Congress beginning in the 1930s he attempted to embarrass U.S. officials by his repeated calls for the independence of Puerto Rico. Marcantonio was also a strong supporter of Pedro Albizu Campos, the Puerto Rican Nationalist Party leader who was Muñoz Marín's major protagonist. When Muñoz Marín became governor, Marcantonio set his polemical sights on the flaws of the new commonwealth structure and the Operation Bootstrap economic program in Puerto Rico. Marcantonio's criticism of Puerto Rico's status with the U.S. and his support for Puerto Rican Nationalists irritated Muñoz Marín, who conspired with O'Dwyer to ruin Marcantonio in New York. The MCPRA was, thus, used to undermine the support of Puerto Rican New Yorkers for Marcantonio by providing them with many services they were getting from Marcantonio's office. This attack on Marcantonio eventually became part of a larger U.S. government effort to exclude and eliminate radical leadership as well as to demobilize the Puerto Rican community in New York.

The MCPRA died in 1955 with the creation of a new agency, the Commission on Intergroup Relations (COIR). Unlike the MCPRA, the COIR worked for all groups in the city and had no Puerto Ricans on its board. COIR could also subpoena witnesses and records as a defender of "minority rights," whereas the MCPRA could not. What was more important, however, was that the COIR was a nonpolitical body. The MCPRA, on the other hand, was reminiscent of the old party machine where votes were exchanged for services. The COIR reflected the rise of the new social work policy in the city that emphasized the need for "healing" over political representation and power to solve the city's minority problem. The impact of going from the MCPRA to COIR was, it could be argued, a step backward in the political development of Puerto Ricans in the city. Puerto Ricans went from being what Jennings has called "clients" to being "recipients." With the MCPRA, Puerto Ricans *transacted* political favors; with COIR, Puerto Ricans *received* them. The differences proved profound for Puerto Rican political development. Antonia Pantoja, a young social worker at the time, joined COIR's staff shortly after its creation as the only Puerto Rican in the agency.

The Liberal Party was also behind another process of exclusion. It was important to Puerto Ricans for several reasons. Since its creation in 1944, the Liberal Party played a decisive role in most city and state elections. It was a major force in local politics. More importantly, the Liberal Party had always served as the political arm of the city garment unions, especially the ILGWU. During the 1950s Puerto Ricans were a substantially large fraction of the garment industry work force. Though the garment industry valued them as cheap labor, Puerto Ricans were abused and manipulated as members of the Liberal Party. The Liberal Party, for instance, blocked Puerto Ricans from leadership positions within the party, ignored the Puerto Rican community's need for elected representation, supported the growth of the municipal work force at the expense of manufacturing and, more importantly, campaigned for lower minimum wages in the state. These actions not only weakened Puerto Ricans politically but dampened their wages and undermined their bargaining position with employers. Thus, while the Liberal Party paraded around as a worker's party, nothing could be further from the truth as far as Puerto Ricans were concerned.

This exclusion from the Liberal Party was, however, far more devastating to Puerto Ricans than the exclusion from the Democratic Party. The Liberal Party was smaller than the Democratic Party. Its smallness could have magnified the impact of Puerto Rican party membership. As a third party, the Liberal Party also carried the "swing vote" in many elections, which gave a potentially greater influence to minority voting blocks. Finally, the partnership between the Liberal Party and the garment unions strengthened electoral votes with union resources, people, and capacity to call work actions. Puerto Ricans were kept away from all that potential power by a union and a party that treated Puerto Ricans as a disposable commodity with no future in the city.

It is possible to attributed Puerto Rican experiences with local government and the Liberal Party to elite manipulation. The conflicts and manipulation generated by the differences between O'Dwyer and Muñoz Marín, on the one hand, and Marcantonio, on the other, seemed designed to leave the masses of Puerto Ricans out of any prominent political role.

The process of selective political exclusion and incorporation of Puerto Ricans also suggests that the pluralist presumption that a process of group action and competition neutrally allocates political power is just plain wrong. Political power seems a lot harder for Puerto Ricans to grab, in part because "insiders" protect it. It is not "out there" like a fruit ready to be plucked from a tree. It is hidden and protected. But is it elites who hide and protect it?

The Ruling-Elite Approach

Ruling-elite theorists believe that only a few people control the political process. C. Wright Mills described the organization of power in the United States as a pyramid. At the top is a complex of rulers comprised of top corporate executives, the Joint Chiefs of Staff of the military, and high-ranking politicians such as the president. This elite, he argued, has "the power to make decisions of national and international consequence" (Mills 1956: 27). Beneath this level is a sector, the "middle layers of power," consisting of interest groups, the Congress, the media, and judges. These people have some influence on the policy-making process but not like that of the ruling elite. At the bottom of the pyramid sit the rest of the population. These "masses" have little political influence and those above largely manipulate them. In fact, Mills said, "the bottom of this society is politically fragmented, and even as a passive fact, increasingly powerless" (1963: 38).

Recent formulations of elite theory rely on a more persuasive empirical foundation. (See, for example, Domhoff 1983; Dye 1986; Dye and Putnam 1976.) The impact was such that even David Truman, a founder of pluralist theory, has had to modify his views. In the preface to the 1971 edition of his *The Governmental Process*, Truman admitted that "in the subtle politics of a developing emergency, the elites are, for all practical purposes, the People" (1971: xiv). He was forced to recognize the degree to which elites monopolize power, even if only during unusual emergency conditions like war and depression.

However, for all its merits, does ruling-elite theory fit the Puerto Rican experience? Several studies on Puerto Ricans subscribe to this model. Journalist Dan Wakefield's *Island in the City* (1959), for example, interprets politics with a ruling-elite vocabulary. Thus, he attributed the political failures of Puerto Ricans in New York during the fifties to "those forces that no one could quite pin down but which were against the Puerto Ricans; those invisible forces of bitterness and disregard" (1959: 278). Like most elite theorists, Wakefield assumes unity of purpose and action among elites, thus their targeting Puerto Ricans for repression. But it's not clear why Puerto Ricans have been so targeted. At other times, he blissfully underestimates the impact of particular government policies on Puerto Ricans. For example, he dismisses the MCPRA, discussed above, as a "harmless propaganda group" without asking why positive propaganda about a poor and weak group became so important to the city's elites (1959: 265).

Most of the literature on Puerto Ricans that deals with elites is concerned with Puerto Rican elites. Who are they? Are they unified? How much power do they have? Herbstein, for example, describes the emergence of a new "elite" leadership cadre among Puerto Ricans during the 1950s. She says that as opposed to the new "ethnic based" leadership that emerged later, in the 1950s individuals either within or closely connected with the administration and political structure of the city made up the traditional authority elite. This elite had an idealogy of assimilation because it was itself assimilated. Moreover, the wider society made the high rank of this elite synonymous with the status of "leaders of the community." The members of this elite certainly pressured for legislation and delivery of services favorable to Puerto Ricans. Yet, they were more concerned with protecting their relationships with institutions of the wider society than with mobilizing the support of the mass of Puerto Ricans. Rather than expecting loyalty in return for the delivery of resources to the ethnic population, this elite viewed their position at the top as their proper role (1983: 41).

The new Puerto Rican elite that replaced the traditional, according to Herbstein, "discovered the advantages of playing the political game using the idiom of ethnicity" (1983: 407). Though she calls the old and new leaders elites, Herbstein also recognizes how inappropriate this category may be for Puerto Ricans who as a community or as leaders control very little power. Thus, she says that while "Functionally, Puerto Rican leaders constitute an elite, as they occupy the highest institutionalized positions in the 'community,' in terms of the wider society, they are not" (1983: 414). Writing in the mid-1960s, Gotsch came to the same conclusion. His analysis of Puerto Rican leadership in New York City recognized that trying to identify the leaders within the Puerto Rican community according to who participates in making decisions about specific policies is very misleading. Gotsch saw that "the nub of the problem, too often for the minority group, is the 'institutionalization of powerlessness'" (1966: 2). The exclusion of Puerto Ricans as a group from the policy process also can be read as an exclusion of Puerto Rican leaders. Indeed, the City Hall decision to create the MCPRA, discussed above, was in part an attempt to discredit and exclude radical leadership elements in the Puerto Rican community like Vito Marcantonio from the political process.

Most of the other studies in this genre simply describe and identify Puerto Rican leaders with little if any reflection on what these leaders mean for the shape of power in the Puerto Rican community. Martin (1975), for example, uses Hunter's "reputational" survey approach to identify those people Puerto Ricans themselves say are their leaders. Falcón conducted similar surveys during the 1970s and 1980s.

Still, there is no one within the Puerto Rican community who is in a powerful enough position to make "vital" decisions about government or the economy to qualify as an "elite." Even the internal organization of Puerto Rican *barrios* is not in the hands of singular individuals. The politicians Ramón Vélez and Borough President Fernando Ferrer in the South Bronx are perhaps the closest any Puerto Ricans come to the elite label, but they are, at most, what C. Wright Mills would have called "middle-level" elites.

Some analysts have attributed ruling-elite type power to non-Puerto Ricans who are active or work in the Puerto Rican community. Fuentes, for instance, makes a case for the existence of a series of elite layers that culminate with the school system as the most immediate instrument of Puerto Rican oppression. His polemical attack on Albert Shanker, the head of the United Federation of Teachers during the late 1960s, claimed the existence of "a kind of piggy-back structure of American oppression . . . with each layer atop the other, and Shanker's union atop the schools of the poor, manipulated by the layers atop it, particularly the corporate-government interests that determine its contracts" (Fuentes 1980: 118).

What ruling-elite arguments such as Fuentes' ignore, however, is how often significant changes in policy occur that conflict with apparent elite interests. The community movement to decentralize control of the New York City school system, which Fuentes helped lead, was generally successful despite Albert Shanker and the long and bitter teacher's strike called by his union in 1968. The community's victory appears shallow today, since the local school boards have become a playground for corrupt and petty politicians rather than a true instrument of community control, and the limits of their power have become evident after two decades of operation. But the 1968 battle represented to many a real victory at the time. And it is not the only one. For example, the interests and demands of the masses were addressed with the enactment of minimum wage laws, unemployment insurance, civil rights laws, and other policies. Pluralists were wrong to assume that the American political system was totally open and accessible to any group. But it is also true that if there is a ruling elite, it does not always rule. What kind of elite is this, then, that permits followers even sporadically to decide policy? The ruling-elite theorist is likely to respond that particular elites support and sponsor such changes in order to appear flexible and satisfy public discontent without jeopardizing the mechanisms that allow them to rule. Social change for popular causes does not invalidate the notion of elite rule, according to this argument, because other factors point to an indomitable rule by elites even with victories by the masses.

Elites are not like average Puerto Ricans or even the average white Americans for that matter. According to ruling-elite theorists, those who run government, the corporations, and the military most frequently are educated at prestigious U.S. institutions and come from families with longstanding wealth and status. Elites with common backgrounds, like those of Jimmy Carter and Jessie Jackson, are exceptions. Elites are distant to the masses not only in background but in accountability. Voters select representatives from a short list narrowed by the decisions of a very select group of people. The process of candidate nomination and campaign financing gives a few people rather than the public tremendous influence. And once elected, government officials become hard to remove: over 95 percent of incumbents to House and Senate seats get reelected.

On top of that, corporate and military elites rarely get or keep their positions through public approval. Besides being unaccountable, elites (both corporate and government) influence the public more than the public influences them, primarily because they have greater access to and capacity to use the mass media. As Dye and Ziegler argue, the "policy questions of government are seldom decided by the masses" (1978). Although they suggest that the masses have some influence over policy, Dye and Ziegler insist on putting the weight of policy-making in the hands of a select group. This insistence on their part, however, raises rather than answers questions.

Pluralists respond to the elite model in several ways. They challenge the alleged dissimilarity between elites and the masses, the degree of access individuals have to become members of the "elite circle," as well as the notion that elites are not accountable to the public. These responses by pluralists don't go very far in rebutting the ruling-elite thesis. They ignore the weakest link in the elite argument; that is, the allowance recent elite theory makes for policy influence by the masses. This allowance raises a number of issues. When do the masses have their way? Do elites measure the quantity or quality of the demands by the masses in order to decide when to back off? Does the content of the demands make any difference? Do elites take action individually or collectively in order to make victories by the masses possible? Ruling elite theorists generally can't answer these questions because they have never specified what, apart from their desire to rule, elites really are trying to protect.

If elites act simply to protect their individual right to rule, then, when faced with challenges from below, they have little to guide them. How do they know which new law or policy demanded from below will merely appease public discontent and not undermine their power? The answer is that some elites will know and some won't. Since power is so personal, according to the ruling-elite model, its protection depends on the intelligence, wisdom, and will of the elite, as well as on unknown and unpredictable factors. But the problem with this scenario is that it suggests a turbulence and instability to the elite maintenance of power that has not been the historical experience. There are few wild upheavals in the topography of power. There are few revolutions in history, especially in the Western capitalist countries. And the reason for that may be that power resides more in structure than in elites.

Social structures and institutions both enable and limit the actions of individuals, whether they belong to the masses or the elite. This is the power that structures, like the institution of private property or the Federal Reserve, have. Thus, it is against those social structures that new social demands are measured and denied or accepted. Theoretical recognition of the structural foundations of power, however, cannot be found in either the pluralist or ruling-elite perspectives. The ruling-elite theorists ignore the structural foundations of power, seeing only individuals as important in the quest for and control of power; while pluralists ignore it by taking such structures for granted as the "background" against which groups compete with each other for power.

The Political-Economy Approach and Its Reformulation

This approach connects political power to economic structures. But how? López wrote, in a now classic book, about the development of Puerto Rican nationalism in New York City that "as the question of political self-determination becomes important, the question of economic control rises. Economic control is the power to run, maintain, and, consequently, benefit from the means of production"

(1973: 126). He, thus, suggested that we locate the sources of political power not in voting or representation but in the more general category of popular control. The control of substantial amounts of money clearly creates a basis for political power. But what López suggests is that control over other institutions and resources is important as well. Schools, workplaces, and government agencies are some examples.

Is López correct to say that "political power is the power to control all institutions that are basic to a people's survival" (1973: 267)? If survival is not the primary aim in life, it is at least the means to all others. Control over basic sources of survival is, indeed, then the major source of power. Yet, López and others in the political-economy tradition have not developed that idea of control very far. What, for instance, accounts for the fact that Puerto Ricans don't control institutions that are necessary for their survival? What social factors explain this? And how can they go about getting such control?

The answers to these questions can be found within the political-economy perspective, especially in the reformulation outlined here. The political-economy perspective has gained some acceptance recently within mainstream academia, but this acceptance has apparently tamed and neutralized it. The political economy of Marx and Engles was concerned with blunt issues of class power and state coercion. But the modern formulation of political economy talks more abstractly about "the economic role of government" and the "market economy" (*a la* Alt and Crystal 1983). This neutral theoretical stance obscures what is often a deeply partisan conservative bias, even if these studies do on occasion provide, sometimes inadvertently, important insights into the nature and operation of power.

Lindblom's research is within the modern political-economy tradition. He has done much to discredit the pluralist argument that all interest groups have equal access and space within the policy process. Business, he says, has a "privileged position" because it makes the important decisions in society about what is going to be produced, how, and for whom. As a result, "any government official who understands the requirements of his position and the responsibilities that market-oriented systems throw on businessmen will therefore grant them a privileged position" (1977: 175). The privileges granted to business are the requirements of doing politics in a market system. The power of business is thus not the product of competing interest groups, nor is it the result of "a power elite established by clandestine forces" (1977: 175). The power of business is almost invisible. Business leaders need say or do very little to get what they want, since government is generally prepared to give them what they need. As Lindblom argues:

> [B]usinesses only rarely threaten any collective action such as a concerted restriction of function. Ordinarily, they need only point to the costs of doing business, the state of the economy, the dependence of the economy's stability and growth on their profits or sales prospects—and simply predict, not threaten, that adverse consequences will follow on a refusal of their demands. (1977: 185)

Business needs, therefore, have a high priority within the policy process of government. This is one part of the answer to the question posed earlier about what it is that elites try to protect when they act to preserve their power. But it is also true that business does not always get what it wants or needs. Sometimes, the needs of business are too fragmented and complex for government leaders to understand or respond to effectively. At other times government may—for its own reasons or in response to the pressure of other subordinate classes—ignore or contest business interests. Lindblom appears strangely oblivious to the influence of nonbusiness sectors over government policy. Thus, he attributes policies that are not consistent with business interests to the mere "failure" of government "to respond to business demands" (1977: 183).

Recent Marxist research has generally done a better theoretical job of dealing with the complex class sources of public policy. Thus, some Marxist theorists today admit that policymakers don't listen to businesspersons only. Bloch, for instances, states that "in its struggles to protect itself from the ravages of a market economy, the working class has played a key role in the steady expansion of the state's role in capitalist societies" (1984: 41). However, these more sophisticated portraits of the contradictory social forces behind policy still lack insight into the nature of workers' power.

What makes the influence of labor over business and government possible? Some Marxists explain the power workers sometimes have to get the government to respond to their interests (e.g., minimum wage, public housing programs, etc.) as a function of the fact that capitalist societies need workers to exploit to produce commodities (Therborn 1982). This systemic need for workers translates into a "power capacity" that gives workers and their organizations (i.e., unions) access and influence over policy-making. In these terms, business or capital still enjoy a privileged position within policy-making circles, but their influence is not absolute.

All too often, both traditional and Marxist political economy treat power as a "thing" individuals and institutions possess, carry, lose, or acquire. For traditional political economy, power is equivalent to money or the coercive aspect of state rule. It is quantifiable, discreet, and transferable. For Marxists, power rests on control of the means of production. Thus, it is capital that basically has power. The state has coercive power, but it generally serves the needs of capital. In addition, most Marxists presume that, except for the process of production, there are no other foundations of power.

A "Social Power" Reformulation of the Political-Economy Approach

The reformulation of power presented here expands on the conceptions found in both political-economy traditions. Power exists only in relations. It consists, as Stamm and Ryff describe, of "the ability of an individual to influence or exert control over resources, actions, or social relationships that are valued by the community or groups in which she/he participates" (1984: 3). The important elements of this reformulation of power are the need for relations and the control of resources that are valued. Thus, there can be no power when no relationship exists, just as there can be no romantic love between strangers. And for an individual or group to have power over others, not only must there be a relationship between them but the former must control resources, actions, or relations that the others value. What society, the state, or individuals value, in a sense, is not limited to productive activity, however important this might be. Public opinion in a media-saturated era is a value that many people besides politicians want and need to influence and control. Similarly, government employees have become a "value" and thus have become more powerful as government has become larger and such a functional part of the economy. Where nothing of value exists, neither does power. A butane lighter brings no power to its owner in Hell, since the other residents simply have no reason to value the fire the lighter can produce. Alternatively, the story would be far different were the lighter the only source of fire in a campsite on the North Pole. Thus, where a relationship or value is missing, any resource or action is likely to be void of power.

Despite the ongoing debate within the political-economic tradition, very little of it filters into the study of Puerto Rican politics. Much of the literature on Puerto Ricans remains stuck on pluralist and ruling-elite models, with all of their limitations. But what is interesting about this literature is the extent to which some of the discussions of political power found there lend themselves naturally to a reformed political-economic explanation. An analysis of the organizational capacity of the Puerto Rican community, for instance, usually helps substantiate an argument about this community's pluralist assertions. But this analysis of organizational capacity also can help shed light on the extent to which Puerto Ricans, as workers, can or are challenging capitalist relations of production. Puerto Rican attempts to organize themselves can fulfill pluralist ambitions to compete for the spoils of group political competition as well as impact on this community's ability to negotiate its place within the class system of production.

Much of what can be redeemed for use by a political-economy perspective in the literature on Puerto Rican politics consists of treatments of political power as material or moral "resources." What is important about these resources, from a political-economy perspective, is the effect their use has "on the (re)production of a given ... mode (or modes) of production" (Therborn 1982:241). Thus, these resources do not have to be directly or explicitly used in efforts to confront capitalist domination of workers in or out of the workplace. What is important is the extent to which their use challenges the operations of individual capitalists or the larger capitalist system. To do that, these "resources" must somehow be of value to others in the society, especially capitalists. That way they become important contributors to the organization of class power.

Some researchers have suggested that the ethnic notion of

being Puerto Rican was not always present and only later became an important political resource for the Puerto Rican community. This is not as nonsensical as it may appear. Puerto Ricans did not always have a sense that they were one ethnic (almost racial) minority community possessing a collective experience with discrimination. Puerto Ricans in the U.S. at one point no doubt thought of themselves as exiled members of their towns of origin in Puerto Rico, as links in a kinship network, or as individual migrants from the "nation" of Puerto Rico. Herbstein claims, perhaps too narrowly, that the notion of being a Puerto Rican "minority" emerged during the 1960s because Puerto Ricans "discovered the advantages of playing the political game using the idiom of ethnicity" (1978:407). The idea to unite on the basis of a common Puerto Rican national origin, Herbstein says, became an important basis for community organization for three reasons:

1. It represented important nationalist sentiments among Puerto Ricans;
2. It was a response to discrimination and,
3. It was a response to the development in the larger society of "an ideology and a structure of resources that rewarded organizational manifestations of an ethnic 'community'" (Herbstein 1978:408).

While Herbstein's observation of the historically contingent nature of ethnic identity is important, her conclusions that Puerto Rican self-consciousness as an ethnic minority is relatively recent and a leadership construct appear to be based on a selective reading of Puerto Rican history in New York City. The evidence reveals a community that did view itself as a racial-ethnic minority at least since the 1920s, when Puerto Rican communities of significant size began to make themselves felt in Manhattan and Brooklyn (Vega; Sánchez Korrol).

The proclamation of a "Puerto Rican" identity separates Puerto Ricans from other (working-class) groups, at least to get government attention. However, it does not preclude Puerto Ricans from joining other groups in political and economic acts of resistance toward landlords and bosses. But, in general, the expenditure of energy and attention to group-related concerns at the community level did create serious obstacles to such alliances during the War on Poverty period of the 1960s (Savitch 1972).

If ethnicity became a resource for Puerto Ricans, it's not clear what it became a resource for, beyond resisting discriminatory practices. Some research shows, for instance, that the larger political system has not rewarded Puerto Ricans as much as other groups because of their mobilization as an ethnic community. Puerto Rican wage and employment levels, for example, lag behind those of Afro-Americans (Torres 1989; Stafford 1985). Ethnicity has thus been an important factor in the relations between the Puerto Rican working-class community and the larger world, but it is not clear that it has been a definitive source of power.

There are many reasons why ethnicity does not always translate automatically into political power. Some researchers, for instance, attribute this failure to organization. It is the political organization of ethnic consciousness that fails in this sense and not ethnic self-identification. Baver, for example, criticized the Migration Office established by the government of Puerto Rico in 1948 in New York City precisely because it "slowed the growth of a Puerto Rican leadership cadre in New York City" (1948: 45). The lack of indigenous leadership hampered the effective development and deployment of Puerto Rican ethnicity. Others, however, find fault with the ideology these leaders have, rather than with the leadership cadre itself. Along these lines, Lapp agrees with Jennings that the Migration Division "valued assimilation above cultural and political assertiveness" (1986:11). So these researchers argue that the organizational involvement of the Migration Division either retarded Puerto Rican political leadership or affected the cultural style.

Other researchers, however, target leaders rather than organizations for blame. Pantoja, for example, a founder of many Puerto Rican organizations in New York City, charges that "the existence of an unethical leadership threatens to destroy the institutions we have and to create a climate of distrust, in our people" (1989: 28). But while good leadership is a resource, it is probably more important to focus on organizations, since it is organizations that nurture leaders and provide the environment for action. The focus must, in fact, be shifted from leaders to the relationship between organization and community. This is a focus in Jennings' research.

Case Study 3: Organizational Resources

Using terminology developed by Charles V. Hamilton to describe Black urban politics, Jennings describes the changes in organization Puerto Ricans experienced during the 1960s as a move from patron-client to patron-recipient relationships. In patron-client relationships, clients capture some important institutional basis of power. Traditionally, many ethnic communities exchanged their vote for control of local party positions, government jobs, or influence over agencies. The old political machine operated on this simple principle: votes for parts of the machinery of government or its products.

On the other hand, the focus of the patron-recipient relationship is on "soft" or "grant"-generated budgets (Jennings 1984:92). Programs, offices, and jobs created by "soft" money are unstable because they require repeated assertions of official support or law to continue. They are not part of the constitutional framework of government. By being subjected to a patron-recipient model of community organization, Puerto Ricans absorbed "a dependent politics, one in which independent political power is not developed" (ibid.: 92). Because of these changes, the Puerto Rican policy agenda ended in the hands of outsiders. Community organizations based on the patron-recipient model cannot make very many contributions to achieving the independent ethnic and class interests of the Puerto Rican community.

Jennings' description of how the focus of Puerto Rican community organization changed during the 1960s is very useful. It helps to explain why the militancy and activism of Puerto Ricans in the 1960s was intense and yet so ineffective. For example, many community organizations created in the 1960s are still around today. Despite that long record of organization, Puerto Ricans are poorer today, have worse housing, and are less healthy. Though the notion of patron-recipient relations helps to explain this, it does not explain why the change from client to recipient occurred in the first place. Jennings simply attributes this to the Democratic Party decision not to invite or encourage Puerto Ricans to become part of the party machinery. As a result of "ignoring the Puerto Ricans, the Democratic Party helped to keep this community from developing the bloc vote as a political resource peculiar to other ethnic groups in

New York City" (Jennings 1984:87). What weakens this explanation is that Jennings admits in the same paragraph that "overtures have been made throughout the years to other ethnic groups, including blacks, to develop political relationships with the established power structure" (ibid.).

But why blacks and not Puerto Ricans? Jennings adds that the Democratic Party turned away from incorporating Puerto Ricans because the party needed to control votes and believed that "Puerto Ricans, as a non-European people, could create problems for the Democratic Party leaders" (ibid.). The problem with this response is that blacks are homegrown products of American culture and even less European than Puerto Ricans. Why would the Democratic Party invite one in and not the other? Part of the problem is Jennings' assumption that Puerto Ricans would register a gain in power upon joining the Democratic Party. But just the opposite may be true.

New immigrant groups and blacks were invited into the party, for example, not so that they might finally share party power. They were invited in because they had developed an independent source of power the party wished to channel and control for its own purposes. The Democratic (and in some cities, the Republican) Party incorporated immigrant groups like the Irish and the Italians because they had begun to amass social and economic power rather than because they lacked it. Harrigan writes, for example, that "already bound together symbolically, geographically, and economically by the church, the Irish developed into a cohesive voting bloc that eventually gained great influence over the Democratic party in city after city" (1989: 51).

A central feature in the developing social power of Irish communities in the nineteenth century was the creation of a system of Catholic parish churches that maintained geographic concentrations of the Irish, provided an alternative, independent Irish educational system, transferred cultural and moral symbols of Irish identity, and spurred the autonomous economic development of Irish business by requiring the construction of schools, parishes, rectories, cathedrals, retirement homes, and seminaries. Thus, the Irish had developed the capacity to transform the physical and social environment and create wealth. That was social power. The incorporation of the Irish into the Democratic Party occurred during, if not after, this period of social and economic development. Puerto Ricans were not incorporated into the Democratic Party because they have lacked the social and economic power to scare or tempt party officials into admitting them to party structures and processes. Social power is, thus, often a prerequisite for political power. But is social power only developed from economic developments like what the Irish created?

Carmichael and Hamilton argued in their now classic book *Black Power* that: "the concept of Black Power rests on a fundamental premise: *Before a group can enter the open society, it must first close ranks.* By this we mean that group solidarity is necessary before a group can operate effectively from a bargaining position of strength in a pluralistic society" (1967: 44). Puerto Ricans, like blacks, also aspire to achieve the solidarity necessary to speak and act with some measure of political unanimity. The militant community and student groups of the past (e.g., Young Lords and the Puerto Rican Student Union) no longer exist. But in organizational forms that vary from the grassroots group (The National Congress for Puerto Rican Rights) to the interest group (the National Puerto Rican Coalition) and to professional networks (the National Association of Hispanic Journalists), the hope remains very much alive that Puerto Rican political power can be leveraged from group solidarity.

Although the attempts of solidarity continue, the historical results have been spotty. The early 1970s confrontation between the Puerto Rican community and the Housing Authority is one example. No amount of solidarity is enough when social and economic conditions worsen. Closing ranks brings Puerto Ricans closer to their problems and each other but it doesn't necessarily make them more effective in competing with other groups. That effectiveness depends on many other factors. Solidarity is probably more important for weak groups than for strong groups, but, by itself, it is no guarantee of anything. Strong groups have social power behind them. They control values others in the society need or want. Solidarity is a social process but it is not a social power in that sense. Solidarity can focus the actions of a group, but it does not normally create social values. Solidarity can wrap a community as tight as a fist, but it does not make the blows that fist delivers more accurate or harder.

The disappointment that comes from this limitation can lower expectations. Some writers today seem content to predict political power for Puerto Ricans down the road because of demographic changes rather than group solidarity. The expansion of Puerto Rican and other minority populations in cities like New York suggests the development of predominantly minority cities and with that an unstoppable process of empowerment for these minorities. Browning and his colleagues have argued that "a successful multiracial coalition will form and take control of city government where the minority population plus support from liberal whites approaches 50 percent of the population" (1990: 216). Though the creation of "minority-majority" cities has already occurred in a number of places and is imminent in many others, Falcón has cautioned that though cities like New York are likely to become "minority-majority," "the political consequences of this development are . . . not well understood" (1985: 1). While a population dominance in the city by Puerto Ricans and other minorities is likely to change the dynamics of political activity, there is no guarantee that the outcome will be more beneficial for these groups. It may not ensure, for instance, that government policies will in general benefit this community.

The problem with the demographic scenario is that demography translates into political power primarily at the time representatives are elected to office. The makeup and size of a population is an electoral source of power that naturally lies dormant once elections are over. Unorganized and unled outside the electoral process, large and diverse populations have very little impact. They may even be a problem. A reliance on demographic change as a source of power may, in fact, close other options. By making demographic size an "end," for instance, attention may be diverted from efforts to reform policy. This is similar to the problem the black community had as they began to achieve their goal of expanding the number of black elected representatives. Black activists discovered that they may hope "eagerly for black political incorporation, but when it arrives, find that it is an obstacle to achievement of a broader set of goals" (Browning 1990: 224).

Case Study 4: The 'National Question'

One broad goal of many Puerto Ricans for some time now is to make Puerto Rico an independent nation. In the U.S., this goal is often associated with a continuing debate on whether Puerto Ricans in the U.S. are a national minority or part of the Puerto Rican "nation." If Puerto Ricans in the U.S. are a national minority then they are a subdivision of the U.S. nation and have economic and political goals that are more intertwined with those of the U.S. rather than with Puerto Rico. Without getting into this long and complicated debate, there are some aspects of this nation versus national minority issue that are important to an analysis of power. For one thing, the issue of whether Puerto Ricans in the U.S. are rightfully a part of the U.S. nation or part of Puerto Rico is by itself very uninteresting if the effort is merely to create analytical categories. Much of this discussion, for example, has sought to define whether Puerto Ricans suffer political and national oppression. Others have cataloged various characteristics of Puerto Ricans in order to determine what they have in common that would allow them to be called a "nation." Most of this analysis is sterile.

In a 1977 article, Blaut suggested that we resolve the nation/ national minority issue by asking one simple question: Are these (Puerto Rican) workers engaged in a struggle to liberate their nation? Do they share with their compatriots a "will toward national existence?" For Puerto Ricans, Blaut says, the answer is yes (1977: 54). Blaut's solution may not simplify the 'national question' issue, especially since recent developments in the U.S. demonstrate that there is tremendous ambivalence on the part of Puerto Ricans about their desire for a "Puerto Rican national existence" (Falcón 1990). What is useful about Blaut's solution, however, is that it rests on what Puerto Ricans want and do rather than on what outsiders think about them. Taking this "internal" perspective allows us to proceed to ask a very different question: Of what value is the idea of Puerto Rican nationhood to Puerto Rican attempts to augment their power?

The idea that Puerto Ricans in the U.S. are part of the Puerto Rican nation has certain implications for relations of power. By placing themselves as members of a Puerto Rican nation, Puerto Ricans in the U.S. are not necessarily making a real promise to return to the island should it become independent. What the assertion of Puerto Rican nationhood does, however, is to create a psychic detachment among Puerto Ricans about U.S. issues and problems. It also suggests that Puerto Ricans in the U.S. have an ally in the nation and government of Puerto Rico. Each factor can make Puerto Ricans in the U.S. feel stronger . . . but not always.

The assertion of nationhood creates distance between Puerto Ricans and other groups in the U.S. Like many newly arrived immigrants, the conscious belief by Puerto Ricans that they are a part of a Puerto Rican "national entity" would divert the focus of their political and cultural attention to Puerto Rico. What goes on "there" would assume greater importance than what goes on "here." It also can create the thinking that problems here don't have to be taken on, since Puerto Rico exists as a real alternative and paradise. But it is also true that, within limits, this stance can also empower. To the extent that Puerto Ricans are being oppressed here, real psychic and cultural benefits can be gained by a community that shifts its attention away from its oppressors. That stance creates opportunities for dissident voices to be raised, heard, and eventually organized. It devalues that which is most American and thus breaks the relationship of power that exists when Puerto Ricans (or any others) want, need, or desire most that which is in the U.S. Ultimately, this stance can undermine the significance and durability of oppressive conditions of life here for Puerto Ricans. It suggests a real-life salvation in the attainment of national independence and unification.

But the "Puerto Rican nation" position also weakens Puerto Ricans. It creates barriers to their full participation and cooperation with others in the U.S. and thus weakens their capacity to work toward common solutions. It is true that movements for political and social transformation on the island have sometimes given coherence and a historical project to Puerto Ricans in the U.S. with national sentiments. One example of this is the mobilization of Puerto Ricans in the U.S. for charitable efforts to relive the suffering caused by the devastation caused by Hurricane Hugo in 1989. But when such coherence is absent, the "Puerto Rican nation" thesis becomes an empty, symbolic gesture that separates Puerto Ricans not only from oppressors but from fellow citizens in the U.S. who share common conditions of life. That separation diminishes the chances for empowerment by reducing the opportunities for others to find value in what Puerto Ricans control or have to offer.

There is another way that the nation thesis can empower Puerto Ricans. Puerto Rico has over three million people. With the two million or so Puerto Ricans in the U.S., that creates a large consumer market that influences many corporate investment and marketing decisions. That population also creates a substantial voting bloc. The recent establishment of a Democratic Party presidential primary in Puerto Rico is a recognition of that. More importantly, the idea of a Puerto Rican nation makes the government of Puerto Rico an ally if not the relevant sovereign authority over Puerto Ricans in the U.S. While the establishment of such a relationship can dampen the political development of Puerto Ricans in the U.S., as Jennings (1984) has argued, it also can put the large economic and political resources of the Puerto Rican government at the potential service of Puerto Ricans in the U.S.. Thus, as Jennings recognized, "the Puerto Rican community in New York City is different from other ethnic groups in that, for a time, Puerto Ricans were represented by a government outside of the stae and city political spheres" (1984: 83). At times, this makes Puerto Ricans not only different but stronger.

Puerto Ricans in the U.S. can be made stronger by this relationship with the government of Puerto Rico if it serves to enhance their ability to assert the interests of the Puerto Rican community here. That has not always been the case. The Puerto Rican government has often taken a very patronizing and manipulative position toward Puerto Ricans in the U.S. A recent example includes the creation by the government of Puerto Rico of a cabinet-level Department of Puerto Rican Community Affairs in the United States, headquartered in New York with offices in other U.S. cities. Thus, though the idea of Puerto Rican nationhood may facilitate the utilization by Puerto Ricans here of Puerto Rican government resources, the relationship between a Puerto Rican community here and a government elected by voters over there creates real problems of accountability that complicates the chances that real empowerment can take place in this way.

Nationalist sentiments may create spiritual and political solidarity among Puerto Ricans in the U.S., but it does not always strengthen Puerto Rican workers in their struggles with U.S. employers, landlords, or government. More generally, Puerto Ricans in the U.S. don't hold an either/or position about being a nation or national minority. They hold both together. The nation idea is usually an adjunct to a more dominant belief by Puerto

Ricans that they are a national minority. A number of recent empirical studies suggests this. In summary, by utilizing a social power perspective, the 'national question' takes on a very different meaning and import. This approach may not make answers come any easier but it can help us to better understand the consequences of our choices.

An important but overlooked source of power is work and the productive process itself. Employers have power: to hire, fire, change the process of work, as well as to invest and relocate productive facilities. In general, most of these economic powers don't translate easily into direct political power. But they are "social powers" that transform the social and physical environment of work, residence, and transportation. Economic decisions are indirectly political in the sense that they allocate and distribute values and are purposely excluded from government control. The corporate capacity to make these decisions also draws government attention and respect.

Periods of labor shortage also create a demand for labor and, thus, improve labor's bargaining position with employers over wages and conditions of work. Unions give workers organization and a common voice that augments the market power created by shortages. The fact that workers control their own bodies also means that employer control of the process of production has some (small) limits. Worker dissatisfaction occasionally expresses itself in production slowdowns and in diminished worker concentration and performance. Labor's social power also doesn't translate easily into political power. But much of what we call the "social welfare state" (welfare, public housing, social security, etc.) can be attributed to government responses to the social power labor exercised through demonstrations and rallies in the 1930s and more specifically to the "Keynesian" role labor played as a "consumptive sponge" that sopped up the economic surplus creating the Depression (Cloward and Piven 1976).

The idea that productive processes are a foundation of social power is largely unrecognized in the Puerto Rican politics literature. However, Vega, the Puerto Rican labor activist who lived in New York City in the first half of the twentieth century, expressed familiarity with the complex and uneven nature of the power relations between labor and employers. He found himself deeply frustrated in his role as a cigar-makers' union official because he was required to defend "the interests of the workers, without at the same time forcing the factories to move to other cities" (Vega 1984: 116). Vega was, thus, very much aware that ownership of productive facilities provides businessmen with the ultimate trump card. Any negotiation with labor or government includes the ever-present and real threat that employers will close shop or move to another location if they don't get what they want. Workers and government officials understand and respond to this hidden power of employers. It is the "privilege" that Lindblom says business enjoys in the policy process. Labor is not without some "privilege" in the policy process. Production, after all, if it is to continue in the same place, cannot proceed without it. But since labor is neither as mobile or as easily converted (e.g., retrained, socialized, etc.) as capital, labor's influence and power is, in general, more limited and circumscribed.

The thesis that social power has an important foundation in the productive process suggests an outline of a possible explanation of Puerto Rican powerlessness. One answer, for example, can be found in Puerto Rican poverty and employment levels. Compared to other groups in this society, Puerto Ricans are overwhelmingly workers rather than employers or managers. A large proportion of Puerto Rican workers is, furthermore, idle and out of work. Over 25 percent of Puerto Rican males in the U.S. during 1988 worked as operators and laborers, another 10 percent in managerial positions, and the rest in service and related occupations (Institute for Puerto Rican Policy 1990). More importantly, only 54 percent of all Puerto Ricans (sixteen years and older) in the U.S. were active in the labor market in 1988, compared to 68 percent of Mexicans and over 65 percent of all non-Latinos (ibid.). Unemployment, meanwhile, was over 12 percent for U.S. Puerto Ricans against 8 percent for Mexicans and 6 percent for all non-Latinos (ibid.). The concentration in working-class occupations and extended periods of idleness makes Puerto Ricans poorer than other groups. In 1988, about 34 percent of the U.S. Puerto Ricans were below the poverty rate, compared to 29 percent of Mexicans and 12 percent of non-Latinos (ibid.). These conditions not only limit Puerto Rican consumption and purchasing power but undermine social power. Business and government are not likely to be very threatened by the demands and actions of idle and unnecessary workers. Puerto Ricans have little social power because authorities are unattentive to their needs and are not dependent on their services as workers or their votes as citizens.

Unions have traditionally served as the principle mechanism by which dissatisfied workers make their demands known to employers and government. Historically, Puerto Ricans have been very receptive to trade-unions, both in Puerto Rico and New York City. Studies show, for instance, that 51 percent of all adult Puerto Ricans in New York City during 1948 were members of labor unions (González and Gray 1984: 118). By 1959, 66 percent of all Puerto Ricans and Latino households in the City of New York included a union member (ibid.). The preponderance of Puerto Ricans in working-class occupations increases union membership. The problem for Puerto Ricans is that union membership has not yet resulted in either economic or political advancement. The poverty and economic hardships Puerto Ricans have experienced in New York City are one consequence of union failure.

The organizational and financial resources of unions have historically been very instrumental in achieving labor interests in the political process. But these resources have not generally been put to use on behalf of Puerto Ricans. In general, as González and Gray conclude, "organized labor has reacted adversely to Puerto Rican political mobilization" (1984: 120). Thus Puerto Ricans have had little influence over union decisions to contribute money and manpower to electoral campaigns or political endorsements and lobbying. In addition, Puerto Rican garment workers in New York City were unable to gain access to the decision-making structures of the ILGWU-dominated Liberal Party.

The combination of these experiences for Puerto Rican workers in New York City has reduced even the small amount of social power that working-class status generates. Poverty, unemployment, as well as manipulative and abusive experiences with labor organizations made Puerto Ricans into a "disposable" labor force. Puerto Ricans work cheaply, but not cheaply enough to complete with other immigrant labor or labor in overseas locations. As a result, both employers and labor organizations are likely today to view Puerto Ricans as unnecessary to the main currents of production. Because of that superfluousness, Puerto Ricans are not especially sought after or able to demand very much from the political or economic spheres in this society.

Conclusion

The benefits of the reformulated political economic approach outlined above are, we hope, clear. The notion of social power is broader than the traditional Marxist tenet that power is basically located in the means of production. This is much too limited, since power is found additionally in the state and many other social relations. Such an expanded conceptualization of power is valuable in the study of Puerto Rican politics, for this community has experienced a great deal of exclusion from work (means of production) and from state-oriented social institutions like unions and political parties. The social power concept helps to explain both why these things happened and what needs to change for Puerto Ricans to gain power. The idea that power more generally rests on relationships where something is valued also provides a useful way to interpret political issues that have been historically important to Puerto Ricans in the U.S. The controversy over whether Puerto Ricans are a national minority or a nation, for instance, should only be relevant when being one or the other creates real differences in power for Puerto Ricans.

This reformulated political economy or social power approach also has distinct advantages over pluralist and ruling-elite approaches. Unlike the ruling-elite model, the social power approach posits the existence of power in relationships and the social structures that make them relatively permanent features of the social landscape. It avoids the weakness of making power an individual possession. Thus it provides an answer to the question "what do elites try to protect when they rule?" The social power model suggests that what elites should and often do succeed in protecting are social structures and relations that make their power possible. Individual elites may not always know what to do or when. But it is these social structures that measure and determine the success of their efforts.

Against the pluralist model, the political economy approach presented above recognizes a basic truth about power in this society—that it is unevenly distributed. Power is not a fruit that all members of society have equal access to. Nor can power be manufactured simply by the bulldogged assertion of will. Wanting and striving are not enough. Power, in fact, comes to those who are wanted and desired, or can make themselves so. A beggar with the only camel in the desert is decidedly more powerful in that situation than the millionaire alone and without one.

Voting and lobbying, for example, do permit individuals and groups to exert some power. A politician's need and want of votes and financing creates a relationship of power for voters and political financiers. But bereft of greater social power (other relationships where values are in need or want), voting and lobbying have little long-term effectiveness. That is what the pluralist model cannot see.

The outline of the social power approach presented here is only a tentative attempt to deal with some of the issues in the Puerto Rican political experience in the U.S. As a theory, it obviously needs much further development. And in application, many other aspects of Puerto Rican politics need to be considered. Unlike all too many of the other studies of Puerto Rican politics, our efforts here were not to accept, in an uncritical and secondhand way, the theoretical and empirical assumptions of other approaches: a usefully realistic understanding of the Puerto Rican experience has been delayed for too long by such assumptions.

REFERENCES

Alt, James, and K. Alec Chrystal. 1983. *Political Economics*. Berkeley: University of California Press.

Baver, Sherrie. 1984. "Puerto Rican Politics in New York City: The Post-World War II Period." In James Jennings and Monte Rivera, eds., *Puerto Rican Politics in Urban America*. Westport, Conn.: Greenwood Press.

Blaut, James. 1977. "Are Puerto Ricans a National Minority?" *Monthly Review*, May.

Bloch, Fred. 1984. "The Ruling Class Does Not Rule: Notes on the Marxist Theory of the State." In Thomas Ferguson and Joe Rogers, eds., *The Political Economy: Readings in the Politics and Economics of American Public Policy*. Armonk, N.Y.: M. E. Sharpe, Inc.

Browning, Rufus, P., D. R. Marshall, and D. H. Tabb. 1990. *Racial Politics in American Cities*. New York: Longman Press.

Buggs, John A. (Staff Director). 1972. Letter to Luis Nieves, Executive Director of Aspira, Inc., in New York City LaGuardia Archives.

Carmichel, Stokely, and Charles V. Hamilton. 1967. *Black Power*. New York: Random House.

Cloward, Richard A., and Francis F. Piven. 1976. *Poor People's Movement: Why They Succeed, How They Fail*. New York: Random House.

Cohen, Steven M., and Robert E. Kapsis. 1978. "Participation of Blacks, Puerto Ricans, and Whites in Voluntary Associations: A Test of Current Theories." *Social Forces* 56, June.

Cornacchia, Eugene J. 1985. "Ethnicity and Modes of Participation: White Ethnics, Blacks and Hispanics in New York City." Ph.D. diss. Fordham University.

Dahl, Robert. 1956. *A Preface to Democratic Theory*. Chicago: University of Chicago Press.

Domhoff, G. William. 1983. *Who Rules America Now?: A View for the '80s*. Englewood Cliffs, N.J.: Prentice-Hall.

Dye, Thomas R. 1986. *Who's Running America?: The Reagan Years*, 3rd ed. Englewood Cliffs, N.J.: Prentice-Hall.

——— and R. Putnam. 1976. *Who's Running America? Institutional Leadership in the United States*. New York: Prentice-Hall.

——— and L. Harmon Ziegler. 1978. *Irony of Democracy*, 4th ed. Belmont, Calif.: Duxbury Press.

El Diario-La Prensa. 1972a. "Poor Participation of Puerto Ricans in New York's Public Housing," February 14.

———. 1972b. "Nine's Law Eliminates the Last Vestiges of Discrimination in Housing Projects," May 25.

Estades, Rosa. 1978. *Patterns of Political Participation of Puerto Ricans in New York City*. Puerto Rico: University of Puerto Rico.

Falcón, Angelo. 1980. "Puerto Rican Political Participation: New York City and Puerto Rico." Paper presented at the American Political Science Convention.

———. 1985. "Black and Latino Politics in New York City: Race and Ethnicity in a Changing Urban Context," *New Community*.

Fuentes, Luis. 1980. "The Struggle for Local Political Control." In Clara E. Rodríguez et al., *The Puerto Rican Struggle: Essays on Survival in the U.S.* New York: Puerto Rican Migration Research Consortium, Inc.

González, Eddie, and Lois Gray. 1984. "Puerto Ricans, Politics and Labor Activism." In Jennings and Rivera 1984.

Gómez, Aramis. (Housing Authority Staff) 1972. July 5th Report to Simeon Golar, Chair of Housing Authority, titled "Complaints of Puerto Rican Community—Tenant Selection and Apartment Assignments," LaGuardia Archives.

Gotsch, John Warren. 1966. "Puerto Rican Leadership in New York." M.A. Thesis, New York University.

Gutiérrez, Juan M. 1987. "The Political Dynamics of Bilingual Education: A Retrospective Study of Interest Groups." Ph.D. diss., Stanford University.

Harrigan, John J. 1989. *Political Change in the Metropolis*. 4th ed. Boston: Scott, Foresman.

Herbstein, Judith F. 1978. "Ritual and Politics of the Puerto Rican 'community' in New York City." Ph.D. diss., City University of New York.

———. 1983. "The Politicization of Puerto Rican Ethnicity in New York: 1955–1975," *Ethnic Groups* 5, July.

Hester, Paul H. 1976. "The Educational Benefits of Four Puerto Rican Communities as Indicators of Political Interaction: A Comparative Study." Ph.D. diss., University of Connecticut.

Institute for Puerto Rican Policy, Inc. (IPR). 1990. Data Note, "Puerto Ricans and Other Latinos in the United States 1989," July.

Janeway, Elizabeth. 1980. *Powers of the Weak*. New York: Knopf.

Jennings, James, and M. Rivera, eds. 1984. *Puerto Rican Politics in Urban America*. Westport, Conn.: Greenwood Press.

Lapp, Michael. 1986. "The Migration Division of Puerto Rico and Puerto Ricans in New York City, 1948–1969." Unpublished paper at Johns Hopkins University.

Lindblom, Charles E. 1977. *Politics and Markets: The World's Political-Economic Systems*. New York: Basic Books.

López, Alfredo. 1973. *The Puerto Rican Papers: Notes on the Re-emergence of a Nation*. New York: Bobbs-Merrill Publishers.

Martin, George E. 1975. "Ethnic Political Leadership: The Case of the Puerto Ricans." Ph.D. diss., Fordham University.

Mattuck, Joseph (Acting Director of Research). 1972. August 3rd Memo to Marcus Levy, General Manager of the NYCHA. LaGuardia Archives, Box 3707/09.

Mayor's Committee on Puerto Rican Affairs. 1953. "Interim Report of the MCPRA in New York City: September 1949 to September 1953." New York City Municipal Archives.

Mills, C. Wright. 1956. *The Power Elite*. New York: Oxford University Press.

————. 1967. *Power, Politics, and People*. I. Louis Horowitz, ed. New York: Oxford University Press.

Nelson, Dale. 1980. "The Political Behavior of New York Puerto Ricans: Assimilation or Survival?" In C. E. Rodríguez et al., eds., *The Puerto Rican Struggle: Essays on Survival in the United States*. New York: Puerto Rican Migration Consortium, Inc.

New York City Housing Authority. 1972. "Tension Report for March 31." LaGuardia Archives.

New York State Comptroller, Office of. 1976. "Audit Report on Tenant Selection by the New York City Housing Authority."

New York Times. 1975a. "New York City Housing Authority Raising Maximum Income." January 22.

————. 1975b. "Increasing Numbers of Problem Families in Public Housing." June 29, Section VIII, 1:4.

Padilla, Félix M. 1987. *Puerto Rican Chicago*. Notre Dame, Ind.: University of Notre Dame Press.

Pantoja, Antonia. 1989. "Puerto Ricans in New York: A Historical and Community Development Perspective." *Centro Boletín* 2(5).

Putnam, Robert D. 1976. *The Comparative Study of Political Elites*. Englewood Cliffs, N.J.: Prentice-Hall.

Rodríguez-Fraticelli, Carlos, and Amilcar Tirado. 1989. "Notes Toward a History of Puerto Rican Community Organizations in New York City." *Centro Boletín* 2(6).

Roye, Wendell (Director of Community Affairs, NYCHA). 1969. March 20 memo to Albert Walsh (Chair, NYCHA). LaGuardia Archives.

Sánchez, José Ramón. 1986. "Residual Work and Residual Shelter: Housing Puerto Rican Labor in New York City from WW II to 1983." In Bratt et al., eds., *Critical Perspectives on Housing*. Philadelphia: Temple University.

————. 1990. "Housing Puerto Ricans in New York City, 1945 to 1984: A Study in Class Powerlessness." Ph.D. diss., New York University.

Sánchez-Korrol, Virginia. 1983. *From Colonia to Community: The History of Puerto Ricans in New York City*. Westport, Conn.: Greenwood Press.

Savitch, Harold V. 1972. "Powerlessness in an Urban Ghetto: The Case of Political Biases and Differential Access in New York City." *Polity* 5 (Fall): 19–56.

Stafford, Walter. 1985. *Closed Labor Markets*. New York City: Community Service Society.

Stamm, Liesa, and Carol D. Ryff, eds. 1984. *Social Power and Influence of Women*. Boulder, Colo.: Westview Press.

Therborn, Goran. 1982. "What Does the Ruling Class Do When It

Rules?" In A. Giddens and D. Held, eds., *Classes, Power, and Conflict*. Berkeley: University of California Press.

Torres, Andres. 1989. "Labor Segmentation and Political Power: African American and Puerto Rican Labor in New York City." Unpublished paper, Center for Puerto Rican Studies, Hunter College, New York City.

Truman, David B. 1971. *The Governmental Process*. New York: Knopf Publishers.

Vega, Bernardo. 1984. *Memoirs of Bernardo Vega: A Contribution to the History of the Puerto Rican Community in New York*. New York: Monthly Review Press.

Wakefield, Dan. 1959. *Island in the City: The World of Spanish Harlem*. New York: New York University Press.

Weiss, Mel, and Ester Tenner. 1973. "Everything You Wanted to Know about Tenant Selection," January. [An internal training manual for NYCHA employees.] LaGuardia Archives.

10

New York's Latinos and the 1986 Immigration Act: The IRCA Experience and Future Trends

SHERRIE L. BAVER

On May 5, 1987, the Immigration Reform and Control Act (IRCA) went into effect. This law represented the first change in U.S. immigration policy in twenty-two years. By the early 1980s the national perception was that the United States had lost control of its borders. Thousands of boat people from Cuba and Haiti were landing in Florida at the same time that Mexicans and Central Americans were illegally crossing the southern border. Congress was pushed to act prompted by two types of popular concerns. First, constituents feared potential job losses to illegal immigrants, a fear no doubt fueled by the recession of the early 1980s. Second, a widespread resentment existed against all immigrants but especially, perhaps, Spanish-speaking immigrants, for a seeming unwillingness to assimilate. A clear symptom of this resentment, in addition to calls for immigration reform, was the passage of "official English" bills in several areas throughout the country. Therefore, by the mid-1980s the United States joined other advanced industrial countries in trying to regain the upper hand on immigration.[1]

The primary intent of this article is to examine how the 1986 immigration law with its key features of amnesty and employer sanction affects the Latino community of New York City. We begin with an overview of the IRCA legislation, and then examine the makeup of New York's Latino immigrant community with a brief discussion of the Dominicans, the largest group of immigrants of Latino national origin. (Puerto Ricans are the largest Latino national origin group in New York but they are U.S. citizens, hence, technically not immigrants.) The next section focuses on the legalization process and potential explanations for the seemingly low amnesty application rate in New York City as compared to other parts of the country, followed by a brief overview of the effects of employer sanctions. The final sections offer an analysis of IRCA's effectiveness and general conclusions on immigration reform. The analysis suggests that the law has not achieved its stated goals of ending the marginalization of the undocumented in the United States and significantly reducing the flow of new illegal aliens. Furthermore, the legislation has caused an added degree of hardship for legal residents and citizens in the Latino and other minority communities.

Background

The immigration law that was passed by Congress in November 1986 represented several years of work. In 1979 President Carter established a Select Commission on Immigration Policy, chaired by Notre Dame President Father Theodore Hesburgh. Armed with the findings of the Select Commission, the legislative campaign to change U.S. immigration policy was spearheaded in the Senate by Alan Simpson of Wyoming and in the House by Romano Mazzoli of Kentucky, the legislators who jointly submitted a bill in 1983. The 1986 bill, which ultimately became law, was coauthored by Senator Simpson and Congressman Peter Rodino of New Jersey, chair of the House Judiciary Committee.

The new immigration law had two key features. First, it contained a plan to grant amnesty to all illegal aliens who could document continuous residence in the United States since January 1, 1982. The amnesty legalization period would last for one year starting on May 5, 1987, and ending on May 4, 1988. It is noteworthy that the five-year residence requirement for eligibility made the U.S. program the most restrictive of all nations that had recently instituted similar programs, specifically Canada, France, Australia, Argentina, and Venezuela. The U.S. amnesty, however, did contain a separate and more liberal plan for granting legal residence and citizenship to seasonal agricultural workers (SAWS).[2]

The other key feature of the IRCA was that for the first time in U.S. history, employers who knowingly hired undocumented workers could be sanctioned with fines, prison terms, or both. The obvious intent of these employer sanctions was to reduce the attractiveness of the U.S. labor market to people considering entering the country illegally. The law also provided additional funds to the Immigration and Naturalization Service (INS) to hire new personnel.

Like most legislation passed in the United States, IRCA was based partly on carefully crafted policy analyses conducted by scholars and partly on political compromises. Throughout the legislative debate on immigration reform, several social interest groups were actively involved in promoting their strongly felt positions. Not unexpectedly, the leading national Latino organizations took a keen interest in the legislative reform efforts. While the Mexican-American community probably has had the most frequent dealings with U.S. immigration authorities, the INS has played an important role for other Spanish-speaking communities since the large increase in Latin American migration starting in the mid-1960s. Therefore, Latino advocacy groups tried to play a forceful role in shaping policy.

The advocacy groups supported the general amnesty for undocumented workers but were strongly opposed to employer sanctions. Representatives of the Latino community feared that the sanctions would lead to increased discrimination against Spanish speakers who were citizens or legal permanent residents of the United States. The scenario that groups such as the Mexican American Legal Defense and Education Fund (MALDEF) envisioned was that of an employer wary of hiring someone who looked or sounded foreign, even if the worker had proof of legal residence or citizenship.

The spokesmen of other key interests were equally active in expressing their members' fears. Organized labor, at least initially, supported employer sanctions but opposed the legalization of undocumented foreign workers. Small business opposed employer sanctions, while ideological conservatives, represented by groups such as the Federation for American Immigration Reform (FAIR) and espousing the nativist position of "closing the door to foreigners," opposed the legalization provision and supported employer sanctions.[3] Ultimately, the law that passed in 1986 could be described as "generous but not too generous, tough but not oppressive."[4]

New York's Immigrant Latino Community

Immigration has been a dominant institution in the Latino community nationally as well as for Latinos in the New York area. Between

Table 1
Immigrants to New York City by Country of Birth,
and as a Percentage of all Immigrants to the City,
in Fiscal Year 1986

Dominican Republic	18.1	Soviet Union	1.2
Jamaica	9.8	Poland	1.2
Guyana	8.2	Hong Kong	1.2
China	7.7	Britain	1.2
Haiti	6.8	El Salvador	1.2
Colombia	3.3	Pakistan	1.2
Korea	3.0	Romania	1.2
India	2.9	Barbados	1.1
Ecuador	2.4	Peru	1.0
Philippines	1.9	Cuba	0.9
Trinidad and Tobago	1.5	Iran	0.9
Taiwan	1.3	Grenada	0.9
Honduras	1.3	Italy	0.8
Israel	1.2		

SOURCE: Immigration and Naturalization Service

1980 and 1987 1 million Latin American immigrants arrived in the United States and accounted for 27 percent of all legal immigration during the period. During the same period, about 250,000 of these Spanish-speaking immigrants settled in metropolitan New York with more than half (167,500) settling in New York City. In 1980, 32 percent of Latinos were foreign born, compared to a figure of 13 percent foreign born among non-Latinos in the metropolitan New York region.[5] An especially large number of Spanish-speaking immigrants who settle in New York come from the Dominican Republic. (An in-depth discussion of Dominican immigration is found in the chapter by Hernández and Torres-Saillant in this volume.)

The Dominican Community

Dominican immigration to the United States began on a large scale in the early to mid-1960s due to internal political and economic changes on the island along with changes in U.S. policies. The most fundamental historical factor triggering Dominican emigration was the death of the dictator Trujillo in 1961. Other factors to be considered in a thorough analysis of Dominican emigration are specific political events such as the 1965 uprising in the republic and the change in U.S. immigration policy afterwards. It has been argued that after the Dominican rebellion in April 1965, which ended with the intervention of U.S. Marines, Washington helped facilitate emigration from the island to provide the U.S.-backed government with a "safety valve." The flow of thousands of Dominicans to the States in the postrebellion era was seen as a strategy to promote political stability and economic growth in the republic and thereby avoid the threat of another Cuba in the region.[6] Furthermore, more general socioeconomic explanations for the Dominicans' large-scale exodus lie in the models of industrialization and agricultural commercialization adopted by the Balaguer government after 1966 and the imposition of International Monetary Fund stabilization programs in the 1980s.[7]

Statistics clearly show the increase in Dominican arrivals to the United States since the 1960s. While fewer than 1,000 Dominican immigrants entered the country annually between 1951 and 1960, the annual averages for each later decade have risen dramatically. The average was 9,000 per year through the 1960s; 14,000 per year in the 1970s; and 20,000 in the first half of the 1980s with a total of 372,817 Dominicans legally admitted to the United States between 1961 and 1986. Also, due to family reunification, since 1983 the number of immigrant visas granted by the State Department exceeded the annual 20,000 ceiling. Finally, according to the 1990 census data, New York City's Dominican population was 332,713, which made up 18.7 percent of all Hispanic New Yorkers. This figure of 332,713 represented a 165.4 percent increase in the number of Dominicans since the 1980 census, which reported 207,333 Dominicans in the City. Another way to state the magnitude of the increase is that between 1982 and 1989, one out of every six immigrants to New York City was Dominican.[8]

Based on the DIAGNOS survey done in the Dominican Republic in the 1970s, it would seem that the bulk of the Dominican emigrants, at least through the late 1970s, were of urban background. Furthermore, in terms of social status, the new arrivals to New York were considered middle or lower-middle class by Dominican standards.[9] Since the economic crisis in the republic after 1982, however, coupled with the effects of International Mone-

tary Fund stabilizati
lated through all class
of the middle class b
however, have often
United States via the
Puerto Rico first and 1

Since Dominican
grants to New York in
that they also comprise
in the City. Researcher
found that the same se
illegal entrants and that
bers of the same family.
mented Dominicans gai
because of all Hispanics,
of amnesty applications

308

and thorough knowledge of th
residence in the United S
required extreme ingen
tion. Then, to becom
an English and civ
and history cl
only to bec
for perm
police
fin

The Legalization Process

The national amnesty for undocumented workers began on May 5, 1987. It should be underscored that the "amnesty" was perceived by illegal aliens as a difficult, somewhat punitive means for legalizing their status in the United States. Adjusting one's status by marriage or petitioning for political asylum represented a decidedly preferable way to obtain the same goal of permanent residence.

It also would have been preferable for illegal aliens to apply as a Seasonal Agricultural Worker (SAW), an option not open to many *indocumentados* in New York but open to many in California and the Southwest. SAWs had a much easier time applying than did regular amnesty applicants because of the strength of the U.S. farmers' lobby, which wanted to maintain its labor force. To qualify as a SAW, one would have had to work in U.S. agriculture for at least three months between May 1, 1985, and May 1, 1986. SAWs were given six extra months to apply and were made eligible for food stamps and Medicaid, unlike the amnesty applicants. Of the approximately 1.3 million SAW applicants nationally, only 50,400 or 3.9 percent came from New York State.

To apply for the amnesty required a high degree of motivation

e law. Applicants had to prove their
ates from January 1982, which often
ity in marshaling appropriate documenta-
a permanent resident, applicants had to pass
ics test or enroll in forty to sixty hours of language
sses. Normally immigrants have to pass these tests
me citizens. In addition to other general requirements
anent residence in the United States—such as no serious
record, testing negative for the AIDs virus, and proof of
ancial responsibility—amnesty applicants had to wait five years
between gaining legal status and receiving any public assistance
such as Aid for Families with Dependent Children (AFDC), Medicaid, or food stamps. Also, applicants could not leave the country
for more than thirty days at a time or a total of ninety days during
the period between temporary and permanent residence. Perhaps
most painful for the applicants was that although they had lived
in the United States since 1982, they could not sponsor close relatives
for immigration until they became permanent residents.

New York's Low Application Rate

A major issue troubling immigration advocates and analysts in New
York was why the City had such a seemingly low rate of legalization
applicants compared to the rest of the country. The simplest explanation may be that all INS estimates for potential applicants were
too high, a belief that is held by many students of U.S. immigration.[12]
The agency initially predicted that 3.9 million people would apply
nationally, but program applications never reached that level. This
begs the question for New York City, however, where an especially
marked gap existed between the estimated and actual number of
applicants. The initial prediction for New York City was that 500,000
would apply, about one-half of the 1 million people estimated to
be eligible.

In addition to exaggerated estimates of the number of eligible
aliens, specific problems with the amnesty also occurred. At first,
a widespread distrust of the legalization program existed on the
part of illegal aliens nationally. The INS had been known in poor
immigrant communities primarily in its enforcement role of tracking
down and deporting the undocumented. Now "la migra," as the

INS is referred to in Spanish slang, was offering legal status to the undocumented. Not surprisingly, then, the amnesty was initially perceived by illegals as a new strategy for entrapment. In New York, however, the cost of entrapment, specifically deportation, is seen as higher than the cost in many other parts of the country. Simply put, it is much more difficult to return to the United States if one is deported to the Caribbean or South America (where most of New York's Latin American population originates) than to drive or walk across the U.S.-Mexican border. Along the border those deported to Mexico typically try again, often within days.[13]

Nationally, it took at least several weeks to dispel the fear that the amnesty was a way to trick illegal aliens into revealing themselves. In New York City, however, local officials and immigrants' rights advocates maintained that the INS sponsored public information campaign to lessen fear of entrapment was ineffective for more than half of the legalization period. Part of the problem stemmed from the challenge of publicizing the amnesty to the city's diverse undocumented population that spoke an estimated forty-six languages. Also in New York the INS had a somewhat strained relationship with the voluntary agencies that were designated to aid immigrants in preparing amnesty applicants. During the first half of the legalization period, for example, the INS did not make clear to eligible applicants in New York that they did not have to come to the INS directly but could go to unions, churches, or community groups for help.

The lack of publicity in New York may have been exacerbated by the relative newness of many of the city's immigrant communities. The relatively recent arrival of a community—for example, the Dominicans in New York as compared to the Mexicans in Texas and California—implies a lower density of ethnic associations that could have helped in the information campaign.[14] Therefore, in the beginning of 1988, when it became clear that New York had a dramatically low application rate, local government and nonprofit agencies organized their own extensive publicity and outreach campaign. It should be underscored that city officials and representatives of the nonprofit sector were motivated to act not only to make a good faith effort to carry out the intent of the law. They were also motivated by the knowledge that federal and state funds are distributed to cities based on population. It behooved New York

City, therefore, to help legalize as many undocumented residents as possible.

The outreach campaign did increase the number of applications from targeted groups significantly. Spanish-language television and radio stations and other ethnic media were asked to run stories about successful applicants who had received temporary residence and work permits. Dominican neighborhoods in Washington Heights in Manhattan and Kingsbridge, Tremont, and High Bridge in the Bronx received the most media attention. Not surprisingly Dominicans showed a 209 percent increase in applications, the largest increase shown by any single group.[15] They also represented the national-origin group with the largest number of applications in New York City. Because of public and voluntary agency efforts, it is probable that most of the undocumented had at least heard of the amnesty program before the application deadline. Due to its early publicity failure, the INS allowed a six-month extension for completing applications after the initial filing.

Other problems that were national in scope may or may not have had a particular *denouement* in the New York context. By the end of the legalization period, most illegal aliens probably were convinced that the program was not a trap. This did not mean, though, that they were free to take advantage of the opportunity. The most likely reason for not applying was the inability to get papers to document their life in this country since January 1, 1982. This group of immigrants, made up of experts at hiding their existence in the United States, were now being asked to provide rent stubs, paid electricity bills, and other proof in their own names. Furthermore, employers were often reluctant to provide affidavits for these workers, not wanting to admit to the government that they had employed illegal aliens. Employers were most likely to help an amnesty applicant if they had a personal relationship.

Another common problem was that applicants had to live in the country more or less continuously since January 1, 1982. One could not have been out of the country for more than 180 days since January 1982. This, then, ruled out undocumented aliens who had gone back to their home countries, typically to deal with family problems.

Some undocumented aliens may not have applied for fear of exposing other family members to deportation if they, the applicant, gained legal residence but the others did not or were not eligible. Throughout the legalization period, no nationally applicable policy existed on the issue of deportation of noneligible family members; it was up to the discretion of INS district officials to judge specific cases. Only in February 1990 did the INS make a formal ruling that spouses and children of successful applicants could stay if they had been in the country since November 1, 1986. The earlier, vague INS guidelines had stated that illegal family members could stay only if "compelling humanitarian reasons" could be proven. While only a few people were actually deported, because no clear-cut policy existed on this issue, the possibility of family separation generated fear and confusion within the immigrant community.[16]

Finally, two hypotheses regarding New York's seemingly low legalization rate were offered during the amnesty year in a study sponsored by the Carnegie Endowment for International Peace. The first hypothesis suggested was that New York's undocumented aliens typically worked in ethnic business enclaves; therefore, they felt sheltered from the threat of employer sanctions and had little incentive to apply. The Carnegie study also suggested that illegals in New York City may have felt relatively safe from the INS because of Mayor Koch's directive to city agencies not to cooperate with INS enforcement.[17] Neither hypothesis was borne out in the numerous interviews that this researcher conducted with amnesty applicants in New York. Everyone wanted a green card if it were possible.[18]

Who Applied for Amnesty in New York?

In the summer of 1989, this researcher conducted a study of 171 Latin American amnesty applicants in New York City. Respondents were interviewed in amnesty-related English and civics classes sponsored by the City College of New York and the McBurney YMCA on West 23rd Street. Since the classes were held in Manhattan, a majority of respondents lived in Manhattan, although some respondents came from the other boroughs except Staten Island. While those interviewed were not randomly selected for the study, the findings offer a snapshot of the characteristics of the Spanish-speaking population of New York that legalized under IRCA.

Among respondents, 57 percent were male and 43 percent were female. This parallels exactly the national findings on sex of applicants compiled by the INS on January 9, 1990. Twenty-eight percent of New York respondents were aged twenty to twenty-nine, 35 percent were aged thirty to thirty-nine, 24 percent were between the ages of forty and forty-nine, and 13 percent were fifty and above. In the national statistics, 31 percent were in their twenties, 34 percent were in their thirties, 9 percent were in their early forties, and 12 percent were over forty-five. The age breakdown supports the widely noted demographic pattern that most people migrate during their prime working years. Most likely the large majority of amnesty applicants had come in their twenties, but because they had to have been in the United States for at least seven years when answering the survey in 1989, the largest number were in their thirties.

In assessing their English fluency, 19 percent had a good to excellent command of the language, 29 percent had limited fluency, and 52 percent had little or no ability to speak English. Forty-nine percent had completed some primary school, 27 percent had completed some secondary school, 11 percent had received a high school diploma, and 12 percent had received some university training. This group contained at least one engineer, one dentist, and one physician.

Sixty-five percent of respondents had been employed in their home country. Of the rest, several had been students, housewives, or had farmed their own land. The overwhelming majority of those surveyed, 89 percent, had jobs in New York. Most, 49 percent, worked in the service sector. The second largest group, 25 percent, worked in manufacturing.

The largest number of those interviewed in this survey of Spanish-speaking amnesty applicants came from the Dominican Republic. Ecuadoreans were the second largest national-origin group and Mexicans were the third. To compare this ranking with the numbers for all Hispanic amnesty applicants citywide, Dominicans were the largest group applying citywide, with Mexicans second, Colombians third, and Ecuadoreans ranking fourth in 1994 (table 2).

The biggest surprise for immigration watchers in New York was the large number of Mexicans who submitted applications for legalization. Mexicans applied in large numbers than Salvadorans, Colombians, or Ecuadoreans, indicating a large underground popu-

Table 2

Individuals Approved under IRCA (Legalized Applicants and Seasonal Agricultural Workers) by Country of Birth (Top Sending Countries) for New York City

Dominican Republic	11,898	Jamaica	6,006
Mexico	9,259	India	5,565
Haiti	8,590	Korea	4,495
Colombia	8,576	Bangladesh	4,193
Pakistan	7,094	El Salvador	3,638
Ecuador	6,767	Other	43,285
China	6,335		
	Total IRCA, United States	2,758,526	
	Total IRCA, New York City	125,701	

SOURCE: A. Peter Lobo and Joseph J. Salvo, *The Newest New Yorkers: 1900–1994* (New York: New York City Department of City Planning, 1996).

lation. The Department of City Planning and the researcher Robert Smith estimated the total legal and undocumented population at close to 100,000 by the end of the 1980s.[19] In suggesting why they had been unaware of large numbers of undocumented Mexicans, local officials explained that this group would be more hidden than most others in New York, since they had crossed the border undetected rather than overstaying tourist visas. Furthermore, the large Mexican presence had been missed because, unlike certain other ethnic groups, Mexicans were not highly concentrated in one neighborhood in the City.

At the end of fiscal year 1991, by which time the bulk of eligible amnesty applicants would have been legalized, New York State accounted for approximately 118,210 successful applicants, or about 6.7 percent of the national total. About 89 percent of successful New York applications, or 105,905, came from people living in the City. Nevertheless, some percentage of the eligibles did not apply, for reasons cited earlier. One study done in 1988 suggested that less than half of the eligibles may have applied in New York; although given the extension allowed by the INS, this estimate is probably high.[20] In addition, it is estimated that the undocumented population in the United States increased at a rate of 6.8 percent per year since 1982. At that pace, at least 220,000 undocumented immigrants entered New York State between 1982 and 1993, 90 percent of whom chose to live in New York City.

In sum, the amnesty was intended to reward with legal residence those people who had been oiling the cogs in the American economy by working in its most menial jobs. The program achieved this goal to the extent that some proportion of those eligible to apply did receive temporary legal status. Yet the law resulted in a set of complicated procedures which generated "confusion and anxiety on the part of the populations affected."[21] Surely, a less complex process could have been devised if lawmakers wanted to show more generosity toward the nation's least-protected workers.

Legalization Stage Two: The Hurdles Continue

Applying for amnesty and receiving temporary residence and work authorization did not mean assurance of permanent residence in the United States. After passing through the first stage (i.e., gaining temporary legal status), applicants had thirty months to apply for permanent residence. The first problem raised by immigrants' rights advocates was that some percentage of the generally poorly educated, non-English-speaking applicants were not aware of the second stage of the amnesty process. And if they did not apply for permanent residence within the thirty month period, they again would become illegal and subject to deportation. The INS budgeted little money for an information campaign about the second stage of the legalization process and simply sent all first-stage applicants notices. New immigrants, however, are an extremely mobile population, so it is likely that at least some amnesty applicants would not be notified of the deadline.

Also, to qualify for permanent residence, applicants were required to pass either an INS English and civics test or to prove they had attended forty to sixty hours of language and history courses. Both nationally and in New York, though, applicants had to face a serious shortage of amnesty classes.[22] In January 1990, the INS reported that, nationally, 63.9 percent of amnesty recipients had applied for permanent residence, while the figure for New York was only 58.4 percent. Because of the program's overall complexity and the pitfalls in its implementation, therefore, it is possible that only the immigrants with the greatest financial resources—for example, to hire an immigration lawyer or, possibly, to pay for private language classes—would have viewed the process as within their means.[23]

IRCA and Employer Sanctions

The feature of IRCA that caused extreme concern for the Latino community both nationally and locally was the provision for employer sanctions. Employer sanctions had been sought by organized labor since the early 1970s and the issue had been spearheaded by Congressman Peter Rodino (Democrat, New Jersey). Latino advocacy groups feared that the sanctions would cause employers to discriminate against anyone who looked or sounded foreign, even if that person could prove legal residence or citizenship. Furthermore, Latino community representatives argued that large numbers of undocumented aliens, who were not eligible for the amnesty but had lived here for years, would not return to their home countries but rather would be pushed "even further into the shadows" and face even harsher working conditions.

With the passage of IRCA, all employers must attempt to verify that employees hired after November 6, 1986, are legal residents of the United States. The law provided for one year, between June 1987 and June 1988, to educate business owners about the sanctions program. After 1987, though, employers were subject to fines, prison sentences or both if they continued to hire illegal workers. The federal legislation also called for a Special Prosecutor in the Justice Department to monitor discrimination complaints, and Congress requested three annual reports from the General Accounting Office (GAO) between 1987 and 1989 as another means to assess the incidence of discrimination. If the GAO reports found a pattern of discrimination in its three-year study, Congress would be required either to modify or repeal the sanctions provision.

The GAO, however, was not the only agency monitoring the effects of employer sanctions. Other public and private bodies also began monitoring IRCA-related bias at the federal, state, and local levels. The U.S. Equal Employment Opportunity Commission, for example, monitored discrimination complaints nationwide. In New York State, an Inter-Agency Task Force on Immigration Affairs chaired by the commissioner of Social Services, César Perales, studied complaints and published its first report in November 1988. The New York City Commission on Human Rights was also active in hearing IRCA-related discrimination complaints in the five boroughs.

Both the Inter-Agency Task Force and the Human Rights Commission found evidence of discrimination. The study commissioned by the state Task Force, which examined 400 businesses in the metropolitan New York area, found three types of discrimination by employers: (1) refusal to accept legally valid proof of residence; (2) denial of employment to those who experienced minor but legally allowable delays in gathering work documents; and (3) screening out of applicants who looked or sounded foreign.[24]

The city's Human Rights Commission also uncovered evidence of discrimination. The commission collected data using a variety of testing procedures commonly used in discrimination investigations, specifically hearings, a survey of discrimination victims, and a hiring audit. The commission not only found discrimination in hiring practices but also found bias in terms of housing and purchasing goods and services from stores, banks, and insurance companies. The most common complaints, however, did involve job-related issues. In a 1988 hearing, for example, commissioners learned from a Commonwealth of Puerto Rico Migration Division official that employers were asking Puerto Ricans, all of whom are U.S. citizens, for their green cards. Furthermore, the Commission's 1989 hiring audit found that 41 percent of employers treated job applicants with accents differently from those without accents. The Commission sent its findings of widespread discrimination against immigrants and legal residents "who looked or sounded foreign" to the GAO in 1989 for that agency's final report to Congress.[25]

The Human Rights Commission's findings were also supported by data from New York's Immigration Hotline and the New York-based Center for Immigrants Rights (CIR). Immigration Hotline workers reported that between July 1988 and July 1989, they received about four hundred calls involving employer discrimination. The most frequent problem involved amnesty applicants who had lost jobs. By law, all amnesty applicants were allowed to work while their case was being decided, but because of slow processing of applications by the INS or because of employer confusion about the law, workers were fired.

In June 1988, the Center for Immigrants Rights also started an employer sanctions hotline and, after eleven months in operation, CIR submitted its findings in written testimony to a congressional hearing on IRCA. The Center reported 225 calls on sanctions-related abuse, noting that 35 percent of calls involved citizens, permanent residents, temporary residents, (or applicants), and refugees who had valid work documents. The remaining 65 percent involved undocumented workers without valid work documents who called to report work abuses and deteriorating work conditions. The CIR testimony concluded that sanctions were:

> promoting anti-immigrant and racist sentiments against those who are perceived as foreign because of their appearance or language abilities. Citizens, legalized immigrants, or other authorized workers who are minorities are regarded by employers as especially suspect. [Furthermore, sanctions have] heightened the vulnerability of undocumented workers by imposing an additional level of illegality on their status. The grievances from callers include nonpayment of wages, long hours without overtime pay, irregular night hours, subminimum pay, loss of benefits or seniority, and sexual harassment.[26]

As a result of the findings of discrimination in New York, Mayor Koch agreed to support a 1989 City Council bill amending the City's Human Rights law. For the first time, undocumented aliens would be allowed to take complaints of bias in housing and government services to the Human Rights Commission. The bill also included a provision to grant some licenses, such as those for food vendors, without requiring applicants to prove legal authorization to work in the United States.[27] The mayor also agreed to make permanent a 1985 directive that required city agencies to provide services to undocumented immigrants and barred city agencies from turning information over to the INS.

To the surprise of many observers, and in contrast to its first two reports to Congress, the GAO's third report, published in March 1990, found widespread discrimination against potential employees who "looked or sounded foreign."[28] Given this assessment, Congress had to review the IRCA's employer sanctions provision. Most likely federal legislators will call for increased education of employers on the requirements of the law and a reduction of the number of acceptable work authorization documents that potential job-seekers may present. With fewer acceptable documents, employers may have less concern that they are fraudulent, hence less reason to discriminate. It is highly unlikely, though, that the sanctions will be dropped, since the General Accounting Office also urged that, to some extent, they were reducing illegal immigration.

Analysis

The 1986 Immigration Reform and Control Act had two major goals: (1) to offer the undocumented population of the nation a chance to legalize their status and (2) to slow the rate of further illegal migration to the United States, primarily with employer sanctions. How well have both of these goals been met, especially in New York City?

At the end of fiscal year 1991, about 1.76 million people had applied nationally for temporary residence under the amnesty; another 1.27 million people applied as SAWs. By the end of 1991, over 1.5 million people had received permanent residence status as a result of the amnesty and 966,000 received permanent residence as SAWs. New York State accounted for approximately 118,210 successful amnesty applicants or about 6.7 percent of the national total. About 89 percent of the state's successful applications or 105,905 came from people living in New York City. In terms of SAWs, New York state had an additional 52,776 applicants, with 47,037 coming from New York City. It is assumed that the majority of New York State and City SAW applicants were also successful in gaining permanent residence. Nevertheless, some percentage of eligibles did not apply for the reasons cited earlier. Recall that a 1988 study suggested that large numbers of eligibles did not apply in New York (see note 19).

In addition to offering amnesty to some undocumented workers, IRCA was also supported to cut down on illegal immigration through more stringent enforcement at the borders and especially through employer sanctions. Yet within a little more than a year of IRCA implementation, the INS was virtually alone in claiming that employer sanctions had cut down significantly on illegal

Table 3
Largest Illegal Alien Groups in New York State
as of September 30, 1992 (in thousands)*

Ecuador	27.1	Haiti	21.4
Italy	26.8	Jamaica	21.2
Poland	25.8	Trinidad & Tobago	20.5
Dominican Republic	25.6	Ireland	16.9
Colombia	24.5	El Salvador	15.3

* The INS cautioned, however, that because their count is based on the use of passports, it may be less accurate for those people who do not need passports, like Canadians, and people who cross the border without passports, such as Mexicans.

Source: INS, New York City Department of City Planning, as quoted in the *New York Times*, September 2, 1993.

entrants. While a slowdown in apprehensions at the U.S.-Mexican border did occur in the first year after the law took effect in 1987, since 1989 the apprehension rate, used as an indirect measure of illegal border crossings, was on the rise again, approaching the numbers recorded in late 1986, before IRCA's implementation.[29]

Furthermore, by the later 1980s, before any systematic study existed, many local officials and immigrant rights activists concurred in their view that employer sanctions have had little deterrent effect in New York City for at least two reasons. First, the INS enforcement arm was understaffed. Therefore only large potential employers of illegals, such as big restaurant chains, would most likely be investigated, and large employers would be the most likely to be aware of the law and to comply with it. Second, undocumented workers who were in New York City when IRCA went into effect would not necessarily go home nor would new undocumented immigrants stop coming. They would, however, be even more marginalized than before and would have experienced even more aggressive erosions of labor laws and protections. Before IRCA, these workers might have had full-time jobs in large, unionized firms. Since IRCA passage, the undocumented would more likely be found in small ethnic enterprises, as day laborers, or at home doing piecework.[30]

These theories were underscored by data from the 1990s. A 1993 New York City Planning Commission study, based on INS figures, estimated that about 490,000 undocumented aliens lived in New York State, the largest illegal population of all states except

California. About 80 percent of the undocumented or 392,000 people lived in New York City.[31]

Overall, by granting permanent residence to almost 3 million people nationally, IRCA must be evaluated as an impressive feat of policy-making by Congress. The process, however, still must be described as onerous and required an enormous degree of motivation from applicants and immigration advocacy groups. Furthermore, the implementation of IRCA by the INS placed a major burden on the agency to redesign and redeploy resources to meet the implementation deadline. In addition to coordination problems that any bureaucracy might face in this situation, it can be argued that implementing an amnesty was especially difficult for an agency that saw its role primarily as one of enforcement, that is, keeping illegal aliens out. The result is that as this is being written in 1994, several court cases involving IRCA implementation involve as many as 500,000 people. Two pending cases, *Catholic Social Services vs. Reno*, and *League of United Latin American Citizens (LULAC) vs. INS* have been reviewed by the U.S. Supreme Court and were remanded to lower courts for further review. Until these cases and others are resolved, an accurate figure will not exist for the number of undocumented workers who ultimately gained permanent residence through IRCA.

In sum, between 1988 and 1989 researchers from the University of California at San Diego studied the effect of IRCA on several rural Mexican communities. Although their data focus on Mexicans who were migrating to California, their conclusions seem applicable to the Latin Americans migrating to the New York region as well.

> IRCA has not yet eliminated the basic economic incentive to migrate clandestinely to the United States [or overstay tourist visas], nor has it undermined the powerful social mechanisms that facilitate the process. In communities that have long been dependent on income earned in the U.S., our data show that most people have an *essentially* positive view of the U.S. opportunity structure: not as wide-open as before, but still accessible to those with determination, perhaps assisted by *papeles chuecos* (false documents), and even more importantly, by family contacts. Even with employer sanctions increasing the difficulty of finding work—especially steady, full-time employment—in the United

States, for large numbers of Mexicans it is still not worth it to stay in Mexico and try to make ends meet.[32]

Conclusion

The Immigration Reform and Control Act of 1986 dealt only with illegal immigration to the United States. Also important for the Latino community, however, is that the same forces propelling Congress to address undocumented immigration in 1986 have also pushed lawmakers to rework the nation's legal immigration policy. The new policy that began taking shape in the late 1980s was ultimately passed and signed into laws as the Immigration Act of 1990.

This change, considered the most comprehensive modification of legal immigration policy in twenty-five years, was spearheaded by Alan Simpson and Ted Kennedy. It had as one of its major goals redressing the seeming "Third World bias" in the immigrant stream since passage of the 1965 law. Senator Kennedy's role in this effort and his calls for migration from the "old seed sources of our heritage" no doubt were explained by the large number of Irish-Americans with ties to Ireland among his constituents and the large number of undocumented Irish in the United States. Indeed, by reserving 40 percent of green cards for Irish citizens, the legislation effectively offered a three-year amnesty to many thousands of the undocumented Irish in this country.[33]

The Latino community and immigrants' rights advocates, more generally, can be satisfied that the 1990 law was a reasonable compromise resulting from competing pressure on Congress. At its simplest, lawmakers devised a bill that maintained a generous family reunification policy, the heart of the 1965 law and the main means for immigrants from Latin America, Asia, and the Caribbean to enter the United States. The 1990 law also reduced the lengthy waits typical for reunifying spouses and minor children of U.S. permanent residents.[34] The act gave a one-year extension for 1986 amnesty applicants to complete their second-stage requirements; and, finally, it granted temporary protection to undocumented Salvadorans in the country.

Still, aspects of the law may well be of concern to Latino

activists and others interested in immigrants' rights. The 1990 legislation reintroduced national origin as a basis for entry into the United States. Preference for northern Europeans first became part of federal immigration policy in 1924; this preference was finally removed in 1965 and hailed as a major victory against ethnic and racial prejudice. The 1990 law called for "diversity" in the immigrant stream with "diversity" generally meaning European immigrants. Furthermore, the law made special provision for highly skilled workers and entrepreneurs or, as one analysis succinctly characterized it, "give me your professionals, your experts, your investors."[35]

It is reasonable for the U.S. government to search for a systematic immigration policy, and the 1990 Immigration Act represents fair legislation that addresses several concerns raised by those in the immigration policy community: a need for diversity in the immigrant stream, workers with specialized skills, and continued family reunification. It is through the avenue of family reunification that thousands of Latin Americans will continue to immigrate to the United States each year.

Still policy-makers must also contend with the reality of people from the Third World faced with structurally imbalanced economies at home and the pull of global cities like New York, which demand the cheap labor of immigrant workers. Thus, if potential immigrants find legal channels for entry unavailable, they will continue to take the chance of entering the country illegally.

It is likely, then, that federal lawmakers will continue to feel pressure to find strategies to cut down especially on undocumented Latin American workers. One option, which some officials might consider having the political appeal of a "quick fix," is to increase INS capabilities by adding larger numbers of border guards, and agents to raid businesses suspected of hiring illegal aliens. The "quick fix" notion may gain momentum in the 1990s as states such as Florida and California bring suits against the federal government to pay for costs associated with the undocumented.[36]

Immigration policy, however, offers a window into the national psyche and touches deep feelings about what kind of country the United States is. A massive step-up in INS enforcement would increase a siege mentality, create a police-state atmosphere, and be destructive to our ideology that we are a nation of immigrants who offer the beacon of freedom and opportunity to others.

Another option exists to cut the flow of illegal aliens that is both morally justified and offers the only real possibility of success. Much recent analysis of international migration suggests that it is core country penetration into the periphery that is the initial determinant of migration to the core. In this case, the assertion is understood to mean that U.S. penetration of Latin America and the Caribbean was the initial impetus for migrants from the region to come to the United States. It follows then that Washington needs to implement a policy to encourage social and economic development for Latin America and the Caribbean that would be more creative than earlier attempts at this goal; and with the end of the cold war, it should be a policy unburdened by military concerns. In the long run, a generous and coherent foreign policy toward our hemispheric neighbors will assure the most success in regaining control of U.S. borders.

NOTES

1. For obvious reasons, all statistics on the undocumented population are approximate and often given as broad ranges. In 1987 the Census Bureau estimated between 3 and 5 million illegal aliens in the United States, while the Immigration and Naturalization Service (INS) estimated the figures at 6.4 to 7.5 million.

2. Doris Meissner and Demetrios Papademetriou, *The Legalization Countdown: A Third Quarter Assessment* (Washington, D.C.: Carnegie Endowment for International Peace, 1988), p. 8.

3. See discussion in Terry L. McCoy, "A Primer for U.S. Policy on Caribbean Migration: Responding a Pressures," in Barry B. Levine, ed., *The Caribbean Exodus* (New York: Praeger, 1987), 225–41. Also see Joan Moore and Harry Pachon, *Hispanics in the United States* (Englewood Cliffs, N.J.: Prentice Hall, 1985), pp.. 134–44.

4. "Amnesty for Aliens: The Curtain Rings Down to Some Mixed Reviews," *New York Times*, May 7, 1988.

5. See Regional Plan Association, *Outlook: The Growing Latino Presence in the Tri-State Region*, New York, 1988.

6. Christopher Mitchell, "U.S. Foreign Policy and Dominican Migration to the United States," in Christopher Mitchell, ed., *Western Hemisphere Immigration and United States Foreign Policy* (University Park: Pennsylvania State Press, 1992), pp. 89–123.

7. David Bray, "The Dominican Exodus: Origins, Problems, Solutions," in Levine, ed., *The Caribbean Exodus*, pp. 152–70. Also, Sherri Grasmuck and Patricia Pessar, *Between Two Islands: Dominican International Migration* (Berkeley: University of California Press, 1991).

8. From *The Newest New Yorkers: An analysis of Immigration into New York City during the 1980s (DCP # 92–16)*, New York: Department of City Planning, June 1992, p. 32.

9. The data of the DIAGNOS survey is presented in Antonio Ugalde, Frank Bean, and Gilbert Cárdenas, "International Migration from the Dominican Republic: Findings from a National Survey," *International Migration Review* 13 (1979): 235–54. The accuracy of that survey, however, is coming into question.

10. Bray, "The Dominican Exodus," p. 164. Also, the San Juan INS office noted that arrests of the undocumented rose from 1,100 in 1982 to 4,500 in 1986 and nearly all arrested were Dominican. The INS estimates that for every illegal alien apprehended, several go undetected. See "INS Experiences Limited Success," *San Juan Star*, November 20, 1988.

11. Vivian Garrison and Carol Weiss, "Dominican Family Networks and United States Immigration Policy," in Constance Sutton and Elsa Chaney, eds., *Caribbean Life in New York City: Sociocultural Dimensions* (New York: Center for Migration Studies, 1987), pp. 235–54. Also Demetrios Papademetriou and Nicholas DiMarzio, *Undocumented Aliens in the New York Metropolitan Area: An Exploration into Their Society and Labor Market Incorporation* (New York: Center for Migration Studies, 1986).

12. On the INS's exaggerated estimates of illegal immigrants nationally, see, for example, Frank Bean and Marta Tienda, *The Hispanic Population of the United States* (New York: Russell Sage Foundation, 1987), pp. 117–21.

13. See, for example, John Crewdsen, *The Tarnished Door: The New Immigrants and the Transformation of America* (New York: New York Times Books, 1983).

14. On the associational development within New York's Dominican Community see Eugenia Georges, *New Immigrants in the Political Process: Dominicans in New York*, Occasional Paper No. 45, New York University Center for Latin American and Caribbean Studies, April 1984.

15. Josh DeWind, "The Legalization of Undocumented Immigrants in New York City: The Impact of Publicity and Outreach," study prepared for the Office of the Mayor of the City of New York and the Fund for New Citizens, September 1, 1988.

16. "New Measure Opens the Door a Bit Wider to Aliens," *New York Times*, February 3, 1990.

17. Meissner and Papademetriou, *The Legalization Countdown*, p. 101.

18. My survey contained the following question to which respondents had to agree to disagree. "It is easy to live in New York City without being discovered, so why bother to apply for the amnesty." To this, 156 respondents strongly disagreed, 9 somewhat agreed, and 6 strongly agreed. The question was taken from an earlier study commissioned by the INS to ascertain why *indocumentados* in New York were not applying to the extent expected. See Coronado Communications, "Qualified Designated Entities in the New York Metro Area: Report of Findings," Los Angeles, December 1987.

19. See the Robert Smith essay in this volume on the New York Mexican community. Nationally, Mexicans made up the largest number of amnesty applicants, by far. According to INS statistics, of the national total of 1.76 million legalization applicants, the overwhelming majority were from Mexico (1,228,084 or 69.8%). The next largest group was composed of Salvadorans (142,995 or 8.1%), followed by Guatemalans (52,542 or 3.0%), Colombians (26,350 or 1.5%), Filipinos (19,066 or 1.1%), Dominicans (18,271 or 0.9%), Poles (17,068 or 0.9%), and Nicaraguans (16,000 or 0.9%). Applicants from North America accounted for about 87 percent of the total, including Mexico (69.8%), Central America (13.4%), and the Caribbean (3.4%). From Immigration and Naturalization Service, *Statistical Yearbook of the Immigration and Naturalization Service 1991* (Washington, D.C.: U.S. Government Printing Office, 1992), p. 70.

20. New York Community Trust, *The Immigration and Control Act of 1986: Making It Work* (New York: New York Community Trust, 1988).

21. Dewind, "The Legalization of Undocumented Immigrants in New York City: The Impact of Publicity and Outreach," p. 41.

22. "Immigrants Swell Language Classes," *New York Times*, January 7, 1990.

23. "Immigrants Face a Threat to Amnesty," *New York Times*, August 1, 1989.

24. *Workplace Discrimination under the Immigration Reform and Control Act of 1986: A Study of Impacts of New Yorkers*, New York State Inter-Agency Task Force on Immigration Affairs, November 4, 1988. The Inter-Agency Task Force published a second study in February 1990, again finding a widespread pattern of employer discrimination against people born outside the United States or those with temporary work

authorization. See, "Immigration Laws Linked to Job Bias," *New York Times*, February 26, 1990.

25. *Tarnishing the Golden Door: A Report on the Widespread Discrimination Against Immigrants and Persons Perceived as Immigrants which has resulted from the Immigration Reform and Control Act of 1986*, New York City Commission on Human Rights, August 1989.

26. Shirley Lung, Center for Immigrant Rights (CIR), "Written Testimony on the Impact of Employer Sanctions," submitted to the House Subcommittee on Immigration, Oversight Hearings on IRCA, May 9, 1989. With four more years of data, the CIR continued to advocate the repeal of employer sanctions. See, CIR, "Written Testimony on the Repeal of Employer Sanctions," submitted to the House Subcommittee on International Law, Immigration, and Refugees, Hearing on the Implementation of Employer Sanctions, June 16, 1993.

27. "Bill to Safeguard Rights of Aliens Passed by Panel," *New York Times*, June 20, 1989.

28. U.S. General Accounting Office, *Immigration Reform: Employer Sanctions and the Question of Discrimination*, Washington, D.C., March 1990.

29. For early discussions of a lack of efficacy in IRCA see "Immigration Law Is Failing to Cut Flow from Mexico," *New York Times*, June 24, 1988; and Michael White, Frank Bean, and Thomas Espenshade, "The U.S. Immigration Reform and Control Act and Undocumented Migration to the United States," Washington, D.C.: The Urban Institute, 1989. For more recent data, see "Law Fails to Stem Abuse of Migrants," *New York Times*, October 22, 1992.

30. See, for example, Muzaffar A. Chishti, "The Impact of IRCA's Employer Sanctions Provision of Workers and Workplace," in Lydio F. Tomasi, ed., *In Defense of the Alien*, vol. XII (New York: Center for Migration Studies, 1990), 189–91; also, "Illegal Salvadorans Fight Poverty, Winter and Fear on L.I.," *New York Times*, December 25, 1989.

31. "Study Sees New York's Illegal Immigrants in a New Light," *New York Times*, September 2, 1993.

32. Wayne A. Cornelius, "Impacts of the 1986 U.S. Immigration Law on Emigration from Rural Mexican Sending Communities," paper presented at the XV International Congress of the Latin American Studies Association, Miami, December 4–6, 1989.

33. "Landmark Accord Promises to Ease Immigration Curbs," *New York Times*, October 26, 1990; "40,000 Aliens to Win Legal Status in Lottery," *New York Times*, September 25, 1991.

34. Warren R. Leiden, "The New Preference Categories of the Immigration Act of 1990," in Lydio F. Tomasi, ed., *In Defense of the*

Alien, vol. XV (New York: Center for Migration Studies, 1993), pp. 36–44. Also, Advance Report, "Immigration Statistics: Fiscal Year 1992" (Washington, D.C.: Statistics Division, Immigration and Naturalization Service, May 1993), pp. 1–6.

35. "The Immigration Act of 1990," *Center for Immigrants Rights Report*, no. 13, March 1991.

36. "California Sues U.S. Government Over Costs Tied to Illegal Aliens," *New York Times*, May 1, 1994.

Part Three

CONCLUSION

11

Puerto Rican and Latino Culture
at the Crossroads

JUAN FLORES

> Puerto Rico mi isla querida de amor
> tus cantares vengo a revivir
> son tus hijos cantando la historia de tu son
> y tu tan lejos la puedes oir
> > Los Pleneros de la 21

1.

Years ago, back in the 1920s and 30s, you used to be able to tell where the Puerto Rican families lived by the green plants and colored flowers on their windowsills. Of all the immigrant nationalities settling in New York in those times, it was the Puerto Ricans who would freshen up their humble tenement walls with splashes of nature and provide themselves, neighbors, and passersby some relief from the dreary grays and browns of the big-city streets.

At least that's how the venerable Puerto Rican poet Juan Avilés remembers it, and his memories are confirmed by many other pioneers of the Puerto Rican community in New York. They also recall the lilting songs of Rafael Hernández and the bustling plena rhythms of Manuel Jiménez, known as "El canario," as they resounded from storefronts and fifth-floor walk-up in Chelsea, below Fourteenth Street and in the neighborhoods along the Brooklyn waterfront. And in times closer to our own who doesn't remember the "kikirikí" of the cocks crowing at daybreak, and that moment of disbelief when we realize that we're huddled in the inner city and not out on a mountain farm somewhere?

With the thousands of families streaming into the city from the Dominican Republic, Colombia, Mexico, and all over Latin

America and the Caribbean, there seems to be less talk these days
of the Puerto Rican community. Yet the Puerto Ricans are still not
only the most numerous of the Latino groups, they also, along with
the Cubans, are the ones who introduced the sights and sounds of
tropical cultures to New York City. An early novel about Puerto
Rican life here, published in 1951, was *Trópico en Manhattan* ("Manhattan Tropics") by Guillermo Cotto-Thorner, and the title was
apt: the "sabor" of our city, that special Caribbean flavor we sense
all around us, we owe to the pioneering presence of the Puerto
Rican population.

For Puerto Ricans, the struggle to maintain and re-create cultural and artistic traditions has been a matter of survival. In the
face of crushing poverty, political exclusion, and frequent discrimination, most Puerto Ricans in New York find an indispensable
source of self-affirmation and joy in celebrating roots, origins, and
reminiscences. Whether it's a classical play at the Puerto Rican
Travelling Theater, an exhibit of recent or folkloric art at the Museo
del Barrio, a Mother's Day dance at a hometown social club, shop-
ping for yuca and plátanos verdes at La Marqueta on 116th Street,
or just listening to stories told by parents and grandparents, Puerto
Ricans never lose touch with the creative life-ways they brought
with them, or inherited, for their beloved homeland.

As vital as these attachments may be, though, New York Puerto
Ricans are fully aware that they are here, in the Big Manzana, and
that their cultural concerns cannot be just an extension or replay
of experiences on the island. As the word implies, "Nuyorican"
culture is at the crossroads, drawing key inspiration from the
"Rican" background but responding most directly to experiences
here in "Nuyor." There is great pride in those celebrarted compatriots who have gained recognition for their contributions to American
culture, like José Ferrer, Rita Moreno, Freddie Prinze, and Raul Juliá
in the entertainment field, Tito Puente and José Feliciano in popular
music, and the many Puerto Rican stars in professional sports.
Pride mixes with disdain as Puerto Rican New Yorkers have had
to respond to depictions of their experience in Broadway musicals,
Hollywood movies, and on network television.

The *West Side Story* stereotype haunts the New York Puerto
Rican community. Unable to hope for more sympathetic treatment
from the commercial media, the only reliable answer has been for

Puerto Ricans to portray things themselves, from their own point of view. In the 1950s and 60s, when the influx of Puerto Ricans was at its peak, some of the major writers and artists from the island turned to life in "el barrio" as a central theme in their plays, stories, and painting. But even here, in the works of René Marqués, José Luis González, and others who visited but never lived here for long, distortions were still rampant.

More accurate and sensitive treatment only occurs in the hands of those who participated directly in the migration and settlement, as in the books of Bernardo Vega, Jesús Colón, Piri Thomas, Nicholasa Mohr, and Ed Rivera, the poetry of the Nuyorican poets Pedro Pietri, Sandra María Esteves, Victor Hernández Cruz, and Tato Laviera, the paintings of Rafael Tufiño, Jorge Soto, and others from the "Taller Boricua, " the salsa music of Eddie Palmieri, Ray Barreto, and Willie Colón.[1]

Here we gain a closer and deeper sense of culture at the border between Puerto Rico and New York. Over the past twenty years Nuyorican and New York Latino art has shown the importance and beauty of bilingual and bicultural expression.

The traditions that gave rise to Latin jazz and Nuyorican poetry attest to the strong influence of African-American culture on Puerto Ricans in the New York setting. Just as African Americans and Puerto Ricans have long lived and worked side by side, their artistic expressions have intermingled and found common roots.

In our own times, Puerto Ricans in New York continue to invent new ways of reconnecting to homeland traditions while taking active part in New York trends and styles.

In hip-hop, young Puerto Ricans and other Latinos have once again joined their African-American peers in forging new styles of popular performance. Puerto Ricans were among the first rappers, graffiti writers, and breakdancers to appear on the scene in the late 1970s. Today groups like Latin Empire, POW, and the Rock Steady Crew are freely mixing Latin rhythms, words, and images into their rhymes and dance beats.[2]

Another striking example of Puerto Ricans breaking new artistic ground are the *casitas*, or "little houses," that have sprung up in abandoned lots in the South Bronx and El Barrio. The *casitas* are modeled directly after working-class dwellings on the island from over fifty years ago. With their characteristic front porch and farm-like atmosphere in the surrounding yard, these remarkable little structures are intended for recreation and cultural association among neighbors. They are like oases in the desert of urban blight: the architecture and natural setting are throwbacks to the rural tropics, while the sociability they inspire contrasts sharply with the neglect and hostility facing life in the neighborhood.

Up on Brook Avenue and 159th Street the casita named Rincón Criollo (roughly "Hometown Corner") stands its ground against periodic threats from developers and the housing authorities. Members and neighbors are proud of Rincón Criollo, which evokes powerful memories of Puerto Rico while serving as a lively community center. In addition to the parties and special occasions, classes in folkloric bomba and plena music and dance all happen right there at the casita on the corner.[3]

In recent years the casitas have finally gained the attention of the wider society, serving as the featured subject of newspaper articles, radio shows, and community research projects. From February to June of 1991, casita culture was on elaborate display at the inaugural exhibition of the Smithsonian's new Experimental Gallery in Washington, D.C. And the whole show, complete with a life-size casita, was then the featured exhibit at the Bronx Museum.

In a way, casitas just go to show that Puerto Ricans are still busy putting flowers in their windows.

2.

The broader significance of assessing Puerto Rican and Latino culture in New York becomes most evident when attention is given to vernacular expressions and practices. For here, more than in an account of the established and recognized representatives and representations, the Latino "contribution" constitutes more than simply what it might add to the prevailing culture by way of exotic or quaint elements. The social clubs and festivities, street drumming and home-style cuisine, botánicas and domino games which form part of everyday life in the barrios comprise not just "another way" of being American, but also an alternative to being American in any narrow, culturally delimited sense. Beyond its place in the pluralist mosaic, Latino culture harbors a deeper challenge to mainstream U.S. society in the form of a different, and potentially divergent, ethos and aesthetic.[4]

The struggle for group and personal identity, which has been the abiding project of Puerto Rican cultural practice over the decades, the active recourse to Latin American and Caribbean history and culture as a real and imagined locus of reference. Relentless exclusion and discrimination at the economic and political levels have gone to reinforce this continued gravitation to "external" sources of cultural value, much to the dismay of the die-hard assimilationists and even some of the most "inclusionary" of the multicultural pluralists. Of course this apparent separatism or resistance to assimilation needs to be viewed in historical terms, especially with regard to the circumstances of emigration and arrival. Only in this full social context is it possible to recognize the contrast with the cultural experience of earlier immigrant groups.

For despite their growing presence here since early in the century, Puerto Rican experience in the United States has been prototypical of the "new," post-World War II immigrants. Unlike their predecessors from the European poor, those arriving since mid-century have predominantly originated from colonial and semicolonial countries and migrated in response to the needs of an economy caught up in postindustrial shrinkage rather than industrial takeoff. In addition to the obvious difference in the ensuing racial dynamic, the result has been a new and markedly less felicitous pattern of incorporation and exclusion. It is this altered sociohistorical context which has rendered obsolete that paradigm of cultural analysis based on the "immigrant analogy," that is, on the dogma that newly arriving cultures, no matter how "foreign," will by force of social necessity and inclination eventually shed their old ways and attachments and find their niche in the new field of identity options.

Yet the situation of Puerto Rican and Latino culture is not reduceable to "resistance," either. In continuing to identify as Puerto Rican rather than American or even "Puerto Rican American," the attitude that prevails across lines of economic status, time of arrival, age, gender, race, and political affiliation signals not only a choice *not* to be something, but a choice to *be* something as well. Beyond the sense of negation and any spirit of opposition there is an affirmation of an available alternative. What I have termed the "ethos" latent in the Latino cultural project has to do with the relative autonomy of vernacular identity-formation, its at least partial indifference to the demands of the impinging dominant culture. Reaction, whether by way of defiance or accommodation, is not the only, and perhaps not even the guiding, impulse in this process of preferred cultural determination.

The point is that Puerto Rican culture in the United States, like that of other Latinos and colonial immigrants, calls for a focused and situational analysis; that is, one which proceeds from the perspective of the culture taken in its own terms and not simply as a reflex of reigning parameters and constraints. Choosing a location at the seams and interstices of the existing cultural geography, as is so vividly evident in expressive practices like the casitas and bilingual rhyming and speech, points up the collective construction of new, uncharted spaces. Though hounded by the conflicting pressures of paternalistic tolerance and racist rejection, these emergent enclaves are defined as much by interactions within and among themselves as by their more familiar negotiation with the official culture or cultures, whether of the U.S. or of their homelands, whether elite or mass-mediated.

What implications these "imagined communities" and "invented traditions" may carry for the ongoing culture wars in the United States can only surface in the course of further theoretical and ethnographic work. Current discussions of transnational culture and processes of deterritorialization and re-indigenization would certainly appear to suggest some fertile new ground, as does, though somewhat more problematically, the debate over the cultural consequences of post colonialism.[5] In any case, the study of Nuyorican and other Latino vernacular experience demands a break from any facile correlation between socioeconomic conditions and cultural vitality.

Moving beyond the nagging influence of notions of "subcultures of poverty," the "underclass," and "ghettoization" need not involve a lapse into some form of cultural essentialism, nor the extraction of the cultural dimension or realm from the context of political and economic oppression. Rather, it is precisely the lived reality of colonial social conditions, with its simultaneous pressures toward uniformity and hierarchy at the cultural level, that impel the constitution of alternative communities and structures of identity-formation. The ethos of Nuyorican and other Latino culture of course comprises the self-destructive and regressive tendencies so commonly pathologized in mainstream social science and in the media and overlooked or even glorified in paternalistic political and ethnographic approaches. But difference only equates with "deviance," deficiency, or deprivation when an assessment and representation of the culture in question is based on the normative measures of the dominant society. The ethical strategy of Latino popular culture, understood in the terms of its own geographical and historical dynamic, points up a collective relation to place, memory, and tradition the intensity and pertinence of which are systematically blunted by the sweep of prevailing national and international cultures.

NOTES

1. For a brief overview, see my "Puerto Rican Literature in the United States: Stages and Perspectives," in *Redefining American Literary History*, ed. A. LaVonne Ruoff and Jerry W. Ward, Jr. (New York: Modern Language Association, 1990), pp. 210–18. See also Eugene Mohr, *The Nuyorican Experience: Literature of the Puerto Rican Minority* (Westport, Conn.: Greenwood, 1982).

2. For an early discussion of the role of Puerto Ricans in the hip-hop, see my "'Rappin', Writin' and Breakin': Black and Puerto Rican Street Culture in New York," *Dissent* (Fall 1987): 580–84. See also my more recent essays "'Puerto Rican and Proud, Boyee!': Rap, Roots and Amnesia," in *Microphone Fiends: Youth Music and Youth Culture*, ed. Andrew Ross and Tricia Rose (New York: Routledge, 1994), pp. 89–98, and "Puerto Rocks: New York Ricans Stake Their Claim," in *Droppin Knowledge: Critical Essays on Rap and Hip-Hop Culture*, ed. Eric Perkins (Philadelphia: Temple, 1995).

3. See my essay "''Salvación Casita': Puerto Rican Performance and Vernacular Architecture in the South Bronx," in *Negotiating Performance: Gender, Sexuality, and Theatricality in Latin/o America*, ed. Diana Taylor and Juan Villegas (Durham, N.C.: Duke University Press, 1994), pp. 121–36.

4. For a theoretical discussion of Latino culture and identity, see my essay, co-authored with George Yúdice, "Living Borders/Buscando América: Languages of Latino Self-Formation," *Social Text* 24 (Fall 1990): 57–84. See also my earlier papers "'La Carreta Made a U-Turn':

Puerto Rican Language and Culture in the United States," *Daedalus* 10 (2) (Spring 1991): 193–217 (co-authored with John Attinasi and Pedro Pedraza), and "'Qué Assimilated, Brother, Yo Soy Asimilao': The Structuring of Puerto Rican Identity in the United States," *Journal of Ethnic Studies* 13 (3) (1985): 1–16. All are now included in my collection of articles entitled *Divided Borders: Essays on Puerto Rican Identity* (Houston: Arte Público, 1993).

5. In addition to the references in note 4 above, see Arjun Appadurai, "Disjuncture and Difference in the Global Cultural Economy," *Public Culture* 2 (2) (1990): 1–24, and Robert J. Foster, "Making National Cultures in the Global Ecumene," *Annual Review of Anthropology* 20 (1991): 235–60.